D0205300

Careers in Physics

Careers in Physics

Editor

Donald R. Franceschetti

The University of Memphis

SALEM PRESS
A Division of EBSCO Publishing
Ipswich, Massachusetts

GREY HOUSE PUBLISHING

Careers in Physics, 2013, published by Grey House Publishing, Inc., Amenia, NY, under exclusive license from EBSCO Publishing, Inc.

∞ The paper used in these volumes conforms to the American National Standard for Permanence of Paper for Printed Library Materials, Z39.48-1992 (R1997).

Library of Congress Cataloging-in-Publication Data

Careers in physics.
    pages cm
 Includes bibliographical references and index.
 ISBN 978-1-58765-992-8 (hardcover)
 1. Physics--Vocational guidance.
 QC29.C37 2013
 530.023--dc23

                                                          2012044525

 ebook ISBN: 978-1-4298-3761-3

PRINTED IN THE UNITED STATES OF AMERICA

Contents

Publisher's Note   xi
Contributors   xvii

> *✐ - Designated as a Green Occupation by the US Department of Labor, Employment and Training Administration.*

Acoustics   3
  Basic Principles   3
  Core Concepts   4
  Applications Past and Present   9
  Impact on Industry   13
  Social Context and Future Prospects   15
  Sound Engineering Technician   17

Aeronautics and Aviation   25
  Basic Principles   25
  Core Concepts   26
  Applications Past and Present   29
  Impact on Industry   33
  Social Context and Future Prospects   36
  Aerospace Engineer ✐   38

Astrophysics   47
  Basic Principles   47
  Core Concepts   48
  Applications Past and Present   52
  Impact on Industry   56
  Social Context and Future Prospects   58
  Astrophysicist   60

Atmospheric Physics   69
  Basic Principles   69
  Core Concepts   70
  Applications Past and Present   74
  Impact on Industry   78
  Social Context and Future Prospects   80
  Meteorologist ✐   82

Atomic and Molecular Physics   91
  Basic Principles   91
  Core Concepts   92
  Applications Past and Present   95
  Impact on Industry   98
  Social Context and Future Prospects   100
  Atomic and Molecular Physicist   102

Biophysics   109
  Basic Principles   109
  Core Concepts   110
  Applications Past and Present   112
  Impact on Industry   115
  Social Context and Future Prospects   117
  Biophysicist   119

Civil Engineering   128
  Basic Principles   128
  Core Concepts   129
  Applications Past and Present   131
  Impact on Industry   136
  Social Context and Future Prospects   139
  Civil Engineer✐   140

Classical or Applied Mechanics   148
  Basic Principles   148
  Core Concepts   149
  Applications Past and Present   153
  Impact on Industry   156
  Social Context and Future Prospects   159
  Mechanical Engineer ✐   161

Condensed Matter Physics   169
  Basic Principles   169
  Core Concepts   170
  Applications Past and Present   174
  Impact on Industry   177
  Accelerator Physicist   181

Cryogenics   190
  Basic Principles   190

Core Concepts 191
Applications Past and Present 192
Impact on Industry 196
Social Context and Future Prospects 198
Cryogenic Engineer ✐ 199

Electrical Engineering 205
Basic Principles 205
Core Concepts 206
Applications Past and Present 208
Impact on Industry 212
Academic Research and Teaching 215
Social Context and Future Prospects 215
Electrical Engineer ✐ 217

Environmental Physics 226
Basic Principles 226
Core Concepts 227
Applications Past & Present 230
Impact on Industry 234
Environmental Engineer ✐ 240

Fluid Dynamics 249
Basic Principles 249
Core Concepts 250
Applications Past and Present 254
Impact on Industry 256
Hydrologist ✐ 260

Geophysics 268
Basic Principles 268
Core Concepts 269
Applications Past and Present 272
Impact on Industry 276
Social Context and Future Prospects 278
Oceanographer ✐ 279

Nanotechnology 288
Basic Principles 288
Core Concepts 289
Applications Past and Present 291

Impact on Industry   293
Social Context and Future Prospects   295
Nanosystems Engineer ✐   296

Nuclear Medicine   305
Basic Principles   305
Core Concepts   306
Applications Past and Present   309
Impact on Industry   313
Social Context and Future Prospects   314
Nuclear Medicine Technologist   317

Nuclear Physics   324
Basic Principles   324
Core Concepts   325
Applications Past and Present   328
Impact on Industry   332
Social Context and Future Prospects   335
Nuclear Monitoring Technician ✐   336

Optics   344
Basic Principles   344
Core Concepts   345
Applications Past and Present   347
Impact on Industry   351
Social Context and Future Prospects   353
Photonics Engineer ✐   355

Quantum Physics   361
Basic Principles   361
Core Concepts   362
Applications Past and Present   365
Impact on Industry   368
Social Context and Future Prospects   370
Quantum Physicist   371

Solid Mechanics   379
Basic Principles   379
Core Concepts   380
Applications Past and Present   384
Impact on Industry   386

Social Context and Future Prospects   387
Materials Physicist 🖉   389

Systems Engineering   397
Basic Principles   397
Core Concepts   398
Applications Past and Present   401
Impact on Industry   405
Social Context and Future Development   406
Robotics Engineer 🖉   407

Thermodynamics   414
Basic Principles   414
Core Concepts   416
Applications Past and Present   418
Impact on Industry   422
Social Context and Future Prospects   425
Thermodynamics Engineer   426

Appendixes

Bibliography   435
Detailed STEM Undergraduate Majors   445
Colleges to Consider   448
Career Guidance Portals   454
Occupational Resources   460
Noble Prizes in Physics   464

Indexes

Occupational Index   469
Index   471

Publisher's Note

It is estimated that the United States will have over 2.1 million job openings in STEM-related (Science, Technology, Engineering, and Mathematics) fields and occupations by 2020. More specifically, within that ten-year period, the US Bureau of Labor Statistics (BLS) projects that employment within the scientific, professional, and technical services industries will grow by approximately 29 percent. Along with these positive growth trends, employees in STEM occupations also earn higher salaries than workers in other fields and have lower unemployment rates than fellow college graduates, and STEM students are seeing an increase in grants and funding through burgeoning government and educational initiatives. Further, STEM students are highly targeted for recruitment by major cutting-edge companies such as Google, while companies such as Microsoft are starting to recruit for STEM careers at an early educational level by working to spark an interest in science and technology, especially among female students. The growth of STEM-related careers and the investment in science education will play a key role in the future of our nation.

Despite these trends and the steady growth across all STEM fields, the United States is experiencing a significant deficit in the number of STEM workers, or those holding technical jobs within the fields of science, technology, engineering, and mathematics. Not enough students are graduating with STEM backgrounds to fill the open positions in the marketplace, leading many schools across the country to engage in STEM advocacy campaigns to encourage student interest in STEM subjects.

To that end, this publication, *Careers in Physics*, contains over twenty alphabetically arranged articles describing specific fields of interest in physics with an accompanying discussion of a particular STEM-related career or occupation within that area. These occupational profiles provide a current overview and a future outlook, including green technologies where applicable. Merging scholarship with occupational development, this single comprehensive guidebook provides physics students and readers alike with the necessary insight into potential scientific pursuits and provides instruction on what job seekers can expect in terms of training and advancement, earnings, job prospects, working conditions, relevant associations, and more. *Careers in Physics* is specifically designed for a high school and under-graduate audience and is edited to align with secondary or high school curriculum standards.

Scope of Coverage

Understanding the interconnected nature of the different and varied branches of science and technology is important for anyone preparing for a career or endeavor in STEM fields. *Careers in Physics* comprises more than twenty lengthy and alphabetically arranged essays on a broad range of branches and subfields within physics and over twenty corresponding occupational profiles that highlight a particular career within that branch or subfield. The overview essays include traditional and long-established fields such as civil engineering and applied mechanics to in-demand and cutting-edge fields such as cryogenics, environmental physics, and nuclear medicine. This excellent reference work then presents possible career paths and occupations within high-growth and emerging fields as diverse as aerospace technologies, hydrology, nanotechnology, oceanography, quantum physics, robotics engineering, and thermodynamics. While occupations requiring Green Enhanced Skills are marked with a "green leaf" symbol, the future applications of all occupations are thoroughly discussed.

Careers in Physics is also enhanced with numerous charts and tables, including US Bureau of Labor Statistics projections and median annual salaries or wages for applicable physics-based occupations. The Transferable Skills section notes those skills that can be applied across STEM occupations, and Interesting Facts provides insights into fields that are often overlooked. Rounding out these profiles are questionnaires completed by professionals in physics-related occupations. The respondents share their personal career paths, detail their potential paths for career advancement, and offer advice for students and readers—a must-read for those embarking on a career in science.

Essay Length and Format

Science overviews range in length from 3,500 to 4,500 words and all entries begin with ready-reference top matter, including fields of study and a clear definition of the physics branch or subfield. Essays then place the major field or area of study in historical or technological perspective by examining basic principles and core concepts, including the discipline's development, such as historic and current applications. The articles also cover the impact that each particular field has had on industry—a comprehensive section that includes private industry and business, government agencies and the military, and academic research and teaching, as well as the field's social context and future prospects and applications. Further reading suggestions and detailed author profiles accompany all articles.

Occupational profiles range in length from 1,500 to 2,000 words and include an "employment snapshot" in the top matter that presents the occupation's median yearly earnings; employment outlook (sourced from the BLS *Occupational Outlook Handbook*); O*NET-SOC Code (an eight-digit code assigned to each occupation through the US Department of Labor); and related "career clusters" that name occupations in the same field of work that require similar skills. Each occupation then receives the following detailed sections:

- **Scope of Work** presents a brief introduction to the occupation, including the applications of the work.

- **Education and Coursework** addresses the educational path and the basic coursework needed to go on to more advanced research or professional positions within this occupation or field.

- **Career Enhancement and Training** details the certification or licensing necessary to secure employment and advancement in a given occupation, if applicable, and discusses the benefits of professional associations and societies.

- **Daily Tasks and Technology** describes the typical set of daily activities of the occupation and the technology employed in the occupation.

- **Earnings and Employment Outlook** provides an overview of the wages and job growth associated with the occupation.

- **Related Occupations** lists similar or related occupations within the field.

- **Future Applications** discusses the impact this field or occupation will have on future jobs and careers.

- **More Information** lists websites that students can turn to for further research and information about the occupation.

In addition, unique highlights of these occupational profiles include:

- **Transferable Skills,** a list of six to eight commonly recognized skills considered to be transferable across multiple careers and work environments.

- **Careers Questionnaire,** a 150- to 300-word questionnaire completed by a professional within a particular field, relating his or her respective career path, advice, and possible advancement opportunities. This special feature canvasses a diverse range of professionals working in the fields of—or with a background in—physics, ranging from academia to the private sector, from small business owners to CEOs, and from young professionals to accomplished individuals.

Special Features

Several features continue to distinguish this reference series from other career-oriented reference works. The back matter includes several appendixes and indexes, including a general bibliography, a collated collection of annotated suggested readings, and an awards appendix listing the Nobel Prize winners in physics. Colleges to Consider presents an alphabetically arranged list of the most highly selective four-year colleges in the United States for pursuing and attaining a bachelor's degree in physics, using select criteria. A career guidance appendix presents a comprehensive listing of career-oriented portals maintained by preeminent and influential societies and organizations advocating on behalf of physicists and other scientists and science-related workers. Additionally, an occupational websites directory notes those websites with specific relevance to the pursuit of a career in physics.

Additional features are provided to assist in the retrieval of information. An index illustrates the breadth of the reference work's coverage, listing people, scientific concepts and theories, technologies, terms, principles, and other topics of discussion, while an occupational index directs the reader to all discussions of a specific occupation throughout both the science and occupational profile articles.

Acknowledgments

Many hands went into the creation of this work. Special mention must be made of consulting editor Donald R. Franceschetti, who played a principal role in shaping the reference work and its contents. Thanks are due to the many academicians and professionals who worked to communicate their expert understanding of physics to the general reader; a list of these individuals and their affiliations appears at the beginning of the volume. Finally, thanks are also due to the professionals who communicated their work experience through our careers questionnaires. Their frank and honest responses have provided immeasurable value to our careers product. The contributions of all are gratefully acknowledged.

Introduction

It is a truism that the pace of change in industry and technology has been rapidly increasing. The atomic nucleus was discovered a little over a century ago, the first primitive transistor built in 1947, and earth satellites a mere decade later. Today's student may use cell phone or VoIP technology to share information with a friend almost anywhere in the world, and the owner of an inexpensive computer has at his or her command more computing resources than the United States government had access to a scant sixty-five years ago. While the process of growth has experienced setbacks from time to time, the student who has some command of the hard sciences—particularly physics and chemistry—along with a modicum of communications skills can expect to have an interesting and well-remunerated career.

This book is intended to serve as a guide to career options in these technical fields for students in high school or the early years of college. Generally, the careers available will depend on the breadth and depth of training. A few important general observations can be made at the outset. The most important outcome of schooling is learning how to learn. Today's high school graduates can expect a working lifetime of forty years or more and will need to acquire new knowledge throughout their careers from a wide variety of sources, many of them electronic. Communications skills—speaking, writing and the production of visual media—will continue to be important in the workplace, and basic computer competency will be essential. Additionally, understanding of mathematics is essential for any career in science. So in addition to the obvious courses in physics or chemistry, attention to coursework in English composition, computer programming, and mathematics is critical. Increasingly, people working in the sciences will find themselves working with individuals from different cultures and different nations. Courses that provide multicultural perspectives, including courses in foreign languages, might be a good investment.

The level of education obtained will help to delimit career prospects. Attending a vocational high school or community college could qualify you as a laboratory technician, but having a college degree will broaden career prospects considerably. Students interested in chemistry or physics should talk with science teachers about the programs available at the college of their choice. Students wanting to attain the bachelor's degree in chemistry should try to select a program accredited by the American Chemical Society and take advantage of this status to become student affiliates of that organization. The physics community in the United States has chosen not to accredit individual degree programs as some quite small departments have excellent programs. Finding a college with an active chapter of the Society of Physics Students, affiliated with the American Institute of Physics, is almost indispensable for the aspiring professional physicist. Student organizations in chemistry and physics have national and regional meetings, and plan field trips on a local level to industrial sites and national laboratories, while inviting speakers to campus to describe employment opportunities.

The Bachelor of Science degree takes the equivalent of four years to acquire and generally includes courses in the major, as well as in supporting areas such as mathematics, and includes a healthy dose of general education (English, history, foreign language, and social science). There are many employment opportunities for physicists and chemists at the bachelor's level, and many choose to enter the workforce at this point, though most employers will expect, and many will pay for, some amount of continuing education. Some graduates may go to professional school to become physicians, dentists, veterinarians, and optometrists, or to law school to enter one of the many fields of legal practice, including patent law (for which a bachelor's degree in one of the STEM areas is required). Additional opportunities for STEM graduates can be found in the armed forces, where they can obtain commissions as officers, and in secondary teaching, after obtaining an amount of professional preparation in pedagogy (the requirements differing greatly from state to state).

Further education for STEM graduates generally amounts to earning the Master of Science (MS) or Doctor of Philosophy (PhD) degree. This can be done on a full-time or part-time basis and often involves teaching or research duties that provide a stipend as well as remission of tuition, so that the graduate student can be a self-supporting adult. In contrast to bachelor's degree programs, which can involve taking courses in many different departments, graduate students generally take their advanced work in a single department or a few closely related ones. The majority of MS programs include a certain amount of graduate coursework in preparation for a comprehensive examination and a research project or thesis, which serves as the candidate's first introduction to research and often results in a scientific publication. MS programs require eighteen months to two years of full-time effort, but allow the student to enter the workforce at a more advanced level.

The doctorate degree has existed for many centuries though the requirements have changed vastly. In modern practice, the PhD requires passing a stringent general examination in the field of specialization and the submission of a PhD dissertation, a book-length manuscript describing a single research study. Obtaining the PhD can take four or more years beyond the bachelor's degree. The degree is required to teach on a permanent basis at most four-year colleges, and many universities will expect most of their new hires to have completed a stint as a paid postdoctoral research fellow before beginning the probationary period that leads to tenure. Many PhDs choose to enter industry instead, where the salaries are somewhat higher and there is greater opportunity to enter managerial positions and eventually become corporate executives.

Whatever career path is chosen, the young STEM student will find interesting work in the company of like-minded individuals. New fields of study will emerge and new research tools will appear. It is impossible to say now, in the second decade of the twenty-first century, where such careers will lead in thirty to forty years, but the probability of an engaging and satisfying career is high indeed for the student with an aptitude for science and math learning and the maturity to persist in a physics or chemistry career.

Donald R. Franceschetti
Departments of Physics and Chemistry
The University of Memphis

Contributors

Michael P. Auerbach
Marblehead, Massachusetts

Harlan H. Bengtson
Southern Illinois University, Edwardsville

Daniel Castaldy
Marlborough, Massachusetts

Keith M. Finley
Southeastern Louisiana University

Molly Hagan
New York, New York

Gina Hagler
Washington, DC

Micah L. Issitt
Philadelphia, Pennsylvania

Amanda R. Jones
Burgaw, North Carolina

Vincent Jorgensen
Sunnyvale, California

Marylane Wade Koch
University of Memphis

Narayanan M. Komerath
Georgia Institute of Technology

R. C. Lutz
Bucharest, Romania

Steve Miller
Somerville, Massachusetts

Cassandra Newell
Somerville, Massachusetts

Ellen E. Anderson Penno
Western Laser Eye Associates

George R. Plitnik
Frostburg State University

Sibani Sengupta
American Medical Writers Association

Rose Young
Ipswich, Massachusetts

Careers in
Physics

Acoustics

FIELDS OF STUDY

Electrical, chemical, and mechanical engineering; architecture; music; speech; psychology; physiology; medicine; atmospheric physics; geology; oceanography.

DEFINITION

Acoustics is the science dealing with the production, transmission, and effects of vibration in material media. If the medium is air and the vibration frequency is between 18 and 18,000 hertz (Hz), the vibration is termed "sound." Sound is used in a broader context to describe sounds in solids and underwater and structure-borne sounds. Because mechanical vibrations, whether natural or human induced, have accompanied humans through the long course of human evolution, acoustics is the most interdisciplinary science. For humans, hearing is a very important sense, and the ability to vocalize greatly facilitates communication and social interaction. Sound can have profound psychological effects; music may soothe or relax a troubled mind, and noise can induce anxiety and hypertension.

Basic Principles

The words "acoustics" and "phonics" evolved from ancient Greek roots for hearing and speaking, respectively. Thus, acoustics began with human communication, making it one of the oldest if not the most basic of sciences. Because acoustics is ubiquitous in human endeavors, it is the broadest and most interdisciplinary of sciences; its most profound contributions have occurred when it is commingled with an independent field. The interdisciplinary nature of acoustics has often consigned it to a subsidiary role as a minor subdivision of mechanics, hydrodynamics, or electrical engineering. Certainly, the various technical aspects of acoustics could be parceled out to larger and better established divisions of science, but then acoustics would lose its unique strengths and its source of dynamic creativity. The main difference between acoustics and more self-sufficient branches of science is that acoustics depends on physical laws developed in and borrowed from other fields. Therefore, the primary task of acoustics is to take these divergent principles and integrate them into a coherent whole in order to understand, measure, and control vibration phenomena.

The Acoustical Society of America subdivides acoustics into fifteen main areas, the most important of which are ultrasonics, which examines high-frequency waves not audible to humans; psychological acoustics, which studies how sound is perceived in the brain; physiological acoustics, which looks at human and animal hearing mechanisms; speech acoustics, which focuses on the human vocal apparatus and oral communication; musical acoustics, which involves the physics of musical instruments; underwater sound, which examines the production and propagation of sound in liquids; and noise, which concentrates on the control and suppression of unwanted sound. Two other important areas of applied acoustics are architectural acoustics (the acoustical design of concert halls and sound reinforcement systems) and audio engineering (recording and reproducing sound).

Core Concepts

Ultrasonics. Dog whistles, which can be heard by dogs but not by humans, can generate ultrasonic frequencies of about 25 kilohertz (kHz). Two types of transducers, magnetostrictive and piezoelectric, are used to generate higher frequencies and greater power. Magnetostrictive devices convert magnetic energy into ultrasound by subjecting ferric material (iron or nickel) to a strong oscillating magnetic field. The field causes the material to alternately expand and contract, thus creating sound waves of the same frequency as that of the field. The resulting sound waves have frequencies between 20 Hz and 50 kHz and several thousand watts of power. Such transducers operate at the mechanical resonance frequency where the energy transfer is most efficient.

Piezoelectric transducers convert electric energy into ultrasound by applying an oscillating electric field to a piezoelectric crystal (such as quartz). These transducers, which work in liquids or air, can generate frequencies in the megahertz region with considerable power. In addition to natural crystals, ceramic piezoelectric materials, which can be fabricated into any desired shape, have been developed.

Physiological and Psychological Acoustics. Physiological acoustics studies auditory responses of the ear and its associated neural pathways, and psychological acoustics is the subjective perception of sounds through human auditory physiology. Mechanical, electrical, optical, radiological, or biochemical techniques are used to study neural responses to various aural stimuli. Because these techniques are typically invasive, experiments are performed on animals with auditory systems that are similar to the human system. In contrast, psychological acoustic studies are noninvasive and typically use human subjects.

A primary objective of psychological acoustics is to define the psychological correlates to the physical parameters of sound waves. Sound waves in air may be characterized by three physical parameters: frequency, intensity, and their spectrum. When a sound wave impinges on the ear, the pressure variations in the air are transformed by the middle ear to mechanical vibrations in the inner ear. The cochlea then decomposes the sound into its constituent frequencies and transforms these into neural action potentials, which travel to the brain where the sound is evidenced. Frequency is perceived as pitch, the intensity level as loudness, and the spectrum determines the timbre, or tone quality, of a note.

Another psychoacoustic effect is masking. When a person listens to a noisy version of recorded music, the noise virtually disappears if the music is being enjoyed. This ability of the brain to selectively listen has had important applications in digitally recorded music. When the sounds are digitally compressed, such as in MP3 (MPEG-1 audio layer 3) systems, the brain compensates for the loss of information; thus one experiences higher fidelity sound than the stored content would imply. Also, the brain creates information when the incoming signal is masked or nonexistent, producing a psychoacoustic phantom effect. This phantom effect is particularly prevalent when heightened perceptions are imperative, as when danger is lurking.

Psychoacoustic studies have determined that the frequency range of hearing is from 20 to about 20,000 Hz for young people, and the upper limit progressively decreases with age. The rate at which hearing acuity declines depends on several factors, not the least of which is lifetime exposure to loud sounds, which progressively deteriorate the hair cells of the cochlea. Moderate hearing loss can be compensated for by a hearing aid; severe loss requires a cochlear implant.

Speech Acoustics. Also known as acoustic phonetics, speech acoustics deals with speech production and recognition. The scientific study of speech began with Thomas Alva Edison's phonograph, which allowed a speech signal to be recorded and stored for later analysis. Replaying the same short speech segment several times using consecutive filters passing through a limited range of frequencies creates a spectrogram, which visualizes the spectral properties of vowels and consonants. During the first half of the twentieth century, Bell Telephone Laboratories dedicated considerable time and resources to the systematic understanding of all aspects of speech, including vocal tract resonances, voice quality, and prosodic features of speech. For the first time, electric circuit theory was applied to speech acoustics, and analogue electric circuits were used to investigate synthetic speech.

Musical Acoustics. A conjunction of music, craftsmanship, auditory science, and vibration physics, musical acoustics analyzes musical instruments to better understand how the instruments are crafted, the physical principles of their tone production, and why each instrument has a unique timbre. Musical instruments are studied by analyzing their tones and then creating computer models to synthesize these sounds. When the sounds can be recreated with minimal software complications, a synthesizer featuring realistic orchestral tones may be constructed. The second method of study is to assemble an instrument or modify an existing instrument to perform nondestructive (or on occasion destructive) testing so that the effects of various modifications may be gauged.

Underwater Sound. Also known as hydroacoustics, this field uses frequencies between 10 Hz and 1 megahertz (MHz). The deployment of submarines in World War I provided the impetus for the rapid

Interesting Facts about Acoustics

- Scientists have created an acoustic refrigerator, which uses a standing sound wave in a resonator to provide the motive power for operation. Oscillating gas particles increase the local temperature, causing heat to be transferred to the container walls, where it is expelled to the environment, cooling the interior.

- A cochlear implant, an electronic device surgically implanted in the inner ear, provides some hearing ability to those with damaged cochlea or those with congenital deafness. Because the implants use only about two dozen electrodes to replace 16,000 hair cells, speech sounds, although intelligible, have a robotic quality.

- MP3 files contain audio that is digitally encoded using an algorithm that compresses the data by a factor of about eleven but yields a reasonably faithful reproduction. The quality of sound reproduced depends on the data sampling rate, the quality of the encoder, and the complexity of the signal.

- Sound cannot travel through a vacuum, but it can travel four times faster through water than through air.

- The "cocktail party effect" refers to a person's ability to direct attention to one conversation at a time despite the many conversations taking place in the room.

- Continued exposure to noise over 85 decibels (dB) will gradually cause hearing loss. The noise level on a quiet residential street is 40 dB, a vacuum cleaner 60–85 dB, a leafblower 110 dB, an ambulance siren 120 dB, a rifle shot 160 dB, and a rocket launching from its pad 180 dB.

development of underwater listening devices (hydrophones) and sonar (sound navigation ranging), the acoustic equivalent of radar. Pulses of sound are emitted and the echoes are processed to extract information about submerged objects. When the speed of underwater sound is known, the reflection time for a pulse determines the distance to an object. If the object is moving, its speed of approach or recession is deduced from the frequency shift of the reflection, or the Doppler effect.

Returning pulses have a higher frequency when the object approaches and lower frequency when it moves away.

Noise. Physically, noise may be defined as an intermittent or random oscillation with multiple frequency components, but psychologically, noise is any unwanted sound. Noise can adversely affect human health and well-being by inducing stress, interfering with sleep, increasing heart rate, raising blood pressure, modifying hormone secretion, and even inducing depression. The physical effects of noise are no less severe. The vibrations in irregular road surfaces caused by large rapid vehicles can cause adjacent buildings to vibrate to an extent that is intolerable to the buildings' inhabitants, even without structural damage. Machinery noise in industry is a serious problem because continuous exposure to loud sounds will induce hearing loss. In apartment buildings, noise transmitted through walls is always problematic; the goal is to obtain adequate sound insulation using lightweight construction materials.

Traffic noise, both external and internal, is ubiquitous in modern life. The first line of defense is to reduce noise at its source by improving engine enclosures, mufflers, and tires. The next method, used primarily when interstate highways are adjacent to residential areas, is to block the noise by the construction of concrete barriers or the planting of sound-absorbing vegetation. Internal automobile noise has been greatly abated by designing more aerodynamically efficient vehicles to reduce air turbulence, using better sound isolation materials, and improving vibration isolation.

Aircraft noise, particularly in the vicinity of airports, is a serious problem exacerbated by the fact that as modern airplanes have become more powerful, the noise they generate has risen concomitantly. The noise radiated by jet engines is reduced by two structural modifications. Acoustic linings are placed around the moving parts to absorb the high frequencies caused by jet whine and turbulence, but this modification is limited by size and weight constraints. The second modification is to reduce the number of rotor blades and stator vanes, but this is somewhat inhibited by the desired power output. Special noise problems occur when aircraft travel at supersonic speeds (faster than the speed of sound), as this propagates a large pressure wave toward the ground that is experienced as an explosion. The unexpected sonic boom startles people, breaks windows, and damages houses. Sonic booms have been known to destroy rock structures in national parks. Because of these concerns, commercial aircraft are prohibited from flying at supersonic speeds over land areas.

Construction equipment (such as earthmoving machines) creates high noise levels both internally and externally. When the cabs of these machines are not closed, the only feasible manner of protecting operators' hearing is by using ear plugs. By carefully designing an enclosed cabin, structural vibration can be reduced and sound leaks made less significant, thus quieting the operator's environment. Although manufacturers are attempting to reduce the external noise, it is a daunting task because the rubber tractor treads occasionally used to replace metal are not as durable.

Applications Past and Present

Ultrasonics. High-intensity ultrasonic applications include ultrasonic cleaning, mixing, welding, drilling, and various chemical processes. Ultrasonic cleaners use waves in the 150 to 400 kHz range on items (such as jewelry, watches, lenses, and surgical instruments) placed in an appropriate solution. Ultrasonic cleaners have proven to be particularly effective in cleaning surgical devices because they loosen contaminants by aggressive agitation irrespective of an instrument's size or shape, and disassembly is not required. Ultrasonic waves are effective in cleaning most metals and alloys, as well as wood, plastic, rubber, and cloth. Ultrasonic waves are used to emulsify two nonmiscible liquids, such as oil and water, by forming the liquids into finely dispersed particles that then remain in homogeneous suspension. Many paints, cosmetics, and foods are emulsions formed by this process.

Although aluminum cannot be soldered by conventional means, two surfaces subjected to intense ultrasonic vibration will bond—without the application of heat—in a strong and precise weld. Ultrasonic drilling is effective where conventional drilling is problematic, for instance, drilling square holes in glass. The drill bit, a transducer having the required shape and size, is used with an abrasive slurry that chips away the material when the suspended powder oscillates. Some of the chemical applications of ultrasonics are in the atomization of liquids, in electroplating, and as a catalyst in chemical reactions.

Low-intensity ultrasonic waves are used for nondestructive probing to locate flaws in materials for which complete reliability is mandatory, such as those used in spacecraft components and nuclear reactor vessels. When an ultrasonic transducer emits a pulse of energy into the test object, flaws reflect the wave and are detected. Because objects subjected to stress emit ultrasonic waves, these signals may be used to interpret the condition of the material as it is increasingly stressed. Another application is ultrasonic emission testing, which records the ultrasound emitted by porous rock when natural gas is pumped into cavities formed by the rock to determine the maximum pressure these natural holding tanks can withstand.

Low-intensity ultrasonics is used for medical diagnostics in two different applications. First, ultrasonic waves penetrate body tissues but are reflected by moving internal organs, such as the heart. The frequency of waves reflected from a moving structure is Doppler-shifted, thus causing beats with the original wave, which can be heard. This procedure is particularly useful for performing fetal examinations on a pregnant woman; because sound waves are not electromagnetic, they will not harm the fetus. The second application is to create a sonogram image of the body's interior. A complete cross-sectional image may be produced by superimposing the images scanned by successive ultrasonic waves passing through different regions. This procedure, unlike an x-ray, displays all the tissues in the cross section and also avoids any danger posed by the radiation involved in x-ray imaging.

Physiological and Psychological Acoustics. Because the ear is a nonlinear system, it produces beat tones that are the sum and difference of two frequencies. For example, if two sinusoidal frequencies of 100 and 150 Hz simultaneously arrive at the ear, the brain will, in addition to these two tones, create tones of 250 and 50 Hz (sum and difference, respectively). Thus, although a small speaker cannot reproduce the fundamental frequencies of bass tones, the difference between the harmonics of that pitch will re-create the missing fundamental in the listener's brain.

Another psychoacoustic effect is masking. When a person listens to a noisy version of recorded music, the noise virtually disappears if the individual is enjoying the music. This ability of the brain to selectively listen has had important applications in digitally recorded music. When sounds are digitally compressed, as in MP3 systems, the brain compensates for the loss of information, thus creating a higher fidelity sound than that conveyed by the stored content alone.

As twentieth-century technology evolved, environmental noise increased concomitantly; lifetime exposure to loud sounds, commercial and recreational, has created an epidemic of hearing loss, most noticeable in the elderly because the effects are cumulative. Wearing a hearing aid, fitted adjacent to or inside the ear canal, is an effectual means of counteracting this handicap. The device consists of one or several microphones, which create electric signals that are amplified and transduced into sound waves redirected back into the ear. More sophisticated hearing aids incorporate an integrated circuit to control volume, either manually or automatically, or to switch to volume contours designed for various listening environments, such conversations on the telephone or where excessive background noise is present.

Speech Acoustics. With the advent of the computer age, speech synthesis moved to digital processing, either by bandwidth compression of stored speech or by using a speech synthesizer. The synthesizer reads a text and then produces the appropriate phonemes on demand from their basic acoustic parameters, such as the vibration frequency of the vocal cords and the frequencies and amplitudes of the vowel formants. This method of generating speech is considerably more efficient in terms of data storage than archiving a dictionary of prerecorded phrases.

Another important, and probably the most difficult, area of speech acoustics is the machine recognition of spoken language. When machine recognition programs are sufficiently advanced, the computer will be able to listen to a sentence in any reasonable dialect and produce a printed text of the utterance. Two basic recognition strategies exist, one dealing with words spoken in isolation and the other with continuous speech. In both cases, it is desirable to teach the computer to recognize the speech of different people through a training program. Because recognition of continuous speech is considerably more difficult than the identification of isolated words, very sophisticated pattern-matching models must be employed. One example of a machine recognition system is a word-driven dictation system that uses sophisticated software to process input speech. This system is somewhat adaptable to different voices and is able to recognize 30,000 words at a rate of 30 words per minute. The ideal machine recognition system would translate a spoken input language into another language in real time with correct grammar. Although some progress is being made, such a device has remained in the realm of speculative fantasy.

Musical Acoustics. The importance of musical acoustics to manufacturers of quality instruments is apparent. During the last decades of the twentieth century, fundamental research led, for example, to vastly improved French horns, organ pipes, orchestral strings, and the creation of an entirely new family of violins.

Underwater Sound. Applications for underwater acoustics include devices for underwater communication by acoustic means, remote control devices, underwater navigation and positioning systems, acoustic thermometers to measure ocean temperature, and echo sounders to locate schools of fish or other biota. Low-frequency devices can be used to explore the seabed for seismic research.

Although primitive measuring devices were developed in the 1920s, it was during the 1930s that sonar systems began incorporating piezoelectric transducers to increase their accuracy. These improved systems and their increasingly more sophisticated progeny became essential for the submarine warfare of World War II. After the war, theoretical advances in underwater acoustics coupled with computer technology have raised sonar systems to ever more sophisticated levels.

Noise. One system for abating unwanted sound is active noise control. The first successful application of active noise control was noise-canceling headphones, which reduce unwanted sound by using microphones placed in proximity to the ear to record the incoming noise. Electronic circuitry then generates a signal, exactly opposite to the incoming sound, which is reproduced in the earphones, thus canceling the noise by destructive interference. This system enables listeners to enjoy music without having to use excessive volume levels to mask outside noise and allows people to sleep in noisy vehicles such as airplanes. Because active noise suppression is more effective with low frequencies, most commercial systems rely on soundproofing the earphone to attenuate high frequencies. To effectively cancel high frequencies, the microphone and emitter would have to be situated adjacent to the user's eardrum, but this is not technically feasible. Active noise control is also being considered as a means of controlling low-frequency airport noise, but because of its complexity and expense, this is not yet commercially feasible.

Impact on Industry

Acoustics is the focus of research at numerous governmental agencies and academic institutions, as well as some private industries. Acoustics also plays an important role in many industries, often as part of product design (hearing aids and musical instruments) or as an element in a service (noise control consulting).

Industry and Business. Many businesses (such as the manufacturers of hearing aids, ultrasound medical devices, and musical instruments) use acoustics in their products or services and therefore employ experts in acoustics. Businesses are also involved in many aspects of acoustic research, particularly controlling noise and facilitating communication. Raytheon BBN Technologies in Cambridge, Massachusetts, has developed low-data-rate Noise Robust Vocoders (electronic speech synthesizers) that generate comprehensible speech at data rates considerably below other state-of-the-art devices. Acoustic Research Laboratories in Sydney, Australia, designs and manufactures specialized equipment for measuring environmental noise and vibration, in addition to providing contract research and development services.

Government Agencies and Military. Acoustics is studied in many government laboratories in the United States, including the US Naval Research Laboratory (NRL), the Air Force Research Laboratory (AFRL), the Los Alamos National Laboratory, and the Lawrence Livermore National Laboratory. Research at the NRL and the AFRL is primarily in the applied acoustics area, and Los Alamos and Lawrence

Occupation	Sound Engineering Technicians
Employment 2010	19,000
Projected Employment 2020	19,100
Change in Number (2010–20)	100 .
Percent Change	1%

Bureau of Labor Statistics, 2012

Livermore are oriented toward physical acoustics. The NRL emphasizes fundamental multidisciplinary research focused on creating and applying new materials and technologies to maritime applications. In particular, the applied acoustics division, using ongoing basic scientific research, develops improved signal processing systems for detecting and tracking underwater targets. The AFRL is heavily invested in research on auditory localization (spatial hearing), virtual auditory display technologies, and speech intelligibility in noisy environments. The effects of high-intensity noise on humans, as well as methods of attenuation, constitute a significant area of investigation at this facility. Another important area of research is the problem of providing intelligible voice communication in extremely noisy situations, such as those encountered by military or emergency personnel using low data rate narrowband radios, which compromise signal quality.

Academic Research and Teaching. Research in acoustics is conducted at many colleges and universities in the United States, usually through physics or engineering departments, but, in the case of physiological and psychological acoustics, in groups that draw from multiple departments, including psychology, neurology, and linguistics. The Speech Research Laboratory at Indiana University investigates speech perception and processing through a broad interdisciplinary research program. The Speech Research Lab, a collaboration between the University of Delaware and the A. I. duPont Hospital for Children, creates speech synthesizers for the vocally impaired. A human speaker records a data bank of words and phrases that can be concatenated on demand to produce natural-sounding speech.

Academic research in acoustics is also being conducted in laboratories in Europe and other parts of the world. The Laboratoire d'Acoustique at the Université de Maine in Le Mans, France, specializes in research in vibration in materials, transducers, and musical instruments. The Andreyev Acoustics Institute of the Russian Acoustical Society brings together researchers from Russian universities, agencies, and businesses to conduct fundamental and applied research in ocean acoustics, ultrasonics, signal processing, noise and vibration, electroacoustics, and bioacoustics. The Speech and Acoustics Laboratory at the Nara Institute of Science and Technology in Nara, Japan, studies diverse aspects of human-machine communication through speech-oriented multimodal interaction. The Acoustics Research Centre, part of the National Institute of Creative Arts and Industries in New Zealand, is concerned with the impact of noise on humans. A section of this group, Acoustic Testing Service, provides commercial testing of building materials for their noise attenuation properties.

Academic positions dedicated to acoustics are few, as are the numbers of qualified applicants. Most graduates of acoustics programs find employment in research-based industries in which acoustical aspects of products are important, and others work for government laboratories.

Social Context and Future Prospects

Acoustics affects virtually every aspect of modern life; its contributions to societal needs are incalculable. Ultrasonic waves clean objects, are routinely employed to probe matter, and are used in medical diagnosis. Cochlear implants restore people's ability to hear, and active noise control helps provide quieter listening environments. New concert halls are routinely designed with excellent acoustical properties, and vastly improved or entirely new musical instruments have made their debut. Infrasound from earthquakes is used to study the composition of Earth's mantle, and sonar is essential to locate submarines and aquatic life. Sound waves are used to explore the effects of structural vibrations. Automatic speech recognition devices and hearing aid technology are constantly improving.

Many societal problems related to acoustics remain to be tackled. The technological advances that made modern life possible have also resulted in more people with hearing loss. Environmental noise is ubiquitous and increasing despite efforts to design quieter machinery and pains taken to contain unwanted sound or to isolate it from people. Also, although medical technology has been able to help many hearing- and speech-impaired people, other individuals still lack appropriate treatments. For example, although voice generators exist, there is considerable room for improvement.

Further Reading

Bass, Henry E., and William J. Cavanaugh, eds. *ASA at Seventy-Five*. Melville, NY: Acoustical Society of America, 2004. An overview of the history, progress, and future possibilities for each of the fifteen major subdivisions of acoustics as defined by the Acoustical Society of America.

Beyer, Robert T. *Sounds of Our Times: Two Hundred Years of Acoustics*. New York: Springer-Verlag, 1999. A history of the development of all areas of acoustics. Organized into chapters covering twenty-five to fifty years. Virtually all subfields of acoustics are covered.

Crocker, Malcolm J., ed. *The Encyclopedia of Acoustics*. 4 vols. New York: Wiley, 1997. A comprehensive work detailing virtually all aspects of acoustics.

Everest, F. Alton, and Ken C. Pohlmann. *Master Handbook of Acoustics*. 5th ed. New York: McGraw-Hill, 2009. A revision of a classic reference work designed for those who desire accurate information on a level accessible to the layperson with limited technical ability.

Rossing, Thomas, and Neville Fletcher. *Principles of Vibration and Sound*. 2d ed. New York: Springer-Verlag, 2004. A basic introduction to the physics of sound and vibration.

Rumsey, Francis, and Tim McCormick. *Sound and Recording: An Introduction*. 5th ed. Boston: Elsevier/Focal Press, 2004. Presents basic information on the principles of sound, sound perception, and audio technology and systems.

Strong, William J., and George R. Plitnik. *Music, Speech, Audio*. 3d ed. Provo, UT: Brigham Young University Academic, 2007. A comprehensive text, written for the layperson, which covers vibration, the ear and hearing, noise, architectural acoustics, speech, musical instruments, and sound recording and reproduction.

Swift, Gregory. "Thermoacoustic Engines and Refrigerators." *Physics Today* (July, 1995): 22–28. Explains how sound waves may be used to create more efficient refrigerators with no moving parts.

About the Author: George R. Plitnik, BA, BS, MA, PhD, is a professor of physics at Frostburg State University. He received bachelor's degrees from Lebanon Valley College, a master's degree from Wake Forest University, and a doctorate from Brigham Young University. His academic specialty is acoustics, and he is interested in anthropogenic climate modification, energy, pollution control, and music. He lives in a passive solar house, which he designed and built. He teaches courses on solar energy and global warming.

Sound Engineering Technician

Earnings (Yearly Median): $47,080 (Bureau of Labor Statistics, 2012)

Employment and Outlook: Slower than average growth (Bureau of Labor Statistics, 2012)

O*NET-SOC Code: 27-4014.00

Related Career Clusters: Arts; Audio/Video Technology & Communications; Information Technology; Marketing

Scope of Work

Sound engineering technicians operate the machinery and equipment used to record, mix, and produce music, voices, or sound effects for a variety of purposes. They are employed by recording studios, sporting arenas, theater productions, and film studios in addition to any number of jobs in which sound recording or reproduction is required. They are the technological backbone of the sound engineering industry, playing an important role in developing musical-instrument digital-interface programs, live audio systems, and postproduction audio equipment.

Sound engineering technicians work in dynamic, fast-paced environments such as radio and television broadcasting and live concert entertainment, mixing sound and maintaining equipment to keep shows running. Technicians have a high level of technical dexterity and understand the finer mechanisms of audio production.

Education and Coursework

A bachelor's degree is not required for most sound engineering technician positions. At minimum, a high school diploma or General Educational Development (GED) certificate is required for most entry-level positions. It is common, however, for technicians to have associate's degrees or certification from trade schools or one-year vocational programs. High school students hoping to enter the sound engineering field should familiarize themselves with extracurricular and school-affiliated vocational training options offered in their community. High school courses in audiovisual production and music theory are another good outlet for establishing basic sound engineering skills.

Audio engineering programs are offered on the collegiate level, and earning a degree from a four-year program could give a prospective technician a competitive edge when seeking employment. Skills gained through firsthand experience and on-the-job training, however, are at least as important as formal education in the sound engineering field. Prospective technicians should seek internship and apprenticeship positions that provide significant opportunities to work one-on-one with experienced technicians.

Audio production has nearly completed a full shift to digital means of recording, editing, and broadcasting. Therefore, sound engineering technicians are required to have exemplary computer skills. Prospective technicians should take high school courses in math, physics, and computer science in addition to participating in extracurricular audiovisual clubs to gain practical experience. Continuing education courses in computer software used for audio production are available through a variety of channels, and technicians should remain abreast of new technologies as they are integrated into the industry.

Career Enhancement and Training

Most employers do not require industry certification, though obtaining certificates does make candidates more competitive. For example, the Society of Broadcast Engineers offers an audio engineer certificate

---

> ### **Transferable Skills**
> - Interpersonal/Social Skills: Listening (SCANS Basic Skill)
> - Interpersonal/Social Skills: Working as a member of a team (SCANS Workplace Competency – Interpersonal)
> - Organization & Management Skills: Paying attention to and handling details
> - Work Environment Skills: Working in a noisy atmosphere
> - Technical Skills: Applying technology to a task (SCANS Workplace Competency – Technology)
> - Technical Skills: Working with machines, tools, or other objects

exam for sound engineering technicians with at least five years of experience working in the television and radio industries.

InfoComm International, one of the leading audiovisual professional organizations, also offers certification programs in design, installation, and general skills. In addition to certificate exams, InfoComm hosts online and onsite continuing education courses on live-event engineering, project management, sales, and more.

Given the dynamic nature of the audio engineering field, it is recommended that technicians take training courses on new technologies and techniques as frequently as possible so as to maintain a competitive edge within the industry. The Audio Engineering Society maintains an extensive online directory of universities, technical schools, and independent professional organizations that provide continuing education in a variety of audio production fields.

Daily Tasks and Technology

The daily tasks of a sound engineering technician vary with the field of application. In general, however, the workload includes setting up microphones and other audio equipment; recording speech, music, and sounds; troubleshooting equipment problems; and converting audio for editing. Technicians working in the broadcasting industry might be charged with regulating volume levels and sound quality during a live

A Conversation with a Management Consultant

Job Title: Principal at a top global management consulting firm

What was your career path?

Seven years in graduate school (astrophysics, Caltech), followed by three years as post doctorate (U. Chicago).

What are three pieces of advice you would offer someone interested in your profession?

1. Know why you want to become a management consultant. Have a long-term vision for where you want to be professionally in five or ten years, and have a view on how consulting will advance these goals. Be able to explain your motivation crisply. And, believe it as well—it is critical that your interest is authentic, not just to be more persuasive, but also to be sure this step is the right one. Talk to other PhDs who have made this career step and listen to their stories to develop a sense of whether it is right for you.

2. Excel at case interviews. We interview everyone, PhDs included, through multiple rounds of case interviews; case interviews are a proven approach for evaluating talent and fit with our business model. Case interviews are challenging and arduous, but fortunately, case interviewing is a learnable skill. Practice with like-minded folks—e.g., MBAs or PhDs who understand the expectations and rigors of the case interview, and who can provide you with good feedback. This is also a good way to learn more about the business and build your professional network.

3. Once you join the firm, be prepared to learn. You may have many significant accomplishments in your scientific career, but when you join a management consulting firm, you will likely find yourself back at the bottom of the learning curve. This is expected. Management consulting will stretch you in new and different ways;

you will learn new skills in problem-solving, verbal, and written communications, collaborating with clients, and driving client value. The good news is that most leading firms recognize this need and will invest time and energy to train their staff and make them successful. Human capital is our primary asset, so we take extraordinary pains to develop our talent. More to the point, consulting is a truly an apprenticeship business, and even MBAs can have significant learning curves. So bring an open mind, park your ego at the door, and jump in.

What paths for career advancement are available to you?

In my firm, the next step is partner. If I were moving to industry, I would target senior firector or VP-level positions.

program. Similarly, sound engineering technicians working in live music entertainment perform equivalent duties, but in concert settings. Theater productions require sound engineers to equip multiple actors with independent wireless microphones that they must then monitor for volume level and functionality throughout the performance.

Many sound engineers work as third-party contractors, providing equipment and audio services for many kinds of events. Sound engineering technicians are responsible for the setup, tear-down, and operation of microphones, public-address systems, soundboards, and other necessary audio equipment during the course of an event. Technicians work closely with producers, performers, and event planners to achieve the desired sound for the project. On-location work requires a substantial amount of manual labor and occasional heavy lifting.

Sound engineering technicians use advanced computer software to control audio equipment and to edit recorded material during postproduction in films, music, and television. Commonly used audio editing programs such as Avid Pro Tools and Logic are a crucial component of the sound engineering technician's job. Digital multimedia platforms such as Final Cut Pro are also used for certain projects, and a general understanding of computer science would be beneficial to any sound engineering technician.

Earnings and Employment Outlook

The median annual wage for sound engineering technicians in 2010 was $47,080 according to the US Bureau of Labor Statistics (BLS). Technicians working in major cities or for established institutions typically earn more than those working in small-market positions. Evening, weekend, and holiday work is common for sound engineering technicians working in fields with inherently sporadic schedules. Some broadcast media runs twenty-four hours a day, requiring sound technicians to be on hand at all times.

As of 2010, nineteen thousand people were employed as sound engineering technicians in the United States, according to the BLS. Employment numbers are projected to increase only 1 percent by 2020 because of the high rate of competitive applicants, radio and television station consolidation, and laborsaving advances in technology.

Related Occupations

- **Broadcast Technician:** Broadcast technicians operate and maintain the electronic equipment used to transmit radio and television programs.

- **Film and Video Editor:** Film and video editors edit moving images on film and other media, synchronizing soundtracks with images.

- **Motion Picture Projectionist:** Projectionists set up, maintain, and operate motion-picture projection and sound-reproduction equipment.

- **Musical Instrument Repair Technician:** Instrument repair technicians fix stringed, reed, percussion, and wind instruments, and they may specialize in tuning pianos or other large instruments.

Future Applications

As audio production technology is becoming more advanced, it is also becoming more accessible and affordable. Mixing boards used to be the domain of well-trained engineers, but now anyone with a laptop can lay down tracks of near-professional quality. No amount of self-taught prowess, however, can rival the depth of industry experience provided by a career as a sound engineering technician.

Live events will always require the skilled hands of sound engineering technicians. Furthermore, high schools and universities are implementing more digital and interactive services within the classroom than ever before, all of which will require the help of sound engineering technicians. Also, the film and television industries are evolving toward near-exclusive use of digital-based software and equipment, meaning that sound engineer technicians will continue to be in demand. Though the industry is projected to experience only 1 percent growth between 2010 and 2020, it will remain a highly competitive field that will require the ongoing acquisition and implementation of knowledge.

—Steve Miller

More Information

Audio Engineering Society
International Headquarters
60 East 42nd Street, Room 2520
New York, NY 10165
www.aes.org

InfoComm International
11242 Waples Mill Road, Suite 200
Fairfax, VA 22030
www.infocomm.org

Society of Broadcast Engineers
9102 North Meridian Street, Suite 150
Indianapolis, IN 46260
www.sbe.org

The Recording Academy
Producers and Engineers Wing
3030 Olympic Boulevard
Santa Monica, CA 90404
www.grammy.org/recording-academy

Recording Connection Audio Institute
1201 West 5th Street, Suite M130
Los Angeles, CA 90017
www.recordingconnection.com

Aeronautics and Aviation

Algebra; calculus; inorganic chemistry; organic chemistry; physical chemistry; optics; modern physics; statics; aerodynamics; thermodynamics; strength of materials; propulsion; propeller and rotor theory; vehicle performance; aircraft design; avionics; orbital mechanics; spacecraft design.

DEFINITION

Aeronautics is the science of atmospheric flight. Aviation is the design, development, production, and operation of flight vehicles. Aerospace engineering extends these fields to space vehicles. Transonic airliners, airships, space launch vehicles, satellites, helicopters, interplanetary probes, and fighter planes are all applications of aerospace engineering.

Basic Principles

Aeronautics is the science of atmospheric flight. The term ("aero" referring to flight and "nautics" referring to ships or sailing) originated from the activities of pioneers who aspired to navigate the sky. These early engineers designed, tested, and flew their own creations, many of which were lighter-than-air balloons. Modern aeronautics encompasses the science and engineering of designing and analyzing all areas associated with flying machines.

Aviation (based on the Latin word for "bird") originated with the idea of flying like the birds using heavier-than-air vehicles. "Aviation" refers to the field of operating aircraft, while the term "aeronautics" has been superseded by "aerospace engineering," which specifically includes the science and engineering of spacecraft in the design, development, production, and operation of flight vehicles.

A fundamental tenet of aerospace engineering is to deal with uncertainty by tying analyses closely to what is definitely known, for example, the laws of physics and mathematical proofs. Lighter-than-air airships are based on the principle of buoyancy, which derives from the law of gravitation. An object that weighs less than the equivalent volume of air experiences a net upward force as the air sinks around it.

Two basic principles that enable the design of heavier-than-air flight vehicles are those of aerodynamic lift and propulsion. Both arise from Sir Isaac Newton's second and third laws of motion. Aerodynamic lift is a force perpendicular to the direction of motion, generated from the turning of flowing air around an object. In propulsion, the reaction to the acceleration of a fluid generates a force that propels an object, whether in air or in the vacuum of space. Understanding these principles allowed aeronauts to design vehicles that could fly steadily despite being much heavier than the air they displaced and allowed rocket scientists to develop vehicles that could accelerate in space. Spaceflight occurs at speeds so high that the vehicle's kinetic energy is comparable to the potential energy due to gravitation. Here the principles of orbital mechanics derive from the laws of dynamics and gravitation and extend to the regime of relativistic phenomena. The engineering sciences of building vehicles that can fly, keeping them stable, controlling their flight, navigating, communicating, and ensuring the survival, health, and comfort of occupants, draw on every field of science.

Core Concepts

Force Balance in Flight. Five basic forces acting on a flight vehicle are aerodynamic lift, gravity, thrust, drag, and centrifugal force. For a vehicle in steady level flight in the atmosphere, lift and thrust balance gravity (weight) and aerodynamic drag. Centrifugal force due to moving steadily around the earth is too weak at most airplane flight speeds but is strong for a maneuvering aircraft. Aircraft turn by rolling the lift vector toward the center of curvature of the desired flight path, balancing the centrifugal reaction due to inertia. In the case of a vehicle in space beyond the atmosphere, centrifugal force and thrust counter gravitational force.

Aerodynamic Lift. Aerodynamics deals with the forces due to the motion of air and other gaseous fluids relative to bodies. Aerodynamic lift is generated perpendicular to the direction of the free stream as the reaction to the rate of change of momentum of air turning around an object, and, at high speeds, to compression of air by the object. Flow turning is accomplished by changing the angle of attack of the surface, by using the camber of the surface in subsonic flight, or by generating vortices along the leading edges of swept wings.

Propulsion. Propulsive force is generated as a reaction to the rate of change of momentum of a fluid moving through and out of the vehicle. Rockets carry all of the propellant onboard and accelerate it out through a nozzle using chemical heat release, other heat sources, or electromagnetic fields. Jet engines "breathe" air and accelerate it after reaction with fuel. Rotors, propellers, and fans exert lift force on the air and generate thrust from the reaction to this force. Solar sails use the pressure of solar radiation to push large, ultralight surfaces.

Static Stability. An aircraft is statically stable if a small perturbation in its attitude causes a restoring aerodynamic moment that erases the perturbation. Typically, the aircraft center of gravity must be ahead of the center of pressure for longitudinal stability. The tails or canards help provide stability about the different axes. Rocket engines are said to be stable if the rate of generation of gases in the combustion chamber does not depend on pressure stronger than by a direct proportionality, such as a pressure exponent of 1.

Flight Dynamics and Controls. Static stability is not the whole story, as every pilot discovers when the airplane drifts periodically up and down instead of holding a steady altitude and speed. Flight dynamics studies the phenomena associated with aerodynamic loads and the response of the vehicle to control surface deflections and engine-thrust changes. The study begins with writing the equations of motion of the aircraft resolved along the six degrees of freedom: linear movement along the longitudinal, vertical and sideways axes, and roll, yaw, and pitch rotations about them. Maneuvering aircraft must deal with coupling between the different degrees of freedom, so that roll accompanies yaw, and so on.

The autopilot system was an early flight-control achievement. Terrain-following systems combine information about the terrain with rapid updates, enabling military aircraft to fly close to the ground, much faster than a human pilot could do safely. Modern flight-control systems achieve such feats as reconfiguring control surfaces and fuel to compensate for damage and engine failures; or enabling autonomous helicopters to detect, hover over, and pick up small objects and return; or sending a space probe at thousands of kilometers per hour close to a planetary moon or landing it on an asteroid and returning it to Earth. This field makes heavy use of ordinary differential equations and transform techniques, along with simulation software.

Orbital Missions. The rocket equation attributed to Russian scientist Konstantin Tsiolkovsky related the speed that a rocket-powered vehicle gains to the amount and speed of the mass that it ejects. A vehicle launched from Earth's surface goes into a trajectory where its kinetic energy is exchanged for gravitational potential energy. At low speeds, the resulting trajectory intersects the Earth, so that the vehicle falls to the surface. At high enough speeds, the vehicle goes so far so fast that its trajectory remains in space and takes the shape of a continuous ellipse around Earth. At even higher kinetic energy levels, the vehicle goes into a hyperbolic trajectory, escaping Earth's orbit into the solar system. The key is thus to achieve enough tangential speed relative to Earth. Most rockets rise rapidly through the atmosphere so that the acceleration to high tangential speed occurs well above the atmosphere, thus minimizing air-drag losses.

Hohmann Transfer. Theoretically, the most efficient way to impart kinetic energy to a vehicle is impulsive launch, expending all the propellant instantly so that no energy is wasted lifting or accelerating propellant with the vehicle. Of course, this would destroy any vehicle other than a cannonball, so large rockets use gentle accelerations of no more than 1.4 to 3 times the acceleration due to gravity. The advantage of impulsive thrust is used in the Hohmann transfer maneuver between different orbits in space. A rocket is launched into a highly eccentric elliptical trajectory. At its highest point, more thrust is added quickly. This sends the vehicle into a circular orbit at the desired height or into a new orbit that takes it close to another heavenly body. Reaching the same final orbit using continuous, gradual thrust would require

---

Interesting Facts about Aeronautics and Aviation

- The X-29 test vehicle demonstrated that an aircraft could be built to be statically unstable and yet maintain stable flight. The flight control computer reliably provides rapid updates of control surface actuators to compensate for disturbances before they amplify. Modern fighter aircraft are marginally unstable but use control systems to augment stability, thereby increasing maneuver performance.

- A long conductor trailed from a spacecraft generates an electric current when moving through Earth's magnetic field. Conversely, a current passed through a tether between two objects in different orbits generates a force. This is a proposed electrodynamic space broom, which will drag debris into orbits where they will quickly burn up in the atmosphere.

- When aerodynamic lift is generated, the flow around the body is pushed down (against the direction of lift), while the flow outside the body's span gets lifted up. The energy in this updraft is wasted unless another aircraft benefits from following in close proximity off to one side. Birds use this feature routinely and so have air forces since World War I to save fuel. Swarms of small unmanned aerial vehicles, or micro spacecraft, can generate the same resolution and efficiency as a very large antenna by maintaining relative position in flight.

roughly twice as much expenditure of energy. However, continuous thrust is still an attractive option for long missions in space, because a small amount of thrust can be generated using electric propulsion engines that accelerate propellant to extremely high speeds compared with the chemical engines used for the initial ascent from Earth.

Applications Past and Present

Aerospace Structures. Aerospace engineers always seek to minimize the mass required to build the vehicle but still ensure its safety and durability. Unlike buildings, bridges, or even (to some degree) automobiles, aircraft cannot be made safer merely by making them more massive, because they must also be able to overcome Earth's gravity. This exigency has driven development of new materials and detailed, accurate methods of analysis, measurement, and construction. The first aircraft were built mostly from wood frames and fabric skins. These were superseded by all-metal craft, constructed using the monocoque concept (in which the outer skin bears most of the stresses). The Mosquito high-speed bomber in World War II reverted to wood construction for better performance. Woodworkers learned to align the grain (fiber direction) along the principal stress axes. Metal offers the same strength in all directions for the same thickness. Composite structures allow fibers with high tensile strength to be placed along the directions where strength is needed, bonding different layers together.

Aeroelasticity. Aeroelasticity is the study of the response of structurally elastic bodies to aerodynamic loads. Early in the history of aviation, several mysterious and fatal accidents occurred wherein pieces of wings or tails failed in flight, under conditions where the steady loads should have been well below the strength limits of the structure. The intense research to address these disasters showed that beyond some flight speed, small perturbations in lift, such as those due to a gust or a maneuver, would cause the structure to respond in a resonant bending-twisting oscillation, the perturbation amplitude rapidly rising in a "flutter" mode until structural failure occurred. Predicting such aeroelastic instabilities demanded a highly mathematical approach to understand and apply the theories of unsteady aerodynamics and structural dynamics. Modern aircraft are designed so that the flutter speed is well above any possible speed achieved. In the case of helicopter rotor blades and gas turbine engine blades, the problems of ensuring aeroelastic stability are still the focus of leading-edge research. Related advances in structural dynamics have enabled development of composite structures and of highly efficient turbo machines that use counter-rotating stages, such as those in the F135 engines used in the F-35 Joint Strike Fighter. Such advances also made it possible for earthquake-resistant high-rise buildings to be built in cities such as San Francisco, Tokyo, and Los Angeles, where a number of sensors, structural-dynamics-analysis software, and actuators allow the correct response to dampen the effects of earth movements even on the upper floors.

Smart Materials. Various composite materials such as carbon fiber and metal matrix composites have come to find application even in primary aircraft structures. The Boeing 787 is the first to use a composite main spar in its wings. Research on nano materials promises the development of materials with hundreds of times more strength per unit mass than steel. Another leading edge of research in materials is in developing high-temperature or very low-temperature (cryogenic) materials for use inside jet and rocket engines, the spinning blades of turbines, and the impeller blades of liquid hydrogen pumps in rocket engines. Single crystal turbine blades enabled the development of jet engines with very high turbine inlet temperatures and, thus, high thermodynamic efficiency. Ceramic designs that are not brittle are pushing turbine inlet temperatures even higher. Other materials are "smart," meaning they respond actively in some way to inputs. Examples include piezoelectric materials.

Wind Tunnels and Other Physical Test Facilities. Wind tunnels, used by the Wright brothers to develop airfoil shapes with desirable characteristics, are still used heavily in developing concepts and proving the performance of new designs, investigating causes of problems, and developing solutions and data to validate computational prediction techniques. Generally, a wind tunnel has a fan or a high-pressure reservoir to add work to the air and raise its stagnation pressure. The air then flows through means of reducing turbulence and is accelerated to the maximum speed in the test section, where models and measurement systems operate.

The power required to operate a wind tunnel is proportional to the mass flow rate through the tunnel and to the cube of the flow speed achieved. Low-speed wind tunnels have relatively large test sections and can operate continuously for several minutes at a time. Supersonic tunnels generally operate with air blown from a high-pressure reservoir for short durations. Transonic tunnels are designed with ventilating slots to operate in the difficult regime where there may be both supersonic waves and subsonic flow over the test configuration.

Hypersonic tunnels require heaters to avoid liquefying the air and to simulate the high stagnation temperatures of hypersonic flight and operate for millisecond durations. Shock tubes generate a shock from the rupture of a diaphragm, allowing high-energy air to expand into stationary air in the tube. They are used to simulate the extreme conditions across shocks in hypersonic flight. Many other specialized test facilities are used in structural and materials testing, developing jet and rocket engines, and designing control systems.

Avionics and Navigation. Condensed from the term "aviation electronics," the term "avionics" has come to include the generation of intelligent software systems and sensors to control unmanned aerial vehicles (UAVs), which may operate autonomously. Avionics also deals with various subsystems such as radar and communications, as well as navigation equipment, and is closely linked to the disciplines of flight dynamics, controls, and navigation.

During World War II, pilots on long-range night missions would navigate celestially. The gyroscopes in their aircrafts would spin at high speed so that their inertia allowed them to maintain a reference position as the aircraft changed altitude or accelerated. Most modern aircraft use the Global Positioning System (GPS), Galileo, or GLONASS satellite constellations to obtain accurate updates of position, altitude, and velocity. The ordinary GPS signal determines position and speed with fair accuracy. Much greater precision and higher rates of updates are available to authorized vehicle systems through the differential GPS signal and military frequencies.

Gravity Assist Maneuver. Yuri Kondratyuk, the Ukrainian scientist whose work paved the way for the first manned mission to the moon, suggested in 1918 that a spacecraft could use the gravitational attraction of the moons of planets to accelerate and decelerate at the two ends of a journey between planets. The Soviet Luna 3 probe used the gravity of the Moon when photographing the far side of it in 1959. American mathematician Michael Minovitch pointed out that the gravitational pull of planets along the trajectory of a spacecraft could be used to accelerate the craft toward other planets. The Mariner 10 probe used this "gravitational slingshot" maneuver around Venus to reach Mercury at a speed small enough to go into orbit around Mercury. The Voyager missions used the rare alignment of the outer planets to receive gravitational assists from Jupiter and Saturn to go on to Uranus and Neptune, before doing another slingshot around Jupiter and Saturn to escape the solar system. Gravity assist has become part of the mission planning for all exploration missions and even for missions near Earth, where the gravity of the Moon is used.

Impact on Industry

Aeronautics and aviation have had an immeasurable impact on industry and society. Millions of people fly long distances on aircraft every day, going about their business and visiting friends and relatives, at a cost that is far lower in relative terms than the cost of travel a century ago. Additionally, every technical innovation developed for aeronautics and aviation finds its way into improved industrial products. Composite structural materials are found in everything from tennis rackets to industrial machinery. Bridges, stadium domes, and skyscrapers are designed with aerospace structural-element technology and structural-dynamics instrumentation and testing techniques. Electric power is generated in utility power plants using steam generators sharing jet engine turbo machine origins.

Growth within the aeronautics and aviation industry is generally expected to grow more slowly than average for a range of occupations. As a sampling, employment of both aerospace engineers and aircraft mechanics is expected to grow more slowly than the average for all occupations through the year 2020, which means employment is projected to increase 3 percent to 9 percent. However, employment of pilots is expected to grow about as fast as the average for all occupations through the year 2020, which means employment is projected to increase 10 percent to 19 percent.

Aerospace Engineering. Aerospace engineers work on problems that push the frontiers of technology. Typical employers in this industry are manufacturers of aircraft or their parts and subsystems and the defense services, as well as airlines. Many aerospace engineers are also sought by financial services and other industries seeking those with excellent

Occupation	Aerospace engineering and operations technicians
Employment 2010	8.700
Projected Employment 2020	8,600
Change in Number (2010–20)	-100
Percent Change	-2%

*Bureau of Labor Statistics, 2012

quantitative (mathematical and scientific) skills and talents. New designs and new technologies involved in the creation of commercial and military aircraft will encourage demand for aerospace engineers.

Defense Industry. The defense industry is moving toward using aircraft that do not need a human crew and can perform beyond the limits of what a human can survive, so the glamorous occupation of combat jet pilot may be heading for extinction. Airline pilot salaries are also coming down from levels that compared with surgeons toward those more comparable to bus drivers. Aircraft approach, landing, traffic management, emergency response, and collision avoidance systems may soon become fully automated and will require maneuvering responses that are beyond what a human pilot can provide in time and accuracy.

Other Industries. Satellite antennae are found everywhere. Much digital signal processing, central to digital music and cell phone communications, came from research projects driven by the need to extract low-level signatures buried in noise. Similarly, image-processing algorithms that enable computed tomography (CT) scans of the human body, eye and cardiac diagnostics, image and video compression, and laser printing came from aerospace image-processing projects. The field of geoinformatics has advanced immensely, with most mapping, navigation, and remote-sensing enterprises assuming the use of space satellites. The GPS has spawned numerous products for terrestrial drivers on land and navigators on the ocean.

Government Agencies. Government agencies employing within the aeronautics and aviation fields include the Department of Defense, the National Aeronautics and Space Administration (NASA), and government laboratories. Aerospace engineers may specialize in one type of aerospace product, such as aircraft, missiles, or space vehicles. They may also specialize in engineering specialties such as product design, testing, or production

Occupation	Aerospace engineers
Employment 2010	81,000
Projected Employment 2020	85,000
Change in Number (2010–20)	4,000
Percent Change	5%

Bureau of Labor Statistics, 2012

research. Depending on their specialty, they may be called aeronautical engineers, aeronautical test engineers, or stress analysts.

Military. Although private companies build the military's aerospace equipment, military engineers are responsible for seeing that all equipment meets service needs. Aerospace engineers in the military also design and direct the development of military aircraft, missiles, and spacecraft. Newly commissioned aerospace engineers are usually assigned to engineering research and development units or laboratories. They work under the direction of experienced officers conducting research. With experience, they may serve as research and development managers or laboratory managers.

Academic Research and Teaching. There is opportunity for teaching at aviation institutes and within aeronautics programs and aerospace engineering and similar departments. For research, aerospace medicine research has developed advances in diagnosing and monitoring the human body and its responses to acceleration, bone marrow loss, muscular degeneration, and their prevention through exercise, hypoxia, radiation protection, heart monitoring, isolation from microorganisms, and drug delivery.

Social Context and Future Prospects

Airline travel is under severe stress in the first part of the twenty-first century. This is variously attributed to airport congestion, security issues, rising fuel prices, predatory competition, reduction of route monopolies, and leadership that appears to offer little vision beyond cost cutting. Meanwhile, the demand for air travel is rising all over the world. Global demand for commercial airliners is estimated at nearly 30,000 aircraft through 2030 and is valued at more than $3.2 trillion—in addition to 17,000 business jets valued at more than $300 billion.

Detailed design and manufacturing of individual aircraft are distributed between suppliers worldwide, with the wings, tails, and engines of a given aircraft often designed and built in different parts of the world. Japan and China are expected to increase their aircraft manufacturing, while major US companies appear to be moving more toward becoming system integrators and away from manufacturing.

The human venture in space is also under stress as the US space shuttle program ends without another human-carrying vehicle to replace it. The future of the one remaining space station is in doubt, and there are no plans to build another. Opportunities for spaceflight may also be minimal unless commercial and military spaceflight picks up to fill the void left by the end of government-run space exploration programs.

On the other hand, just over one century into powered flight, the human venture into the air and beyond is just beginning. Aircraft still depend on long runways and can fly only in a very limited range of conditions. Weather delays are still common because of uncertainty about how to deal with fluctuating winds or icing conditions. Most airplanes still consist of long tubes attached to thin wings, because designing blended wing bodies is difficult with the uncertainties in modeling composite structures. The aerospace and aviation industry is a major generator of atmospheric carbon releases. This will change only when the industry switches to renewable hydrogen fuel, which may occur faster than many people anticipate.

The human ability to access, live, and work in space or on extraterrestrial locations is extremely limited, and this prevents development of a large space-based economy. This situation may be expected to change over time, with the advent of commercial space launches. New infrastructure will encourage commercial enterprises beyond Earth.

The advancements in the past century are truly breathtaking and bode well for the breakthroughs that one may hope to see. Hurricanes and cyclonic storms are no longer surprise killers; they are tracked from formation in the far reaches of the oceans, and their paths are accurately predicted, giving people plenty of warning. Crop yields and other resources are accurately tracked by spacecraft, and ground-penetrating radar from Earth-sensing satellites has discovered much about humankind's buried ancient heritage and origins. Even in featureless oceans and deserts, GPS satellites provide accurate, reliable navigation information. The discovery of ever-smaller distant planets by orbiting space telescopes, and of unexpected forms of life on Earth, hint at the possible discovery of life beyond Earth.

Further Reading

Anderson, John D., Jr. *Introduction to Flight.* 5th ed. New York: McGraw-Hill, 2005. This popular textbook, setting developments in a historical context, is derived from the author's tenure at the Smithsonian Air and Space Museum.

Bekey, Ivan. *Advanced Space System Concepts and Technologies, 2010–2030+.* Reston, VA: American Institute of Aeronautics and Astronautics, 2003. Summaries of various advanced concepts and logical arguments used to explore their feasibility.

Design Engineering Technical Committee. *AIAA Aerospace Design Engineers Guide.* 5th ed. Reston, VA: American Institute of Aeronautics and Astronautics, 2003. A concise book of formulae and numbers that aerospace engineers use frequently or need for reference.

Gann, Ernest K. *Fate Is the Hunter.* 1961. Reprint. New York: Simon, 1986. Describes an incident that was the basis for a 1964 film of the same name. Autobiography of a pilot, describing the early days of commercial aviation and coming close to the age of jet travel.

Hill, Philip, and Carl Peterson. *Mechanics and Thermodynamics of Propulsion.* 2d ed. Upper Saddle River, NJ: Prentice Hall, 1991. A classic textbook on propulsion that covers the basic science and engineering of jet and rocket engines and their components. Also gives excellent sets of problems with answers.

Jenkins, Dennis R. *X-15: Extending the Frontiers of Flight.* NASA SP-2007-562. Washington, DC: US Government Printing Office, 2007. Contains various copies of original data sheets, memos, and pictures from the days when the X-15 research vehicle was developed and flown.

Lewis, John S. *Mining the Sky: Untold Riches from the Asteroids, Comets and Planets.* New York: Basic Books, 1997. The most readable answer to the question, "What resources are there beyond Earth to make exploration worthwhile?" Written from a strong scientific background, it sets out the reasoning to estimate the presence and accessibility of extraterrestrial water, gases, minerals, and other resources that would enable an immense space-based economy.

Liepmann, H. W., and A. Roshko. *Elements of Gas Dynamics*. Mineola, NY: Dover, 2001. A textbook on the discipline of gas dynamics as applied to high-speed flow phenomena. Contains several photographs of shocks, expansions, and boundary layer phenomena.

O'Neill, Gerard K. *The High Frontier: Human Colonies in Space*. 3d ed. New York: Morrow, 1977. Reprint. Burlington, Ontario, Canada: Apogee, 2000. Sets out the logic, motivations, and general parameters for human settlements in space. This formed the basis for NASA/ASEE (American Society for Engineering Education) studies in 1977–1978 and beyond, to investigate the design of space stations for permanent habitation. Fascinating exposition of how ambitious concepts are systematically analyzed and engineering decisions are made on how to achieve them, or why they cannot yet be achieved.

Peebles, Curtis. *Road to Mach 10: Lessons Learned from the X-43A Flight Research Program*. Reston, VA: American Institute of Aeronautics and Astronautics, 2008. A contemporary experimental flight-test program description.

About the Author: Narayanan M. Komerath, PhD, is a professor of aerospace engineering at Georgia Institute of Technology in Atlanta, where he directs the John Harper Wind Tunnel and the Micro Renewable Energy Laboratory. He has more than twenty-five years of experience in teaching and conducting research on aerospace and energy engineering. He has served as a fellow of the NASA Institute of Advanced Concepts and as a Boeing Welliver Faculty Fellow.

Aerospace Engineer 🖋 *

Earnings (Yearly Median): $97,480 (Bureau of Labor Statistics, 2012)

Employment and Outlook: Slower than average growth (Bureau of Labor Statistics, 2012)

O*NET-SOC Code: 17-2011.00

---

*   Designated as a Green Occupation by the US Department of Labor, Employment and Training Administration..

> **Related Career Cluster(s)**: Manufacturing; Marketing; Government & Public Administration; Business, Management & Administration

Scope of Work

Aerospace engineers are involved in the design and construction of aircraft, spacecraft, satellites, and missiles. Aerospace engineers who work with spacecraft are called astronautical engineers, while those who work with aircraft are called aeronautical engineers. Whichever their specialty, an aerospace engineer's work can focus on propulsion systems, defense systems, jets, controls, guidance systems, stealth technology, or thermodynamics, with the goal of designing and testing prototypes of manned and unmanned craft as well as advanced weapons systems.

Aerospace engineers also develop new concepts for the propulsion of the craft they design. After testing their theories on paper and in computer models, they build prototypes for further testing. The projects an aerospace engineer works on can be quite large and often involve teams of engineers, each one working in his or her area of specialty.

Education and Coursework

During high school, students interested in a career in aerospace engineering should study physics, chemistry, and biology. Math courses such as algebra, geometry, trigonometry, and calculus are essential. Robotics and math clubs would be good extracurricular activities, as would clubs that focus on aviation and space.

A bachelor's degree in aerospace engineering is one route into the field. Students may also elect to study mechanical engineering, chemical engineering, civil engineering, materials engineering, or electrical engineering as undergraduates and then pursue a degree in aerospace engineering at the graduate level, with a focus on such topics as wind tunnel testing or fluid mechanics.

Typically, during the first two years of college, an undergraduate aerospace engineering major will take courses in humanities, aviation history, and general engineering. The final two years will include work in thermodynamics, differential calculus, fluid mechanics, heat transfer, applied aerodynamics, analytical mechanics, and trajectory dynamics. Students will also conduct research in order to analyze and interpret data. If the research involves work with robots, students will need to have completed coursework in computer science.

Internships with major aviation firms or companies involved in the development of commercial space transportation allow students to gain valuable experience the field of aerospace engineering before completing undergraduate work. Internships can also provide insight into the type of graduate work that would be most advantageous to a chosen career path.

Aerospace engineering is a rigorous major. The requirements for acceptance into undergraduate aerospace programs are high. For graduate programs, candidates must demonstrate an understanding of aerospace engineering applications and problems, as well as the solutions to those problems. They must be able to function on multidisciplinary teams and be able to design components that will perform as specified within the constraints given.

A graduate degree in aerospace engineering can lead to a teaching position at a university, a research position within a company, or a position as an aerospace engineer. As commercial space transportation becomes more established, it may lead to the development of new areas of study.

Career Enhancement and Training

Aerospace engineers can join and network within several professional associations and societies. The American Institute of Aeronautics and Astronautics (AIAA), founded in 1963 after a merger of the American Interplanetary Society and the Institute of Aeronautical Science, sponsors conferences, courses, and workshops around the globe. Corporate, individual, and student memberships are available. The AIAA currently offers professional-enrichment tools such as distance-learning opportunities, webcasts, and books and journals that cover topics such as propulsion and power, spacecraft and rockets, thermophysics and heat transfer, and aircraft. The website includes a career center with tips for interviewing, social networking, and résumé writing. It

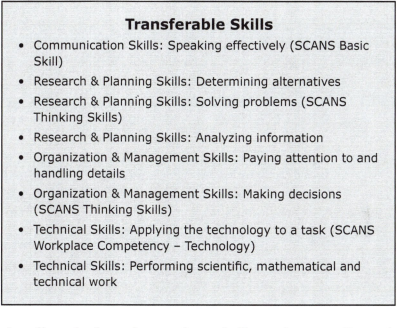

Transferable Skills

- Communication Skills: Speaking effectively (SCANS Basic Skill)
- Research & Planning Skills: Determining alternatives
- Research & Planning Skills: Solving problems (SCANS Thinking Skills)
- Research & Planning Skills: Analyzing information
- Organization & Management Skills: Paying attention to and handling details
- Organization & Management Skills: Making decisions (SCANS Thinking Skills)
- Technical Skills: Applying the technology to a task (SCANS Workplace Competency – Technology)
- Technical Skills: Performing scientific, mathematical and technical work

also offers e-books, and a new electronic library, Aerospace Research Central (ARC), is being developed for member use.

AIAA also has opportunities for members to join committees, which is an excellent way to serve the aerospace industry while learning more about the field and making contacts that may lead to networking opportunities. Another especially useful tool on the AIAA website is the Professional Career Time Line, which is a series of checklists and helpful actions that are designed to help college students as well as established aerospace engineers set career goals. The time line is designed by the AIAA Career and Workforce Development Committee and helps the user track career goals throughout his or her career until he or she retires from the field.

Certification as a professional engineer (PE) may or may not be required by an employer, but being a certified PE can make an applicant more desirable and set him or her apart from one who is not certified. Certification is granted by a state board of registration after the successful completion of four steps: First, a student must graduate from an engineering program accredited by the Accreditation Board for Engineering and Technology (ABET). The student must then pass the Fundamentals of Engineering (FE) exam and work as an engineer for four years. The final step in certification is to pass the Principles and Practice of Engineering (PE) exam.

Daily Tasks and Technology

Aerospace engineers are often part of multidisciplinary teams that function independently but meet frequently to set shared goals and timelines. Engineering professionals may give presentations at meetings or update the team on their progress to date. Reports on new findings may also be given at these meetings.

The aerospace engineers working on a project will typically be assigned project-specific tasks to complete. These tasks may include the design of a new payload system or landing apparatus or the design of a prototype for testing. Wind-tunnel tests are often conducted to ascertain the aerodynamic efficiency of a design. Virtual tests may also be run using computational fluid dynamics (CFD) models. Any of these tasks may be part of the day-to-day work of an aeronautical engineer. Familiarity with computer models and the use of CFD software is essential for an aeronautical engineer testing a new design because they allow engineers to view simulated airflow. Areas of inefficiency can then be reported, which provides valuable feedback before a physical prototype is constructed.

An aerospace engineer must also work within the constraints of performance, price, and materials when envisioning and testing new designs and prototypes. These constraints may include the use of certain materials instead of others or a price point that has to be met. It is the job of the aerospace engineer to take constraints into consideration while designing and testing craft and other objects intended for flight through air or space.

Earnings and Employment Outlook

The demand for aeronautical engineers has slowed with the economic downturn and the decreased demand for civilian aircraft projects. There is still a need for aeronautical engineers in military aircraft design, but as funds are reallocated among the various branches of the military, fewer engineers are needed. Employment for aeronautical engineers is expected to increase as airline fleets age and new technologies are developed for civilian and military applications. Aeronautical engineers will be needed to integrate these new technologies into the next generation of aircraft.

Employment for aeronautical engineers is expected to increase as airline fleets age and new technologies are developed for civilian and military applications. Aeronautical engineers will be needed to integrate these new technologies into the next generation of aircraft.

The demand for astronautical engineers has slowed proportionally with the cuts in National Aeronautics and Space Administration (NASA) funding. However, several private companies are making a bid for commercial space travel. As these programs become established, there will be a need for astronautical engineers to design and test the craft used for these private-sector missions. Astronautical engineers will also be involved in the design and implementation of robots in unmanned space missions, and it is expected that their expertise will be needed in future defense applications in space, as well as for mining on distant planets.

Related Occupations

- **Mechanical Engineers:** Mechanical engineers design and manufacture mechanical systems and analyze and maintain a system's performance.
- **Hydraulic Engineers:** Hydraulic engineers plan and design structures such as channels, power plants, and harbors.
- **Electrical Engineers:** Electrical engineers work with electrical devices and systems in a variety of industries.

A Conversation with Narayanan M. Komerath

Job Title: Professor of Aerospace Engineering

What was your career path?

I received a Bachelor of Technology in aeronautical engineering, Master of Science and PhD in aerospace engineering, then worked one year as a postdoctoral fellow, and two years as a research engineer, both with a very active experimental research program in the areas of turbulent combustion diagnostics, ramjet combustion acoustics, and rotorcraft aerodynamics. I was then invited to apply for an academic position, becoming assistant professor, associate professor, and eventually promoted to professor in 1994.

What are three pieces of advice you would offer someone interested in your profession?

1. Find something that really appeals to you, not what other people think you like. Essential to stay interested later in life.
2. Work really hard at the beginning—"hit the ground running." It will get you used to working hard, and you will be moving fast enough to catch opportunities.
3. Talk to everyone you can about your field, but do your own thinking to make decisions.

What paths for career advancement are available to you?

- I could apply to become a university administrator (school director, Dean)
- I could apply for positions with the Federal or State government agencies
- I could start a company.

However, the advice I receive suggests that the freedom that I have to pursue new interests as a professor is hard to achieve in any other line of work.

- **Manufacturing Engineers:** Manufacturing engineers are involved in all aspects of the manufacturing process and are knowledgeable of assembly methods, production, and quality standards.

Future Applications

The future promises an increased use of automated systems in aircraft and spacecraft design. Aerospace engineers will design these systems because their understanding of payload systems, propulsion, heat transfer, and trajectory dynamics is crucial to the design of special-purpose robots, satellites, and aircraft. Whether the craft will be manned or unmanned, the input of aerospace engineers will be essential to the success of these projects.

In the event that private or commercial space travel becomes commonplace, aerospace engineers will be in demand for their expertise. They will be the professionals who design the craft that carry people, robots, equipment, and materials to and from Earth, and their knowledge and experience of component design and testing will be integral parts of any mission.

—Gina Hagler

More Information

Aerospace Industries Association
1000 Wilson Boulevard, Suite 1700
Arlington, VA 22209
www.aia-aerospace.org

American Institute of Aeronautics and Astronautics
1801 Alexander Bell Drive, Suite 500
Reston, VA 20191-4344
www.aiaa.org

International Association of Machinists and Aerospace Workers
9000 Machinists Place
Upper Marlboro, MD 20772-2867
www.iamaw.org

National Society of Professional Engineers
1420 King Street
Alexandria, VA 22314-2794
www.nspe.org

SAE International
400 Commonwealth Drive
Warrendale, PA 15096-0001
www.sae.org

Society of Flight Test Engineers
44814 N. Elm Avenue
Lancaster, CA 93534
www.sfte.org

Astrophysics

FIELDS OF STUDY

Astronomy; astrophysics; physics; mathematics; computer science; classical physics; quantum mechanics; electromagnetism; particle physics; optics; thermodynamics; solar astrophysics; planetary astrophysics; stellar and galactic astrophysics; cosmology; chemistry.

DEFINITION

Astrophysics applies the principles of physics to astronomy. It is a science concerned with the universe beyond Earth. Astrophysics analyzes the physical constitution and interaction of celestial objects and matter that range from the sun to solar and extrasolar planets, stars, nebulae, galaxies, black holes, and cosmic particles. Astrophysics seeks to provide answers to how the universe began, developed, and continues to operate, based on an understanding of the physics governing these processes. Understanding the physical properties of the universe and its content can lead to better knowledge of both Earth itself and humanity's place in the universe.

Basic Principles

Modern astrophysics, which combines the laws of physics with the discipline of astronomy, originated with German astronomer Johannes Kepler. Kepler considered the sun and the planets as physical bodies, and he accepted the heliocentric worldview reintroduced in the West by German Polish astronomer Nicolaus Copernicus in 1543. In 1609 and 1619, Kepler published his three laws governing the motion of the planets around the sun. The scientific validity of astrophysics was confirmed once Isaac Newton's law of universal gravitation, published in 1687, proved the application of physical laws to all bodies in the sky.

The next advance in astrophysics came with the discovery, by 1860, that the chemical composition of stars could be deduced from the dark absorption lines in the spectra of light they emitted. In 1893, Wien's displacement law, named after German physicist Wilhelm Wien, allowed measurement of a star's temperature based on the wavelength analysis of its light. By the early twentieth century, analysis of stellar spectral lines and application of the laws of quantum mechanics created a vast new area of inquiry in astrophysics.

Astrophysics has developed into two fields, observational astrophysics and theoretical astrophysics. Because observational astrophysics relies on collection and analysis of all forms of energy emitted from celestial objects, ranging, for example, from infrared to ultraviolet light and beyond, it has become part of nearly all fields of classical astronomy. Theoretical astrophysics developed out of the observation that the universe is expanding. It combines mathematics and computer modeling with analysis of physical evidence and relies on the results of observational astrophysics for verification. Theoretical astrophysics has made great advances since the 1990s, with key issues in the field being the quests for dark matter and energy and for proof of gravitational waves.

Core Concepts

Astrophysics relies on both the physical observation of the universe and the articulation of mathematical models and scientific theories to explain the origin, current state, and development of the universe and all of its contents. It is closely related to astronomy, physics, and mathematics. Computer science has become essential for data analysis and modeling. Optics and materials science support development of customized observation instruments. Project management organization has become indispensable for multimillion-dollar "big science" projects in astrophysics, such as space-based telescopes.

Observational Astronomy—Optical Astronomy. The classic basis of astrophysics, optical astronomy looks at celestial bodies within the visible light spectrum of electromagnetic radiation. The most important instrument in the field is the telescope. Originally, all observations aside from solar were made by the naked eye at night. In the twentieth century, photography of the images caught by telescopes became standard. By the early twenty-first century, computer-controlled charge-coupled devices (CCDs), invented in 1969, were generally used to capture digital images from the telescopes. The practice enabled astrophysicists to analyze their data via computers at their leisure during the day. In addition to earthbound telescopes, optical astronomy has used space-based telescopes since 1990, when the Hubble Space Telescope began operations. Other optical space telescopes include the Hipparcos, launched in 1989, and the spacecrafts COROT (*Convection rotation et transits planétaires*, 2006) and *Kepler* (2009). Because of the advantages of space-based optical astronomy, which avoids looking through Earth's atmosphere, there are plans to put additional optical telescopes into space, including the spacecrafts *Gaia* (2013) and *Euclid* (2019).

Observational Astronomy—Radio Astronomy. Radio astronomy began by accident in 1933, when American physicist Karl G. Jansky detected a strong radio source in the center of the Milky Way. Since then, radio astronomy has led to the discovery of a variety of previously unknown celestial bodies, objects, and phenomena that can be detected only as radio sources. By 2012, the world's largest single-dish radio telescope was the Arecibo Observatory in Puerto Rico. Radio telescopes are often built with multiple dishes, such as the twenty-seven interconnected radio-telescope dishes of the Very Large Array observatory in Socorro County, New Mexico. As of 2012, there were no radio telescopes in space.

Observational Astronomy—Ultraviolet Astronomy. Because electromagnetic radiation with very short wavelengths is absorbed by Earth's atmosphere, ultraviolet, x-ray, and gamma-ray astronomy became possible only in the age of balloon- and satellite-based astronomy observations in the second half of the twentieth century. Ultraviolet astronomy began with the observations of the first Orbiting Solar Observatory (OSO) in 1962; the Hubble Space Telescope was also equipped for ultraviolet observation.

Observational Astronomy—X-Ray Astronomy. X-ray astronomy started in 1948 when instruments atop a German-made V-2 rocket in the service of the US Army detected x-ray emissions from the sun. Italian American astrophysicist Riccardo Giacconi is considered the father of x-ray astrophysics. Giacconi won the 2002 Nobel Prize in

Physics for his 1962 discovery of the first extrasolar x-ray source, Scorpius X-1. By 2012, Giacconi was the principal investigator of the Chandra X-ray Observatory, a source of major discoveries in x-ray astronomy that was launched into orbit in 1999.

Observational Astronomy—Gamma-Ray Astronomy. Gamma-ray astronomy began in 1961 with a detector atop the Explorer 11 satellite. A series of gamma-ray observatories was launched into space thereafter. By 2012, the International Gamma-Ray Astrophysics Laboratory (INTEGRAL), launched in 2002, and the Fermi Gamma-Ray Space Telescope, launched in 2008, were being used for space-based study. In 2002, the High Energy Stereoscopic System (HESS) observatory in Namibia began conducting earthbound gamma-ray astronomy.

Observational Astronomy—Infrared Astronomy. Infrared astronomy began in the 1830s, but major scientific contributions have come only since the 1950s. Earthbound infrared astronomy is hindered by the high absorption rate of infrared radiation by the atmosphere and is preferably done at observatories installed at great heights, such as the W. M. Keck Observatory, close to the summit of Mauna Kea on Hawaii. The two Keck telescopes can be combined to form a single interferometer suitable for infrared astronomy. However, best results are obtained from space-based telescopes. Optical telescopes have been given infrared detectors, such as the 1997 addition of the Near Infrared Camera and Multi-Object Spectrometer (NICMOS) to the Hubble Space Telescope. By 2012, there existed several space-based telescopes for infrared astronomy, such as the Herschel Space Observatory and the Spitzer Space Telescope. Infrared astronomy is also performed with instruments mounted on high-flying aircraft.

Observational Astronomy—Cosmic-Ray Particles, Neutrinos and Antineutrinos, Gravitational Waves. The quest to capture and measure cosmic-ray particles, neutrinos, antineutrinos, and gravitational waves is one of the most recent efforts of astrophysics. The highly energetic cosmic particles, such as high-energy electrons, protons, and atomic nuclei or unstable neutrons and mesons, could reveal information about the chemical composition of the universe on a grand scale. Since its installation in 2011, the $1.5 billion space-based Alpha

Magnetic Spectrometer has recorded billions of cosmic-ray events for further analysis. Neutrinos could convey information about the universe's past, as they change little over time because they almost never interact with other particles. From 1999 to 2006, the Sudbury Neutrino Observatory in Ontario sought to detect neutrinos emitted by the sun in an underground tank of heavy water. Once gravitational waves are detected, they should yield information about the motion of the most massive celestial objects.

Theoretical Astronomy—Physical Cosmology. Physical cosmology developed as a consequence of the general theory of relativity and the physical observation that other galaxies are moving away from the Milky Way, thus proving the expansion of the universe. Since the 1920s, astrophysicists have been trying to model the origin, development, and ultimate fate of the universe. Physical cosmologists seek to determine these things and test their theories against experiments and observations.

Theoretical Astronomy—Stellar Dynamics and Evolution, Galaxy Formation. The field of stellar dynamics seeks to model and determine the movement of stars in large aggregations such as star clusters. It represents a development of the oldest form of astrophysics, celestial mechanics, toward statistic modeling. Advances were supported by the European satellite Hipparcos, which measured star positions from 1989 to 1993. Those studying stellar evolution seek to determine how stars are formed and the development they undergo until their extinction. Scholars of galaxy formation seek to understand how large systems of stars developed in the aftermath of the big bang.

Theoretical Astronomy—Large-Scale Structure of the Universe. Astrophysicists have tried to develop a model of the overall structure of the universe in order to understand how the universe is built and which rules govern its development.

Instrument Design. Astrophysics has always been closely related to instrument design. Specialized instruments are needed for a varied observation of objects in the sky, including celestial bodies and other features of the universe beyond Earth. Astrophysicists have been deeply involved in the design of various telescopes and other instruments to observe the skies. With the advent of space-based telescopes, instrument design entered a new era. The design of astrophysical instruments has been an essential part of what are often considered "big science" projects, costing more than $1 billion. One such project was the Alpha Magnetic Spectrometer, conceived by American physicist Samuel C. C. Ting, which was put into orbit on the penultimate space-shuttle mission in 2011.

Applications Past and Present

Navigation. One of the first applications of astrophysics was in the celestial navigation of ships on the high seas. The acceptance of the heliocentric worldview and application of Newton's laws for celestial bodies allowed navigators to use stars, together with a reliable maritime chronometer such as the one perfected first by English watchmaker John Harrison in 1761, to positively determine a ship's longitudinal position at sea. Two centuries later, astrophysics aided the development of the Global Positioning System (GPS), developed by the US Department of Defense and operational since 1994. GPS has revolutionized navigation at land and at sea. It is based on a system of satellites that provide accurate positioning and time measurement for all users. GPS applications have become common for navigation systems in cars and mobile telephones.

Discovery of New Celestial Bodies. Astrophysics, in combination with mathematical modeling and innovative instrument design, has led to the discovery of celestial objects previously unknown to humanity. In 1610, Italian scientist Galileo Galilei pointed a telescope at Jupiter and discovered three objects, and later a fourth, moving in front of the planet. By applying celestial mechanics, Galileo determined correctly that these were moons of Jupiter. After the discovery of Uranus as a planet in 1781, astrophysical and mathematical calculations predicted the existence of another planet. Accordingly, Neptune was identified in 1846.

In the twentieth century, expansion of the spectrum and technological means of observational astrophysics led to a series of spectacular

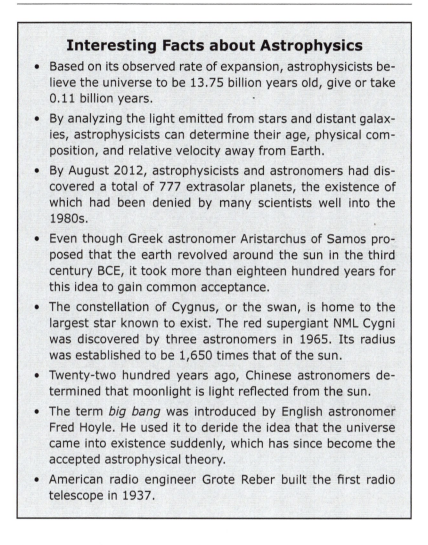

Interesting Facts about Astrophysics

- Based on its observed rate of expansion, astrophysicists believe the universe to be 13.75 billion years old, give or take 0.11 billion years.

- By analyzing the light emitted from stars and distant galaxies, astrophysicists can determine their age, physical composition, and relative velocity away from Earth.

- By August 2012, astrophysicists and astronomers had discovered a total of 777 extrasolar planets, the existence of which had been denied by many scientists well into the 1980s.

- Even though Greek astronomer Aristarchus of Samos proposed that the earth revolved around the sun in the third century BCE, it took more than eighteen hundred years for this idea to gain common acceptance.

- The constellation of Cygnus, or the swan, is home to the largest star known to exist. The red supergiant NML Cygni was discovered by three astronomers in 1965. Its radius was established to be 1,650 times that of the sun.

- Twenty-two hundred years ago, Chinese astronomers determined that moonlight is light reflected from the sun.

- The term *big bang* was introduced by English astronomer Fred Hoyle. He used it to deride the idea that the universe came into existence suddenly, which has since become the accepted astrophysical theory.

- American radio engineer Grote Reber built the first radio telescope in 1937.

discoveries. After the initial 1933 discovery of a strong radio source in Sagittarius A, radio astronomy in the 1950s detected strong radio emissions for which no visible source could be found at first. In 1960, through interferometry, the source—object 3C 48—was identified for the first time. This and similar objects were called quasars, short for "quasi-stellar" objects. In the 1980s, astrophysicists discovered that quasars are formed by the matter around a massive black hole at the center of its galaxy. Radio astronomers discovered the first pulsar in

1967 and found it was a rotating neutron star emitting a strong beam of electromagnetic radiation in the radio spectrum.

The quest to discover the first extrasolar planet orbiting a star other than the sun was achieved in 1992. Polish astronomer Aleksander Wolszczan and Canadian astronomer Dale A. Frail used radio astronomy observation at the Arecibo Observatory to discover two planets orbiting the pulsar PSR 1257+12. Since that time, infrared astronomy has also been used to aid in the discovery and examination of extrasolar planets, which often have a peak in the infrared spectrum.

On the other end of the spectrum, x-ray astronomy has been used to find evidence of black holes. The first candidate object for a black hole, Cygnus X-1, was discovered in 1964; it became a candidate in 1971, after further observation and analysis. In the early twenty-first century, x-ray and infrared astronomy worked together to identify supermassive black holes at the center of galaxies. In October 2002, near-infrared observations allowed Sagittarius A* to be identified as the supermassive black hole at the center of the Milky Way Galaxy. In 2002, the Chandra X-ray Observatory captured evidence for two supermassive black holes at the center of the galaxy NGC 6240, a result of the two smaller galaxies that merged to form it. NGC 6240 emits not only strong x-ray but also strong infrared radiation.

Especially since the Hubble Space Telescope was put into orbit by a space shuttle in 1990, there have been remarkable discoveries of new celestial bodies by space-bound telescopes. It is indicative of its broad applications that the Hubble has led to the discovery of both galaxies in deep space, billions of light years away from Earth, and a fifth moon of the dwarf planet Pluto, which was identified in June and July 2012.

Planetary Science. Astrophysical exploration and examination of the physical properties of the planets (including dwarf planets, moons, and smaller objects of the solar system) as well as of extrasolar planets have affected the study of Earth. In particular, analysis of the atmosphere of planets of the solar system, and even moons such as Titan and Triton, has yielded information concerning climate and weather issues on Earth. Space plasma physics, a subdiscipline of astrophysics, has contributed to planetary science by examining plasma within the solar system. Key plasma sources in the solar system are the sun and its solar winds, the planets with their magnetospheres and iono-spheres, and cosmic rays traveling through the system. Analysis of so-called space weather leads to applications affecting satellites designed for communication and terrestrial weather observation.

Knowledge of the Origin, Structure, Dynamics, and Evolution of the Universe. Since the early twentieth century, astrophysics has been instrumental in establishing and enlarging what humanity knows about the origin, structure, dynamics, and development of the observable universe. While of little immediate practical application, this knowledge has prompted humanity to learn more about its place in the cosmos.

The 1912 discovery by American astronomer Vesto Slipher that galaxies, like stars, emit a measurable spectrum of light enabled him to determine that distant galaxies are all moving away from Earth. This was proved through the redshift in galactic spectrums. After Albert Einstein developed his theory of general relativity in 1916, two other scientists, Russian cosmologist Alexander Friedmann and Belgian physicist and priest Georges Lemaître, used general relativity and Slipher's observation to independently develop the theory, in 1922 and 1927, that the universe is not steady but expanding. The controversial discovery represented a tremendous paradigm shift in humanity's understanding of the universe.

Even more controversial was Lemaître's 1931 proposal that if one traced the expansion of the universe back in time, there would be a point where the universe began. This idea was supported by the evidence collected by American astronomer Edwin Hubble, who had discovered that galaxies move away from Earth faster the further away they are—a relationship he defined in 1929 in what is now called Hubble's law.

Despite Lemaître and Hubble's work, the idea that the universe had an origin was still distasteful to many. However, the discovery of cosmic microwave background radiation by German American physicist Arno Penzias and American astronomer Robert Woodrow Wilson in 1964 provided strong physical evidence for the big bang theory. To gather further proof in light of some challenges, the National Aeronautics and Space Administration (NASA) launched the Cosmic Background Explorer (COBE) aboard a space shuttle in 1989. On April 23, 1992, American astrophysicists George Smoot and John C.

Mather, the principal investigators, announced they had successfully completed measuring the cosmic microwave background radiation, confirming its existence and the expansion of the universe.

By 2012, theoretical astrophysicists had joined forces with observational astrophysicists, relying on ever more powerful earth- and space-bound observation instruments to address some outstanding and challenging unsolved questions. Foremost was the pursuit of dark matter and dark energy, which appeared to account for the vast amount of the mass of the observable universe but had not yet been proved by observation or circumstantial evidence. Another goal was to capture and thus prove the existence of gravitational waves. In orbit, the Alpha Magnetic Spectrometer sought to measure cosmic rays, capture an antihelium nucleus as proof of the existence of antimatter in space, and support the astrophysical quest for dark matter and energy. Findings in this era would again expand humanity's knowledge of its universe.

Impact on Industry

Because of the rather limited immediate practical and economic applications of astrophysics, nearly all astrophysicists worldwide work either for government agencies, including national laboratories, or in a university setting. To do research work as an astrophysicist almost certainly requires a PhD in a science discipline, specifically physics, astrophysics, or astronomy. Students who finish their university education with either a bachelor's or a master of science degree in astrophysics or astronomy are most likely to find work outside research in astrophysics, often as technicians in astrophysics or teachers at the nongraduate level, including high schools. According to the US Bureau of Labor Statistics (BLS), in 2010, there were about twenty-two hundred astrophysicists and astronomers employed in the United States. This figure was predicted to rise by 11 percent by 2020. Factoring in projected retirements during that time, this means that about nine hundred new vacancies in the field should be created by that date. This corresponds fairly well to the estimated 116 new PhDs in the field that are earned from an American university each year, allowing for some of those to seek employment abroad.

Government Agencies. By 2010 in the United States, federal government agencies employed about five hundred astrophysicists and astronomers. Key agencies were NASA, federal research laboratories, the US Department of Energy, and the US Department of Defense. According to a 2011 survey by the American Institute of Physics that covers students graduating between 2007 and 2009, US government agencies accounted for only about

Occupation	Physicists and Astronomers
Employment 2010	20,600
Projected Employment 2020	23,400
Change in Number (2010–20)	2,800
Percent Change	14%

Bureau of Labor Statistics, 2012

15 percent of postgraduate research positions accepted by recent PhDs in astrophysics and astronomy. One reason for this relatively low number is that astrophysicists working for federal agencies were primarily engaged in "big science" projects, such as space-based telescopes. To some extent, their work included project-management activities requiring professional experience rather than pure scientific research.

Because of the vast, multimillion- and even billion-dollar budgets for many astrophysics observatories, whether on Earth or in space, the US government has been a key sponsor of astrophysics in the United States. Whether in collaboration with universities and other nongovernment research agencies or through international astrophysics projects, US government funds have been vital for the work of astrophysicists in the United States and globally.

Military. Because responsibility for the GPS satellite network has been assigned to the Second Space Operations Squadron of the US Air Force, there are a handful of astrophysicists with PhDs employed by the US military. Astrophysicists and astronomers who hold terminal master's degrees in their field can serve as Air Force officers. For example, American four-star general William Shelton, who became leader of the US Air Force Space Command in 2011, earned both bachelor's and master of science degrees in astronautical engineering.

University Research and Teaching. By 2010 in the United States, according to the BLS, more than half of all astrophysicists and astronomers were employed by universities, colleges, nongovernment research institutions, or junior colleges. The stronger the institution's focus on research, particularly at universities and research institutions, the more emphasis there was on the academic work of the astrophysicists and astronomers employed. However, teaching remained a core task in all of academia, with the exception of strict research institutions such as the Institute for Advanced Studies at Princeton, New Jersey. Typically in academia, astrophysicists with recent PhD degrees either focus on their own original research or join established research teams. As they advance their careers from postdoctoral positions and assistant professorships, they more often become research team leaders and work with their best students.

Social Context and Future Prospects

By the early twenty-first century, astrophysics had vastly enlarged humanity's understanding of the universe and its celestial bodies and phenomena. Thus, astrophysics has contributed some of the most important scientific discoveries since the 1960s. At the same time, direct practical applications of astrophysics have been minimal, perhaps with the exception of GPS, which has revolutionized navigation on Earth.

Because many astrophysical research projects cost vast sums of money, government sponsorship of astrophysics has been essential. Whereas theoretical astrophysics does not demand much hardware beyond computers to develop its models and theories, finding experimental proof, or disproof, of advanced astrophysical theories requires very expensive instruments. The reliance on public funds has forced top astrophysicists to lobby the public and its elected representatives in often-acrimonious battles. Even in the United States, corporate sponsorship of big astrophysics projects has been small compared to public funding. A notable exception was the $70 million gift of the W. M. Keck Foundation in 1985 to build the Keck I telescope, leading to the construction of the Keck Observatory in Hawaii.

There has also been somewhat of a controversy between proponents of less expensive and easier-to-service ground-based telescopes and those of vast-reaching space-based telescopes. Great advances in adaptive optics, making up for the disadvantages of observation through Earth's atmosphere, have given a new edge to ground-based telescopes. By 2012, the last of NASA's planned large space projects was the infrared James Webb Space Telescope. The project was nearly canceled in 2011 due to funding difficulties, but it persisted, scheduled for a possible launch into space by 2018 or 2020. In their quests to find answers to the problems of dark matter and dark energy, capture evidence for gravitational waves, and observe farther-away (and thus older) galaxies to learn more about the origin, the development, and the future of the universe, astrophysicists have to compete constantly for sufficient funding.

Further Reading

Carroll, Bradley, and Dale Ostlie. *An Introduction to Modern Astrophysics.* 2nd ed. San Francisco: Pearson, 2007. Comprehensive and accessible for readers with interest in and basic understanding of astronomy and physics. Covers tools of astronomy, the nature of stars, the solar system, galaxies, and cosmology.

Hawking, Stephen, and Roger Penrose. *The Nature of Space and Time*. Princeton: Princeton UP, 2010. Overview of contemporary issues in cosmology, including reconciling classical and quantum physics in astrophysics to understand the structure and organization of the universe. Illustrated.

Irwin, Judith. *Astrophysics: Decoding the Cosmos.* Hoboken: Wiley, 2007. Description of the processes by which astrophysics captures and analyzes signals received through a variety of observational means. Looks at how astrophysics works on a practical level.

LeBlanc, Francis. *An Introduction to Stellar Astrophysics.* Hoboken: Wiley, 2010. Useful survey of an essential aspect of astrophysics; ranges from introduction of basic concepts to stellar formation and evolution. Includes exercises and appendix of tables.

Mészáros, Péter. *The High Energy Universe*. New York: Cambridge UP, 2010. Survey of contemporary issues in high-energy astrophysics and cosmology, with chapters ranging from building blocks and the dynamics of the universe to gamma rays, gravitational waves, cosmic rays, neutrinos, and the quest for dark matter. Requires some knowledge in physics.

About the Author: R. C. Lutz, PhD, is an instructor of business English at an international consulting company. His students include professionals in science and engineering. He is the author of survey and encyclopedia articles in the applied sciences. After obtaining his MA and PhD degrees in English literature from the University of California, Santa Barbara, he worked for a few years in academia before moving to a consulting company. He has worked in the United States, Oman, the United Arab Emirates, Turkey, and Romania.

Astrophysicist

Earnings (Yearly Median): $95,500 (Bureau of Labor Statistics, 2012)

Employment and Outlook: Average growth (Bureau of Labor Statistics, 2012)

O*NET-SOC Code: 19-2011.00

Related Career Clusters: Education & Training; Government & Public Administration; Information Technology

Scope of Work

Astrophysicists research the physical properties of the universe beyond the earth. In their work, astrophysicists apply the principles of physics to the discipline of astronomy. Astrophysicists seek to enlarge humanity's understanding of what celestial bodies and cosmic particles and matter are made of, and how the universe and its parts operate and function. For their research, astrophysicists rely on analyses of data provided to them via observation of electromagnetic radiation, cosmic ray particles, neutrinos, antineutrinos, and possibly gravitational waves in the future. This data is captured by both earthbound and space-based telescopes and other detectors. Astrophysicists may participate in the design and testing of measuring instruments. Some astrophysicists focus on theoretical astrophysics, developing models for describing physical processes and properties of the cosmos, and aligning their models with freshly discovered data.

Education and Coursework

A person desiring to become an astrophysicist should be willing to earn a PhD. While it is possible and common to find employment with a bachelor's degree in astronomy, or a master's degree in astronomy or astrophysics, without a PhD one cannot expect to pursue a research career in the field.

In high school, classes should be taken in the natural sciences, especially in physics, as well as classes in mathematics and computer science. A love of astronomy and an interest in the universe serves as strong motivation to pursue a career as an astrophysicist. If a high school or a community has an astronomy club, it is helpful for the student to join. Even though direct physical observation of celestial bodies is being increasingly replaced by computer-based analysis, familiarity with the basic tool of astronomy, the telescope, is very useful.

By 2012 in the United States, there were seventy-six departments granting bachelor degrees in astronomy. Half of them offered degrees in astronomy and physics. This combination is of special value because traditionally, many astrophysicists earned their bachelor's degree in physics. A double major in astronomy and physics is another option, taken by 41 percent of the about one thousand students graduating with a BS in astronomy between 2007 and 2009.

Undergraduate courses should cover subjects such as general astronomy, as well as advanced courses in planetary physics, stellar and galactic astrophysics, and cosmology. Students need to focus strongly on physics. Within this subject, courses in classical and quantum mechanics, electromagnetism, optics, and thermodynamics are important. A solid understanding of advanced mathematics is indispensable for astrophysicists. Above average skills in computer science are necessary. Often, astrophysicists are expected to write their own computer programs to analyze and model their data.

Approximately forty American universities were offering a master's or PhD degree in astronomy and astrophysics by 2012. At the postgraduate level, students begin to specialize in a particular branch of astrophysics. They should develop a close research relationship with a faculty mentor. Possible subfields to specialize in include topics

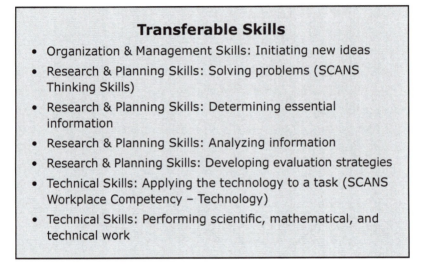

Transferable Skills

- Organization & Management Skills: Initiating new ideas
- Research & Planning Skills: Solving problems (SCANS Thinking Skills)
- Research & Planning Skills: Determining essential information
- Research & Planning Skills: Analyzing information
- Research & Planning Skills: Developing evaluation strategies
- Technical Skills: Applying the technology to a task (SCANS Workplace Competency – Technology)
- Technical Skills: Performing scientific, mathematical, and technical work

in high energy astrophysics, laboratory astrophysics, or heliophysics. While some students graduate with a master's degree, the great majority of astrophysicists pursue their PhD. Postgraduate work to obtain a PhD in astrophysics, through a contribution of original research, typically takes students about five to seven years. Students can also pursue PhDs in physics with their theses focused on astrophysics.

Career Enhancement and Training

From 2007 to 2009, 75 percent of all those who earned their PhDs in astronomy or astrophysics took up postdoctoral positions afterward. In a 2011 survey of the American Institute of Physics (AIP), half of the postdoctoral researchers who responded told AIS that their choice was pragmatic, because the postdoctoral was seen as a required step toward a desirable permanent position. The two other most common reasons were to obtain more research experience in the field and to work with a chosen senior scientist or research team. About half of the postdoctoral appointments were for three years, the others for two years or less. A median age of twenty-nine years for most young astrophysicists shows a commitment to this postdoctoral work and the importance of completing further training before seeking a permanent position.

As a postdoctoral researcher—or as one of the 20 percent of astrophysicists who are hired for a potentially permanent position directly after earning their PhDs—presenting original research at conferences and in professional journals is essential, whether the astrophysicist's own research or from a combined effort with his or her team. Conferences also provide necessary opportunities for networking. These conferences are often organized by professional societies, such as the American Astronomical Society (AAS), the American Institute of Physics (AIP), and the American Physical Society (APS). Membership in these organizations is therefore a necessary part of advancing one's career as an astrophysicist.

Daily Tasks and Technology

As astrophysicists advance in their careers, they receive more opportunities to develop their own research goals and to formulate their own theories. Research in astrophysics is very diverse. It can range, for instance, from articulating a theory explaining the dynamics of solar wind or the composition of exoplanets—also called extrasolar planets, meaning outside the solar system—to searching for evidence of dark matter in the universe.

Once an astrophysicist is committed to a research project, whether as principal investigator or as member of a research team—which is generally the case for junior astrophysicists—data analysis becomes a daily task. Data comes from a variety of earthbound and increasingly space-based telescopes and measuring devices. There is professional competition to gain access time to work with the world's largest telescopes, such as the twin Keck telescopes on Mauna Kea, Hawaii, or space telescopes such as the Hubble Space Telescope and the Chandra X-Ray Observatory. Access to such major instruments is a highlight in the lives of many astrophysicists.

Due to remote data transmission, astrophysicists need to spend less and less time at actual telescopes or research centers controlling space-based measurement devices. This also means that data gathered by telescopes at night can be analyzed during the day.

The more senior an astrophysicist becomes, the more time has to be devoted to writing grant applications and pursuing funding for expensive astrophysical instruments. Participation in the development and design of these instruments is another task for some astrophysicists. They are also expected to publish the results of their research and review the work of colleagues. Those working in academia teach courses and mentor their postgraduate students.

Astrophysicists work daily with advanced products of computer and information technology. They operate with analytical and scientific software and often write their own programs. Astrophysicists use a variety of measuring instruments, ranging from those at their own research institutions, to those at major national and international installations, to those in space.

Earnings and Employment Outlook

In the United States, the primary employers of astrophysicists are universities and public research institutions. The US Bureau of Labor Statistics (BLS) estimates that from 2010 to 2020, employment of astrophysicists and astronomers will rise by 11 percent, from 2,200 to 2,500 positions. Incorporating retirement and attrition, the BLS predicts that this should translate into 900 new job openings for astronomers and astrophysicists during that time period. The AIS reports that from 2007 to 2009, about 140 people earned a PhD in astronomy and astrophysics in the United States each year. Seventeen percent of these students left the country after graduation, leaving about 116 new potential job entrants per year. This statistic indicates that the balance between new jobs and job seekers should be almost even for astrophysicists through 2020.

The US Bureau of Labor Statistics estimates that from 2010 to 2020, employment of astrophysicists and astronomers will rise by 11 percent, from 2,200 to 2,500 positions.

According to the BLS, the median salary for astronomers and astrophysicists was $95,500 in 2011. There was a considerable bandwidth, with the top 10 percent earning above $155,500 and the bottom 10 percent earning below $48,700. One cause is the high number of post-doctoral researchers.

The AIS reported that entry level salaries for PhDs remained relatively constant from 2007 to 2009. During this time, the median entrance salary for an astrophysicist or postdoctoral astronomer was $50,000 at a university and $55,300 at a government institution. BLS data shows a widening gap between university and government salaries. The 2011 median wage for all astronomers and astrophysicists at universities was $64,070, compared to $137,400 in government positions. There has been no trend to close this gap.

Related Occupations

- **Astronomers:** Astronomers have traditionally studied the motions, positions, and brightness of celestial objects, as well as observed celestial events such as eclipses; astronomers are less focused on the physical properties of the universe.

- **Natural Sciences Managers:** Natural sciences managers are often recruited from among senior scientists to lead the work of other scientists and manage large projects or programs, often at government agencies; this generally comes with a large salary increase.

- **Physicists:** Physicists study the physical properties of life and matter, often in the form of basic research or applied research in industry positions.

- **Biophysicists and Biochemists:** Biophysicists and biochemists research fundamental scientific principles of life, often at the cellular level.

- **Computer and Information Research Scientists:** Computer and information research scientists seek to develop new computing technologies or improve existing ones.

Future Applications

To carry out their research, astrophysicists depend on public and university funding. To secure funding means to convince the American

A Conversation with Scott Randall

Job Title: Astrophysicist

What was your career path?

I followed the traditional path for astrophysics, earning an undergraduate degree with majors in astronomy and physics, followed by a MS and Ph.D. in Astronomy. After a few years as a postdoctoral researcher, I took my current position as an astrophysicist at the Harvard-Smithsonian Center for Astrophysics. I work in the High Energy Astrophysics Division, where my research focuses on galaxy clusters, large scale structure, cosmology, and the physics of the intra-cluster medium. I am also a member of the Science Operations Team for NASA's Chandra X-ray Observatory.

What are three pieces of advice?

1. Get involved with research early. Summer internships are a great way for an undergraduate to get some research experience.
2. Be active in the community. Got to journal clubs at your university, talk with professors who are active in research, if possible go to conferences and talk with scientists who work in fields you are interested in.
3. Diversify, especially early in your career. This will make you a more attractive candidate for postdocs, fellowships, and the like.

What paths for career advancement are available to you?

Once you obtain a more or less permanent position, career advancement comes with time, so long as you maintain an active research program and a strong publication record. Professors will become eligible for tenure, whereas staff scientists like myself can be promoted to, e.g., senior astrophysicist positions. However, there are many options one could pursue, including becoming the director of a lab, getting involved with the development of an upcoming mission, or transitioning to the private sector and using the skills you've learned to get involved with proprietary research.

A Conversation with Gregory Herczeg

Job Title: Bairen Professor, Kavli Institute for Astronomy and Astrophysics, Peking University, China

What was your career path?

BS from Notre Dame; MS/PhD from Colorado in astrophysics; Postdoc at Caltech ;Postdoc at Max-Planck-Institut für extraterrestriche Physik, Garching, Germany; Bairen Professor, Kavli Institute for Astronomy and Astrophysics, Peking University, China.

What are three pieces of advice you would offer someone interested in your profession?

1. Unless you are at one of the top 2-3 schools, few people get professor jobs that they would want in a location that they want. Prepare for industry jobs during graduate school and consider alternative jobs as a success rather than a failure of a PhD.

2. For an academic career, either be prepared to move around frequently or recognize that an academic career will likely be limited to a teaching job at your local community college.

3. Communication and networking is as important as the quality of your work. Most successful people succeed in both of these areas.

What paths for career advancement are available to you?

I have no idea. Lateral moves are difficult and advancement at my current institute is limited for me.

---

public of the excitement and value of their research. An emerging field of astrophysics is to study the properties of exoplanets, especially to look for any suitability to host extraterrestrial life. Additionally, astrophysicists are working toward a fuller understanding of the effects of solar properties. This research contributes to climate studies of the earth itself.

Because of the potentially vast cost of instruments for astrophysical research, and the resulting scientific contribution to global human knowledge, there has been great international cooperation in astrophysics. For example, the Alpha Magnetic Spectrometer—which cost close to $1.5 billion to design, build, and send into space—has been a joint North American, European, and Asian project. Housed at the International Space Station since May 19, 2011, it provides astrophysicists with the scientific means to search, for example, for antimatter or evidence of dark matter in the universe.

As long as humanity keeps an interest in the questions of the universe and the material it is made of—and is willing to spend money on scientists and their research to find answers—astrophysicists will continue to conduct research for projects both old and new.

—R. C. Lutz, PhD

More Information

American Astronomical Society
2000 Florida Avenue NW, Suite 400
Washington, DC 20009-1231
aas.org

American Institute of Physics
1 Physics Ellipse
College Park, Maryland 20740-3843
www.aip.org

American Physics Society
1 Physics Ellipse
College Park, MD 20740-3844
www.aps.org

National Aeronautics and Space Administration (NASA)
Public Communications Office
NASA Headquarters
Suite 5K39
Washington, DC 20546-000
www.nasa.gov

Atmospheric Physics

FIELDS OF STUDY

Aeronomy; acoustics; applied physics; atmospheric dynamics; calculus; chemistry; climatology; cloud physics; computer modeling; engineering; environmental physics; fluid dynamics; fluid mechanics; mathematics; meteorology; physics; radiation; remote sensing; statistics; statistical mechanics; spatial statistics; thermodynamics.

DEFINITION

Atmospheric physics is a subfield of atmospheric science that studies the physics at work in atmospheric phenomena. Atmospheric physicists study the flow of energy as cold and warm air masses collide and as fast and slow rivers of air interact. Mathematics is an integral part of studying these processes, as physics itself depends on mathematics. In atmospheric physics, the goal is to mathematically model, and therefore predict, what occurs in the atmospheric layers that surround the earth and other planets. Statistics and computers play an important role in studying the atmosphere, as does chemistry; the chemical makeup of the atmosphere affects its activity. To gather data, the field depends on the advanced design and manufacture of sensing devices.

Basic Principles

Historically, atmospheric research has been two-pronged. Physical meteorology studies what is seen and heard in the atmosphere, such as cloud formation, rainfall, lightning, tornadoes, and other tangible phenomena. The dynamics side of atmospheric research studies large-scale atmospheric motions, such as those that are hundreds of miles or many days long. This includes frontal systems, tropical storms, jet streams, and related effects. Also central to atmospheric physics are air pressure, density, and the capture of water, especially from oceans.

These two historical approaches are best merged in an interdisciplinary approach. The study of climate change, for instance, involves advanced dynamics, chemistry, and radiation research. The mathematics of physics, especially fluid flow equations, remains essential to this study. For example, scattering theory uses mathematics to understand the behavior of atmospheric matter scattering in particles and/or waves. The study of atmospheric physics also uses mathematics to model wave propagation, or the ways that waves travel.

The application of physics to atmospheric studies has grown in recent decades. The late twentieth and early twenty-first centuries brought advances in atmospheric physics thanks to satellites and computers. The gaseous envelope of atmosphere that makes life on earth possible is never fully at rest, so much of scientists' knowledge of it still relies on Newton's laws of motion, formulated in the seventeenth century. The constant motion of air makes it difficult to capture facts without the application of continuum mechanics, which studies the behavior of solids and fluids as entire masses rather than separate particles. Joseph-Louis Lagrange (1736–1813) was the next scientist after Isaac Newton (1643–1727) to make an in-depth study of mechanics. Lagrange's work enabled the development of mathematical physics, and his approach has become widespread ever since. In the Lagrangian description of fluid motion, a physicist examines a parcel or several parcels of air to learn how properties transform and interact as a single system within those bounds and with the environment beyond the parcels.

Core Concepts

The atmosphere is a complicated mixture of chemicals, water, and solid matter. A relatively thin layer compared to the mass of the planet, it has far more horizontal than vertical movement. The atmosphere, like the ocean, has tides. For the most part, they are created through daily heating by the sun's radiation, solar gravitation, and molecular resonance, in which a molecule vibrates among several alternate structures. Though solar radiation has an effect on atmospheric physics, gravity, compressing most of the air to within ten miles of the surface, has more effect. The pressure exerted by gravity causes air to become denser at sea level than in the mountains or on airplanes.

Density decreases exponentially with altitude, and pressure changes in the troposphere create flows of air mass. These air masses are also affected by the rotation of the planet. Planetary rotation impacts the upper atmosphere too, by creating waves that affect the movement of heat, chemicals, and aerosols.

Atmospheric Composition. The earth's atmosphere contains mostly nitrogen and oxygen. The remaining gases, including carbon dioxide (CO_2) and ozone (O_3), make up only 1 percent of the air. One of the most important components of the atmosphere is water, occurring both in molecular form and in fine aerosols. Aerosols are tiny solid or liquid particles suspended in gas. The air carries natural aerosols, coming from volcanic ash, sea spray, pollen, and other sources; the air also carries human-produced aerosols.

Ozone is made in the stratosphere when solar rays collide with O_2 molecules and break them into two O_1 atoms. These then combine with O_2, resulting in O_3—ozone. Stratospheric ozone is good, as it protects the earth from harmful ultraviolet rays coming from the sun. Harmful ozone is a type of surface pollution, which happens in the troposphere when sunlight and heat trigger chemical reactions involving nitrogen oxides—often created by human activity, such as cars—and volatile organic chemicals. Harmful ozone can make breathing difficult for people with respiratory ailments.

Water Movement. Water movement in the air is a central concern for meteorologists. Water vapor, considered only a trace of what makes up the atmosphere, is found almost exclusively in the troposphere. It is produced at the surface and in the tropics, drying out increasingly toward the upper troposphere and the poles. Convection, or the movement of molecules within fluids, builds cells (clouds) vertically near the tropics, but most cloud motion is horizontal. As trained physicists, weather forecasters need to understand the basic elements of motion. For example, speed differs from velocity. Speed describes how fast in time an object moves (e.g., miles per hour), whereas velocity describes both the speed and particular direction of an object's movement. Acceleration in units per second per second, and force, including the force of gravity, are part of understanding cloud physics and other parts of

Interesting Facts about Atmospheric Physics

- The mesosphere contains night-shining clouds. Also called noctilucent clouds, they show up after sunset at higher latitudes, glowing an icy blue color. Believed to be formed from ice crystals, noctilucent clouds have in recent years been seen farther south than previous records specify, perhaps indicative of climate change.

- Heat from one nuclear bomb multiplied by about ten thousand approximates the thermal energy of one single hurricane.

- Over thirty-five million objects launched from the earth are floating in orbit.

- Aurora borealis displays are associated with storms in the ionosphere caused by solar flares. Flares can travel from the sun to the ionosphere in eight minutes, causing massive electric currents (one million amperes or more) to ionize and emit light.

- Oceanic currents and temperatures, both tied to the principles of atmospheric physics, involve significantly overlapping areas of study. For instance, the study of ocean temperatures is an emerging and challenging field; data collection of ocean temperatures began around 1990.

- The formation of lightning has long been a mystery to scientists. Scientists previously believed that the water of thunderstorms has no electrical charge. This would make it neutral and therefore have no connection with lightning's massive release of electricity. However, some researchers from Brazil reported in 2010 that water vapor may hold an electrical charge. In tests, they exposed metals to water vapor, and the metals did take on a small negative charge.

the atmosphere. The earth's rotation adds centripetal (inward-pulling) and centrifugal (outward-pushing) forces. In addition, the Coriolis effect causes atmospheric masses to sway with relation to the ground, as viewed from above. Northern Hemisphere air masses swerve right, and Southern appear to go left; thus, cyclones spin clockwise north of the equator, and counterclockwise south of it.

Thermodynamics. The study of thermodynamics focuses on the relationship between energy and work and the transfer of energy between systems. One aspect of thermodynamics in atmospheric physics is thermal equilibrium, in which a transfer of heat has occurred between two systems to the point at which there is no longer an exchange of energy; the systems' temperatures are now the same. Another thermal effect of the atmosphere is that it makes water change states. Water can be liquid, gas, solid, or plasma. The discipline of thermodynamics supplies the necessary formulae and conceptual mathematics to study the phase changes of water, such as how vapor transforms into water or ice. An understanding of thermodynamics also helps physicists to calculate the condensation of vapor, which must occur faster than evaporation in order to form liquid water. These are just two basic examples of the applications of thermodynamics to atmospheric physics.

Atmospheric Zones. The earth's atmosphere is considered to be about three hundred miles thick, though gravity concentrates most of it to within ten miles of the surface of the earth. The atmosphere also does not end at a particular height. Rather, it continuously thins until it has merged with space. It is helpful to understand the earth's atmosphere by dividing it into different zones.

- The thermosphere is the highest layer of the earth's atmosphere. Temperature within it increases with altitude, because a smaller amount of gas is absorbing a large amount of solar radiation. The top portion of the thermosphere, right before space begins, is called the exosphere. The exosphere extends from about four hundred miles high up to a thousand miles or more, depending on solar activity. The second part of the thermosphere is the ionosphere, which stretches up from approximately fifty miles high from the earth's surface. The ionosphere contains a large amount of ions—the sun's radiation is so powerful here that it breaks electrons free, producing ions out of molecules—which, when impacted by solar wind, cause aurora light displays. The ionosphere is also where NASA's space shuttle orbits; radio waves are reflected here, making radio communication possible.

- Below the thermosphere is the mesosphere, the coldest layer of earth's atmosphere, stretching from about thirty miles to fifty miles high. The air here, while thin, is thick enough that it can burn up meteoroids and cause meteor showers to be visible. The mesosphere is too high for airplanes and weather balloons, but too low for orbital satellites.

- The next layer, the stratosphere, stretches between approximately ten and thirty miles high. The stratosphere's temperature increases the higher it goes, due to heating ozone. This is where "good" ozone acts as a protective shield, keeping away ultraviolet rays from the sun.

- The zone closest to the earth's surface and where most of the earth's atmosphere is concentrated is called the troposphere. This is where weather happens. The sun warms the earth's surface, then the surface warms air masses, which rise as cool air masses fall. The troposphere cools with gains in altitude; its vertical instability is one major cause of weather. Between the troposphere and the stratosphere is the tropopause, which acts as a soft boundary. High-altitude jet streams race along this level. The height of the tropopause is affected by vertical instability from convection, meaning that it lies closer to the cold of the poles than the warmth of the equator. The tropopause is very dry and caps the weather zone; just above it is the best place for commercial airplanes to fly.

Applications Past and Present

Remote Sensing. On October 4, 1957, the Soviet Union launched *Sputnik I*, the first earth-orbiting, human-built satellite; this started the space race of the 1950s and 1960s. Since the launch of *Sputnik I*, satellites have come a long way. Remote sensor satellites, basically platforms carrying sensors that orbit the earth and send back data, have become so common that debris associated with those no longer functioning—space junk—is a navigational hazard. Even so, remote sensing has revolutionized communications, intelligence gathering, weather forecasting, and atmospheric research. NOAA, the National

Oceanic and Aeronautic Administration, operates satellites that track storms, gather ocean temperatures, take innumerable data readings, and make these readings available around the clock to scientists in the field. Every satellite reports to an earth base, where scientists receive the data, process it, and make it available to others. The US Office of Satellite Products and Operations, OSPO, can provide data on such topics as atmospheric profiles, rain, clouds, wind, ozone, aerosols, and the radiation budget.

The satellites that remote sensing technology rides on are platforms that exist in the harsh conditions of space. Their data gathering cameras or other sensors are dependent on power systems and antennae, and none of it can be maintained once the unit is in orbit. Even when a satellite is performing well, it can be thrown off course by gravitational forces and will lose altitude over time. Correcting for position is often done with gas canisters; the usable life of the satellite may depend less on its advanced technology than on how many gas canisters can be packed onto the platform. Despite this difficulty, satellites provide information that cannot be obtained in other ways. Scientists continually work toward the improvement of satellite technology so that more accurate and detailed data, about the weather and other atmospheric concerns, can be provided.

Meteorology. Meteorology, the study of the phenomena in the atmosphere collectively known as weather—changes in air pressure, moisture, temperature, and wind direction—has been part of atmospheric physics since long before the satellite age. Since antiquity, for example, people with rheumatism have been said to feel pressure changes in their joints. "Weather" in the atmospheric physics community is a fluid term, but an important focus. Weather can be defined as air flow patterns miles long, occurring in the troposphere over the course of days rather than weeks. Meteorologists can track weather patterns, given that they show some regularity over months and in annual cycles. However, weather can still be random on any given day and generally remains unpredictable. Beyond meteorology, other fields of study and their corresponding data sets, such as ocean temperature change, impinge on atmospheric research. Atmospheric physics is part of the overall study of climate change. The field therefore must keep advancing so that civilization-impacting effects—such as droughts, hurricanes, and the effects of climate change—can be predicted and appropriate planning can take place.

Flight. As society demands increasingly fuel-efficient airplanes and effective military aircraft, aerodynamic design depends on increasing knowledge of atmospheric physics. Wings of aircraft "fly" because the speeding up of airflow over the top surface of a certain shape creates a difference in air pressure between the top and bottom of the surface. Orville and Wilbur Wright were the first test this concept when their *Flyer* rose in the air above Kitty Hawk, North Carolina, in 1903. Pilots know that air pressure differences and motions cause winds and turbulence, requiring skill and experience to negotiate. Aircraft must withstand greater atmospheric temperatures the faster they fly. The space shuttle *Columbia*, for example, was destroyed in 2003 by hot gases that penetrated its exterior in one spot that was under intense pressure during reentry through the atmosphere. Such challenges concerning altitude and speed are a significant part of atmospheric physics' importance to aircraft design.

Acoustics. Sound waves are one type of atmospheric wave that physicists study. Acoustics, the effect of sound in a certain space, affects modern living in a number of ways. One is noise control. In an increasingly noisy world, the design and manufacture of materials that can, for example, separate highway noise from homes or appliance noise from one apartment to the next, are important. Acoustics affects architecture in transmitting sound as well. Public arenas, such as concert and lecture halls, represent Lagrangian parcels, each with their own needs. Acoustics is also important in industrial and military diagnostics, as high powered engines can be tested for imperfections by listening for a rattling sound. Finally, the study of acoustics is needed for the ever-better transmission of communications over wireless areas, as these areas steadily grow.

Climate Change. Weather occurs over large spaces and in short amounts of time. Climate, however, occurs across the planet over decades and centuries. The study of climate change is a relatively new field, in the sense that its effects are more pressing than they have been in past centuries. The United States Environmental Protection Agency (EPA) reported that the first decade of the twenty-first century had a planet-wide average temperature rise of 1.4 degrees Fahrenheit. The summer of 2012 saw widespread drought in the United States' grain-growing regions, resulting in record-high prices for corn and soybeans. These staple crops are used for more than just food; ethanol, certain plastics, and other products are made with corn and soy. Climate change has also caused storms to rage worldwide and with increased ferocity. Atmospheric carbon dioxide and other greenhouse gases are widely held to be causes of global warming. The study of atmospheric physics, therefore, is used in most efforts made by industry or government to address climate change and to secure the well-being of future generations.

Energy Balance and Thermal Equilibrium. The first law of thermodynamics states that in a closed system, such as the atmosphere, energy can never be created nor destroyed, but it does transition from one form to another. Additionally, the amount of work done by a system is equal to the amount of energy available. According to this law, the atmosphere will heat or cool internal to itself to the degree equal to heat supplied by the sun, minus work done by the atmosphere. That work is the radiation of excess heat back out into space. If the earth simply absorbed heat from the sun, it would be like Venus, a boiling ball. Instead, the earth's atmosphere accepts the sun's shortwave radiation and emits longwave, or infrared radiation (IR). A portion of shortwave radiation, known as albedo, is reflected off the ground and off clouds. Clouds play an important role in the earth's thermal equilibrium because they are highly reflective. Heat bouncing off the ground can sometimes hit the bottoms of clouds. When this happens, the clouds will still reflect albedo, but this time back to the earth's surface. In addition to this complexity, aerosol particles help form clouds by providing places for water vapor to coagulate. They also absorb IR from anywhere and scatter shortwave solar rays. Aerosols' effect on thermal equilibrium has been documented throughout history in association with volcanic ash emitted from massive eruptions. However, the full effects of aerosols are believed to be more complex than scientists yet know, since the amounts and kinds of aerosols in a given atmospheric parcel are often impacted by human activity.

To achieve equilibrium, incoming solar energy is distributed throughout the atmosphere as the earth turns. Outgoing longwave radiation (OLR) is complicated by the greenhouse effect, in which the troposphere turns half the OLR back to the earth's surface to bounce again. The troposphere is a heat sink—meaning that it absorbs heat—that both drives atmospheric circulation and acts as a blanket to trap heat and make life on the earth possible. As atmospheric chemical and water vapor levels change, atmospheric physicists are needed to determine the effects this will have.

Impact on Industry

Government Agencies. The US government conducts a great amount of atmospheric research. The National Aeronautics and Space Administration (NASA) collects atmospheric data, with satellites measuring such things as rainfall in the tropics and surface salinity in the oceans. NOAA is in charge of the nation's Doppler radar, through the National Weather Service (NWS). The Office of Oceanic and Atmospheric Research (OAR) also employs many atmospheric researchers. Research typically involves computer modeling of some kind.

The international community is rich in government-sponsored atmospheric research organizations. For instance, there is the Met Office in the United Kingdom and the Institute for Space Aeronomy in Belgium. Scientists from institutions in Peru, India, Brazil, Japan, and the United States attended the Thirteenth International Symposium on Equatorial Aeronomy (ISEA13) in March 2012, sponsored by the Climate and Weather of the Sun-Earth System (CAWSES) academic organization. Governments around the world are interested in climate change—and therefore physicists who specialize in studying the atmosphere—particularly since the signing of the Kyoto Protocol in 1997. The protocol seeks to control nations' emissions of greenhouse gases to improve sustainability across the globe.

Military. The weather has been important to military campaigns for centuries. Knowledge of weather has grown, partly due to advances in atmospheric physics. Armies and navies of the past were mainly concerned with the troposphere, whereas the modern US military

Occupation	Atmospheric and space scientists
Employment 2010	9,500
Projected Employment 2020	10,500
Change in Number (2010–20)	1,000
Percent Change	14%

Bureau of Labor Statistics, 2012

takes an interest in atmospheric activity all the way to the plasma of the ionosphere. Much of the focus of the Space Physics and Atmospheric Research Center (SPARC) at the US Air Force Academy (USAFA) is on how plasmas on the outer limits of the ionosphere affect air force systems. Satellites for communications and remote sensing are used in the military as much as or more than in civilian organizations. Guidance systems for manned or drone aircraft are also used. Any system that can be disabled in the atmosphere is of military interest. USAFA builds its own small satellites to collect data. Scientists then analyze this data to study the behavior of plasma in the upper atmosphere when exposed to solar events and other space weather phenomena.

The applied physics efforts of SPARC include studies of the mesosphere. SPARC also works on making new advances in camera speed and light filters, extending the ability to collect data. The ultra-high levels of the atmosphere are not its only interest, however. Hurricane predictability has been a problem for meteorologists; SPARC has been working toward fixing that problem. In addition, SPARC researches the effect of complex landscapes on atmospheric layering. As mentioned above, pilots prefer to fly just above the tropopause. Learning how the tropopause deforms in relation to mountain ranges, for example, is one practical problem that the Air Force studies.

University Research and Teaching. Atmospheric physics is increasingly interdisciplinary and therefore a promising field for those interested in research and teaching. An undergraduate degree in mathematics, physics, chemistry, computer modeling, or a related discipline would help a student prepare for advanced studies in atmospheric physics at the postgraduate level. A student may then decide to continue to research at a university and/or to teach courses related to atmospheric physics.

Teaching atmospheric science is an option at the postgraduate, undergraduate, or even grade school level. The National Math and Science Initiative (NMSI) was formed after a 2005 study found students' participation in the sciences in American high schools to be problematically low. This meant a lack of preparation for college-level courses in mathematics and the sciences. Training capable science teachers for grade and high schools is one NMSI goal; to train successful teachers, successful college professors are required. Both have been in shorter supply than NMSI would like. The University of Texas at Austin spearheaded a program called UTeach, which has been adopted, with financial help from NMSI, at thirty universities. NMSI also seeks to raise advanced placement (AP) scores in science, mathematics, and English.

Social Context and Future Prospects

Climate Change. The issue of climate change is often approached from two areas: forcings and feedbacks. Forcings are what impact or initiate change, whether anthropogenic (caused by human activity) or natural. Aerosols are considered forcing agents. Some types of aerosols initiate atmospheric cooling, while others initiate warming. Other forcings include anthropogenic changes in the atmosphere's composition, changes in land use, volcanic eruptions, alterations in solar output, and long-term changes of the earth's orbital parameters. Though research into these effects has been conducted since the beginning of the twenty-first century, much more needs to be done.

The second area that scientists watch closely is called feedback. Feedbacks are the results of forcings. They are either positive, by increasing warming, or negative, by decreasing warming. Feedbacks, which have been studied more than forcings, come from water vapor, albedo, atmospheric lapse-rate (the rate at which temperature decreases upward), and clouds. For example, an increase in greenhouse gases may increase the amount of bright, low-level clouds. This, in turn, leads to less absorption of the sun's rays and thus an increase solar radiation hitting the earth. The Intergovernmental Panel on Climate Change (IPCC) has called for research into clouds as a top priority. Studies of precipitation feedback have been in the earliest stages of mathematical modeling; models vary so widely that more atmospheric researchers who focus in cloud physics and precipitation are needed.

Communications. Storms in the ionosphere disrupt radio, electronic navigation, and GPS (Global Positioning Systems). Modern living has become increasingly dependent on electronic navigation and GPS. Satellites that serve cell phone communications depend on electronic navigation to stay balanced, stay in orbit, and keep away from space junk. Large-scale agriculture has become more dependent on tractor-mounted GPS to plant and maintain crops. Better knowledge of the earth's ionosphere will matter more and more as human reliance on technology, whether large or small, continues to increase into the future.

Air Quality. More people live in densely-populated areas than ever before. As the world's population grows, concerns about urban air quality also grow. Ground-level ozone is one pollutant associated with industries and automobiles. Another pollutant is the particular matter of urban atmospheric aerosols, such as dust and ash. Particulate matter is one of the most harmful pollutants for people. While scientists have been working to lower ozone-creating emissions, controlling dust is also important. Atmospheric physicists who understand the motion of particles at the very lowest levels of the troposphere are needed for this purpose.

Further Reading

Dessler, Andrew E., and Edward A. Parson. *The Science and Politics of Global Climate Change: A Guide to the Debate*. New York: Cambridge UP, 2010. Print. Introduction to the issue of climate change, including atmospheric chemistry and other atmospheric properties research. Also discusses the potential future of research in the area of climate change.

Frederick, John E. *Principles of Atmospheric Science*. Sudbury, MA: Jones & Bartlett, 2008. Print. Introductory text describing the various fields of atmospheric sciences, including atmospheric chemistry, atmospheric physics, and climatology. Describes techniques and research methods utilized in modern climate and atmospheric research.

Houghton, John T. *The Physics of Atmospheres*. 3rd ed. Cambridge: Cambridge UP, 2002. Print. Revised textbook with chapters on topics such as remote sensing, numerical modeling, climate change, chaos, and predictability.

NASA Goddard Institute for Space Studies. National Aeronautics and Space Administration, 2012. Web. 21 Aug. 2012. Describes a variety of current research programs in the environmental sciences, physics, and atmospheric chemistry. Also contains descriptions of using atmospheric physics in the study of climate change and global warming.

Spencer, Roy. *Global Warming*. Roy Spencer, 2012. Web. 23 Aug. 2012. Spencer, a climatologist, used to work for NASA. His website offers alternative ideas to the common view that global warming is caused by human activity.

About the Author: Amanda R. Jones has an MA from Virginia Tech and a PhD in English from the University of Virginia. She has written several articles for EBSCO and has published in the *Children's Literature Association Quarterly*.

Meteorologist

Earnings (Yearly Median): $87,780 (Bureau of Labor Statistics, 2012)

Employment and Outlook: Average growth (Bureau of Labor Statistics, 2012)

O*NET-SOC Code: 19-2021.00

Related Career Cluster(s): Agriculture, Food & Natural Resources; Arts, Audio/Video Technology & Communications; Government & Public Administration; Health Science

Scope of Work

Also known as atmospheric scientists, meteorologists study atmospheric phenomena, conditions, and trends, including the weather and climate change. They analyze data gathered by ground, air, and satellite technologies such as barometers, radars, and thermometers. Based on this data, meteorologists prepare reports used for forecasting the weather, analyzing air and surface conditions, and studying certain types of atmospheric phenomena. Atmospheric scientists also use maps, photographs, and different models to predict long-term weather patterns. Many meteorologists present their findings and forecasts to the general public using television, radio, print, and Internet media. Others apply the data collected and models they generate to the study of agricultural conditions, the effects of pollution on the environment, and global warming.

Education and Coursework

Aspiring meteorologists must receive at least a bachelor's degree in meteorology, atmospheric science, or a related discipline from a federally recognized program at an undergraduate institution. A broader undergraduate degree in science or mathematics can also be useful if the student intends to pursue graduate school. Students attending undergraduate institutions should take courses of relevance to the field, including physics, mathematics, chemistry, and geography. Because meteorologists rely heavily on computer-based technology, course work in computer science is also an essential component of an undergraduate student's training. Furthermore, a large number of aspiring atmospheric scientists seek to become media-based meteorologists. These candidates would benefit from additional course work in public speaking, communications, and journalism to enhance their skills in the media-oriented fields.

Many meteorologists are primarily researchers working for scientific foundations and agencies, including those of the US federal and other national governments. In order to pursue a career in this arena, students are strongly encouraged to obtain a master's degree in meteorology or a similar discipline at an accredited graduate-school program. There, they will take courses in more specified areas, such as oceanography, geophysics, atmospheric chemistry, and climatology. A master's degree usually takes about two to three years to complete. In addition to in-depth course work, students are usually required to pass a comprehensive examination or complete and defend an independent research paper, or thesis, in order to acquire their master's degree.

Those who seek a career in atmospheric science research are well advised to obtain a doctorate, or PhD, in addition to a master's degree.

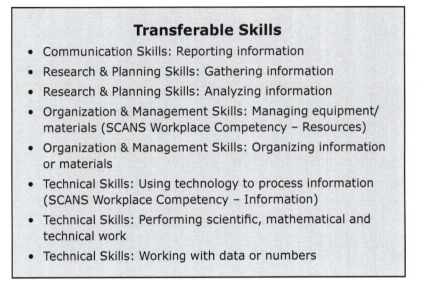

This advanced degree gives a candidate greater competitive value when pursuing a job with a major institution or government agency. A PhD may be obtained at the same university at which a student would receive his or her master's degree. Following the structured course work at the master's level (and usually after passing an exam), the student would pursue an independent research project, or dissertation. Upon completion, this research paper would be presented to the faculty of the institution and eventually published. The dissertation is often used as a supporting document in the job search.

Career Enhancement and Training

Aspiring meteorologists can enhance their career tracks through internships and entry-level work with media outlets, research organizations, and other employers. Many such positions are available to students who are still in undergraduate or graduate programs in meteorology.

Individuals who seek to become media meteorologists are advised to begin their careers at small-market stations, where they will become familiar with the practices and technologies used by successful weather forecasters. Once they become more experienced in this arena, they may apply for positions in larger markets.

Those who seek to become researchers typically enter the workforce at a basic level as well, sometimes while still in graduate school, as a research assistant or in a similar position. In this capacity, they learn the technologies and research practices utilized by the institution at which they work, developing the experience necessary to advance to higher-level positions.

Many atmospheric scientists seek to work at universities rather than research facilities or media outlets. In order to become professors, they must gain teaching experience, which is often initiated while still in graduate school, in positions such as research assistant or teaching assistant.

All meteorologists, regardless of their specific career paths, benefit from connecting with atmospheric science–oriented professional associations and societies. Here, these scientists share information with one another, learn new research techniques, study data, and learn about new employment opportunities. Among the many such organizations are the National Weather Association, the American Meteorology Society, and the International Association of Meteorology and Atmospheric Science.

Daily Tasks and Technology

The daily responsibilities of a meteorologist vary based on the field in which he or she applies his or her knowledge. In general, however, meteorologists collect and study atmospheric data using sensory equipment on airborne, ground-based, and satellite vehicles. The technology used in this arena has evolved considerably over the last few decades. Radar systems, for example, now include Doppler radar, synthetic aperture radar, and the Next-Generation Radar (NEXRAD) network, providing imagery of weather phenomena in greater detail than ever before. Additionally, the meteorologist has at his or her disposal geographic information system (GIS) technology, which uses a global network of interconnected satellite systems to provide broad-scale images that can be used to predict and track weather phenomena.

Based on the information gathered, meteorologists then compile the data and form models. These models help atmospheric scientists forecast the life cycles and paths of large storms, as well as the types of conditions those storms will create. The data can also be used for models that

A Conversation with Sean Potter

Job Title: Certified Consulting Meteorologist; Certified Broadcast Meteorologist; Specialist

What was your career path?

I began my career as a broadcast meteorologist and, after returning to graduate school to complete my Master's degree, continued on a path of communicating about weather and meteorology that led me to where I am today. Along the way, I developed skills, certifications, and relationships that proved invaluable to advancing my career. Not only do I have a fulfilling "day job" managing online news and social media for the National Weather Service, but I also get to flex my meteorological muscles in my spare time by doing consulting work in the field of forensic meteorology, as well as writing for publications such as Weatherwise magazine, of which I am a contributing editor.

What are three pieces of advice you would offer someone interested in your profession?

Spend as much time as you can getting to know people currently working in the field—ask them about their careers and how they got there. I've found networking to be an important part of my career development. It's also important to focus on an aspect of the field that plays on your strengths, be it forecasting, research, broadcasting, outreach, etc. There are many paths available besides the obvious ones. Finally, don't give up! Getting a degree in meteorology requires lots of calculus, physics, and other subjects that can be daunting, but keeping your goals in mind and persevering will pay off in the end.

What paths for career advancement are available to you?

For the freelance consulting and writing work I do, there isn't much room for advancement, except in terms of doing more of it and for a broader range of clients. With my job at the National Weather Service, the paths for advancement would involve getting into management, such as becoming the director or deputy director of communications for the agency. If I were to move into a forecast office setting (as opposed to the national headquarters, where I work now), it would likely involve working as the office's warning coordination meteorologist, who serves in a management role as the local public face of the agency, and, ultimately, the meteorologist-in-charge for the office.

predict long-term climate changes such as the ongoing global-warming trend. Modeling is predominantly performed on computers using statistical programs—scientific software capable of managing extremely large quantities of data—as well as imaging and map-creation programs that generate illustrations of weather trends. Among the types of this latter software are AccuWeather Galileo and Esri's ArcGIS.

Depending on the area in which they work, meteorologists may use the models generated to present short- and long-term forecasts on camera or to develop scientific reports. Here, too, databases and computer systems capable of showing and transferring detailed images and large amounts of data, including updated e-mail and publishing systems, are important tools.

Earnings and Employment Outlook

Meteorologists' salaries vary based on the sector and organization in which they work, be it the media, research foundations, or government institutions. Some atmospheric scientists earn as much as nearly $131,000 per year, while others earn just over $55,000 per year. The average pay rate for meteorologists is growing steadily at a rate of about 11 percent annually, about as fast as salary rates in other industries.

Meteorology has long been a specialized field, and as such, the job market for these scientists has traditionally been relatively small. However, the evolution and greater availability of meteorological technology has helped many private companies to grow their operations to include meteorological analysis. For example, a shipping business may employ a meteorologist to better predict dangerous weather that could threaten its operations.

Meteorology has long been a specialized field, and as such, the job market for these scientists has traditionally been relatively small. However, the evolution and greater availability of meteorological technology has helped many private companies to grow their operations to include meteorological analysis.

Public institutions, nonprofit research foundations, and government agencies have of late been subject to increasingly strict budget constraints. Without room for staff expansion, jobs in these settings are difficult to obtain, and many require candidates to have a minimum of a PhD and relevant experience in order to be considered. The job market in the private sector is expected to show greater expansion than the public sector, which means that meteorologist positions will likely be relatively more available and attainable.

Related Occupations

- **Geoscientists:** Geoscientists analyze the earth's structure, characteristics, and natural processes. They also track and predict changes that have occurred and will occur to the earth over time.

- **Hydrologists:** Hydrologists study the earth's oceans, lakes, rivers, and other water bodies. They also monitor the water cycle, which includes weather phenomena.

- **Astronomers:** In addition to studying phenomena and bodies in outer space, astronomers analyze the effects of space weather such as solar flares on the earth's planetary spheres. They also compare weather on Earth with phenomena seen on other planets.

- **Environmental Scientists:** Environmental Scientists study the effects of human civilization on the planet, including acid rain and increases in storm severity caused by climate change.

Future Applications

Although meteorology has long been focused primarily on predicting and tracking weather patterns, the field has seen considerable expansion into other sectors. For example, scientists are increasingly using meteorological concepts and research practices to study the effects of man-made pollution on the environment. They are also using the models developed by meteorologists to study periods of climate change that occurred in the past and to track and forecast future changes in climate. Due to continued budget constraints dictated by an unpredictable economy, it is likely that this expansion will be concentrated more in the private sector than in the public sector.

In addition, meteorology will likely see increased use in commercial and public safety. Using meteorological technology and expertise, airlines and other travel-related industries can successfully track and adjust to atmospheric phenomena with greater speed, thus saving money and time. The continued evolution of radar and other systems will also help public-safety officials track severe weather such as tornadoes and hurricanes, allowing more time for people to get out of storms' paths.

—Michael P. Auerbach, MA

More Information

American Meteorological Society
45 Beacon Street
Boston, MA 02108-3693
www.ametsoc.org

International Association of Meteorology and
Atmospheric Sciences
Deutsches Zentrum fuer Luft und Raumfahrt e.V. (DLR)
Institut fuer Physik der Atmosphaere (IPA)
Muenchner Strasse 20
D-82234 Oberpfaffenhofen
Germany
www.iamas.org

National Oceanic and Atmospheric Administration
1401 Constitution Avenue NW, Room 5128
Washington, DC 20230
www.noaa.gov

National Weather Association
228 West Millbrook Road
Raleigh, NC 27609-4304
www.nwas.org

National Weather Service
1325 East West Highway
Silver Spring, MD 20910
www.weather.gov

Atomic and Molecular Physics

FIELDS OF STUDY

Physics; chemistry; physical chemistry/chemical physics; spectroscopy; optics; photonics; quantum mechanics; statistical mechanics; electromagnetism; condensed-matter physics; nuclear and particle physics; fluid physics; solid-state physics; computational chemistry/physics; atomic and optical physics; biophysics; plasma physics; theoretical particle physics; classical mechanics; mathematics; calculus; differential equations; linear algebra; statistics; numerical analysis; computer science.

DEFINITION

Atomic and molecular physics is as broad a subject as the name implies. In addition to the study of the physics of atoms and molecules—atoms and ions in isolation and in combination, respectively—atomic and molecular physics has close ties to spectroscopy, which is used to study these systems, and to such fields as nanotechnology and biophysics, which extend insights from atomic and molecular physics to particular systems. Applications range from understanding the behavior of atmospheric species contributing to climate change to engineering new pharmaceutical delivery systems and developing sensors to detect trace levels of explosives or contaminants.

Basic Principles

The idea that all matter is composed of fundamental building blocks traces back to ancient Greek and Indian philosophers. However, it was not until the turn of the nineteenth century that John Dalton established atomic theory, which states that all matter is composed of atoms and that atoms are the smallest unit of matter. One hundred years later, at the turn of the twentieth century, atomic theory was confirmed by Albert Einstein, who used it to explain the random motion of a particle suspended in a liquid or gas. Einstein was also one of the fathers of quantum mechanics, the model of physics used to explain how atoms and molecules behave.

In its original incarnation, atomic theory states that atoms are the smallest units of matter. However, scientists later discovered that atoms are composed of protons, electrons, and neutrons, which are in turn composed of quarks; the six types of quarks are called up, down, strange, charm, bottom, and top. These subatomic particles are relevant to atomic and molecular physics, but their study as entities in and of themselves is the province of particle physics. Molecular physics sometimes bleeds into the realm of chemical physics or physical chemistry. Although there is no cut-and-dried distinction between the two, physical chemistry generally concerns molecules only and approaches the topic with a focus on its application to the broader realm of chemistry. Chemical physics lies somewhere between and within atomic and molecular physics and physical chemistry, concerning molecules more than atoms but focusing on the physical phenomena rather than chemical applications.

Core Concepts

Quantum Mechanics. Very small objects, such as atoms and molecules, behave very differently from human experience of the laws of physics. All matter exhibits the same wave-particle duality commonly used to describe photons or electrons; that is, matter is not the perfectly corporeal entity observed on this scale. Rather, all matter has a characteristic wavelength called a de Broglie wavelength. One may observe a human hand as being solid and well defined, but it actually has a wavelength, period, and amplitude, just like light. The quantum world seems strange in other ways, too. If a person were playing with a spring, for example, he or she might think that it could be made to bounce at any frequency chosen; however, the energy used to make the spring bounce is actually only available in discrete packets. Thus, if that person can bounce the spring with energy A, bouncing it at energy A+B is impossible unless B is an integer number of energy units, called quanta. As the term *quantum mechanics* suggests, it was the discovery of the quantization of energy by Einstein and his colleagues that launched scientists' understanding of small-scale physics. Because quantum mechanics dictates how atoms and molecules behave, it is a crucial element of atomic and molecular physics.

Structures of Atoms. High-school science teaches that atoms comprise a small core containing protons and neutrons orbited by electrons, much like the sun is orbited by planets. However, this is a vast simplification, and the omitted details are crucial for understanding atomic and molecular physics. For example, both the electrons and the nuclei have a property called spin. Despite its seemingly straightforward name, this type of spin is a purely quantum-mechanical property and has nothing to do with any kind of actual spinning motion. Electrons also do not orbit around the nucleus per se, often being found in different shapes around the nucleus, such as dumbbell or clover shapes.

Structures of Molecules. Chemical bonds can be covalent, in which electrons are shared; ionic, in which opposing charges attract; or metallic, in which the electrons travel throughout the material, surrounding the nuclei but not being bound to any one nucleus. Although in chemistry the word *molecule* tends to refer to covalently bonded atoms, it is typically used more broadly in physics. Molecules undergo many different types of motion. Translational motion is the movement of an entire molecule in space, vibrational motion is the stretching and bending of chemical bonds, and rotational motion involves rotation around chemical bonds. The concepts of nuclear and electron spin, electronic energy levels, and energy quantization are also relevant for molecules. All of these properties can be studied using spectroscopy, as explained below.

Spectroscopy. Spectroscopy is the use of the interaction between light and matter to gain information about the properties of that matter—or, sometimes, the properties of the light. Spectroscopy is used extensively in atomic and molecular physics because it is often the only way to obtain detailed information about atoms and molecules. The information that can be accessed using spectroscopic techniques includes the connectivity of atoms within molecules, the lattice orientation of a solid, the electron configuration of an atom or molecule, and electron and nuclear spins. Spectroscopy is categorized by the wavelength of

Interesting Facts about Atomic and Molecular Physics

One way to appreciate the complexity of atomic and molecular physics is to consider atoms and molecules containing a single element. The following facts concern exclusively carbon materials.

- Carbon atoms bonded with no macroscale ordering take the form of coal. This material is quite reactive and is used for heating and energy production.

- Diamonds are composed of a cubic arrangement of carbon atoms and are the hardest material known. In addition to a diamond's legendary hardness, it is also a surprisingly good conductor of heat. Pure diamonds are electrical insulators.

- Glassy carbon is a black solid that, in contrast to coal or amorphous carbon, is extremely inert. Combined with its stability at high temperatures, this property makes it an excellent sample holder and electrode.

- Graphene is a single-atom-thick sheet of carbon atoms arranged in hexagonal patterns. Concerning electrical conductivity, it is a semi-metal. Graphene is also one of the strongest materials known.

- Carbon nanotubes are essentially tubes of graphene. The bonds in these tubes are extremely strong, allowing the production of very long, very thin tubes. Carbon nanotubes are semiconductors, unlike graphene.

- Buckminsterfullerene, also called a buckyball, is a soccer ball–like molecule containing sixty carbon atoms bonded into a sphere of hexagons. For its synthesis in the mid-1980s, its creators were awarded the 1996 Nobel Prize in Chemistry. Buckminsterfullerene is a superconductor at the fairly high temperature—relative to other molecular superconductors—of 18 kelvins (-255.15 degrees Celsius, or -427.27 degrees Fahrenheit).

radiation used and by the experimental design. In the case of the former, different parts of the electromagnetic spectrum are able to probe different aspects of an atomic or molecular system. For example, infrared light is often used to study vibrations in molecules, radio waves can be used to elucidate information about spin, and ultraviolet and visible light provide information about the energy levels occupied by electrons in molecules or atoms. Regarding the experimental design, numerous details can differentiate experiments: whether the experiment measures the absorption, reflection, or emission of light by a sample; the use of a single wavelength or a range of wavelengths; the method used to analyze the data; and other details.

Arrangements of Matter. The following terms are used heavily in atomic and molecular physics to describe the phase or arrangement of the matter being discussed. Three of the states of matter—solid, liquid, and gas—should already be familiar to students. A fourth state of matter is plasma, which is gas that has been ionized, producing a gaseous substance that responds strongly to electricity. Plasma globes can be found in many science museums as novelty items; neon-colored tendrils of electricity seem to extend from a center orb (which is actually an electrode) to the glass and respond to hands placed on the outside of the glass. Another common term in atomic and molecular physics is *solid state*, such as in the phrase *solid-state physics*. As the name suggests, it refers to the solid state of matter. Condensed matter incorporates both solids and liquids, as well as other, less common states of matter, such as Bose-Einstein condensates—matter cooled to a point where low-temperature quantum phenomena dictate its behavior. Matter changes states by undergoing a phase transition, involving a change in temperature, pressure, or both. However, matter can be "tricked" into remaining in one phase despite being in a pressure and temperature regime that would favor another phase. For example, water can remain a liquid below zero degrees Celsius (thirty-two degrees Fahrenheit) at standard pressure if it is pure enough that the ice lattice has no imperfection to trigger crystallization; this process is known as supercooling.

Applications Past and Present

Air-Pollution Reduction. Scientists use atomic and molecular physics to study the atmospheric reactions relevant to air pollution, the accumulation of greenhouse gases, and the destruction of the ozone layer. By studying the reactions between key small molecules and radicals, scientists have identified the causes of air pollution. Using this information, regulations can be created to reduce emissions accordingly. For example, research revealed that chlorofluorocarbon, or CFC (e.g., Freon), responds to the intense ultraviolet light found at the top of the atmosphere by decomposing and reacting with ozone in a chain reaction, depleting it in the process. Chlorofluorocarbon was then subjected to intense regulation to reduce and eventually eliminate its use.

Atomic and molecular physics is also applied in finding ways to remove CO_2 from the atmosphere to offset the disproportionate amount of CO_2 being released by humans. For example, a common CO_2 removal and storage strategy known as a carbon sink is the use of amine solutions to trap CO_2 molecules from the air in the solution. Strategies such as this are based on an understanding of the physical properties of small molecules.

Lasers. Lasers are an example of the utilization of a quantum-mechanical phenomenon that would not be possible without the field of atomic and molecular physics. Lasers produce light composed of photons with the same energy, that is, a beam of a single color of light. Since the development of lasers, they have been heavily applied in the medical field as a surgical device; in biological, chemical, and physical research as a way to study a system's response to a very specific energy increment; and in everyday life in DVD players, laser pointers, and barcode scanners. Since their invention in 1960, many different types of lasers have been developed, all utilizing different features of the constituent material to emit light at previously inaccessible wavelengths or with properties useful for a specific application, such as high-intensity radiation. The design of new lasers remains an active research area.

Energy. Atomic and molecular physics, the basis for materials science, plays a crucial role in the development of more energy-efficient devices by applying insights gained from a ground-level understanding of matter to develop more efficient processes. In addition, atomic and molecular physics is used in a similar vein to develop better photovoltaics for capturing solar energy and cleaner coal-burning technology, among others. One of the motivations behind superconductor research is that, by employing a resistance-free, lossless conduction medium, superconductors would vastly improve the efficiency of the grid used to distribute electricity throughout the United States. This technology has not yet arrived; although the number and variety of superconductors continues to increase, they still require quite cold temperatures, making them unfeasible for this type of practical application.

Timekeeping. As science has progressed, recording time in a very precise way has become increasingly important, and precise time measurement requires a standard. Just as there exists a material defined as weighing exactly one kilogram, so too are there clocks used to define exactly how long a second is. However, this is no easy task, as clocks are subject to inaccuracies due to friction and general degradation. To overcome this problem, clocks relying on the intrinsic atomic properties of certain materials have been created. The current US standard is a cesium fountain clock located at the National Institute of Standards and Technology (NIST) in Boulder, Colorado, which takes over 100 million years to lose a second's worth of accuracy. Although this value may seem impressive, research groups continue to work on creating even more accurate clocks. In 2005, Jun Ye's research group at JILA (NIST and the University of Colorado's Joint Institute for Laboratory Astrophysics), also located in Boulder, made a clock using strontium that, improved upon since then, became three times more accurate than the cesium fountain clock.

Medicine. Atomic and molecular physics is crucial in modern medicine, providing scientists with a better understanding of the human body and how different treatments create change. Consider the routine procedure of getting an x-ray, perhaps to image teeth or a broken bone. Atomic and molecular physics provides the information needed to interpret the x-rays, to understand which materials create light spots and which create dark spots. Scientists' understanding of the way that biological tissue reacts to radiation also informs the sparing use of x-rays and the use of appropriate lead protection to isolate the x-rays to the location of interest. This field also helps scientists understand the mechanisms of lead poisoning, radiation sickness, and "the bends," an issue encountered by divers who travel back to the surface more quickly than their body can adapt, causing gas bubbles to form in the blood.

Reaction Control. As scientists become better able to apply light with specific characteristics to matter and predict how the matter will respond, the question arises of whether scientists will ever be able to control reactions using lasers rather than just monitoring them as passive observers. This field is still in development, but the results thus far are promising, particularly given the development of increasingly short, attosecond-scale (10^{-18} s) laser pulses. Reaction control would enable scientists to steer chemical reactions in certain directions using laser pulses, allowing them to study less common reaction pathways and to produce purer products by eliminating undesired side reactions.

Quantum Computing. Quantum computing is another field in development with exciting future applications. Quantum mechanics includes a phenomenon called entanglement, wherein some part of the identity of one particle becomes inherently related to that of another. For example, imagine that atom A is in state 1 and atom B is in state 2. If these two atoms are entangled—specifically such that one of the two is always in each state—then regardless of how far apart the atoms are, changing the state of one instantaneously changes the state of the other. This feature can be used to do basic computing at extremely fast speeds. Some encouraging strides have been made in this area, including the creation of actual, if small and limited, quantum computers that can perform basic logical functions.

Impact on Industry

The US Bureau of Labor Statistics predicts a 14 percent growth in jobs for physicists and astronomers between 2010 and 2020, which is near the national average across all careers. The breadth of this field and its fundamental role in modern science suggest that this estimate is likely to hold for atomic and molecular physics as well as the larger fields of physics and astronomy. Scientists with degrees or backgrounds in atomic and molecular physics can find employment in the private and public sectors, including the military, the government, and academia.

Government Agencies. Many government agencies employ researchers and consultants with backgrounds in atomic and molecular physics. Of particular note is the National Institute for Standards and Technology (NIST), which runs several research centers. One such research center is JILA, located in Colorado, which includes a division dedicated to atomic and molecular physics. Atomic and molecular physics also has applications relevant to the Environmental Protection Agency (EPA), the Department of Homeland Security, and many others. By working for such government agencies, atomic and molecular physicists can perform cutting-edge research in the field while also applying their skills to solving different problems, such as determining pollution risks or developing new explosive or drug detectors.

Academic Research and Teaching. Atomic and molecular physics is a core subject in undergraduate curricula and a popular graduate specialization. Additionally, much of atomic and molecular physics falls into the category of basic science—broad science that is fundamental but not application based—and universities are natural venues for basic research projects because of the lack of pressure to produce high-revenue, short-turnaround products. Thus, atomic and molecular physicists have a wide range of potential job opportunities in academia. However, this sector is notorious for having few availabilities given the number of interested applicants, requiring long hours, and providing little pay, regardless of the particular scientific field. Interested students should research quality-of-life factors to determine whether this lifestyle is one that they are well suited for.

Military. Scientists interested in atomic and molecular physics who desire to work in or alongside the military are encouraged to look at each branch's research laboratories. These laboratories employ researchers with physics backgrounds to do research that is directly tied to developing better technology for the armed forces. For example, Dr. Paul Baker's atomic and molecular physics research group at the US Army Research Laboratory has been studying how to apply atomic and molecular physics to sensors, including navigational equipment, and new ways of creating materials, such as through the use of quantum control.

Private Industry. Physicists in general tend to have excellent job opportunities in the private-industry sector, due to their familiarity with basic science and engineering concepts. Many corporations employ people with backgrounds in atomic and molecular physics as researchers and consultants to keep their product line at the state-of-the-art level and to lead the industry in developing and incorporating new technology. These corpora-

Occupation	Physicists and Astronomers
Employment 2010	20,600
Projected Employment 2020	23,400
Change in Number (2010–20)	2,800
Percent Change	14%

Bureau of Labor Statistics, 2012

tions may be involved in producing scientific equipment, creating new biomedical devices, developing new wastewater treatment strategies, or creating the newest media format. Relative to the other employment sectors, private industry tends to pay well.

Social Context and Future Prospects

As a field of basic science, the impact of atomic and molecular physics in one's daily life is so enormous that it is impossible to find an area of life that has not been affected by advances in this field. Scientists' increasing understanding of the properties of atoms and molecules enables biomedical engineers to design drugs based on their expected efficacy and side effects. Everything from breakfast cereal to transmission fluid to long underwear has been improved by scientists' ability to identify how molecules behave. Without atomic and molecular physics, scientists would be unable to assess air pollution and find remedies for it, and electronics would never have been invented. Due to its importance and expansiveness, there is no danger of this field becoming obsolete. The job outlook for atomic and molecular physicists will fluctuate due to cyclical trends in the importance attached to basic versus applied science and in the relative popularities of biology, chemistry, and physics. The broad range of subdisciplines under the umbrella of atomic and molecular physics ensures opportunities for interested students to specialize in areas of high demand.

Future research directions will most likely involve taking advantage of atomic- and molecular-scale quantum phenomena to create novel devices. For example, the ongoing development of quantum computing relies on quantum entanglement to perform calculations much faster than classical computers, which would constitute a giant leap forward in computer technology. Another promising area of research is the creation and investigation of Bose-Einstein condensates, which can be used to create an atom laser: a material that emits a beam of atoms with approximately the same energy. One potential use of atom lasers is studying surfaces with resolutions of single nanometers or less; surfaces are particularly interesting in applications because they are often the site of chemical reactions and can also be used to form monolayers. In the long term, atomic and molecular physicists seek to completely understand atoms and molecules, and there is no danger of this ambitious goal being achieved anytime soon.

Further Reading

"Atomic and Molecular Physics." *JILA: CU Boulder and NIST*. JILA, 17 May 2010. Web. 3 Oct. 2012. Presents state-of-the-art research in atomic and molecular physics at JILA, a highly respected research center. Includes descriptions of current research topics and their importance.

Cohen-Tannoudji, Claude, Bernard Diu, and Franck Laloë. *Quantum Mechanics*. 2nd ed. 2 vols. New York: Wiley, 1977. Print. Authoritative, renowned text on quantum mechanics and atomic and molecular physics, written by a Nobel laureate in physics. Includes sections dedicated to reviewing or introducing relevant mathematical concepts.

Demtröder, Wolfgang. *Atoms, Molecules, and Photons: An Introduction to Atomic-, Molecular-, and Quantum-Physics*. 2nd ed. New York: Springer, 2010. Print. Contains information about a wide range of topics in atomic and molecular physics, ranging from the historical development of the field to modern applications.

Ford, Kenneth W. *The Quantum World: Quantum Physics for Everyone*. Cambridge: Harvard UP, 2005. Print. Presents the history and basic concepts of quantum mechanics to a general audience, thereby introducing the reader to the landscape of atomic and molecular physics.

Neffe, Jürgen. *Einstein: A Biography*. Baltimore: Johns Hopkins UP, 2009. Print. Puts Einstein's scientific accomplishments in the context of his personal life, painting a vivid picture of both.

Svanberg, Sune. *Atomic and Molecular Spectroscopy: Basic Aspects and Practical Applications*. 4th ed. Berlin: Springer, 2004. Print. Describes the many ways that light is used to study atoms and molecules.

About the Author: Cassandra Newell graduated from Colby College with a bachelor's degree in chemistry and attended MIT for graduate school, completing 2.5 years of work toward a PhD in physical chemistry before leaving to pursue other interests. She worked as a research assistant at both institutions, studying such topics as molecular recognition, guest-host chemistry, computational chemistry, terahertz spectroscopy, acoustic spectroscopy, and proton/electron transfer in chemical systems. She also has experience as a teaching assistant and tutor in the fields of spectroscopy and quantum mechanics. Since leaving academia, she has pursued projects pertaining to science communication, such as editing scientific manuscripts and writing about science for nonspecialists.

Atomic and Molecular Physicist

Earnings (Yearly Median): $105,430 (Bureau of Labor Statistics, 2012)

Employment and Outlook: Average growth (Bureau of Labor Statistics, 2012)

O*NET-SOC Code: 19-2012.00

Related Career Clusters: Health Science; Manufacturing; Transportation, Distribution & Logistics

Scope of Work

Atomic and molecular physicists mainly work in research positions for the government and for universities, but they are also employed by private companies and laboratories. Atomic physics and molecular physics are two specialized concentrations for physicists—scientists who study atoms and molecules and seek to explain how matter functions in the universe—and the two are closely related. Atomic physicists study isolated atoms and electrons, while molecular physicists work with molecules composed of more than one atom. Molecular physicists often work with gaseous molecules, such as oxygen, hydrogen, and carbon dioxide.

The main task of atomic and molecular physicists is to conduct research in a laboratory setting, performing experiments with atoms and molecules, and testing theories on the properties of matter. For example, an atomic physicist may develop a theory on the nature of atoms, how they interact with other atoms, and atom formation. Molecular physicists may apply the study of molecules to chemical interactions in the atmosphere and to important issues such as global warming.

Education and Coursework

A molecular or atomic physicist needs a PhD in order to work in a research position for the government or a university. A bachelor's degree will not qualify an individual for a research position, but it will qualify him or her for an assistant or technician position in a laboratory. A master's degree in physics will open doors to developmental positions in private manufacturing companies and, more often than not, will set a path for a doctorate degree. Depending on the company, an individual with a master's degree and ten or more years of experience in a laboratory setting may be qualified for a research position, but a PhD is strongly preferred.

PhD programs take five to seven years to complete. Students may concentrate in a subfield of physics, such as molecular, atomic, chemical, or applied physics. In order to be successful in this program and in one's subsequent career as a physicist, a candidate must have superior mathematical, analytical, problem-solving, interpersonal, and critical-thinking skills. Course work includes advanced classes in mathematics and science, such as calculus, quantum chemistry and mechanics, physics, statistics, and thermodynamics. Computer courses are commonly required to develop the skills needed to operate laboratory equipment and specialized analytical and simulation software.

A PhD culminates in a dissertation, a professional thesis that makes a new contribution to a field of study. After completing the dissertation

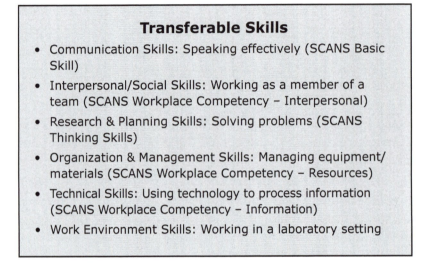

Transferable Skills

- Communication Skills: Speaking effectively (SCANS Basic Skill)
- Interpersonal/Social Skills: Working as a member of a team (SCANS Workplace Competency – Interpersonal)
- Research & Planning Skills: Solving problems (SCANS Thinking Skills)
- Organization & Management Skills: Managing equipment/materials (SCANS Workplace Competency – Resources)
- Technical Skills: Using technology to process information (SCANS Workplace Competency – Information)
- Work Environment Skills: Working in a laboratory setting

and earning a doctorate degree, an atomic or molecular physicist is obligated to pursue postdoctoral research. Postdoctoral positions offer recent PhDs the chance to gain experience in professional research labs and begin their careers as researchers in atomic and molecular physics. During their postdoctoral research, physicists work under the supervision of senior scientists for approximately two to three years.

Career Enhancement and Training

Atomic and molecular physicists do not have to be licensed, but they do need a PhD and postdoctoral experience. To be employed by the US federal government, a physicist needs to be a US citizen. Depending on the nature of the physicist's work—if he or she is involved in research for defense systems or military weapons, for example—the physicist may need high security clearance that allows access to confidential military information.

Networking is an important tool for finding a desirable postdoctoral position in physics; joining an organization that supports the study of atomic or molecular physics can help physicists develop valuable connections with experienced professionals. The American Institute of Physics (AIP), for instance, is a nonprofit organization dedicated to the advancement of the physics industry. This organization connects over 135,000 scientists and working professionals. The AIP also publishes scholarly journals and magazines, making it one of the leaders in the field of physical science.

The American Physical Society (APS) is another useful organization, connecting over 50,000 professionals. The APS organizes programs to foster collaboration among researchers, educators, and scientists in the physics industry. This organization also offers a one-year free trial membership for undergraduate and graduate students. Membership in the APS can help undergraduate and graduate students enhance their careers by exposing them to recent innovations in the physics industry, connecting them with working professionals, and augmenting their résumés. Being a member of the AIP, the APS, or any other professional organization shows an employer or a university admissions committee both commitment and dedication to the field.

Daily Tasks and Technology

The main task of an atomic or molecular physicist is to conduct research in a laboratory setting. From research based on experiments, physicists form theories on the nature and workings of atoms and molecules. This involves working with complex mathematics on a daily basis, such as using calculus to analyze the physical properties of matter.

Atomic and molecular physicists use a variety of technologies and equipment in the laboratory setting. A gas chromatograph, for example, is used to separate compounds via vaporization, which is the evaporation of a liquid. This allows researchers to identify and analyze a compound by isolating the different components of its molecules. Spectrometers and spectroscopes are used to measure electromagnetic waves, which include light, gamma rays, x-rays, and other forms of radiation. Various forms of laser technology are used in laboratories. A Ti:sapphire (titanium-doped sapphire) laser, for instance, emits infra-red light that is used to examine molecules.

Most of an atomic or molecular physicist's time is spent researching and conducting experiments, but these physicists also have important tasks outside of the laboratory. Writing proposals for research grants, for example, is vital for funding research. After completing an experiment in the lab, a physicist will write a scientific paper on his or her findings

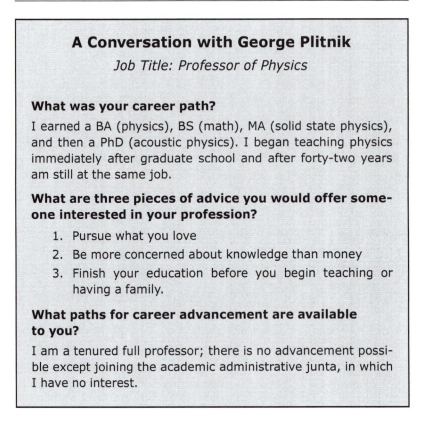

A Conversation with George Plitnik
Job Title: Professor of Physics

What was your career path?

I earned a BA (physics), BS (math), MA (solid state physics), and then a PhD (acoustic physics). I began teaching physics immediately after graduate school and after forty-two years am still at the same job.

What are three pieces of advice you would offer someone interested in your profession?

1. Pursue what you love
2. Be more concerned about knowledge than money
3. Finish your education before you begin teaching or having a family.

What paths for career advancement are available to you?

I am a tenured full professor; there is no advancement possible except joining the academic administrative junta, in which I have no interest.

and attempt to have the articles published in a scholarly journal. Physicists also present their research at conferences and universities.

Earnings and Employment Outlook

The demand for atomic and molecular physicists is expected experience average growth through 2020. In addition to being an important educational component of physics, research in atomic and molecular physics is essential for understanding matter at its most fundamental level. Consequently, research in this area will always play an important role within the scientific community.

According to Recruiter.com, the 2012 average compensation range for atomic and molecular physicists is $88,000 to $132,000. Salaries vary by employer, with physicists in the private sector and the federal government earning the most and those employed by state governments earning the least. Average annual salaries also vary by state: Kansas had the highest in 2012, at $141,570, while South Carolina had the lowest, at $57,730.

Related Occupations

Materials Scientists: Materials scientists study the properties of chemical substances and develop new types of technology. Nanotechnology, in particular, deals with matter at the molecular and atomic levels.

Chemists: A chemist is a scientist who researches the composition of molecules and their chemical properties.

Biophysicists: Biophysicists study the physical properties of living organisms.

Astrophysicists and Astronomers: Astrophysicists and astronomers study the universe, space, and matter. They also develop technology that helps them conduct research in these areas.

Biological Engineers: Biological engineers use the principles of biology, particularly molecular biology, to solve problems and create applications for living organisms.

Future Applications

The world is experiencing rapid growth in science and technology, and an investment in atoms and molecules—the building blocks of life—is essential to all scientific fields of study. Understanding more about atoms and molecules can help scientists understand more about humans and their environment.

Research conducted by atomic and molecular physicists could be applied to a myriad of different industries, products, and technologies in the future. For example, the study of atoms and molecules could be used to enhance medical technology. New laser technology could be used in intricate surgical procedures. In conjunction with accelerator physicists, atomic and molecular physicists could develop new beam-therapy techniques that could precisely target a malignant tumor, thereby decreasing damage to surrounding tissue and organs.

The study of molecules in the atmosphere could help monitor the progression of global warming, uncover the cause of damage to the ozone layer, and access the future implications of climate change. Knowing more about the behavior of molecules in the atmosphere will allow scientists to understand the effects of pollution on the atmosphere and develop techniques that may help slow the progression of global warming.

—Daniel Castaldy

More Information

American Institute of Physics
1 Physics Ellipse
College Park, MD 20740
www.aip.org

European Physical Society
6 rues des Frères Lumière
68200 Mulhouse
France
www.eps.org

Institute of Physics
76 Portland Place
London W1B 1 NT
UK
www.iop.org

Journal of Atomic, Molecular, and Optical Physics
410 Park Avenue
Fifteenth Floor, #287 pmb
New York, NY 10022
www.hindawi.com/journals/jamop/

MIT Department of Physics
77 Massachusetts Avenue
Cambridge, MA 02139
www.web.mit.edu/physics/

Biophysics

FIELDS OF STUDY

Physics; physical sciences; chemistry; mathematics; biology; molecular biology; chemical biology; engineering; biochemistry; classical genetics; molecular genetics; cell biology.

DEFINITION

Biophysics is the branch of science that uses the principles of physics to study biological concepts. It examines how life systems function, especially at the cellular and molecular level. It plays an important role in understanding the structure and function of proteins and membranes and in developing new pharmaceuticals. Biophysics is the foundation for molecular biology, a field that combines physics, biology, and chemistry.

Basic Principles

The word *biophysics* means the physics of life. Biophysics studies the functioning of life systems, especially at the cellular and molecular level, using the principles of physics. It is known that atoms make up molecules, molecules make up cells, and cells in turn make up the tissues and organs that are part of an organism, or a living machine. Biophysicists use this knowledge to understand how the living machine works.

In photosynthesis, for instance, the absorption of sunlight by green plants initiates a process that culminates with the synthesis of high-energy sugars such as glucose. To fully understand this process, one needs to look at how it begins: light absorption by the photosystems. Photosystems are groups of energy-absorbing pigments such as chlorophyll and carotenoids that are located on the thylakoid membranes inside the chloroplast, the photosynthetic organelle in the plant cell. Biophysical studies have shown that once a chlorophyll molecule captures solar energy, it gets excited and transfers the energy to a neighboring unexcited chlorophyll molecule. The process repeats itself, and thus, packets of energy jump from one chlorophyll molecule to the next. The energy eventually reaches the reaction center, where it begins a chain of high-energy electron-transfer reactions that lead to the storage of the light energy in the form of adenosine triphosphate (ATP) and nicotinamide adenine dinucleotide phosphate (NADPH). In the second half of photosynthesis, ATP and NADPH provide the energy to make glucose from carbon dioxide.

Biophysics is often confused with medical physics. Medical physics is the science devoted to studying the relationship between human health and radiation exposure. A medical physicist often works closely with a radiation oncologist to set up radiotherapy treatment plans for cancer patients.

Core Concepts

Biophysicists study life at all levels, from atoms and molecules to cells, organisms, and environments. They attempt to describe complex living systems with the simple laws of physics. Often, biophysicists work at the molecular level to understand cells and their processes.

The work of Gregor Mendel in the late nineteenth century laid the foundation for genetics, the science of heredity. His studies, rediscovered in the twentieth century, led to the understanding that the inheritance of certain traits is governed by genes and that the alleles of the genes are separated during gamete formation. Experiments in the 1940s revealed that genes are made of DNA, but the mechanisms by which genes function remained a mystery. James Watson and Francis Crick's discovery of the double-helix structure of DNA in 1953 revealed how genes could be translated into proteins.

Biophysicists use a number of physical tools and techniques to understand how cellular processes work, especially at the molecular level. Some of the important tools are electron microscopy, nuclear magnetic resonance (NMR) spectroscopy, circular dichroism (CD) spectroscopy, and x-ray crystallography. For example, the discovery of Watson and Crick's double-helix model was possible in part because of the x-ray images of DNA that were taken by Rosalind

Franklin and Maurice H. F. Wilkins. Franklin and Wilkins, both bio-physicists, made DNA crystals and then used x-ray crystallography to analyze the structure of DNA. The array of black dots arranged in an X-shaped pattern on the x-ray photograph of wet DNA suggested to Franklin that DNA is helical.

Electron Microscopy. Electron microscopes use beams of electrons to study objects in detail. Electron microscopy can be used to analyze an object's surface texture (topography) and constituent elements and compounds (composition), as well as the shape and size (morphology) and atomic arrangements (crystallographic details) of those elements and compounds. Electron microscopes were invented to overcome the limitations posed by light microscopes, which have maximum mag-nifications of 500x or 1000x and a maximum resolution of 0.2 mil-limeter. To see and study subcellular structures and processes required magnification capabilities of greater than 10,000x. The first electron microscope was a transmission electron microscope (TEM) built by Max Knoll and Ernst Ruska in 1931. The invention of the scanning electron microscope (SEM) was somewhat delayed (the first was built in 1937 by Manfred von Ardenne) because the field had to figure out how to make the electron beam scan the sample.

NMR Spectroscopy. Nuclear magnetic resonance (NMR) spectros-copy is an extremely useful tool for the biophysicist to study the mo-lecular structure of organic compounds. The underlying principle of NMR spectroscopy is identical to that of magnetic resonance imaging (MRI), a common tool in medical diagnostics. The nuclei of several elements, including the isotopes carbon-12 and oxygen-16, have a characteristic spin when placed in an external magnetic field. NMR focuses on studying the transitions between these spin states. In com-parison with mass spectroscopy, NMR requires a larger amount of sample, but it does not destroy the sample.

CD Spectroscopy. Circular dichroism (CD) spectroscopy measures differences in how left-handed and right-handed polarized light is absorbed. These differences are caused by structural asymmetry. CD spectroscopy can determine the secondary and tertiary structure of proteins as well as their thermal stability. It is usually used to study proteins in solution.

X-Ray Crystallography. X-rays are electromagnetic waves with wavelengths ranging from 0.02 to 100 angstroms (Å). Even before x-rays were discovered in 1895 by Wilhelm Conrad Röntgen, scientists knew that atoms in crystals were arranged in definite patterns and that a study of the angles therein could provide clues to the crystal structure. As is true of all forms of radiation, the wavelength of x-rays is inversely proportional to its energy. Because the wavelength of x-rays is smaller than that of visible light, they are powerful enough to penetrate most matter. As x-rays travel through an object, they are diffracted by the atomic arrangements inside and thus provide a guideline for the electron densities inside the object. Analysis of this electron-density data offers a glimpse into the internal structure of the crystal. As of 2012, about 88 percent of the structures in the Worldwide Protein Data Bank had been elucidated through x-ray crystallography.

Applications Past and Present

Biophysical tools and techniques have become extremely useful in many areas and fields. They have furthered research in protein crystallography, synthetic biology, and nanobiology, and they have allowed scientists to discover new pharmaceuticals and to study biomolecular structures and interactions and membrane structure and transport. Biophysics and its related fields, molecular biology and genetics, are rapidly developing and are at the center of biomedical research.

Biomolecular Structures. Because structure dictates function in the world of biomolecules, understanding the structure of the biomolecule (with tools such as x-ray crystallography and NMR and CD spectroscopy), whether it is a protein or a nucleic acid, is critical to understanding its individual function in the cell. Proteins function as catalysts and bind to and regulate other downstream biomolecules. Their functional basis lies in their tertiary structure, or their three-dimensional form, and this function cannot be predicted from the gene sequence. The sequence of nucleotides in a gene can be used only to predict the primary structure, which is the amino-acid sequence in the polypeptide.

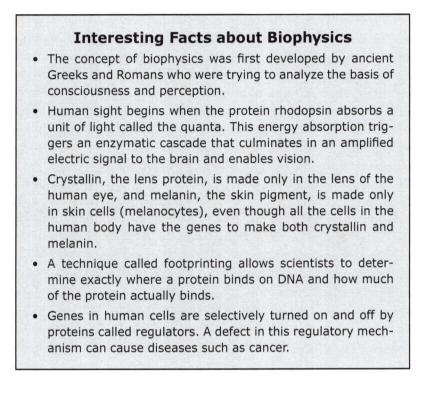

Interesting Facts about Biophysics

- The concept of biophysics was first developed by ancient Greeks and Romans who were trying to analyze the basis of consciousness and perception.
- Human sight begins when the protein rhodopsin absorbs a unit of light called the quanta. This energy absorption triggers an enzymatic cascade that culminates in an amplified electric signal to the brain and enables vision.
- Crystallin, the lens protein, is made only in the lens of the human eye, and melanin, the skin pigment, is made only in skin cells (melanocytes), even though all the cells in the human body have the genes to make both crystallin and melanin.
- A technique called footprinting allows scientists to determine exactly where a protein binds on DNA and how much of the protein actually binds.
- Genes in human cells are selectively turned on and off by proteins called regulators. A defect in this regulatory mechanism can cause diseases such as cancer.

Once the structure-function relationship has been analyzed, the next step is to make mutants or knock out the gene via techniques such as ribonucleic acid interference (RNAi) and confirm loss of function. Subsequently, a literature search is performed to see if there are any known genetic disorders that are caused by a defect in the gene being studied. If so, the structure-function relationship can be examined for a possible cure.

Membrane Structure and Transport. In 1972, biologist S. J. Singer and his student Garth Nicolson conceived the fluid-mosaic model of the plasma membrane. According to this model, the plasma membrane is a fluid lipid bilayer largely made up of phospholipids arranged in an amphipathic pattern, with the hydrophobic lipid tails buried inside and the hydrophilic phosphate groups on the exterior. The bilayer is interspersed with proteins, which help in cross-membrane transport. Because membranes control the import and export of materials into the cell, understanding membrane structure is key to coming up with ways to block transport of potentially harmful pathogens across the membrane.

Electron microscopes were used in the early days of membrane biology, but fluorescence and confocal microscopes have come to be used more frequently. The development of organelle-specific vital stains has rejuvenated interest in evanescent field (EF) microscopy because it permits the study of even the smallest of vesicles and the tracking of the movements of individual protein molecules.

Synthetic Biology. In the 2000s, the term *systems biology* became part of the field of life science, followed by the term *synthetic biology*. To many people, these terms appear to refer to the same thing, but they do not, even though they are indeed closely related. While systems biology focuses on using a quantitative approach to study existing biological systems, synthetic biology concentrates on applying engineering principles to biology and constructing novel systems heretofore unseen in nature. Clearly, synthetic biology benefits immensely from research in systems and molecular biology. In essence, synthetic biology could be described as an engineering discipline that uses known, tested functional components such as genes, proteins, and various regulatory circuits in conjunction with modeling software to design new functional biological systems, such as bacteria that make ethanol from water, carbon dioxide, and light. The biggest challenge to synthetic biologists is the complexity of life-forms, especially higher eukaryotes such as humans, and the possible existence of unknown processes that can affect the synthetic biological systems.

Pharmaceutical Development. In the pharmaceutical world, the initial task is to identify the aberrant protein responsible for generating the symptoms in any disease or disorder. Once that is done, a series of biophysical tools are used to ensure that the target is the correct one. First, the identity of the protein is confirmed using techniques such as N-terminal sequencing and tandem mass spectroscopy (MS-MS). Second, the protein sample is tested for purity (which typically should be more than 95 percent) using methods such as denaturing sodium dodecyl sulfate polyacrylamide gel electrophoresis (SDS-PAGE).

Third, the concentration of the protein sample is determined by chromogenic assays such as the Bradford or Lowry assay. The fourth and probably most important test is that of protein functionality. This is typically carried out by either checking the ligand binding capacity of the protein (with biacore ligand binding assays) or testing the ability of the protein to carry out its biological function. All these thermodynamic parameters need to be tested to develop a putative drug, one that could somehow correct or restrain the ramifications of the protein's malfunction.

Nanobiology. With the aid of biophysical tools and techniques, the field of biology has moved from organismic biology to molecular biology to nanobiology. To get a feel for the size of a nanometer, picture a strand of hair, then visualize a width that is one hundred thousand times thinner. Typically nanoparticles are about the size of either a protein molecule or a short DNA segment. Nanomedicine, or the application of technology that relies on nanoparticles to medicine, has become a popular area for research. In particular, the search for appropriate vectors to deliver drugs into the cells is an endless pursuit, especially in emerging therapeutic approaches such as RNA interference. Because lipid and polymer-based nanoparticles are extremely small, they are easily taken up by cells instead of being cleared by the body.

Impact on Industry

As one would expect, biophysics research worldwide has progressed faster in countries that traditionally have had a large base of physicists. The Max Planck Institute of Biophysics, one of the earliest pioneers in this field, was established in 1921 in Frankfurt, Germany, as the Institut für Physikalische Grundlagen der Medizin. The aim of the first director, Friedrich Dessauer, was to look for ways to apply the knowledge of radiation physics to medicine. He was followed by Boris Rajewsky, who coined the term *biophysics*. In 1937, Rajewsky established the Kaiser Wilhelm Institute for Biophysics, which incorporated the institute led by Dessauer. The Max Planck Institute of Biophysics has become one of the world's foremost biophysics research institutes, with scientists and students analyzing a wide array of topics in biophysics, including membrane biology, molecular neurogenetics,

Occupation	Biochemists and biophysicists
Employment 2010	25,100
Projected Employment 2020	32,800
Change in Number (2010–20)	7,700
Percent Change	31%

Bureau of Labor Statistics, 2012

and structural biology. In addition to Germany, countries active in biophysics research include the United States, Japan, France, Great Britain, Russia, China, India, and Sweden.

The International Union for Pure and Applied Biophysics (IUPAB) was created to provide a platform for biophysicists worldwide to exchange ideas and set up collaborations. The IUPAB in turn is a part of the International Council for Science (ICSU). The primary goal of IUPAB is to encourage and support students and researchers so that the field continues to grow and flourish. By 2012, the national biophysics societies of about fifty countries had become affiliated with the IUPAB.

Government Agencies. In the United States, the Biophysical Society was created in 1957 to facilitate propagation of biophysics concepts and ideas. To further broaden its mission, the Biophysical Society includes members from government research agencies such as the National Institutes of Health (NIH) and National Institute of Standards and Technology (NIST), many of whom are also part of the American Association for the Advancement of Science (AAAS) and the National Science Foundation (NSF). These members provide useful feedback to federal agencies such as the National Science and Technology Council, the National Science Board, and the White House's Office of Science and Technology Policy, which are responsible for formulating national policies and initiatives.

Military. Scientists working within the military generally conduct research within research laboratories, as well as clinical and medical laboratories and facilities. Topics of research for military purposes include the study of diseases, including causes and treatment. As of

2012, according to government statistics, there were approximately two hundred life scientists in the military.

Industry and Business. Most countries at the forefront of pharmaceutical breakthroughs have industries that are heavily invested in biophysical and biochemical research. The pharmaceutical industry has been spending billions of dollars to find treatments and cures for diseases and disorders that affect millions of people, including stroke, arthritis, cancer, heart disease, and neurological disorders. Biophysics is at the forefront of the field of drug discovery because it provides the tools for conducting research in proteomics and genomics and allows the scientific community to identify opportunities for drug design. The next step after drug design is to plan the method of drug delivery, and biophysical research can help provide suitable vectors, including nanovectors. The pharmaceutical industry in the United States—companies such as Novartis, Eli Lilly, Bristol-Myers Squibb, and Pfizer—and the NIH have a combined budget of about $60 billion per year. However, neither the industry nor the government supports basic research at the interface of life sciences with physics and mathematics. Without this support, biophysics is unlikely to produce new tools to revolutionize or accelerate the ten-to-twelve-year drug-development cycle. If this impediment can be overcome, the number of new drugs added to the market every year is likely to grow.

Academic Research and Teaching. While few universities offer undergraduate majors in biophysics, several offer graduate programs in biophysics, with opportunities for teaching. Postdoctoral research, generally lasting several years, is typically the last step before one becomes an independent biophysicist running his or her own laboratory.

Social Context and Future Prospects

The discovery of the structure of DNA set off a revolution in molecular biology that has continued into the twenty-first century. In addition, modern scientific equipment has made study at the molecular level possible and productive. Many biophysicists, especially those who have also had course work in genetics and biochemistry, are working in molecular biology, which promises to be an active and exciting area for the foreseeable future.

Organisms are believed to be complex machines made of many simpler machines, such as proteins and nucleic acids. To understand why an organism behaves or reacts a certain way, one must determine how proteins and nucleic acids function. Biophysicists examine the structure of proteins and nucleic acids, seeking a correlation between structure and function. Once proper function is understood, scientists can prevent or treat diseases or disorders that result from malfunctions. This understanding of how proteins function enables scientists to develop pharmaceuticals and to find better means of delivering drugs to patients. Someday, this knowledge may allow scientists to design drugs specifically for a patient, thus avoiding many side effects. In addition, the scientific equipment developed by biophysicists in their research has been adapted for use in medical imaging for diagnosis and treatment. This transformation of laboratory equipment to medical equipment is likely to continue.

Biophysics applications have played and will continue to play a large role in medicine and health care, but future biophysicists may be environmental scientists. Biophysics is providing ways to improve the environment. For example, scientists are modifying microorganisms so that they produce electricity and biofuels that may lessen the need for fossil fuels. They are also using microorganisms to clean polluted water. As biophysics research continues, its applications are likely to cover an even broader range.

Further Reading

Bischof, Marco. "Some Remarks on the History of Biophysics and Its Future." *Current Development of Biophysics: The Stage from an Ugly Duckling to a Beautiful Swan.* Ed. Changlin Zhang, Fritz Albert Popp, and Marco Bischof. Hangzhou: Hangzhou UP, 1996. 10–22. Print. A paper delivered at a 1995 symposium on biophysics in Neuss, Germany, that examines how the field of biophysics got its start and predicts future developments.

Claycomb, James R., and Jonathan Quoc P. Tran. *Introductory Biophysics: Perspectives on the Living State.* Sudbury: Jones, 2011. Print. A textbook that considers life in relation to the universe. Relates biophysics to many other fields and subjects, including fractal geometry, chaos systems, biomagnetism, bioenergetics, and nerve conduction. Contains a compact disc that allows computer simulation of biophysical phenomena.

Glaser, Roland. *Biophysics*. 5th ed. New York: Springer, 2005. Print. Contains numerous chapters on the molecular structure, kinetics, energetics, and dynamics of biological systems. Also looks at the physical environment, with chapters on the biophysics of hearing and the biological effects of electromagnetic fields.

Goldfarb, Daniel. *Biophysics Demystified*. Maidenhead: McGraw, 2010. Print. Examines anatomical, cellular, and subcellular biophysics, as well as tools and techniques used in the field. Designed as a self-teaching tool.

Herman, Irving P. *Physics of the Human Body*. New York: Springer, 2007. Print. Analyzes how physical concepts apply to human body functions.

Kaneko, K. *Life: An Introduction to Complex Systems Biology*. New York: Springer, 2006. Print. Provides an introduction to the field of systems biology, focusing on complex systems.

About the Author: Sibani Sengupta, PhD, earned a bachelor's degree in physiology and a master's degree in biophysics, molecular biology, and genetics from the University of Calcutta, India. She also holds a doctorate in biomedical sciences from the University of Connecticut. Both her doctoral and postdoctoral research involved extensive use of genetic engineering and various biochemical assays to test for protein and gene function. After completing a postdoctoral stint, she started teaching in an all-female college preparatory school in Connecticut. She has taught advanced placement biology, honors biology, genetics, microbiology, and biotechnology.

Biophysicist

Earnings (Yearly Median): $79,390 (Bureau of Labor Statistics, 2012)

Employment and Outlook: Much faster than average growth (Bureau of Labor Statistics, 2012)

O*NET-SOC Code: 19-1021.00

Related Career Clusters: Agriculture, Food & Natural Resources; Health Science; Human Services

Scope of Work

Biophysicists study the physical properties of living organisms and their cellular components, including electrical, chemical, and mechanical processes, then apply this knowledge to understanding the complex reactions involved in biological processes such as metabolism, heredity, reproduction, and photosynthesis. Biophysicists are often involved in developing new medications and other substances and testing them to determine their effects on the body. They may also analyze the effects of environmental pollutants on an organism. Biophysicists often play a role in the detection and treatment of disease as well as the development of new biomedical products and research technologies. Biophysicists conduct in-depth quantitative analyses that rely on complex mathematical data. These scientists typically work in laboratory settings at universities, pharmaceutical and medical manufacturing facilities, and private research institutions.

Education and Coursework

A career in biophysics requires a bachelor of science degree plus several years of graduate and postgraduate education. Most biophysics jobs will require at least a master's degree. Beginning in high school, students interested in pursuing a career as a biophysicist should take course work across a range of different scientific disciplines, including mathematics, biology, physics, and chemistry. Future biophysicists commonly major in one or more of these scientific disciplines at the undergraduate level, as very few undergraduate programs offer a major in biophysics.

In-depth course work on subjects such as molecular physics and biology, chemistry, engineering, and statistics will prepare undergraduate students for advanced study. They should also hone their writing, public speaking, and researching skills, as later in their careers they will have to perform literature reviews, prepare papers and grant proposals, and present and defend research proposals. Undergraduates are also encouraged to gain hands-on research experience, either through university laboratory sessions or through a summer internship program in a research lab.

Upon graduating from college, aspiring biophysicists pursue either a master's degree or a doctorate degree (PhD). In addition to a PhD,

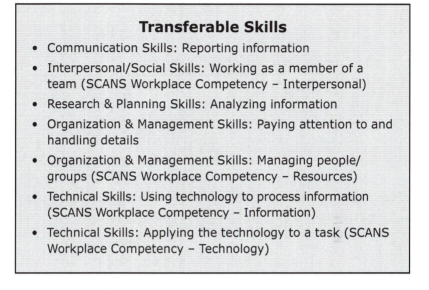

students interested in treating patients or performing research involving humans will also need to pursue a medical doctorate (MD). For the first few years in a PhD program, students must take advanced courses in fields of relevance to biophysics, such as biochemistry, cellular biology, genetics, neurology, and physiology. This course work is structured and accompanied by work in a laboratory setting to give students knowledge of the latest research protocols. Most graduate students also hold positions as teaching or research assistants. Upon completion of the seminar and laboratory phase of their graduate education, candidates must undertake an independent research project. This research will culminate in a dissertation, which, if completed, will be published in a relevant professional scientific journal. The entire process of completing such a degree can take between three and five years, although the dissertation phase could take longer.

Candidates who seek a medical degree in addition to a PhD in biophysics, thereby enabling them to practice medicine while conducting research, must also take structured courses during their first two years of medical school. During the second half of medical school, students also receive training in a hospital setting, working with patients and hospital staff while conducting independent research. Medical school typically lasts four years but is followed by residencies and internships, adding to the continued training of a medical doctor.

Career Enhancement and Training

Many biophysicists who begin their careers with a bachelor's or master's degree are eligible only for entry-level positions, with limited opportunities for advancement. Individuals entering the field with PhDs usually obtain additional training after graduation as postdoctoral researchers for two or three years, working with experienced scientists at academic, pharmaceutical, or other scientific research laboratory facilities. This training helps them to apply the knowledge and experience they obtained in graduate school to researching a specific problem or field of study, such as genetics, cellular mechanics, or pharmaceutical development. It will also help them develop new research techniques, formulate models, and prepare scientific papers for publication.

Biophysicists, like other scientists and medical professionals, benefit greatly by networking with their peers through professional societies and associations. Biophysicists who are also medical doctors, for example, are able to share information with colleagues through the American Medical Association (and their state affiliate associations). The Biophysical Society, based in the United States, and the European Biophysics Societies' Association are examples of networks and associations geared specifically toward these professionals. Membership in a professional association offers a number of benefits, including opportunities and resources for professional development, free access to journals and databases, and representation in outreach and advocacy efforts in the field of biophysics.

Daily Tasks and Technology

Biophysicists' daily tasks vary based on the field in which they apply their knowledge. In general, however, biophysicists collect specimens, analyze their components, collate data, generate models, and use the information to generate reports and scientific papers. The primary goal of biophysicists' research is to understand complex biological processes, such as cell growth or metabolism, in order to develop more effective drugs, biomedical products, and treatment regimes. In addition to utilizing existing research practices, biophysicists may be responsible for refining and developing new analytical techniques. They may utilize many different types of spectrometers, centrifuges, and microscopes. These technologies assist biophysicists in detecting diseases, genetic disorders, mutations, and the effects of pharmaceuticals and food products on an organism's biological processes and structures.

Biophysicists' work is performed mainly in a laboratory setting, and most biophysicists work as part of an interdisciplinary team of researchers that may also include chemists, engineers, and computer scientists. Biophysicists who are senior-level scientists are also responsible for managing laboratory staff, including research assistants, interns, and technology operators. These scientists monitor staff progress on their assignments and ensure that the tasks performed are consistent with the overall project's parameters.

Biophysics is a specialized field, which means that there are a limited number of such professionals in the market. As the need for knowledge about genetics, pharmaceuticals, and disease increases and technology continues to evolve, the demand for biophysicists is expected to grow.

In addition to the research performed, biophysicists must compile and analyze the data collected to generate models and papers. One of the most useful technologies they employ for this purpose is computer-aided design (CAD) software, which is capable of compiling large quantities of data and forming comprehensive models based on that data. They also frequently use graphic and imaging software, which is capable of generating detailed, three-dimensional images of molecular and cellular structures. Furthermore, biophysicists use the data and models generated through their research and compilation to write and publish reports, scientific papers, articles, and books.

A Conversation with Ayman Oweida

Job Title: Biophysicist

What was your career path?

My career path began with an undergraduate degree in medical sciences. In my early years of undergraduate study, I took the core courses of a typical medical science or biology program, in addition to physics and calculus courses. In my third and fourth years of undergraduate study, I chose to specialize in biophysics. After completing my Bachelor of Medical Sciences, I pursued a Master of Science degree in medical biophysics with a research emphasis on medical imaging.

What are three pieces of advice you would offer someone interested in your profession?

Know the difference between the various medical physics and biophysics programs available to you. Some medical physics graduate programs are accredited by a national certifying body. Accredited programs give you the added advantage of being qualified to work in clinical medical physics jobs. Non-accredited programs are usually research-based and lead to academic or industry-inclined jobs. Also, regularly evaluate your areas of interest while going through your studies; it's important to specialize in something you love and are passionate about. Finally, you should be aware that a lot of schooling is required to be able to work in this profession and you should plan your finances accordingly.

What paths for career advancement are available to you?

My opportunities for advancement in medical physics are vast. I have the potential to pursue teaching besides my clinical career in medical physics. There's also the opportunity to pursue research and contribute to the advancement of therapy and diagnosis in cancer patients.

Earnings and Employment Outlook

Biophysicists' annual earnings vary based on the arena in which they work. For example, scientists who work in the public sector or in university settings may earn approximately $51,000 a year. However, those who work in the private sector, such as in pharmaceutical and medical manufacturing companies or privately funded research facilities, may earn as much as $85,000 a year. Biophysicists who are also medical doctors earn much higher salaries, in many cases approaching $200,000.

While salaries for biophysicists can be high, in many cases—particularly for combined PhD/MD holders—these scientists must also pay for school loans, malpractice insurance, and other significant expenses. Many biophysicists involved in research often receive a large portion of their funding through grants (one-time payments from a foundation or the government), which means that annual budgets can be subject to dramatic changes if the anticipated grants are not approved.

Biophysics is a specialized field, which means that there are a limited number of such professionals in the market. As the need for knowledge about genetics, pharmaceuticals, and disease increases and technology continues to evolve, the demand for biophysicists is expected to grow. This trend is particularly evident in the pharmaceutical field, as research into the effectiveness of new medicines requires the expertise of knowledgeable biophysicists.

Related Occupations

- **Biochemists:** Biochemists focus on the chemical processes of living organisms. They follow a similar educational and professional career track to that of biophysicists.

- **Medical Doctors:** Many biophysicists are in fact medical doctors who specialize in biophysical research. However, medical doctors may have other duties related to patient care and hospital administration in addition to the research responsibilities of a biophysicist.

- **Epidemiologists:** Epidemiologists study the spread of disease among humans and other organisms. Like biophysicists, they closely study the cause and characteristics of various diseases.

- **Agricultural and Food Scientists:** Agricultural scientists and food scientists study the development and use of food products, sharing a number of common areas of research with biophysicists.

- **Biological Technicians:** Biological technicians tend to have a more technical education than biophysicists, but both professions make use of the same research technologies, share many activities, and are likely to work together in teams in a laboratory.

Future Applications

The life-sciences field, which includes pharmaceutical research and medical manufacturing, continues to grow, due in no small part to the pressing need to find cures for a number of medical ailments. Additionally, new technologies are being developed that are capable of analyzing biological subjects in greater detail than ever before. In light of these trends, the demand for biophysicists is expected to grow at a significant rate—as much as 31 percent over a ten-year period.

It is expected that the number of biophysicists, which is relatively small in light of the specificity of the field, will also continue to grow over the longer term, especially as the applications for this field expand. Biophysicists are already in demand to research disease treatments, and as research efforts expand in the field of genetic disorders and conditions, this will be even more the case. Furthermore, the development of alternative fuel and food sources, such as genetically modified crops that can produce larger yields with less maintenance, has a number of biophysical applications, and the demand for experienced biophysicists capable of adapting their skills and knowledge to this growing field will likely continue into the near future.

—Michael P. Auerbach, MA

More Information

American Society for Cell Biology
8120 Woodmont Avenue, Suite 750
Bethesda, MD 20814-2762
www.ascb.org

Biophysical Society
11400 Rockville Pike, Suite 800
Rockville, MD 20852
www.biophysics.org

European Biophysical Societies' Association
www.ebsa.org

International Union for Pure and Applied Biophysics
51 Boulevard de Montmorency
75016 Paris
France
www.iupab.org

Civil Engineering

FIELDS OF STUDY

Physics; mathematics; chemistry; engineering mechanics; strength of materials; fluid mechanics; soil mechanics; hydrology; surveying; engineering graphics; environmental engineering; structural engineering; transportation engineering.

DEFINITION

Civil engineering is the branch of engineering concerned with the design, construction, and maintenance of fixed structures and systems, such as large buildings, bridges, roads, and other transportation systems, and water supply and wastewater-treatment systems. Civil engineering is the second-oldest field of engineering, with the term "civil" initially used to differentiate it from the oldest field of engineering, military engineering. The major subdisciplines within civil engineering are structural, transportation, and environmental engineering. Other possible areas of specialization within civil engineering are geotechnical, hydraulic, construction, and coastal engineering.

Basic Principles

Civil engineering is the second-oldest field of engineering, after military engineering. The term "civil engineering" came into use in the mid-eighteenth century and initially referred to any practice of engineering by civilians for nonmilitary purposes. Before this time, most large-scale construction projects, such as roads and bridges, were done by military engineers. Early civil engineering projects were in areas such as water supply, roads, bridges, and other large structures, the same type of engineering work that exemplifies civil engineering in modern times. Today, civil engineering encompasses a very broad field of engineering, ranging from subdisciplines such as structural engineering to environmental engineering, some of which have also become recognized as separate fields of engineering.

Civil engineering, like engineering in general, is a profession with a practical orientation, having an emphasis on building things and making things work. Civil engineers use their knowledge of the physical sciences, mathematics, and engineering sciences, along with empirical engineering correlations to design, construct, manage, and maintain structures, transportation infrastructure, and environmental treatment equipment and facilities.

Empirical engineering correlations are important in civil engineering, because usable theoretical equations are not available for all the necessary engineering calculations. These empirical correlations are equations, graphs, or nomographs, based on experimental measurements, that give relationships among variables of interest for a particular engineering application. For example, the Manning equation gives an experimental relationship among the flow rate in an open channel, the slope of the channel, the depth of water, and the size, shape, and material of the bottom and sides of the channel. Rivers, irrigation ditches, and concrete channels used to transport wastewater in a treatment plant are examples of open channels. Similar empirical relationships are used in transportation, structural, and other specialties within civil engineering.

Core Concepts

In addition to mathematics, chemistry, and physics, civil engineering makes extensive use of principles from several engineering science subjects: engineering mechanics (statics and strength of materials), soil mechanics, and fluid mechanics.

Engineering Mechanics—Statics. As implied by the term "statics," this area of engineering concerns objects that are not moving. The fundamental principle of statics is that any stationary object must be in static equilibrium. That is, any force on the object must be cancelled out by another force that is equal in magnitude and acting in the opposite direction. There can be no net force in any direction on a stationary object, because if there were, it would be moving in that direction. The object considered to be in static equilibrium could be an entire structure or it could be any part of a structure down to a individual member in a truss.

Calculations for an object in static equilibrium are often done through the use of a free body diagram, that is a sketch of the object, showing all the forces external to that object that are acting on it. The principle then used for calculations is that the sum of all the horizontal forces acting on the object must be zero and the sum of all the vertical forces acting on the object must be zero. Working with the forces as vectors helps to find the horizontal and vertical components of forces that are acting on the object from some direction other than horizontal or vertical.

Engineering Mechanics—Strength of Materials. This subject is sometimes called mechanics of materials. Whereas statics works only with forces external to the body that is in equilibrium, strength of materials uses the same principles and also considers internal forces in a structural member. This is done to determine the required material properties to ensure that the member can withstand the internal stresses that will be placed on it.

Soil Mechanics. Knowledge of soil mechanics is needed to design the foundations for structures. Any structure resting on the Earth will be supported in some way by the soil beneath it. A properly designed foundation will provide adequate long-term support for the structure above it. Inadequate knowledge of soil mechanics or inadequate foundation design may lead to something such as the Leaning Tower of Pisa. Soil mechanics topics include physical properties of soil, compaction, distribution of stress within soil, and flow of water through soil.

Fluid Mechanics. Fundamental principles of physics are used for some fluid mechanics calculations. Examples are conservation of mass (called the continuity equation in fluid mechanics) and conservation of energy (also called the energy equation or the first law of thermodynamics). Some fluid mechanics applications, however, make use of empirical (experimental) equations or relationships. Calculations for flow through pipes or flow in open channels, for example, use empirical constants and equations.

Knowledge from Engineering Fields of Practice. In addition to these engineering sciences, a civil engineer uses accumulated knowledge from the civil engineering areas of specialization. Some of the important fields of practice are hydrology, geotechnical engineering, structural engineering, transportation engineering, and environmental engineering. In each of these fields of practice, there are theoretical equations, empirical equations, graphs or nomographs, guidelines, and rules of thumb that civil engineers use for design and construction of projects related to structures, roads, storm water management, or wastewater-treatment projects, for example.

Civil Engineering Tools. Several tools available for civil engineers to use in practice are engineering graphics, computer-aided drafting (CAD), surveying, and geographic information systems (GIS). Engineering graphics (engineering drawing) has been a mainstay in civil engineering since its inception, for preparation of and interpretation of plans and drawings. Most of this work has come to be done using computer-aided drafting. Surveying is a tool that has also long been a part of civil engineering. From laying out roads to laying out a building foundation or measuring the slope of a river or of a sewer line, surveying is a useful tool for many of the civil engineering fields. Civil engineers often work with maps, and geographic information systems, a much newer tool than engineering graphics or surveying, make this type of work more efficient.

Codes and Design Criteria. Much of the work done by civil engineers is either directly or indirectly for the public. Therefore, in most of civil engineering fields, work is governed by codes or design criteria specified by some state, local, or federal agency. For example, federal, state, and local governments have building codes, state departments of transportation specify design criteria for roads and highways, and wastewater-treatment processes and sewers must meet federal, state, and local design criteria.

Applications Past and Present

Structural Engineering. Civil engineers design, build, and maintain many and varied structures. These include bridges, towers, large buildings (skyscrapers), tunnels, and sports arenas. Some of the civil engineering areas of knowledge needed for structural engineering are soil mechanics/geotechnical engineering, foundation engineering, engineering mechanics (statics and dynamics), and strength of materials.

When the Brooklyn Bridge was built over the East River in New York City (1870–1883), its suspension span of 1,595 feet was the longest in the world. It remained the longest suspension bridge in North America until the Williamsburg Bridge was completed in New York City in 1903. The Brooklyn Bridge joined two independent cities, Brooklyn and Manhattan, and helped establish the New York City Metropolitan Area.

The Golden Gate Bridge, which crosses the mouth of San Francisco Bay with a main span of 4,200 feet, had nearly triple the central span of the Brooklyn Bridge. It was the world's longest suspension bridge from its date of completion in 1937 until 1964, when the Verrazano-Narrows Bridge opened in New York City with a central span that was 60 feet longer than that of the Golden Gate Bridge. The Humber Bridge, which crosses the Humber estuary in England and was completed in 1981, has a single suspended span of 4,625 feet and was the longest suspension bridge in the world until 1998, when the Akashi Kaikyo Bridge opened in Japan with a central span of 6,532 feet.

One of the best-known early towers illustrates the importance of good geotechnical engineering and foundation design. The Tower of Pisa, commonly known as the Leaning Tower of Pisa, in Italy started to lean to one side very noticeably, even during its construction (1173–1399). Its height of about 185 feet is not extremely tall in comparison with towers built later, but it was impressive when it was built. The reason for its extreme tilt (more than 5 meters off perpendicular) is that it was built on rather soft, sandy soil with a foundation that was not deep enough or spread out enough to support the structure. In spite of this, the Tower of Pisa has remained standing for more than six hundred years.

Another well-known tower, the Washington Monument, was completed in 1884. At 555 feet in height, it was the world's tallest tower until the Eiffel Tower, nearly 1,000 feet tall, was completed in 1889. The Washington Monument remains the world's tallest masonry structure. The Gateway Arch in St. Louis, Missouri, is the tallest monument in the United States, at 630 feet.

The twenty-one-story Flatiron Building, which opened in New York City in 1903, was one of the first skyscrapers. It is 285 feet tall and its most unusual feature is its triangular shape, which was well suited to the wedge-shaped piece of land on which it was built. The 102-floor Empire State Building, completed in 1931 in New York City with a height of 1,250 feet, outdid the Chrysler Building that was under construction at the same time by 204 feet, to earn the title of the world's tallest building at that time. The Sears Tower (now the Willis Tower) in Chicago is 1,450 feet tall and was the tallest building in the world when it was completed in 1974. Several taller buildings have been constructed since that time in Asia and the Middle East.

Some of the more interesting examples of tunnels go through mountains and under the sea. The Hoosac Tunnel, built from 1851 to 1874, connected New York State to New England with a 4.75-mile railway tunnel through the Hoosac Mountain in northwestern Massachusetts. It was the longest railroad tunnel in the United States for more than fifty years. Mount Blanc Tunnel, built from 1957 to 1965, is a 7.25-mile long highway tunnel under Mount Blanc in the Alps to connect Italy and France. The Channel Tunnel, one of the most publicized modern tunnel projects, is a rather dramatic and symbolic tunnel. It goes a distance of 31 miles beneath the English Channel to connect Dover, England, and Calais, France.

Transportation Engineering. Civil engineers also design, build, and maintain a wide variety of projects related to transportation, such as roads, railroads, and pipelines.

Many long, dramatic roads and highways have been built by civil engineers, ever since the Romans became the first builders of an extensive network of roads. The Appian Way is the best known of the many long, straight roads built by the Romans. The Appian Way project was started in 312 B.C.E. by the Roman censor Appius Claudius. By 244 B.C.E., it extended about 360 miles from Rome to the port of Brundisium in southeastern Italy. The Pan-American Highway, often billed as the world's longest road, connects North America and South America. The original Pan-American Highway ran from Texas to Argentina with a length of more than 15,500 miles. It has since been extended to go from Prudhoe Bay, Alaska, to the southern tip of South America, with a total length

Interesting Facts about Civil Engineering

- The Johnstown Flood in Pennsylvania, on May 31, 1889, which killed more than 2,200 people, was the result of the catastrophic failure of the South Fork Dam. The dam, built in 1852, held back Lake Conemaugh and was made of clay, boulders, and dirt. An improperly maintained spillway combined with heavy rains caused the collapse.

- The I-35W bridge over the Mississippi River in Minneapolis, Minnesota, collapsed during rush-hour traffic on August 1, 2007, causing 13 deaths and 145 injuries. The collapse was blamed on undersized gusset plates, an increase in the concrete surface load, and the weight of construction supplies and equipment on the bridge.

- On November 7, 1940, 42-mile-per-hour winds twisted the Tacoma Narrows Bridge over the Puget Sound in Washington state and caused its collapse. The bridge, with a central span of 2,800 feet, had been completed just four months earlier. Steel girders meant to support the bridge were blocking the wind, causing it to sway and eventually collapse.

- Low-quality concrete and incorrectly placed rebar led to shear failure, collapsing the Highway 19 overpass in Laval, Quebec, on September 30, 2006.

- The first design for the Gateway Arch in St. Louis, Missouri, had a fatal flaw that made it unstable at the required height. The final design used 886 tons of stainless steel, making it a very expensive structure.

- On January 9, 1999, just three years after it was built, the Rainbow Bridge, a pedestrian bridge across the Qi River in Sichuan Province, collapsed, killing 40 people and injuring 14. Concrete used in the bridge was weak, parts of it were rusty, and parts had been improperly welded.

of nearly 30,000 miles. The US Interstate Highway system has been the world's biggest earthmoving project. Started in 1956 by the Federal Highway Act, it contains sixty-two highways covering a total distance of 42,795 miles. This massive highway construction project transformed the American system of highways and had major cultural impacts.

The building of the US Transcontinental Railroad was a major engineering feat when the western portion of the 2,000-mile railroad across the United States was built in the 1860s. Logistics was a major part of the project, with the need to transport steel rails and wooden ties great distances. An even more formidable task was construction of the Trans-Siberian Railway, the world's longest railway. It was built from 1891 to 1904 and covers 5,900 miles across Russia, from Moscow in the west to Vladivostok in the east.

The first oil pipeline in the United States was a 5-mile-long, 2-inch-diameter pipe that carried 800 barrels of petroleum per day. Pipelines have become much larger and longer since then. The Trans-Alaska Pipeline, with 800 miles of 48-inch-diameter pipe, can carry 2.14 million barrels per day. At the peak of construction, 20,000 people worked twelve-hour days, seven days a week.

Water Resources Engineering. Another area of civil engineering practice is water resources engineering, with projects like canals, dams, dikes, and seawater barriers.

The oldest known canal, one that is still in operation, is the Grand Canal in China, constructed between 485 B.C.E. and 283 C.E. The length of the Grand Canal is more than 1,000 miles, although its route has varied because of several instances of rerouting, remodeling, and rebuilding over the years. The 363-mile-long Erie Canal was built from 1817 to 1825 across the state of New York from Albany to Buffalo, thus overcoming the Appalachian Mountains as a barrier to trade between the eastern United States and the newly opened western United States. The economic impact of the Erie Canal was tremendous. It reduced the cost of shipping a ton of cargo between Buffalo and New York City from about $100 per ton (over the Appalachians) to $4 per ton (through the canal).

The Panama Canal, constructed from 1881 to 1914 to connect the Atlantic and Pacific Oceans through the Isthmus of Panama, is only about 50 miles long, but its construction presented tremendous challenges because of the soil, the terrain, and the tropical illnesses that killed many workers. Upon its completion, however, the Panama Canal reduced the travel distance from New York City to San Francisco by about 9,000 miles.

When the Hoover Dam was built from 1931 to 1936 on the Colorado River at the Colorado-Arizona border, it was the world's largest dam, at a height of 726 feet and crest length of 1,224 feet. The technique of passing chilled water through pipes enclosed in the concrete to cool the newly poured concrete and speed its curing was developed for the construction of the Hoover Dam and is still in use. The Grand Coulee Dam, in the state of Washington, was the largest hydrolectric project in the world when it was built in the 1930s. It has an output of 10,080 megawatts. The Itaipu Dam, on the Parana River, along the border of Brazil and Paraguay, is also one of the largest hydroelectric dams in the world. It began operation in 1984 and is capable of producing 13,320 megawatts.

Dikes, dams, and similar structures have been used for centuries around the world for protection against flooding. The largest sea barrier in the world is a two-mile-long surge barrier in the Oosterschelde estuary of the Netherlands, constructed from 1958 to 1986. Called the Dutch Delta Plan, the purpose of this project was to reduce the danger of catastrophic flooding. The impetus that brought this project to fruition was a catastrophic flood in the area in 1953. A major part of the barrier design consists of sixty-five huge concrete piers, weighing in at 18,000 tons each. These piers support tremendous 400-ton steel gates to create the sea barrier. The lifting and placement of these huge concrete piers exceeded the capabilities of any existing cranes, so a special U-shaped ship was built and equipped with gantry cranes. The project used computers to help in guidance and placement of the piers. A stabilizing foundation used for the concrete piers consists of foundation mattresses made up of layers of sand, fine gravel, and coarse gravel. Each foundation mattress is more than 1 foot thick and more than 650 feet by 140 feet, with a smaller mattress placed on top.

Impact on Industry

In view of its status as the second-oldest engineering discipline and the essential nature of the type of work done by civil engineers, civil engineering is well established as an important field of engineering around the world. Civil engineering is the largest field of engineering in the United States. The US Bureau of Labor Statistics estimates

Occupation	Civil engineers
Employment 2010	262,800
Projected Employment 2020	313,900
Change in Number (2010–20)	51,100
Percent Change	19%

*Bureau of Labor Statistics, 2012

that 278,400 civil engineers were employed in the United States in 2008. The bureau also projected that civil engineering employment would grow at the rate of 24 percent rate until 2018, which is much faster than average for all occupations.

Consulting Engineering Firms. This is the largest sector of employment for civil engineers. There are many consulting engineering firms around the world, ranging in size from small firms with a few employees to very large firms with thousands of employees. In 2010, the *Engineering News Record* identified the top six US design firms: AECOM Technology (Los Angeles); URS (San Francisco); Jacobs (Pasadena, California); Fluor (Irving, Texas); CH2M Hill (Englewood, Colorado); and Bechtel (San Francisco). Many consulting engineering firms have some electrical engineers and mechanical engineers, and some even specialize in those areas; however, a large proportion of engineering consulting firms are made up predominantly of civil engineers. About 60 percent of American civil engineers are employed by consulting engineering firms.

Construction Firms. Although some consulting engineering firms design and construct their own projects, some companies specialize in constructing projects designed by another firm. These companies also use civil engineers. About 8 percent of American civil engineers are employed in the nonresident building construction sector.

Other Industries. Some civil engineers are employed in industry, but less than 1 percent of American civil engineers are employed in an industry other than consulting firms and construction firms. The industry sectors that hire the most civil engineers are oil and gas extraction and pipeline companies.

Occupation	Civil engineering technicians
Employment 2010	79,000
Projected Employment 2020	88,400
Change in Number (2010–20)	9,400
Percent Change	12%

Bureau of Labor Statistics, 2012

Government Agencies and Military. Civil engineers work for many federal, state, and local government agencies. For example, the US Department of Transportation uses civil engineers to handle its many highway and other transportation projects. Many road or highway projects are handled at the state level, and each state department of transportation employs many civil engineers. The US Corps of Engineers and the Department of the Interior's Bureau of Reclamation employ many civil engineers for their many water resources projects. Many cities and counties have one or more civil engineers as city or county engineers, and many have civil engineers in their public works departments. About 15 percent of American civil engineers are employed by state governments, about 13 percent by local governments, and about 4 percent by the federal government.

The military has about 7,200 civil engineers. On average, the armed services need about 350 more each year. Newly commissioned civil engineers usually assist senior engineering officers in planning and design. With experience, they may manage construction projects and, eventually, engineering offices. In time, they may advance to senior management or command positions in the engineering field. Duties and responsibilities may typically include the direct surveying of construction areas; the planning and of temporary facilities for emergency use; the management of master plans for purposes of facility updating for military bases; and the selection of contractors for facility construction.

Academic Research and Teaching. Because civil engineering is the largest field of engineering, almost every college of engineering has a civil engineering department, leading to a continuing demand for civil engineering faculty members to teach the next generation of civil engineers and to conduct sponsored research projects. This applies to universities not only in the United States but also around the world.

Social Context and Future Prospects

Civil engineering projects typically involve basic infrastructure needs such as roads and highways, water supply, wastewater treatment, bridges, and public buildings. These projects may be new construction or repair, maintenance or upgrading of existing highways, structures, and treatment facilities. The buildup of such infrastructure since the beginning of the twentieth century has been extensive, leading to a continuing need for the repair, maintenance, and upgrading of existing structures. Also, governments tend to devote funding to infrastructure improvements to generate jobs and create economic activity during economic downturns. All of this leads to the projection for a continuing strong need for civil engineers.

Further Reading

Arteaga, Robert R. *The Building of the Arch*. 10th ed. St. Louis: Jefferson National Parks Association, 2002. Describes how the Gateway Arch in St. Louis, Missouri, was built up from both sides and came together at the top. Contains excellent illustrations.

Davidson, Frank Paul, and Kathleen Lusk-Brooke, comps. *Building the World: An Encyclopedia of the Great Engineering Projects in History*. Westport, CT: Greenwood, 2006. Examines more than forty major engineering projects from the Roman aqueducts to the tunnel across the English Channel.

Hawkes, Nigel. *Structures: The Way Things Are Built*. 1990. Reprint. New York: Macmillan, 1993. Discusses many well-known civil engineering projects. Chapter 4 contains information about seventeen projects, including the Great Wall of China, the Panama Canal, and the Dutch Delta Plan. Contains illustrations and discussion of the effect of the projects.

National Geographic Society. *The Builders: Marvels of Engineering*. Washington, DC: National Geographic Society, 1992. Documents some of the most ambitious civil engineering projects, including roads, canals, bridges, railroads, skyscrapers, sports arenas, and exposition halls. Discussion and excellent illustrations are included for each project.

Weingardt, Richard G. *Engineering Legends: Great American Civil Engineers: Thirty-Two Profiles of Inspiration and Achievement*. Reston, VA: American Society of Civil Engineers, 2005. Looks at the lives of civil engineers who were environmental experts, transportation trendsetters, builders of bridges, structural trailblazers, and daring innovators.

About the Author: Harlan H. Bengtson, BS, MS, PhD, is a licensed professional engineer. He spent thirty years in engineering education, in teaching and administrative positions, and is working as a technical writer in Missouri. He received his bachelor's and master's degrees from Iowa State University and a doctorate from the University of Colorado, all in chemical engineering. Bengtson did consulting work while in academia and had prior industrial experience. He has written numerous publications and technical reports. His areas of expertise are environmental engineering, hydrology, engineering science, and renewable energy.

Civil Engineer

Earnings (Yearly Median): $77,990 (Bureau of Labor Statistics, 2012)

Employment and Outlook: Average growth (Bureau of Labor Statistics, 2012)

O*NET-SOC Code: 17-2051.00

Related Career Cluster(s): Business Management & Administration; Government & Public Administration; Transportation, Distribution & Logistics

Scope of Work

Civil engineers are involved in the design and construction of buildings and other infrastructure, including bridges, dams, roads and highways, sewer systems, power plants, and other fixed structures and systems. Working in close association with architects, civil engineers translate people's needs and desires into physical space by applying a wide range of engineering and other technologies to provide building systems that are functional, safe, economical, environmentally healthy, and in harmony with the architect's aesthetic intent. They assess costs, durability of building materials, and the physical environments in which the project is being constructed. They also direct and help survey sites; analyze all blueprints, drawings, and photographs;

test soil and other materials; and write and present important reports. Most civil engineers specialize in a subfield such as sanitation engineering, structural engineering, or transportation engineering.

Education and Coursework

At the high-school level, students should be engaged in the study of physics, chemistry, and biology, both in the classroom and through extracurricular clubs and societies. Mathematics, including algebra, geometry, trigonometry, and calculus, are also essential courses. Furthermore, high-school students should take computer-science courses and hone their writing and public speaking skills through English and communications classes. Courses that help students understand blueprints and architecture, such as drafting and industrial arts, are also highly useful.

A bachelor's degree in civil engineering is generally the requirement for entry into the field of civil engineering. Registration as a professional engineer is required for many civil-engineering positions. In the United States, a graduate from a bachelor's degree program accredited by the Accreditation Board for Engineering and Technology is eligible to take the Fundamentals of Engineering (FE) exam to become an engineer in training. After four years of professional experience under the supervision of a professional engineer, one is eligible to take the Principles and Practice of Engineering (PE) exam to obtain a professional engineer (PE) license and become a registered professional engineer.

A typical program of study for a bachelor's degree in civil engineering includes chemistry, calculus and differential equations, calculus-based physics, engineering graphics/AutoCAD, surveying, engineering mechanics, strength of materials, and perhaps engineering geology, as well as general education courses during the first two years. This is followed by fluid mechanics, hydrology or water resources, soil mechanics, engineering economics, and introductory courses for transportation engineering, structural engineering, and environmental engineering, as well as civil-engineering electives to allow specialization in one of the areas of civil engineering during the last two years. Students should also take advantage of student chapters and other networking opportunities, such as the American Society of Civil Engineers student chapter, which can offer internship and placement assistance and funding.

A master's degree in civil engineering that provides additional advanced courses in one of the areas of specialization, an MBA, or an engineering management master's degree complements a bachelor of science degree and enables its holder to advance more rapidly. A master of science degree would typically lead to more advanced technical positions, while an MBA or engineering management degree would typically lead to management positions.

Anyone aspiring to a civil engineering faculty or research position must obtain a doctoral degree. In that case, to provide proper preparation for doctoral-level study, any master's-level study should be in pursuit of a research-oriented master of science degree, rather than a master's degree in engineering or a practice-oriented master of science degree.

Career Enhancement and Training

Civil engineers are able to join and network through numerous professional associations and societies, most notably the American Society of Civil Engineers (ASCE). Some professional civil engineering associations, such as the ASCE, the Academy of Geo-Professionals, and the American Academy of Water Resources Engineers, offer specialty certification programs. Leadership in Energy and Environmental Design (LEED) certification may be necessary for some projects. All states have licensing regulations for engineers whose work affects life, health, or property, and each state administers its own examination.

Daily Tasks and Technology

While most civil-engineering jobs are project based, civil engineers' daily responsibilities and duties vary based on their place of employment and specialty. A civil engineer employed by a city government may focus on only one or two major projects per year, while a civil engineer employed by a major architectural firm may be involved in a greater number of projects. Some civil engineers conduct thorough soil studies in addition to testing the structural integrity and strength of building materials. Many civil engineers are also supervisors,

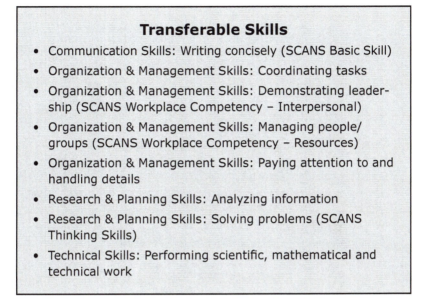

Transferable Skills

- Communication Skills: Writing concisely (SCANS Basic Skill)
- Organization & Management Skills: Coordinating tasks
- Organization & Management Skills: Demonstrating leadership (SCANS Workplace Competency – Interpersonal)
- Organization & Management Skills: Managing people/groups (SCANS Workplace Competency – Resources)
- Organization & Management Skills: Paying attention to and handling details
- Research & Planning Skills: Analyzing information
- Research & Planning Skills: Solving problems (SCANS Thinking Skills)
- Technical Skills: Performing scientific, mathematical and technical work

overseeing construction crews and other engineers at work sites. Civil engineers occasionally act as consultants, providing technical advice and studies to the client as needed.

In general, civil engineers conduct studies and evaluations of existing engineering issues, such as traffic-flow studies for roadway construction projects or flow-rate analyses for water-system upgrades. They prepare public reports, such as environmental-impact assessments, bid proposals for contractors, and detailed descriptions of the proposed project site or sites. Civil engineers write feasibility studies in which they estimate the costs and quantities of building materials, equipment, and labor required for a given project. Then, using drafting tools and software, they create designs for new or improved infrastructure.

During the construction phase, civil engineers visit and inspect work sites regularly, monitoring progress and ensuring compliance with government safety standards and the client's wishes. These inspections also entail testing the strength and integrity of the materials used, as well as the environment in which they are being used.

Civil engineers work with a wide range of technologies and tools during the course of their work. In the office, they use computer-aided

A Conversation with Lisa Deitemeyer

Job Title: Project Manager

What was your career path?

I graduated from Northeastern University with a Bachelor of Science degree in civil engineering. While still in college I passed the Fundamentals of Engineering exam. With this I became an Engineer in Training (EIT). After graduation I worked for a transportation engineering consulting firm. As an EIT you need to work five years (varies in different states) under the supervision of a professional engineer before you can take the professional engineers (PE) exam. My experience working as an EIT was primarily in roadway and drainage design for construction projects varying in size from residential streets to highway interchanges. With good engineering design experience on progressively complex work, I took the PE exam, passed the exam, and officially became a professional engineer. I continued to work as a designer and project engineer on transportation projects. With about nine years of experience, the company I worked for provided the opportunity for me to manage the design of a residential street reconstruction project. From there I continued to have opportunities to manage larger projects. With my increase in management work, my design work decreased and I supervised the design work of others. Today, I am a project manager for the design of a $2 billion design-build construction project in Dallas, Texas.

What are three pieces of advice?

1. Try to work as an intern or get a summer job at a company in the field you are studying. This exposure to real life work will help you confirm that it is the field for you, and it will help apply your college course work to the working world.

2. As and EIT or graduate engineer, try to get as much experience as you can in the areas of your field. For example, in civil engineering, try to get experience in the design of drainage, roadway, traffic, retaining walls, etc. Understanding all aspects of your field will help you become a better manager later, if you choose that path.

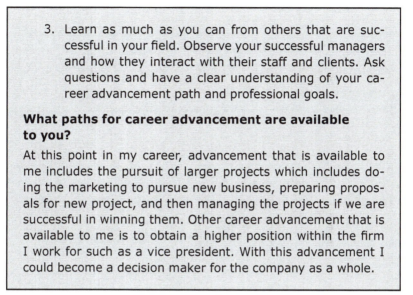

3. Learn as much as you can from others that are successful in your field. Observe your successful managers and how they interact with their staff and clients. Ask questions and have a clear understanding of your career advancement path and professional goals.

What paths for career advancement are available to you?

At this point in my career, advancement that is available to me includes the pursuit of larger projects which includes doing the marketing to pursue new business, preparing proposals for new project, and then managing the projects if we are successful in winning them. Other career advancement that is available to me is to obtain a higher position within the firm I work for such as a vice president. With this advancement I could become a decision maker for the company as a whole.

design (CAD) and other design software, cartography software, project-management systems and databases, and other analytical and scientific programs. At a project site, they use soil-collection equipment, electronic distance-measuring devices, levels, compasses, pressure gauges, and scales.

Earnings and Employment Outlook

The demand for civil engineers remains high, and employment of civil engineers is expected to grow slightly faster than the average for all occupations through the year 2020. Civil-engineering salaries are competitive, and civil engineers typically receive strong benefits. As a result of growth in the population and an increased emphasis on security, more civil engineers will be needed to design and construct safe higher-capacity transportation, water-supply systems, and pollution-control systems, in addition to large buildings and building complexes. They also will be needed to repair or replace existing roads, bridges, and other public structures.

The demand for civil engineers remains high, and employment of civil engineers is expected to grow slightly faster than the average for all occupations through the year 2020.

Earnings depend on the size and geographic location of the employer and the employee's qualifications. In 2011, the average salary offer to college graduates with a bachelor's degree in civil engineering was $55,217 per year, according to the National Association of Colleges and Employers. Civil engineers with a master's degree were offered first-year salaries averaging $64,011, while those with a PhD were offered $68,049 annually.

Related Occupations

- **Transportation Engineers:** Transportation engineers design and prepare plans, estimates, and specifications for the construction and operation of surface transportation projects. Transportation engineers may specialize in a particular phase of the work, such as making surveys of roads, improving road signs or lighting, or directing and coordinating construction or maintenance activity.

- **Structural Engineers:** Structural engineers plan, design, and oversee the erection of steel and other structural materials in buildings, bridges, and other structures that require a stress analysis.

- **Hydraulic Engineers:** Hydraulic engineers design and direct the construction of dams, levees, systems for water distribution and sewage collection, and other projects for the control and use of water.

- **Sanitary Engineers:** Sanitary engineers design and oversee the construction and operation of hygienic projects.

- **Environmental Engineers:** Environmental engineers apply their knowledge of engineering to correcting or improving various areas of environmental concern, such as air, soil, or water pollution.

Future Applications

Given the state of the US transportation infrastructure, civil engineers in the United States will continue to be in high demand as the nation addresses issues relative to the state of repair, improvement, and construction of roads and highways, bridges, ports, air transportation, and rail systems. As the United States heads out of the economic recession and a postwar economy develops, many predict that the second decade of the twenty-first century could be one of significant prosperity for the United States. This economic growth will highlight the necessity for infrastructure improvements and spending. Additionally, civil engineers who have the skills to address those issues facing developing nations, such as clean water, sanitation, waste disposal, and transportation, will also find continued employment.

—Michael P. Auerbach, MA

More Information

Academy of Geo-Professionals
1801 Alexander Bell Drive
Reston, VA 20191
www.geoprofessionals.org

American Society of Civil Engineers
1801 Alexander Bell Drive
Reston, VA 20191
www.asce.org

National Council of Structural Engineers Associations
645 North Michigan Avenue, Suite 540
Chicago, IL 60611
www.ncsea.com

National Society of Professional Engineers
1420 King Street
Alexandria, VA 22314-2794
www.nspe.org

Classical or Applied Mechanics

FIELDS OF STUDY

Physics; mathematics; mechanics; engineering; kinematics; cosmology; kinetics; analytical mechanics; electrical engineering; mechanical engineering; statistical engineering; continuum mechanics; linear algebra; calculus; acoustics; fluid mechanics; thermodynamics; static mechanics; analytical dynamics; Newtonian mechanics.

DEFINITION

An ancient branch of the physical sciences with roots at the foundations of Western scientific thought, mechanics has applications in a variety of modern scientific fields. Classical mechanics studies the physical laws and forces that govern the movements and interactions of objects; it covers the motion and behavior of all bodies, from celestial to biological and engineered. Applied mechanics is the branch of physics and engineering that studies the practical and engineering applications of principles of classical mechanics.

Basic Principles

English physicist and mathematician Isaac Newton is known as the father of mechanics for his formulation of the laws of motion, first published in his book *Philosophiae Mathematica Principia Naturalis* (1687). Newton's laws laid the foundation for the modern scientific understanding of motion using mathematical analysis. Newton also formulated one of the first scientific theories of gravitation, which became the foundation for the scientific understanding of planetary movement and the earth's orbit around the sun.

Between the seventeenth century and the twentieth century, the principles of mechanics were reformulated by leading mathematicians, creating new approaches to mechanical analysis that are still used. French mathematician Joseph-Louis Lagrange presented the first important reformulation of Newtonian mechanics in the 1780s; fifty years later, Irish mathematician William Hamilton presented a reformulation of Lagrange's work that helped to connect classical mechanics with the movement of atoms and molecules. In the twentieth century, physicists developed quantum mechanics to study the motion and behavior of fundamental particles; this soon became the other major branch of mechanics, alongside classical mechanics.

In the twenty-first century, classical mechanics continues to provide the basis for the physical understanding of motion. It has been divided into numerous subfields, including celestial mechanics, which studies the motion of celestial bodies; continuum mechanics, which studies the behaviors of continuous materials; and statistical mechanics, which studies the thermodynamic and mechanical principles of individual molecules and atoms and how those principles translate into the observable behaviors of physical bodies.

Core Concepts

Newtonian Mechanics. Newton's three laws of motion describe the fundamental forces acting upon bodies in motion and define the mathematical relationships between these fundamental forces and observed patterns of movement.

The first law states that an object does not change in its state of either rest or motion unless acted upon by an outside force. Therefore, if an object is at rest, it will remain at rest unless some external force compels it to move; similarly, a moving object will continue moving in the same direction and at the same speed unless its motion is changed by another force. The first law also defines the concept of *inertia*, which is defined as an object's tendency to resist changes in momentum or motion.

The second law defines the concept of force, describing it as equal to the change in an object's momentum of movement. Momentum can be understood as the product of an object's mass multiplied by its velocity, or speed of movement through space. In essence, the second law says that the acceleration of an object through space will be proportional to the force exerted on the object. A greater force will result in greater acceleration.

The third law is often summarized with the phrase "for every action, there is an equal and opposite reaction." In terms of mechanical movement, the law states that when two bodies exert force on one another, the reactions of both objects are equal in terms of intensity but opposite in terms of direction. Reaction engines, such as those that power the flight of jet aircraft and rockets, are based on this principle, using the opposing force created by the firing of jet thrusters to propel an object through space.

Measurement Techniques. Research in classical mechanics relies on methods and tools used to measure the variables that contribute to patterns of movement. Physicists and engineers work together to develop measurement methods and equipment used to derive values for these parameters.

Velocity measurements are generally completed using laser or radar measurements, which gauge velocity by measuring the distance traveled by an object over time. Alternatively, high-speed cameras can be used to measure velocity.

Mass measurements can be conducted by using scales to gauge an object's weight, which can then be compared to the object's size and volume. The mass of gasses and liquids can be obtained using specialized equipment such as a thermal conductivity detector, which estimates the mass of a sample of gas by measuring thermal conductivity compared to a sample of gas with a known mass.

Force measurements are generally conducted using force gauges, which are machines that can translate the force placed on a target sensor into electric signals that provide a digital readout of the force applied.

Acceleration is measured using an accelerometer, an electrochemical device that works by translating the "squeezing" force applied to the device during acceleration into electric signals that can be used to measure the intensity of the movement. Accelerometers can be used to measure both the vibration of an object and its dynamic or directional acceleration.

Differential Equations. Differential equations are mathematical formulations that relate to the differential of a quantity, that is, how quickly the quantity changes with respect to another quantity. Differential equations begin with a function, which is a mathematical process that can be used to yield a certain value. Solving a differential equation yields a different function that describes the relationship between the original function and one or more derivatives. A partial differential equation is a differential equation in which there is more than one independent variable used in the formulation of the equation.

The theory and mathematical processes behind differential equations are central to the study of physics and mechanics. Newton's second law of motion, for example, is based on mathematical formulations using differential equations. Differential equations also form the basis for the scientific understanding of fluid dynamics, which is an important topic in mechanics. A variety of naturally occurring processes, including atmospheric airflow, heat transfer between the earth and the atmosphere, and the movement of ocean currents, can be described and analyzed using differential equations.

Gravity and Gravitational Theory. Newton also contributed to mechanics the formulation of the laws of gravitation, which explain how gravity affects bodies in motion. Newton's law of universal gravitation describes the attraction between two bodies with mass as being both proportional to the product of the masses of the two bodies and inversely proportional to the square of the distance between them. Newton's theory of gravitation was later replaced by Albert Einstein's theory of general relativity, which says that gravity is a result of a curvature in space-time that results from the mass of an object distorting space and time in the object's vicinity.

While the theoretical basis for the gravitational effect was altered by the introduction of Einstein's theory of general relativity, the equations that Newton derived to explain the gravitational attraction of bodies are still used in calculations of physical relationships. Accurate calculations of gravitational relationships are important to a number of scientific fields, including astrophysics and engineering.

Mechanical Work and Thermodynamics. In physics, work is defined as the product of a given force and the distance over which the force takes effect. The concept of work in physics is closely linked to the concept of energy and the equations of thermodynamics, which

Interesting Facts about Classical or Applied Mechanics

- Isaac Newton's concept of gravity was informed by seeing an apple fall from a nearby tree, which led him to contemplate the reasons behind the trajectory of falling objects. The event gave rise to a popular myth that Newton discovered gravity after he was struck in the head by a falling apple.

- Piezoelectricity is an electric current resulting from the energy supplied through pressure. A variety of pressure sensors and other measurement apparatuses use piezoelectric sensors to translate mechanical changes, as do common machines such as the pressure-ignition switches on barbecues.

- The Three Gorges Dam, located on the Chang (Yangtze) River in China, is one of the world's largest hydroelectric dams and one of the world's largest power generating facilities. The dam utilizes hydraulic pumps to generate more than 80 terawatts (1 terawatt = 1 trillion watts) of electricity per year.

- Solid rocket boosters (SRBs) were used to power the flight of NASA's space shuttles during the first two to three minutes of flight. The SRBs were among the largest rocket boosters ever used, each one providing more than 2.8 million pounds of force. More than twenty-five private engineering firms were involved in manufacturing equipment that formed part of the SRB system.

- The newton is the standard unit of force, equivalent to the force required to accelerate one kilogram of material at a rate of one meter per second squared. The concept of the newton was invented in France, at the International Bureau of Weights and Measures, where it was named in honor of Newton's pioneering research in motion and force.

explain the relationship between matter and energy. Equations governing work in physics also must take into account any counterforces that act against the direction of the initial force. For example, to model the distance a bullet will fly when fired from a gun, physicists need to know the initial force applied to the bullet, the gravitational drag on the bullet as the result of the mass of the earth, and the viscosity of the atmosphere through which the bullet is traveling.

Physicists and engineers use the basic equations governing the physical principle of work to calculate the movement of a variety of objects. Aerospace engineers, for example, calculate variables including force, gravity, torque, and displacement to map the trajectory of aircraft, satellites, and other objects propelled through space. Equations related to work are also used in the biological sciences to calculate and model physical movements, producing equations that relate the use of energy to the amount of physical activity that can be completed in a certain situation.

Continuum Mechanics. Continuum mechanics is a subfield of classical and applied mechanics that deals with the behavior of bodies that are modeled as continuous materials, rather than discrete objects. Among the most important subfields of continuum mechanics are the fields of fluid mechanics and fluid dynamics, which study the behavior of liquids and gases, for example. A variety of specific measurement and analysis techniques have been developed for research into fluid and continuum mechanics, including wind tunnels, which allow researchers to model the behavior of airflow and wind currents, and laser Doppler velocimetry (LDV), which uses the reflection of laser beams to measure the speed of a moving liquid.

Applications Past and Present

Celestial Mapping and Exploration. The modern science of astronomy was built on the understanding of gravity and planetary motion developed through classical mechanics research. Newton used his laws of motion and his concept of universal gravitation to complete some of the earliest mathematical models of planetary motion. Lagrange, one of the other major figures in the development of classical mechanics, also applied mechanical principles to orbital movement.

The orbital path of a planet can be represented by a mathematical formula relating the planet's mass to the mass of other astronomical bodies, such as stars, moons, and other planets, to calculate the gravitational pull acting on each body. Further mechanics formulations can be used to represent elliptical orbits and other variations in orbital path based on the gravitational interaction of multiple objects. The behavior of stars and planets as a result of gravitational fluctuations can also be used to study objects in distant solar systems. For example, scientists use variations in the movement of distant planets to detect which planets are surrounded by orbiting moons. Similarly, distant stars exhibit variations in movement when they are orbited by planets, and astronomers can use these minor variations in movement to map other solar systems.

In addition, classical mechanics is used extensively in engineering satellites and spacecraft for space exploration. The design of propulsion systems for rockets and shuttles is based directly on classical mechanics models of force, inertia, acceleration, and other factors that influence bodies in motion through the fluid of the atmosphere. Mechanics specialists also help to plot the trajectory of spacecraft to achieve orbit around the earth or other planets. For a spacecraft to achieve orbit around a planet or satellite, it is necessary to calculate precisely the angle of entry and approach that will be needed to compensate for gravitational pull and will allow the spacecraft to maintain orbital distance from a planet.

Sports Engineering. The design of baseball bats, golf balls, hockey pucks, and footballs is based on engineering that utilizes principles of classical mechanics. For example, the path of a golf ball is determined by energy imparted from the club as it impacts the surface of the ball. As the ball makes its way through the air, its trajectory is determined by the angle of impact, the spin of the ball, and a variety of other factors, including wind speed and direction. The depressions on the surface of a golf ball are designed to reduce drag on the ball by altering the reducing turbulence on the leading edge and therefore increasing initial lift. Engineer William Taylor utilized equations from aerodynamics research to invent the dimpled surface design for modern golf balls. Classical dynamics equations can be used to model each aspect of a golf stroke, from the position of the player's body and angle of swing to the ultimate speed, path, and movement of the ball as it travels through the air.

Another example of applied mechanics in sports technology is the design of shoes for various types of sporting activities. In recreational and professional running, for example, the soles of the shoes must be designed in such a way that they produce friction in contact with the ground surface, so that runners can push away from the ground to gain momentum. However, if the soles produce excess friction, runners will not be able to alternate steps quickly. Equations derived from mechanics research can be used to model the forces and counterforces involved in the impact of shoes against different types of surfaces. Using this data, engineers can attempt to mold the soles of shoes in such a way as to maximize initial friction while still allowing for rapid alternation of steps.

Hydraulic Engineering. Hydraulics is a field of engineering that utilizes the principles of continuum or fluid dynamics for a variety of applications. Hydraulic engineers design methods of extracting energy from fluids by utilizing pressure and heat to produce potential energy, which can then be harvested to produce electric or mechanical energy. One example is the hydraulic pump, a machine that pressurizes and transports liquid through a system of tubes and reservoirs. The pressurized liquid can be used to complete mechanical work, such as turning a rotor or powering the movement of another object. In some applications, hydraulic pumps can be used to power the generation of electricity by transitioning the mechanical energy in the pressurized liquid into electric energy through a generator.

Another application of hydraulic engineering is the design of hydroelectric dams or wave-power generators. Hydroelectric dams use hydraulic pumps to fill a reservoir with water such that the water has potential energy based on the gravitational forces pulling it to the surface. The gravitational and potential energy of the water in the filled reservoir can then be used to rotate turbines connected to an electric generator. In this way, the rotation of the earth, represented by gravitational forces, can be used to generate electric power. Similarly, wave-power generators use hydraulic pumps and rotary generators to translate the kinetic energy in the movement of waves into electric currents. Wave power is an emerging area of research that has the potential to become a major avenue of future energy development.

Materials Science. Materials science and engineering is the branch of classical mechanics research that studies the mechanical properties of various materials, especially with regard to the effects of motion and stress on material components. Thousands of practical applications have emerged from materials science, including the design and composition of automobile frames and bodies and refinements in the shape and structure of airplane wings. Materials-science specialists may study the way that different types of materials deform when subjected to pressure from airflow, for example. This data can be used to enhance the aerodynamic qualities of various vehicles or projectiles. Alternatively, physicists specializing in materials research may investigate the effects of increasing pressure on different materials, which can be used to refine designs used for submersible objects or pipes used in hydraulic engineering.

The design of "smart" materials provides a modern example of materials-science applications. Smart materials are materials that respond to certain external stimuli by undergoing a change in properties. For example, engineers and physicists are working on a variety of "self-healing" materials that automatically correct for minor damage caused by wear and mechanical stress. The design of self-healing materials generally involves utilizing polymers with chemical agents that can re-form chemical and physical bonds broken as a result of stress. While self-healing materials is a relatively new branch of research, there are thousands of potential applications in engineering, biomedical research, and commercial technology. Another example of smart-materials research is the development of thermoelectric technology, or materials that can convert changes in temperature into electric signals. The development of thermoelectric materials has the potential to majorly impact the energy industry, allowing engineers to create more efficient methods of harvesting energy from heat sources, such as solar or geothermal radiation.

Impact on Industry

Mechanics specialists may come from either the research-physics field or the mathematics field and may be employed by the government, universities, or private companies. Applied mechanics is utilized for a wide variety of engineering applications and is supported by a large number of engineering corporations in the United States and around the world.

According to the US Bureau of Labor Statistics, approximately 18,300 individuals were employed as research physicists in 2012, a field that is growing at close to the national average, with 14 percent growth expected between 2010 and 2020. Only a small percentage of those working as research physicists specialize in classical or applied mechanics, and most researchers further specialize in subdisciplines such as fluid mechanics, celestial mechanics, or aerospace mechanics.

Academic Research and Teaching. In 2012, 16 percent of research physicists worked in university research and teaching positions. Many physicists utilize their training to teach classes in general physics or mathematics in addition to conducting research in their chosen fields.

Mechanics research departments at universities often focus on one or more specific issues within the broader field of mechanics. Stanford University's Department of Civil and Environmental Engineering, for example, features a structural engineering and geomechanics program that conducts research focused on, among other areas, the application of computational techniques and computer modeling to various physical phenomena. Among a variety of programs conducted within the department, researchers are investigating techniques for microscale measurement, which allow physicists and engineers to accurately measure a variety of objects on extremely small scales.

Military. Both the US Department of Defense and the US armed forces employ physicists and engineers for a variety of research programs related to issues in classical and applied mechanics. Applied-mechanics research is essential to the development of military vehicles and weapons technology.

The National Research Laboratory (NRL) of the US Navy conducts research programs that use principles of classical mechanics to develop and test aircraft and spacecraft design. NRL researchers utilize specialized equipment to imitate the environment of the upper atmosphere and outer space, thereby allowing for the development of simulations and models to test aircraft design. The US Army Research

Occupation	Mechanical engineers
Employment 2010	243,200
Projected Employment 2020	264,500
Change in Number (2010–20)	21,300
Percent Change	9%

Bureau of Labor Statistics, 2012

Laboratory's Vehicle Technology Directorate also utilizes applied mechanics research in the development of propulsion systems and intelligent systems to enhance maneuverability of ground vehicles.

Government Agencies. Government agencies employ more than 20 percent of research physicists in the United States. The National Aeronautics and Space Administration's (NASA) Goddard Institute for Space Studies is one prominent government agency that employs mechanics specialists for a variety of research programs. NASA physicists utilize classical mechanics to inform calculations and models regarding the movement of planets and celestial objects and to develop technology used in space exploration. In addition, applied mechanics research plays a role in the design of spacecraft, satellites, and propulsion systems used in space exploration. NASA physicists also conduct research in fluid dynamics, which is used to model atmospheric phenomena and climate patterns. NASA is one of the international leaders in efforts to produce accurate models of the mechanical and thermodynamic systems of the earth, including the atmosphere and oceans.

Private Industry Research and Technology. Private research firms and corporations account for more than 32 percent of employment opportunities for research physicists around the world. Mechanics research is essential in the automobile industry, for example, where both classical and applied mechanics equations and techniques are used to investigate a variety of issues surrounding automobile design, including the aerodynamics of auto design, the efficiency of combustion engines and driveshaft construction, and the dynamics of tire-road surface interactions.

Applied mechanics is also utilized in the design of a variety of devices for human use, including sports equipment, kitchen utensils, and other devices that help generate movement. Private corporations may employ mechanics specialists to work with engineers on the design of more ergonomic devices or to evaluate designs for mechanical efficiency. In this regard, mechanics specialists work closely with specialists in mechanical and electrical engineering and those who specialize in human-factors

Occupation	Mechanical engineering technicians
Employment 2010	44,900
Projected Employment 2020	46,700
Change in Number (2010–20)	1,800
Percent Change	4%

Bureau of Labor Statistics, 2012

research, helping to apply the principles of physics and engineering to enhance human capabilities.

Social Context and Future Prospects

Classical and applied mechanics are fundamental to the modern scientific understanding of the world. In modern science, mechanics specialists rarely concentrate solely on classical mechanics, tending instead to specialize in one or more subfields. Because mechanics is applicable to a wide variety of scientific fields and engineering projects, research into basic mechanics still plays an important role in technological development and research.

Modern research in physics often falls into the category referred to as *multiphysics*, which is the application of methods or models from multiple disciplines to create models of complex phenomena. The theoretical and practical innovations of classical mechanics research are being combined with other forms of scientific inquiry and other models of physics to create innovative research techniques. The future of applied physics lies partially in the modern blending of theoretical models.

A relatively recent development in physics research involves the investigation of nonlinear dynamic systems, sometimes called chaotic systems. Such systems appear random in behavior but can be analyzed using complex models and equations that account for subtle variables in initial conditions and track how changes in these variables lead to overall system-wide behaviors. The principles of classical mechanics are essential to the modern understanding of chaotic-systems behavior and help scientists to devise methods used to model complex systems for enhanced predictability. Examples of chaotic systems found in nature include atmospheric gas flow, population dynamics of organisms, and the activity of the brain.

Further Reading

Finn, John Michael. *Classical Mechanics*. Sudbury: Jones, 2009. Comprehensive introduction to the study of classical and applied mechanics, suitable for advanced students of physics and mathematics. Contains sections on statistical dynamics and fluid mechanics.

Kibble, Tom W. B., and Frank H. Berkshire. *Classical Mechanics.* 5th ed. River Edge: World Scientific, 2004. Detailed overview of classical mechanics that introduces Newton's laws of motion, relativity theory, and basic types of motion, with information regarding applications to biology and engineering.

McCall, Martin. *Classical Mechanics: From Newton to Einstein; A Modern Introduction*. New York: Wiley, 2011. Written for undergraduate students of the physical sciences. Presents the history and basic principles of classical mechanics, including applied mechanics research, plus the basics of relativity theory as it applies to celestial mechanics.

Morin, David. *Introduction to Classical Mechanics: With Problems and Solutions*. New York: Cambridge UP, 2008. Introductory text to mechanics written for undergraduate students that provides a guide to solving and interpreting differential equations for classical mechanics problems.

Phillips, Anthony C. *Introduction to Quantum Mechanics* New York: Wiley, 2003. Basic introduction to quantum mechanics that discusses the types of problems researched by quantum-mechanics specialists and discusses the theoretical implications of quantum theory.

About the Author: Micah L. Issitt, BS, is a professional freelance writer and journalist specializing in writing on the life sciences and sociology. He has written numerous articles covering environmental sciences and the history of environmental science in the United States.

Mechanical Engineer 🖋

Earnings (Yearly Median): $99,150 (American Society of Mechanical Engineers, 2012)

Employment and Outlook: Slower than average (Bureau of Labor Statistics, 2012)

O*NET-SOC Code: 17-2141.00

Related Career Clusters: Architecture & Construction; Business, Management & Administration; Manufacturing, Transportation, Distribution & Logistics

Scope of Work

Mechanical engineering is a field of engineering concerned with the design, production, and use of tools and machines, as well as the generation of heat and mechanical power from such devices. Mechanical engineers make use of engineering principles and theoretical equations in the design of machines and tools. They often work in multidisciplinary teams to explore and understand engineering problems that have an impact on a global scale. Engineers may create machines, components, or other devices for use in power generation and manufacturing, among other industries. In addition to creating tools and machines for industrial or scientific use, some mechanical engineers have made key contributions to the design of various vehicles, from aircraft and spacecraft to ships and submarines.

Education and Coursework

At the high-school level, students interested in entering the field of mechanical engineering should study physics and chemistry. Students can gain additional practical experience in these subjects through participation in science-focused extracurricular activities and clubs. Other essential areas of study include mathematics, computer science, writing, and public speaking. Courses in engineering principles,

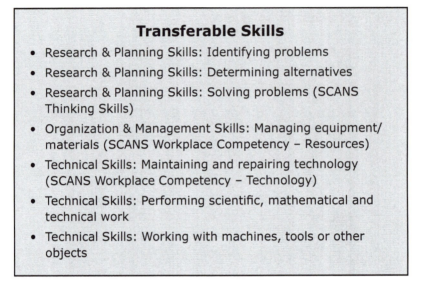

Transferable Skills

- Research & Planning Skills: Identifying problems
- Research & Planning Skills: Determining alternatives
- Research & Planning Skills: Solving problems (SCANS Thinking Skills)
- Organization & Management Skills: Managing equipment/materials (SCANS Workplace Competency – Resources)
- Technical Skills: Maintaining and repairing technology (SCANS Workplace Competency – Technology)
- Technical Skills: Performing scientific, mathematical and technical work
- Technical Skills: Working with machines, tools or other objects

drafting, and industrial design, when available, also provide students with valuable skills.

A bachelor's degree in mechanical engineering is the general requirement for entry into the field, and degree programs accredited by the Accreditation Board for Engineering and Technology (ABET) are preferred. A typical program of study includes course work in mechanics, engineering design, dynamics, and thermodynamics. Classes in fluid mechanics, transfer processes, and electronics and instrumentation may also be required. Electives may include classes in vehicle dynamics, production management, computer-aided design (CAD), and microelectromechanical systems.

A master's degree in mechanical engineering provides the opportunity for additional course work in an area of specialization and will typically qualify a candidate to hold a more advanced technical position. A master's of business administration or engineering management degree may be useful for engineers pursuing management positions. Those who wish to attain a mechanical-engineering faculty or research position must obtain a doctorate, often preceded by a master's degree in a research-oriented field.

Career Enhancement and Training

Licensure as a professional engineer is a requirement for many positions in mechanical engineering. In the United States, a graduate from an ABET-accredited program can take the Fundamentals of Engineering exam and become an engineer in training. After working under the supervision of a professional engineer for a set number of years (the exact number is determined by the candidate's state of residence), the candidate is eligible to take the Principles and Practice of Engineering exam. Passing the exam entitles the candidate to become a licensed professional engineer.

A number of professional associations and societies offer training and networking opportunities for mechanical engineers, including the American Society of Mechanical Engineers (ASME), the National Society of Professional Engineers (NSPE), and the Society of Naval Architects and Marine Engineers (SNAME). Each of these organizations offers training opportunities, workshops, and conferences. In addition to national conferences, these organizations host regional events that provide excellent networking opportunities, as they give members a chance to meet other professionals in their area and discuss shared concerns and interests.

ASME is an international organization with members in more than 150 countries. Its mission is to provide resources for engineers worldwide, including training and professional-development opportunities. The organization carries out research, sets codes and standards for work in the field, and publishes the award-winning magazine *Mechanical Engineering*, as well as several newsletters. ASME also maintains an online knowledge base with articles on industries, disciplines, career development, and other topics of interest to mechanical engineers. ASME is affiliated with a number of nonprofit service organizations, including Engineers without Borders, that provide opportunities for engineers to volunteer their time and skills. Student memberships in ASME are available to undergraduates and graduate students enrolled in approved engineering programs.

Daily Tasks and Technology

Mechanical engineers are responsible for the design, construction, and testing of machines, tools, and mechanical products and systems. Typical daily tasks for a mechanical engineer will depend upon the industry in which he or she is employed. Some engineers work primarily in office environments, where they develop and design machines or parts of machines that are then constructed elsewhere. They may complete this work independently or as part of a team. For instance, a mechanical engineer may be part of a multidisciplinary team responsible for the design of a new type of landing gear for an airplane. In such a case, the engineer may be involved in team meetings as the design is finalized and a prototype is created and may oversee the testing of the prototype to ensure that it meets expectations. Some of the design and testing may be carried out using computer software, so familiarity with CAD and computational fluid dynamics software may be necessary.

Not all of a mechanical engineer's work is done in an office. Some engineers may take a more active role in the construction and testing of a device and therefore may be required to work primarily in a workshop or testing site. Regardless of work environment or industry of employment, a mechanical engineer's priority is the integrity of the machine, tool, or mechanical system and its ability to meet the specifications under a variety of circumstances.

Earnings and Employment Outlook

While the US Bureau of Labor Statistics has predicted that employment in the field will experience slower-than-average growth between 2010 and 2020, mechanical engineering positions offer very competitive starting salaries. According to a salary survey conducted by the National Association of Colleges and Employers (NACE) in 2011, the field of mechanical engineering is one of the highest-paying fields for college graduates. A salary survey published by ASME in 2012 displayed similar results.

While the US Bureau of Labor Statistics has predicted that employment in the field will experience slower-than-average growth between 2010 and 2020, mechanical engineering positions offer very competitive starting salaries.

Within the field, salaries vary greatly based on a number of factors, most notably level of education. Engineers with advanced degrees make significantly more on average than those with bachelor's degrees and, in some cases, earn higher salaries than holders of bachelor's degrees with more years of work experience. The majority of individuals employed in the field hold degrees in engineering; however, those with degrees in other disciplines, such as business administration, earned more on average. Geographic location also affects average salaries. According to ASME, engineers in the Pacific Southwest earned the highest median salary, while those in the states of Idaho, Montana, and Wyoming earned the lowest. A significant salary gap exists between male and female engineers, with women earning only 80 percent of what men earn on average. However, experts predict that this gap will continue to narrow as more women enter the field.

Related Occupations

- **Civil Engineers:** Civil engineers design, construct, and maintain roads, bridges, buildings, and other structures. They often work on projects related to the infrastructure of a community, and some civil engineers are involved in projects that include water resource management.

- **Structural Engineers:** Structural engineers analyze and design structures and are responsible for both the individual structural elements of a building, such as beams and columns, and the structural integrity of the entire building.

A Conversation with Sarah McElrath

*Job Title: Senior Mechanical Associate,
Nuclear Power Technologies*

What was your career path?

My career path started while I was in college and I interned at a nuclear power plant. After I graduated with a degree in mechanical engineering, I went to work full time at the plant as a thermal performance engineer in the Systems Plant Engineering Group. During this time I attended graduate school part-time and received my master's degree in mechanical engineering with a focus in thermal sciences. I had been working at the plant about four years when I got a job as a design engineer for an engineering firm. The group I am in specializes in nuclear power and I currently do design changes for two nuclear power plants in New Jersey. My former experience as a thermal performance engineer helps in this role because it gave me a broad view of the overall plant operation while touching on individual plant equipment and performance. An example of this is the feedwater heaters. As a thermal performance engineer I was responsible for monitoring performance, and now as a design engineer I am currently the responsible engineer for a project to replace the feedwater heaters at a plant now. My former experience helps me to have a practical perspective for the job I am trying to do now and gives me insight as to how the end user might want the heater to perform.

What are three pieces of advice you would offer someone interested in your profession?

1. The first piece of advice is to have an open mind. When I was in college I had no idea what career path I would like to take. I met a recruiter for the nuclear plant at a job fair and interviewed for the intern position. I grew up near a nuclear plant and never considered that as a career option. I found out through my internship that the industry was very interesting and I enjoyed the power generation technology and how it offers an opportunity to continue to learn things every day.

2. The second piece of advice is to find something that you enjoy. It is nice to get a paycheck but it means so much more to be contributing to an industry and profession that I care about.

3. The third piece of advice is to have a learning attitude every day. I continue to challenge myself with new projects and try to diversify my experiences. Even though I am done with school I am open to learning and the more diversified experience you have the more opportunities that may open up in the future.

What paths for career advancement are available to you?

In both working at a utility and at an engineering firm there are two main paths available for people with an engineering background: technical and management. You can continue to gain technical experience and advance through this career path. You could become a subject matter expert on a piece of equipment for example or a consultant that may provide advice to power plants trying to solve a difficult issue. The second career path is management. Following this career path puts you in a position of managing groups of people or even advancing to a position like plant manager, responsible for the entire plant. I have been working about six years and people around my age typically decide what track they would like to follow.

- **Aeronautical Engineers:** Aeronautical engineers design and test aircraft, which can include commercial passenger aircraft, military planes and pilotless craft, and experimental aircraft used for scientific research.

- **Astronautical Engineers:** Astronautical engineers design satellites, probes, rovers, and earth-orbiting space systems for government and private organizations.

- **Manufacturing Engineers:** Manufacturing engineers work in all aspects of the manufacturing process, designing production and assembly methods and tools.

Future Applications

As technology continues to advance in nearly every area, mechanical engineers will likely be needed to develop new ways of building and working with machines. The increasing interest in nanotechnology—technology featuring very small components or systems that can be measured in nanometers—is expected to provide numerous new opportunities for mechanical engineers. With the introduction of very small materials and components, mechanical engineers will be needed to modify existing mechanical designs and incorporate such materials into them, as well as design new technology. For example, mechanical engineers may work to miniaturize the internal components of automobiles, allowing for the manufacture of smaller, more fuel-efficient and environmentally friendly vehicles. Similarly, they may improve the design of aircraft to reduce the size of their components and make them more aerodynamic. The introduction of smaller components and the resulting economies that go with the smaller scale will require the development of new design paradigms. Mechanical engineers will play a crucial role in creating those paradigms and setting the standards for new technology.

—Gina Hagler

More Information

American Society of Mechanical Engineers
3 Park Avenue
New York, NY 10016
www.asme.org

National Society of Professional Engineers
1420 King Street
Alexandria, VA 22314
www.nspe.org

The Society of Naval Architects and Marine Engineers
601 Pavonia Avenue
Jersey City, NJ 07306
www.sname.org

Condensed Matter Physics

FIELDS OF STUDY

Band engineering; biological physics; crystallography; electromagnetism; magnetism; molecular networks; nanoscience; nanotechnology; quantum information; quantum kinetics; quantum mechanics; quantum optics; quantum states of matter; particle physics; semiconductor physics; solid state physics; soft condensed matter physics; statistical mechanics; statistical physics; superconductivity and superfluidity; ultrafast optics.

DEFINITION

The condensed state of matter includes liquids and solids. Laboratory-grown crystals dominate the field of condensed matter physics, and powerful tools for examining their atomic structures are available. Out of the periodic table's more than one hundred elements, there are about 10^8 potential compounds. Some combination crystals have properties such as superconductivity at high temperature, special magnetism, or thermoelectric capability. The binding and structure of these new materials falls generally into lattices, superlattices, nanowires, and quantum dots. One-dimensional matter has been put to practical use, and two-dimensional systems are being fabricated worldwide.

Basic Principles

From the time of Sir Isaac Newton until the second half of the nineteenth century, knowledge of condensed matter was complete on a macroscopic scale. Scientists understood elasticity, hydrodynamics, and thermodynamics as these concepts applied to elements found in nature. Then, in 1916, a Polish metallurgist and chemist, Jan Czochralski, made a discovery about crystals. He was melting some tin and taking notes on crystallization. He had at his elbow an inkwell and a crucible of melted tin for the experiment, and he mistakenly dipped his pen into the melted tin. Drawing out his pen, he saw that a thin thread of metal came with it. He found the thread was a single crystal. It marked the beginning of the process of growing crystals artificially. At the beginning of this process, elements from the periodic table were used, but scientists soon used combinations of those elements, leading to "designer" crystals of paired and grouped atomic elements. In the twenty-first century, scientists have begun to investigate crystalline solids not found in nature. Growing crystals from diverse elements has opened the door to the creation of new materials.

At the end of the twentieth and the beginning of the twenty-first centuries, quantum mechanics introduced new theories; discoveries and research have been primarily at the micro- and nanoscales. The nanoscale is enabled by advances in technology that allow physicists to observe and manipulate matter at meters as small as 10^{-9} (a nanometer is one billionth of a meter). Since so much of modern condensed matter physics takes place at the nano scale, specialized equipment is necessary for nanoscale research. Mathematics, especially statistics, is as essential in condensed matter physics as it is in any branch of physics. However, in addition to mathematics, modern probing equipment has allowed for an explosion of information about condensed matter.

Core Concepts

Solidity. "Solidity" once meant hardness under pressure. Now it is understood that certain metals are indeed solid but also soft. In addition, types of solid glass behave more like liquids in a frozen state, melting slowly over decades. These discoveries are important to condensed matter physics because crystals are atomically regular. Many crystalline structures in condensed matter physics are described in terms of lattices, from one to several atoms thick. Such crystals are studied by the "unit cell," or single atomic structural unit, which can be measured and described in terms of vectors. Whether they occur in nature or are grown in the lab, crystalline structures are, by definition, atomically the same from point to point across an entire sample. Unlike in kinds of alkali or glass, in crystals, a given vector follows a lattice pattern through the same part of each atom across the sample, which is itself conceived of as two-dimensional. Nanowires and nanotubes are lab-grown, one or sometimes two atoms thick, and long enough to be measured in microns. Carbon is an especially interesting material for nanotubes, because its electrical conductivity could make nanostructures of carbon highly practical in electronic components.

Probing Technology—X-Ray. Modern physicists' power to conduct research into condensed matter has depended to some degree on the x-ray microscope, which uses x-ray beams to make visible objects as small as 30 nanometers (room for about 150 atoms). An image is created based on the absorption of the x-rays; darker spots show more absorption, lighter ones less, creating something like an old-fashioned black-and-white photograph, but with 3-D information. X-rays cause electrons to dissociate from the absorbing atom, giving off another x-ray, and with high enough resolution, the patterns of the emitted x-rays allow scientists to also determine chemical features of the material under study.

Probing Technology—Light Scattering. On biological samples, the x-ray must be less penetrating than it can be on chemical samples because, at high resolutions, it can harm living samples. This problem is partly solved by the light-scattering microscope. Being a field of electromagnetic nature, light is a force, and it scatters when it impacts very small material samples. With light-scattering probes, scientists are able to get accurate measurements of atomic-level phenomena. Both size and mass of sample material can be ascertained noninvasively.

Scattering light is a twofold methodology: Static light scattering, or Rayleigh scattering, measures the intensity of scattered light, inferring through angles the characteristics of the material; dynamic light scattering, also known as photon correlation spectroscopy, tracks fluctuations in scattered light, bringing molecular and atomic motion to light.

Probing Technology—Neutron. For some time, scientists have aimed neutron beams at objects. However, early in the twenty-first century, they discovered that neutron beams going through an object could be manipulated to form an image. Neutrons scatter when they collide with an object. Using an array of textured plates, or detectors, scientists catch the neutrons and convert them into photons. Then, optical technology creates electronic information, which can be read on computers. Like the light-scattering device, the neutron microscope promises new advances in biotechnology, as it allows scientists to peer into increasingly small samples of living tissue.

Electricity. Electric conductivity, or insularity, is the property of either allowing or resisting electric flow and is of prime interest to condensed matter physicists. Solid state physics, a relatively old branch of condensed matter physics, studies transistors and applies condensed matter studies to semiconductors. An electron's motion is associated with a corresponding "hole" in the solid. A semiconductor, which both conducts and resists electricity, can be described as a substance in which the holes and electrons are moving in a highly activated manner.

Some natural elements, such as silicon, diamond, and germanium, are semiconductors. Silicon is important because its semiconductivity allows it to perform the binary operations that are the basis of computing. In recent research, physicists were surprised to find that iron, not naturally a conductive metal, is superconductive at super high temperatures. Because iron is a magnetic material and magnetism is a field all its own, the fact that iron is superconductive has excited scientists and has become an emerging area of research. The long-range aim of most research is the search for overarching principles that can be applied universally, creating broad new platforms for further development, which is the case with iron conductivity.

Theory of Energy Bands. Electrons are important for condensed matter physics because condensed matter is explored at the atomic level. In a carbon nanowire, for example, electrons have one-dimensional movements. They can go only up or down the wire because it is so narrow. The motion of electrons, and the energy in play, has led to the discovery of energy bands, which are signature forces for different kinds of material. Energy bands could be likened to bar codes, the black stripes representing "allowed" energy and the white stripes "forbidden" energy. Energy bands can be measured either in a particle accelerator or by photoemission. The structure of bands is used to understand properties of physical material. Bands also have promising practical applications in nanotechnology and electromagnetism. Band

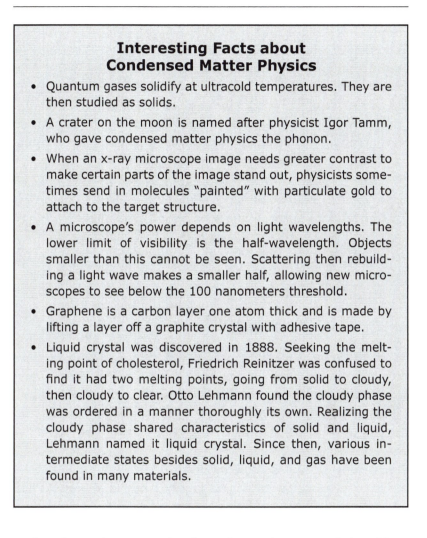

**Interesting Facts about
Condensed Matter Physics**

- Quantum gases solidify at ultracold temperatures. They are then studied as solids.

- A crater on the moon is named after physicist Igor Tamm, who gave condensed matter physics the phonon.

- When an x-ray microscope image needs greater contrast to make certain parts of the image stand out, physicists sometimes send in molecules "painted" with particulate gold to attach to the target structure.

- A microscope's power depends on light wavelengths. The lower limit of visibility is the half-wavelength. Objects smaller than this cannot be seen. Scattering then rebuilding a light wave makes a smaller half, allowing new microscopes to see below the 100 nanometers threshold.

- Graphene is a carbon layer one atom thick and is made by lifting a layer off a graphite crystal with adhesive tape.

- Liquid crystal was discovered in 1888. Seeking the melting point of cholesterol, Friedrich Reinitzer was confused to find it had two melting points, going from solid to cloudy, then cloudy to clear. Otto Lehmann found the cloudy phase was ordered in a manner thoroughly its own. Realizing the cloudy phase shared characteristics of solid and liquid, Lehmann named it liquid crystal. Since then, various intermediate states besides solid, liquid, and gas have been found in many materials.

engineering seeks to create band gaps in certain patterns; being able to do so would allow scientists to control the frequencies of electromagnetism radiating from the substance.

Phonons. The phonon, introduced by Igor Tamm, who won the 1958 Nobel Prize in Physics, is the phenomenon of excited ions vibrating together. Condensed matter physicists calculate the amplitude of phonons using quantum mechanics. Phonon frequencies are also measured by means of Newton's laws of motion. The word "phonon" has the same Greek root as the English word "phone" because sound arises from phonons with long wavelengths. In acoustic phonons, waves are created by all the movement going in the same direction. When excited ions move in opposite directions, they are called optical phonons. They are called optical because infrared light rays impel the phonon.

Acoustic phonon vibrations transfer heat (unless the material is an insulating crystal), and, thus, are important to the thermal systems industry. Because they are used so much in computing and have issues with excess heat, semiconductors, in particular, stand to benefit from further phonon engineering. In an example of ongoing research, a company in North Carolina has tried to use a thin film's phonons to transform excess heat from industrial activity into power-grid-type electricity. The same technology also handles unneeded heat in a process called thermoelectric cooling, which has refrigeration applicability. However, neither process is efficient enough for widespread use as of 2012.

Applications Past and Present

Nanofabrication. In 1925, Percy Bridgman discovered a way to grow large crystals by packing a tube with the desired material then moving the apparatus through a heated area very slowly, melting it directionally and allowing material to recrystallize. Bridgman's method allowed scientists to grow a single crystal of significant size (as opposed to the thin wires discovered by Czochralski). In the early twenty-first century, research emphasis has been on nanocrystals. Growing crystals at the nanoscale was a practice first mastered at Cornell and has since spread to many other universities, including the University of Houston, Stanford, and Penn State. Students and professors explore new materials for valuable properties, including superconductivity, thermodynamic properties, magnetoresistance, and optical characteristics.

In the lab, it is common to grow superlattices, which are essentially crystalline lattices a few atoms thick stacked atop one another. Generally the electrons are sandwiched in one layer, so their movement is one-dimensional within that layer. At Louisiana State University, academics predict nanofabrication will become a trillion-dollar industry by around 2035. Such a vibrant industry could have applications in computers, vaccines, and new materials for everyday products. This growing industry will call for two million trained scientists to fabricate new materials. While the field is international, Germany has one of the larger footprints, with both academic and industrial ties to the United States.

Liquid Crystal Display. The liquid crystal display (LCD) became commercially relevant in the last decades of the twentieth century. Liquid crystals are unique in that their atoms are partly organized and go through two phases, between liquid and solid. Molecules in liquid crystals tend to be shaped in ways that allow them to line up. Molecular rods in a liquid crystal line up similarly to boats in a harbor tied at anchor, which will tend to all point the same way, depending on the current or tide. This phase of liquid crystals is called "smectic" and is close to the solid phase. Characteristically, the smectic phase traps free-floating crystal pieces in layers. In the nematic phase, liquid crystals arrange themselves in a twisted pattern. This phase is similar to the liquid phase, in which molecules float freely; however nematic-phase liquid crystal molecules still float in a pattern. In both phases, the order of the molecules can be mechanically manipulated, or controlled by magnetic forces or electricity.

At a certain point in the nematic phase, the molecules shine brightly in many colors, creating the basic element of the pixel, a tiny liquid crystal package that can emit light. Arrays of pixels made to form images first became commercially available in watches and clocks in the 1970s. In the 1980s, the pocket calculator with an LCD display became standard equipment for students. Computer and television screens are commonly made with LCD technology today.

Both liquid crystals and incommensurate crystals (also called quasicrystals) arrange themselves. In a crystal, atoms repeat their lattices precisely for as far as they go, an action known as "translational periodicity." In gases, atoms float randomly, but in liquids they are arranged loosely; in quasicrystals, the usual crystalline lattice is present but holds its translational periodicity in all but one or perhaps a few directions (if it is a complex lattice). Therefore, a quasicrystal is perfectly precise except for a hidden wobble.

Graphene. Graphene is made by applying adhesive tape to a graphite crystal. When the tape is removed, it takes one or two atomic layers of graphite with it. After the tape is dissolved, the graphite's hexagonal structure translates into a two-dimensional layer of single carbon atoms, producing promising properties. One such property is a high degree of responsiveness to electric current. Thus, graphene makes a good transistor, one that is more efficient and faster than one made of silicon. An electron beam can cut graphene into one-dimensional lengths. If an end is lopped off, a quantum dot (nanocrystal) remains. Graphene has excellent conductive capability for both electricity and heat. Electricity and heat are fundamental powers in the world; therefore, any substance able to conduct them attracts significant attention from scientists. Because a great deal of thermal force is needed to melt graphene, and because graphene is one of the strongest materials known, the material has practical technological applications. For example, thin foil sheets of graphene are used in iPhones.

Biomedicine. In the film *The Fantastic Voyage* (1966), a craft and crew are shrunk to the size of a cell and injected into a human being on a mission to zap a tumor with ray guns. The fantasy of being able to manipulate things inside the human body on a micro scale has become reality with biomedical applications of condensed matter physics, including nanoscience. Though still in their infancy, biomedical applications are highly promising. At Cornell, scientists began their biomedical experiments with condensed matter needing information from trauma sites in the soft tissue of the liver and abdomen. Biological substances already in place in the body were developed into a logic system that would read digitally: 0 for no injury, 1 for injury. The reactions of enzymes were filtered to provide an optical signal.

Inside human bodies, the magnetism of nanoparticles responds to magnetic forces from outside the body, such as those from magnetic resonance imaging (MRI) equipment. In addition, the nanoparticles can be directed inside the body by an outside magnetic field, much the way iron filings are drawn around by magnets in elementary experiments. Furthermore, certain manipulations of the external field will cause nanoparticles with magnetic properties to heat up inside the body. Thus, there is a potential for aiming such particles at tumors for thermal treatment.

Condensed matter studies apply to biological implants, too. New materials mean possible improvements in such things as artificial joints, which, like any manufactured item, show wear and tear as time passes. Diamond surfaces and other "superhard" coatings are the subject of current research. "Superthin" coatings are possible with condensed matter. Implants include more than artificial joints. Some implants are being built as diagnostic or transmission devices, while other implants include structures with porosity that could aid tissue regeneration.

National Security. The US Intelligence Community is a network of sixteen agencies with a collective aim to protect the United States while employing a high level of secrecy. The Intelligence Advanced Research Projects Activity (IARPA) places a strong emphasis on carbon nanotube technology (CNT). Because of their size, nanodevices are especially promising to the intelligence community, where avoiding detection is extremely important. CNT is the subject of IARPA research in electronics. CNT could become so integral to computer and other electronic devices that memory, logic, and transistors may be interchangeable to some extent with standard silicon materials.

Impact on Industry

Government Agencies. Numerous government entities participate in condensed matter research. The US Department of Energy has supported nanofabrication at LSU through a $12.5 million grant. The Department of Energy's focus is on green-energy applications of catalytic materials, and it partners with the National Institutes of Health (NIH) to conduct research into nanotechnology advances in MRI for cancer cells. The Brookhaven National Laboratory, on Long Island, New York, is the center for research into many aspects of condensed matter, including the study of problems arising at boundary areas between two kinds of matter. Some molecular surface films organize themselves in patterns between solid and liquid, moving from a "lying down" phase to a "standing up" phase with increased layering. Some materials exhibit a property in which a very thin layer, measured in molecules, can freeze, while the remaining mass does not. The reason for this phenomenon is unknown. Brookhaven scientists have combined experimentation with theoretical breakthroughs in an attempt

Occupation	Physicists
Employment 2010	18,300
Projected Employment 2020	20,900
Change in Number (2010–20)	2,600
Percent Change	14%

Bureau of Labor Statistics, 2012

to crack the code. They were among very first to employ the procedure of scattering neutrons that enable neutron microscopy to probe ever-smaller imaging. Research at Brookhaven also includes soft condensed matter as it applies to the electronics field and advanced biomaterials.

Military. The US military stands to benefit from research done by IARPA, which is patterned on the design of the Defense Advanced Research Projects Agency (DARPA). IARPA's interest in structural uses for threads made from CNT has military potential. CNT threads, and the yarns into which they can be twisted, form the basic structure of certain kinds of wires, which conduct electricity. These wires can weigh as little as 20 percent as much as their copper counterparts, making them highly desirable in the communications field, for example. At the same time, their conductivity can be quicker and more reliable than copper wires.

An equally important use for CNT yarns is the fabrication of panels for body and vehicle armor. Because of their superior strength, CNT-based or -enriched armor promises to save lives and equipment.

University Research and Teaching. The aim of science, some say, is to provide a field theory that will explain "everything" in the same or similar terms. In physics, for example, electromagnetism and gravity are two different forces; a field theory would find the math for making the two translatable to each other. In condensed matter physics, materials are described in terms of their symmetries. Symmetry is a complicated concept in physics; in oversimplified terms, it refers to those things that do not change when something else does. A classic example is a reflection. The reflected object changes position by showing up in the mirror, but its properties remain the same. Another example is a sphere spun on its axis. It moves, but always looks like a circle. Though the concept might sound simple, it is mathematically involved and worth further study, as researchers believe it may hold the key to a possible field connection between condensed matter physics and the physics of particles. Because of the trend in research toward a universal view of each discipline's place in science, condensed matter physics even has links to cosmology, for example.

Many universities that have the equipment and personnel to study new materials also have theoretical and computational strengths necessary in the field of condensed matter physics. However, experimentation is the heart of the field. For example, in the case of graphene, scientists have considered levitating it to further test its properties, because at this scale of matter the substrate on which it rests tends to slant test results.

There are many opportunities for advanced students of condensed matter physics to pursue academic careers, and the need for strong research, communications, and leadership skills will persist. Also likely to continue is the opportunity for future scientists to work closely with scientists in places such as the Center for Nanophysics and Advanced Materials.

Social Context and Future Prospects

While graphene is already in transistors, it has fascinating future possibilities. It can detect a solitary molecule of gas; thus, gas-sensing devices can be made from graphene. It is very strong, yet netlike in its structure, so it could be used as a support material for other substances under study in electron microscopy, much the way glass slides have been used in conventional microscopes for centuries. In the future, perhaps graphene can be the "slide" for nanoparticles, quantum dots, and microsized samples. Furthermore, in many kinds of nanotubes, those made of carbon are nothing more than rolled graphene, so the strength of graphene translates into tubular wire. This structural strength is complemented by extreme resistance to some strong chemicals, such as hydrofluoric acid. Eventually, graphene coatings a few atoms thick may be able to protect devices in harsh environments.

Many universities are invested in the future of condensed matter physics and its applications. Researchers at Cornell have studied the growth of nanowires on substrate material, a theoretical and practical area that will affect the evolution of computer chips. Cornell students and faculty have also been involved in the computational angle of this growing field. Computers are essential to studying condensed matter physics, and as better algorithms are developed and software becomes more sophisticated, researchers worldwide will benefit.

Academic institutions advance biotechnology also, through departmental research and education. At Wayne State University, for example, scientists are trying to load drugs onto nanoparticles, especially nanoparticles with magnetic properties. If they succeed, a new kind of drug therapy will be possible, because the magnetism of certain nanoparticles will provide physicians with an ability to direct medications to specific sites within the body. Researchers worldwide have held conferences on problems in soft condensed matter because the field is so promising. Scientists, academics, and industrialists envision a new paradigm for drug delivery with strong medical, chemical, and commercial potential.

Further Reading

Chaikin, P. M., and T. C. Lubensky. *Principles of Condensed Matter Physics*. New York: Cambridge UP, 2000. Print. Requires a basic understanding of statistical and quantum mechanics. Outlines the tenets of condensed matter physics, covering conservations laws and symmetries.

"Condensed Matter News." *Phys.org*. Phys.org, 2012. Web. 26 Sept. 2012. Online magazine of condensed matter studies that offers articles for students, interested lay readers, and professionals.

Marder, Michael P. *Condensed Matter Physics*. New York: Wiley, 2000. Modernization of a classic text by Neil W. Ashcroft and N. David Merman. Print. Solid-state physics, bands, magnetism, and quantum theory are among the older parts of the field still covered by Marder. Expands areas of soft condensed matter, surfaces, optics, and more.

About the Author: Amanda R. Jones has an MA from Virginia Tech and a PhD in English from the University of Virginia. She has written several articles for EBSCO Publishing and has published in the Children's Literature Association Quarterly.

Accelerator Physicist

Earnings (Yearly Average): $105,430 (Bureau of Labor, 2012)

Employment and Outlook: About as fast as average (Bureau of Labor, 2012)

O*NET-SOC Code: 19-2012.00

Related Career Clusters: Government & Public Administration; Health Science; Manufacturing; Transportation, Distribution & Logistics

Scope of Work

Accelerator physicists work in laboratories, private companies, research institutions, and for the federal government. Accelerator physicists design and conduct experiments with particle accelerators, devices that use electromagnetic fields to accelerate particles in a vacuum. In large accelerators, these particles are accelerated to a velocity near the speed of light and are sustained in beams that collide with other moving particles. Accelerator physicists analyze the collisions of these subatomic particles and uncover valuable information about the subatomic world: the makeup of matter, the structure and behavior of an atom's nucleus, and the discovery of new elements.

Accelerator physicists also use particle accelerators to simulate the creation of the universe—a process commonly known as the big bang—via the high velocity collision of molecules. From these findings, accelerator physicists are able to uncover further insights into the structure and genesis of the universe. However, only a small number of the world's particle accelerators are used for studying particle physics. More than one-third of accelerators are used as important tools in the medical industry for cancer imaging and therapy. Accelerators are also used for pharmaceutical research, nuclear energy, and national security purposes.

Education and Coursework

Accelerator physicists need PhDs to work in research positions for the government, universities, and other institutions. Bachelor's or master's degrees, in other words, will not qualify individuals for research positions in physics, but they will qualify them for assistant and technician positions (bachelor's) and developmental positions (master's) in a laboratory. For some employers, an applicant with a master's degree in physics with ten or more years of professional experience may qualify for a research position; however, a PhD is strongly preferred.

PhD programs in physics take five to seven years to complete. In addition to spending four years as undergraduate students, many PhD candidates also hold master's degrees in physics or a related field, such as astronomy or engineering. PhD programs in physics are highly competitive, and candidates must have excellent academic records and laboratory experience in academic settings or professional internships. The physics PhD program at Stanford University, for example, receives more than five hundred applications every year and only admits sixty students. In addition to high grade point averages and professional experience, applicants must score high on the GRE and the subject test in physics (PGRE).

To succeed in intensive PhD programs and as professional accelerator physicists, candidates must have superior mathematical, analytical, problem-solving, interpersonal, and critical-thinking skills. Coursework includes advanced classes in math and science—calculus, quantum chemistry and mechanics, theoretical physics, statistics, and thermodynamics. Computer lab courses are also required to develop skills in specialized software used to analyze the results of experiments.

PhDs culminate in dissertations, extensive theses that make new contributions to the physics field. After completing their dissertations and earning their doctorate degrees, accelerator physicists are obligated to pursue postdoctoral research. Postdoctoral positions offer recent PhDs the chance to gain experience in professional research labs. During postdoctoral research, physicists work under the supervision of senior physicists for approximately two to three years.

Transferable Skills

- Communication Skills—Speaking effectively (SCANS Basic Skill)
- Interpersonal/Social Skills—Working as a member of a team (SCANS Workplace Competency – Interpersonal)
- Research & Planning Skills—Solving problems (SCANS Thinking Skills)
- Organization & Management Skills—Managing equipment/materials (SCANS Workplace Competency – Resources)
- Technical Skills—Using technology to process information (SCANS Workplace Competency – Information)
- Work Environment Skills—Working in a laboratory setting

Career Enhancement and Training

Accelerator physicists need PhDs and postdoctoral experience to qualify for research positions, but they do not need to be licensed. If accelerator physicists are employed by the US government, they need to be US citizens and have a high-security clearance—if they are involved in researching nuclear or military weapons, for example—that allows them access to confidential military information.

Cornell University is home to the Cornell Electron Storage Ring (CESR), a world-class particle accelerator that has made Cornell world renowned for its accelerator-physics program. In this program, students have the opportunity to gain hands-on experience working with a particle accelerator. This valuable facility makes Cornell's program not only one of the largest of its kind but also offers first-class training for future accelerator physicists. Another high-energy accelerator is the Stanford Linear Accelerator Center (SLAC), a national laboratory in California.

The European Organization for Nuclear Research (CERN) is home to the Large Hadron Collider (LHC), the largest particle accelerator in the world. In addition to being one of the birthplaces of the Internet, this laboratory is heavily involved in international research and training. CERN employs more than two thousand personnel and is a world-renowned laboratory in the physics world—hosting more than ten thousand scientists and students from more than six hundred universities. More than half of the world's physicists involved in particle accelerators have visited CERN. Training in a facility such as CERN is valuable experience for students on the path to becoming accelerator physicists, and visiting the facility is the ideal opportunity to network at the world's largest physics laboratory.

Another organization for physicists from all disciplines is the American Physical Society (APS). This organization is not as large as CERN, but it connects more than fifty thousand physics professionals on an international platform. The APS is known for hosting programs and exhibitions that promote collaboration among researchers, educators, and scientists. This organization is a valuable resource for future physicists and offers a one-year free trial membership to undergraduate and graduate students. Joining APS as an undergraduate or graduate student will expose individuals to current innovations in the physics industry, connect them with working professionals, and ultimately augment their resume. Being a member of APS, or any professional organization for that matter, shows an employer or a university admissions committee both commitment and dedication to the field.

Daily Tasks and Technology

Accelerator physicists are primarily involved in conducting research and experiments. Laboratory experiments with large particle accelerators conducted by accelerator physicists are central to the understanding of the universe and matter at its most fundamental level. However, accelerator physicists are also involved in the design and production of thousands of smaller accelerators used in the medical industry to diagnose and treat cancer and other illnesses. Moreover, small accelerators are involved in materials research, manufacturing, and homeland security.

Large particle accelerators work by accelerating and colliding charged particles—electrons, protons, and other subatomic particles—at a velocity close to the speed of light. There are two types of particle accelerators: linear and circular. In linear accelerators, a beam is sent through the mechanism only once. Circular accelerators, on the other hand, use magnets to bend the beam, allowing it to move continuously in a circular motion. A linear accelerator uses a fixed location and fires a particle beam at this target. In a circular accelerator, two beams are accelerated at high speeds and collided.

Linear accelerators are used in medicine to treat and diagnose cancer. They do so via positron-emission tomography (PET), a nuclear imaging technique. They are also used to target cancerous tumors by firing a beam of radiation at malignant tumors. The precision of this radiation treatment decreases the chance of damaging surrounding tissues and organs.

The US military uses accelerators to scan for bombs in chemicals and cargo. The accelerators are also used in ships for antimissile detection and in nuclear plants to monitor tests of nuclear weapons. Other applications and technology include the Accélérateur Grand Louvre d'Analyse Elémentaire (better known as AGLAE), an accelerator used in the Louvre to study works of art. Accelerators are also used for ion implantation, in which ions are accelerated and implanted into electronic devices to increase their conductivity and efficiency, thereby decreasing overall cost.

Earnings and Employment Outlook

The demand for atomic and molecular physicists is expected to grow as fast as average through 2020. Scientists agree that accelerator physics is a vital discipline for the scientific community. Particle accelerators are not only being used to conduct research and reveal aspects of matter and the universe but also are being applied to medicine, manufacturing, and nuclear technology. A number of new high-powered accelerators are being developed, including the International Linear Collider (ILC). Fermilab, an organization under the US Department of Energy, has plans to develop large particle accelerators.

According to information accessed from physicsworld.com, in 2012, the average salary for an accelerator physicist with ten years of experience was $98,000. Entry-level salaries were approximately $51,000. Accelerator physicists at the high end of the scale—in the ninth and tenth percentile—earned a mean wage of $108,400. Overall, physicists ranked sixth for highest earning groups for college graduates, just behind economists and electrical engineers, with aerospace and chemical engineers earning the most.

Related Occupations

- **Electrical Engineers:** Electrical engineers design and produce electronic equipment, including broadcast systems and communication technology.

- **Physicists and Astronomers**: Physicists and astronomers develop technology and conduct research by studying the universe, space, and matter.

- **Chemists/Materials Scientists:** Chemists and materials scientists study the properties of chemical substances and develop new technology.

- **Mechanical Engineers:** Mechanical engineers design mechanical systems, such as machines and tools, with the use of physics and materials science.

- **Civil Engineers:** Civil engineers oversee the design and configuration of roads, bridges, and other large natural and physical construction projects.

Future Applications

The research conducted at CERN's Large Hadron Collider is constantly uncovering information on the origin of mass, dark matter, and other materials that compose the universe. The construction of additional particle accelerators, such as the International Linear Collider, will provide further insights into the creation of the universe as well as the structure and behavior of atoms. The Facility for Rare Isotope Beams is expected to develop an updated and larger version of the LHC.

In addition to research with large accelerators, smaller particle accelerators are being applied in a number of ways. The US Navy and Air Force, in collaboration with the Defense Advanced Research Projects Agency (DARPA), are funding the development of new weaponized lasers called free-electron lasers (FEL). The FEL will use a linear particle accelerator and a magnetic field to fire a beam of electrons at

A Conversation with Bob Zwaska

Job Title: Accelerator physicist

What was your career path?

I followed a typical academic path with a Bachelor of Science in physics and mathematics and a PhD in physics (taking six and a half years). My adviser was a High Energy Physics experimentalist, but he had an interest in instrumentation and particle accelerators, allowing me to enter that area. Out of graduate school I was able to directly enter a fellowship at a national laboratory that was a tenure-track position. I have since been at the same laboratory for seven years.

What are three pieces of advice you would offer someone interested in your profession?

Accelerator physics is a relatively high demand area in physics, but has a very small academic preparation community. Thus the challenge is to become appropriately trained—from there entering and persisting within the field is more straightforward. My suggestions are:

1. Choose a university that has some faculty members who practice accelerator physics at either a local or national laboratory.
2. Whether or not studying under an academic accelerator physicist, seek out formal training in accelerator physics at your university or through national and international accelerator schools.
3. Gain competency in many areas, including technology. Particle accelerators are large machines with many specialized components—only those with a broad perspective can truly design and operate them.

What paths for career advancement are available to you?

Particle accelerators are versatile tools used in basic and applied research. They exist at national labs, universities, and in industry. Most potential positions would be as a research scientist at those laboratories. In addition, the skills learned on these machines are transferable to other large science endeavors and the aerospace/defense industry. Finally, there are a small number of academic positions.

high power. The Office of Naval Research released the results of an experiment wherein a laser was capable of disarming a target from more than a mile away. However, the laser used in the experiment was only 15 kilowatts, whereas the free-electron laser will be close to 100 kilowatts in power. The US military expects to implement this weapon by 2020.

Another major obstacle for accelerator physicists is solving the energy crisis. Physicists and scientists are developing a nuclear reactor that uses a particle accelerator and thorium (a less expensive and safer alternative to uranium) to prevent nuclear accidents, decrease cost, and increase the efficiency of nuclear plants. New and improved nuclear plants, called accelerator-driven subcritical reactors, could be operational by 2030.

Cancer is the second leading cause of death in the United States, the first being heart disease. Beam therapy has revolutionized cancer treatment, and scientists continue to enhance existing technology to increase precision and efficiency. A proton-therapy system, for example, which uses a beam of protons to treat cancerous tissue, is a technology under development. Unlike other radiation beams, the proton beam will be more precise and cause less damage to surrounding tissue and organs.

—Daniel Castaldy

More Information

American Physical Society: Division of Physics Accelerators and Beams
One Physics Ellipse
College Park, MD 20740
www.aps.org

Argonne Accelerator Institute
9700 S. Class Avenue
Argonne, IL 60439
www.aai.anl.gov

European Organization for Nuclear Research (CERN)
CERN CH-1211
Geneva 23, Switzerland
www.public.web.cern.ch/public

Institute of Physics: Particle Accelerators and Beam Groups
John Adams Institute
Keble Road, Oxford 0X1 3RH
www.iop.org

SLAC National Accelerator Laboratory
2575 Sand Hill Road
Menlo Park, CA 94025
www.slac.stanford.edu

Cryogenics

FIELDS OF STUDY

Astrophysics; cryogenic engineering; cryogenic electronics; nuclear physics; cryosurgery; cryobiology; high-energy physics; mechanical engineering; chemical engineering; electrical engineering; cryotronics; materials science; biotechnology; medical engineering; astronomy.

DEFINITION

Cryogenics is the branch of physics concerned with the creation of extremely low temperatures. It involves the observation and interpretation of natural phenomena resulting from subjecting various substances to those temperatures. At temperatures near absolute zero, the electric, magnetic, and thermal properties of most substances are greatly altered, allowing for useful industrial, automotive, engineering, and medical applications.

Basic Principles

Cryogenics comes from two Greek words: *kryo*, meaning "frost," and *genic*, "to produce." This science studies the implications of producing extremely cold temperatures and how those temperatures affect substances such as gases and metal. Cryogenic temperature levels are not found naturally on Earth. The usefulness of cryogenics is based on scientific principles. The three basic states of matter are gas, liquid, and solid. Matter moves from one state to another by the addition or subtraction of heat (energy). The molecules or atoms in matter move or vibrate at different rates depending on the level of heat. Extremely low temperatures, as achieved through cryogenics, slow the vibration of atoms and can change the state of matter. For example, cryogenic temperatures are used in the liquefaction of atmospheric gases such as oxygen, nitrogen, hydrogen, and methane for diverse industrial, engineering, automotive, and medical applications.

Sometimes cryogenics and cryonics are mistakenly linked, but the use of subzero temperatures is the only thing these practices share. Cryonics is the practice of freezing a body immediately after death to preserve it for a future time when a cure for a fatal illness or remedy for a fatal injury may be available. The practice is based on the belief that technology from cryobiology can be applied to cryonics. If cells, tissues, and organs can be preserved by cryogenic temperatures, then perhaps the whole body can be preserved for future thawing and life restoration. Facilities exist for interested persons or families, although the cryonic process is not considered reversible as of this writing.

Core Concepts

Cryogenics is an ever-expanding science. The basic principle of cryogenics is that the creation of extremely low temperatures will affect the properties of matter so the changed matter can be used for a number of applications. Four techniques can create the conditions necessary for cryogenics: thermal conduction, evaporative cooling, rapid-expansion cooling (the Joule-Thomson effect), and adiabatic demagnetization.

Creating Low Temperatures. With thermal conduction, heat flows from matter of higher temperature to matter of lower temperature in what amounts, basically, to a transfer of thermal energy. As the process is repeated, the matter cools. This principle is used in cryogenics by allowing substances to be immersed in liquids with cryogenic temperatures or in an environment such as a cryogenic refrigerator for cooling.

Evaporative cooling is another technique employed in cryogenics. Evaporative cooling is demonstrated in the human body when heat is lost through liquid (perspiration) to cool the body via the skin; perspiration absorbs heat from the body, then evaporates after it is expelled. In the early 1920s in Arizona during the summers, people hung wet sheets inside screened sleeping porches and used electric fans to pull air through the sheets, thus cooling the sleeping space. In the same way, a container of liquid can evaporate, thus removing the heat as gas; the repetitive process drops the temperature of the liquid. One example is reducing the temperature of liquid nitrogen to its freezing point.

The Joule-Thomson effect occurs without the transfer of heat. Temperature is affected by the relationship between volume, mass, and pressure. Rapid expansion of a gas from high to low pressure results in a temperature drop. This principle was employed by Dutch physicist Heike Kamerlingh Onnes to liquefy helium in 1908 and remains useful in home refrigerators and air conditioners.

Adiabatic demagnetization uses paramagnetic salts to absorb energy from liquid, resulting in a temperature drop. The principle in adiabatic demagnetization is the removal of the isothermal magnetized field from matter to lower the temperature. This principle is useful in application to refrigeration systems, which may include a superconducting magnet.

Cryogenic Refrigeration. Cryogenic refrigeration, used by the military, laboratories, and commercial businesses, employs gases such as helium (valued for its low boiling point), nitrogen, and hydrogen to cool equipment and related components at temperatures lower than 150 kelvins (K). The selected gas is cooled through pressurization to liquid or solid forms; dry ice used in the food industry is solidified carbon dioxide, for example. The cold liquid may be stored in insulated containers until used in a cold station to cool equipment, either in an immersion bath or with a sprayer.

Cryogenic Processing and Tempering. Cryogenic processing or treatment uses a deep-freezing process to increase the length of wear of many metals and some plastics. In this process, metal objects are introduced to cooled liquid gases such as liquid nitrogen. The computer-controlled process takes about seventy-two hours to affect the molecular structure of the metal. The next step is cryogenic or heat tempering to improve the strength and durability of the metal object.

Applications Past and Present

Early applications of cryogenics targeted the need to liquefy gases. The success of this process in the late 1800s paved the way for more study and research to apply cryogenics to developing life needs and products. Examples include applications in the automobile and health-care industries, the development of rocket fuels, and methods of food

---

Interesting Facts about Cryogenics

- American businessman Clarence Birdseye revolutionized the food industry when he discovered that deep-frozen food tastes better than regular frozen food. In 1923, he developed the flash-freezing method of preserving food at below-freezing temperatures under pressure. The "Father of Frozen Food" first sold small-packaged foods to the public in 1930 under the name Birds Eye Frosted Foods.

- In cryosurgery, super-freezing temperatures as low as -200 degrees Celsius are introduced through a probe of circulating liquid nitrogen to treat malignant tumors, destroy damaged brain tissue in Parkinson's patients, control pain, halt bleeding, and repair detached retinas.

- Cryogenics can be used to save endangered species from extinction. Smithsonian researcher Mary Hagedorn is using cryogenics to establish the first coral seed banks, collecting thousands of sample species and freezing them for the future. Hagedorn refers to this as an insurance policy for natural resources.

- The Joule-Thomson effect, discovered in 1852 by James Prescott Joule and William Thomson (Lord Kelvin), is responsible for the cooling used in home refrigerators and air conditioners.

- Helium's boiling point, 173 kelvins, is the lowest of all known substances.

- Surgical tools and implants used by surgeons and dentists have increased strength and resistance to wear because of cryogenic processing.

- Cryogenic processing is 100 percent environmentally friendly, with no use of harmful chemicals and no waste products.

- In 1988, microbiologist Curt Jones, who studied freezing techniques to preserve bacteria and enzymes for commercial use, created the popular ice-cream treat Dippin' Dots using a quick-freeze process with liquid nitrogen.

---

preservation. Cryogenic engineering has applications related to commercial, industrial, aerospace, medical, domestic, and defense ventures.

Superconductivity. One property of cryogenics is superconductivity. This occurs when the temperature is dropped so low that the electrical current experiences no resistance. In electrical appliances such as toasters, televisions, radios, or ovens, for instance, energy is wasted trying to overcome electrical resistance. Superconductivity is often used in magnetic resonance imaging (MRI) machines, which use a powerful magnetic field generated by electromagnets to diagnosis certain medical conditions. High magnetic field strength occurs with superconducting magnets. Liquid helium, which becomes a free-flowing superfluid, cools the superconducting coils, and liquid nitrogen cools the superconducting compounds, making cryogenics an integral part of this process. Another application of superconductivity is the use of liquefied gases on buried electrical cables to minimize wasted power and energy and to maintain cool cables with decreased electrical resistance.

Medical Technology. The health-care industry recognizes the value of cryogenics. Medical applications of cryogenics include preservation of cells, tissues, blood products, semen, corneas, embryos, vaccines, and skin for grafting. Cryotubes with liquid nitrogen are useful for storing strains of bacteria at low temperatures. Chemical reactions needed to release active ingredients in statin drugs, used for cholesterol control, must be completed at very low temperatures (-100 degrees Celsius). High-resolution imaging, like MRI, depends on cryogenic principles for the diagnosis of disease and medical conditions. Dermatologists uses cryotherapy to treat warts or skin lesions.

Food and Beverages. The food industry uses cryogenic gases to preserve and transport mass amounts of food without spoilage. This is also useful in supplying food to war zones or natural-disaster areas. Deep-frozen food retains color, taste, and nutrient content while increasing shelf life. Certain fruits and vegetables can be deep frozen for consumption out of season. Freeze-dried foods and beverages, such as coffee, soups, and military rations, can be safely stored for long periods without spoilage. Restaurants and bars use liquid gases to store beverages while maintaining the taste and look of the drink.

Automotive Industry. The automotive industry employs cryogenics in diverse ways. One is through the use of thermal contraction. Because materials will contract when cooled, the valve seals of automobiles are treated with liquid nitrogen, which shrinks to allow insertion and then expands as it warms up, resulting in a tight fit. The automotive industry also uses cryogenics to increase strength and minimize wear of metal engine parts, pistons, cranks, rods, spark plugs, gears, axles, brake rotors and pads, valves, rings, rockers, and clutches. Cryogenic-treated spark plugs can increase an automobile's horsepower as well as its gasoline mileage. The use of cryogenics allows a race car to race as many as thirty times without a major rebuild on the motor compared with racing twice on an untreated car.

Aerospace Industry. The National Aeronautics and Space Administration's (NASA) space program utilizes cryogenic liquids to propel rockets. Rockets carry liquid hydrogen for fuel and liquid oxygen for combustion. Cryogenic hydrogen fuel is what enables NASA's workhorse space shuttle to enter orbit. Another application is using liquid helium to cool the infrared telescopes on rockets.

Tools, Equipment, and Instruments. Metal tools can be treated with cryogenic applications that provide wear resistance. In surgery or dentistry, tools can be expensive, and cryogenic treatment can prolong usage. Some sports equipment, such as golf clubs, benefits from cryogenics, as it provides increased wear resistance and better performance. Another application of cryogenics in sports is the ability of a scuba diver to stay submerged for hours with an insulated Dewar flask of cryogenically cooled nitrogen and oxygen. Some claim musical instruments receive benefits from cryogenic treatment; in brass instruments, a crisper and cleaner sound is allegedly produced with cryogenic enhancement.

Other Applications. Other applications are evolving as industries recognize the benefits of cryogenics to their products and programs. The military has used cryogenics in various ways, including infrared tracking systems, unmanned vehicles, and missile-warning receivers. Companies can immerse discarded recyclables in liquid nitrogen to make them brittle, then pulverize them or grind them down into a more eco-friendly form. It is certain that with continued research, many more applications will emerge.

Impact on Industry

Cryogenics continues to grow globally and serve a wide variety of industries. Various groups have initiated research studies to support the expanded use of cryogenics.

Government Agencies and Military. Government agencies have conducted research on various aspects of cryogenics. The military has investigated the applications of cryogenics to national defense, and the NASA space program applies cryogenics to its programs. Cryogenics can be used to preserve food for long periods, which is especially helpful during natural disasters. Additionally, the Air Force Research Laboratory (AFRL) Space Vehicles Directorate addressed applications of cryogenic refrigeration in the area of ballistic missile defense. The study looked at ground-based radars and space-based infrared sensors requiring cryogenic refrigeration. Future research will target the availability of flexible technology such as field cryocoolers. Such studies can contribute significantly to a cost-effective national defense for the United States.**Industry and Business.** In 2006, the Cryogenic Institute of New England (CINE) recognized that although cryogenic processing was useful in many industries, research validating its technologic advantages and business potential was scant. CINE located forty commercial companies that provided cryogenic-processing services and conducted telephone surveys with thirty of them. The survey found that some $8 million were generated by these deep-cryogenic services in the United States, with 75 percent coming from the services themselves and 25 percent from the sales of equipment.

The survey asked participants to identify the list of top metals they worked with in cryogenic processing. These were given as cast

Occupation	Physicists
Employment 2010	18,300
Projected Employment 2020	20,900
Change in Number (2010–20)	2,600
Percent Change	14%

*Bureau of Labor Statistics, 2012

irons, various steels (carbon, stainless, tool, alloy, mold), aluminum, copper, and others. The revenue was documented by market application. Some 42 percent of the cryogenic-processing-plant market was in the motor sports and automotive industry, where cryogenics was used to treat engine components to improve performance, extend life wear, and treat brake rotors. Thirty percent of the application market fell into the category of

Occupation	Biomedical engineers
Employment 2010	15,700
Projected Employment 2020	25,400
Change in Number (2010–20)	9.700
Percent Change	62%

Bureau of Labor Statistics, 2012

heavy metals, tooling, and cutting; examples of these include manufacturing machine tools, dies, piping, grinders, knives, food processing, paper and pulp processing, and printing. Ten percent were listed in heavy components such as construction, in-ground drilling, and mining, while 18 percent of the market was in areas such as recreation, firearms, electronics, gears, copper electrodes, and grinding wheels.

The National Institute of Standards and Technology (NIST) initiated the Cryogenic Technologies Project, a collaborative research effort between industry and government agencies to improve cryogenic processes and products. One goal is the investigation of cryogenic refrigeration. The nonprofit Cryogenic Society of America (CSA) offers conferences on related work areas such as superconductivity, space cryogenics, cryocoolers, refrigeration, and magnet technology. It also has continuing-education courses and lists job postings on its website.

The health-care industry has many possible applications for cryogenics. In 2005, Texas A&M University Health Science Center–Baylor College of Dentistry investigated the effect of cryogenic treatment of nickel titanium on instruments used by dentists. Past research had been conducted on stainless-steel endodontic instruments with no significant increase in wear resistance. This research demonstrated an increase in microhardness but not in cutting efficiency.

Academic Research and Teaching. A primary career track for those interested in working in cryogenics is cryogenic engineering. To become a cryogenic engineer requires a bachelor's or master's degree in engineering. In the United States, some four hundred academic institutions offer graduate programs in engineering, with about forty committed to research and academic opportunities in cryogenics. Schools with graduate programs in cryogenics include the University of California, Los Angeles; the University of Colorado; Cornell University; Georgia Institute of Technology; Illinois Institute of Technology; Florida International University; Iowa State University; Massachusetts Institute of Technology; Ohio State University; the University of Wisconsin–Madison; Florida State University; Northwestern University; and the University of Southampton in the United Kingdom.

Social Context and Future Prospects

The economic and ecological impact of cryogenic research and applications holds global promise for the future. In 2009, Netherlands firm Stirling Cryogenics built a cooling system with liquid argon for the ICARUS project, which is being carried out by Italy's National Institute of Nuclear Physics. In China, the Cryogenic and Refrigeration Engineering Research Centre (CRERC) focuses on new innovations and technology in cryogenic engineering. Both private industry and government agencies in the United States are pursuing innovative ways to utilize existing applications and define future implications of cryogenics. Although cryogenics has proved useful to many industries, its full potential as a science has not yet been realized.

Further Reading

Hayes, Allyson E., ed. *Cryogenics: Theory, Processes and Applications*. Hauppauge: Nova Science, 2010. Details global research on cryogenics and applications such as genetic engineering and cryopreservation.

Jha, A. R. *Cryogenic Technology and Applications*. Burlington: Elsevier, 2006. Deals with most aspects of cryogenics and cryogenic engineering, including historical development and various laws, such as heat transfer, that make cryogenics possible.

Schwadron, Terry. "Hot Sounds from a Cold Trumpet? Cryogenic Theory Falls Flat." *New York Times*. New York Times, 18 Nov. 2003. Web. 9 Oct. 2012. Explains how two Tufts University researchers studied cryogenic freezing of trumpets and determined the cold did not improve the sound.

Ventura, Gugliemo, and Lara Risegari. *The Art of Cryogenics: Low-Temperature Experimental Techniques*. Burlington: Elsevier, 2008. Comprehensive discussion of various aspects of cryogenics, from heat transfer and thermal isolation to cryoliquids and instrumentation for cryogenics.

About the Author: Marylane Wade Koch, MSN, RN, serves as adjunct faculty for Loewenberg School of Nursing, University of Memphis. She was a health-care professional for more than thirty-five years. She has written several health-care books, published various professional health-care articles, and contributed to books published by Elsevier-Mosby, Harcourt Health Sciences, Delmar/Thomson-Cengage, F. A. Davis, Salem Press, and Jones and Bartlett. She works as editor and coach for private clients, including physicians and health-care professionals. She is a member of the American Medical Writers Association.

Cryogenic Engineer 🖋

Earnings (Yearly Median): $84,670 (Bureau of Labor Statistics, 2012)

Employment and Outlook: Much faster than average growth (Bureau of Labor Statistics, 2012)

O*NET-SOC Code: 17-2031.00

Related Career Clusters: Agriculture, Food & Natural Resources; Health Science; Manufacturing

---

Scope of Work

Cryogenics is a broad field that focuses on the production of extremely cold temperatures and the impact of such temperatures on matter. Cryogenic engineers work for the military, the aerospace industry, the health-care community, and other public or private entities in need of more efficient processes facilitated by deep freeze. Practitioners in the field have, for example, brought about revolutionary advances in refrigeration, rocket technology, and medical equipment such as magnetic resonance imaging (MRI) machines. The field is continually expanding as the needs of other disciplines encourage cryogenic engineers to produce innovations with broad applicability.

Education and Coursework

At the high-school level, aspiring cryogenic engineers should take advanced science and mathematics courses, as well as any engineering courses available. Students entering undergraduate engineering programs typically rank in the top half of their high-school class and excel in the quantitative section of the SAT or ACT. A bachelor's degree is the minimum educational requirement for employment in the field. Although colleges and universities generally do not offer a cryogenic-engineering major, many engineering and applied-sciences programs offer relevant courses and allow students to build a major with a cryogenics concentration. Students should pursue extensive course work in physics, chemistry, mathematics, and engineering. Those interested in specializing in a particular application of cryogenics may choose to take courses in relevant areas; for instance, a student interested in cryogenic medical technology may benefit from studying biology, anatomy, and related subjects.

A master's degree in either chemical or mechanical engineering is preferred for advanced positions, and requirements for admission into graduate programs are stringent, with only the highest-ranked undergraduates gaining entry into the most competitive programs. A direct correlation exists between pay grade and educational level attained. Unlike many fields, cryogenics employs graduates of programs in a wide array of concentrations, from mechanical and chemical engineering to physics. Some cryogenic engineers choose to pursue a doctorate in engineering, which may provide individuals with further employment opportunities in industry, academia, or government.

Career Enhancement

Requirements concerning certification and licensing vary based on industry of employment. Cryogenic engineers working for the National Aeronautics and Space Administration (NASA) will be expected to

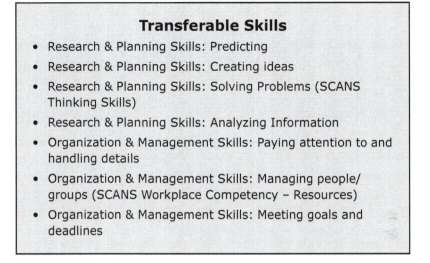

Transferable Skills

- Research & Planning Skills: Predicting
- Research & Planning Skills: Creating ideas
- Research & Planning Skills: Solving Problems (SCANS Thinking Skills)
- Research & Planning Skills: Analyzing Information
- Organization & Management Skills: Paying attention to and handling details
- Organization & Management Skills: Managing people/ groups (SCANS Workplace Competency – Resources)
- Organization & Management Skills: Meeting goals and deadlines

renew their safety certifications frequently and take additional courses to expand their knowledge when necessary. Any cryogenic work performed for other federal agencies will carry similar expectations in terms of both safety and additional training. Engineers employed by private corporations will be held to different standards but will still be expected to hold job-specific safety certifications and pursue additional education commensurate with their work needs.

Those interested in pursuing a career in cryogenics should consider joining a technical society such as the Cryogenic Society of America (CSA). Membership in the CSA includes a subscription to the association's trade magazine, *Cold Facts*, which contains announcements concerning upcoming conferences and networking events, as well as news about advances in the field. Although joining such an association does not ensure employment or greater pay, it does provide interested students and job seekers with access to tools that will make them more competitive applicants.

Daily Tasks and Technology

Whether working for NASA, the US military, or a private firm, cryogenic engineers can expect to spend most of their time in a laboratory researching extremely cold temperatures or developing technology that makes use of such temperatures. Cryogenic engineers may seek new ways to freeze and transport food, work to increase the scientific community's understanding of superconductivity, or design cryogenic fuel systems for rockets. In the medical field, cryogenic engineers may design improved equipment for surgery, medical imaging, or cancer treatment.

Regardless of industry, cryogenic engineers typically use a variety of specialized tools. These may include cryostats, which are devices that keep the substances stored inside at cryogenic temperatures; cryocoolers, which are used to lower the temperature of a substance to cryogenic levels; and thermosiphons, which are used to transfer heat.

Safety is of great concern for all involved in the field, as cryogenic engineers frequently subject matter to extremely low temperatures that can have damaging effects on the human body. Many of the gases and liquids used in cryogenic research, such as hydrogen and carbon monoxide, are flammable or toxic. Preventing accidents remains a major consideration, and cryogenic professionals are often expected to complete various safety classes and hold safety certifications. Despite safety precautions, hazards such as explosions, cold burns, and related health problems make the field potentially dangerous.

Earnings and Employment Outlook

Employment in the field of cryogenic engineering is expected to experience faster-than-average growth between 2010 and 2020. In a field in which only a select number of highly specialized scientists can even meet the minimum requirements for employment, the demand for competent cryogenic engineers remains acute. Experience working in the field is highly desirable, as is technical proficiency with cryogenic systems and related equipment.

Employment in the field of cryogenic engineering is expected to experience faster-than-average growth between 2010 and 2020.

Those who secure entry-level positions with a traditional undergraduate engineering degree and little to no experience can typically expect salaries in at least the $50,000 range. As education and experience increase, so too do rates of compensation. Research laboratories, government agencies, institutions of higher learning, medical-technology firms, and a variety of other entities routinely hire cryogenic engineers at all levels to carry out research, plan and manage projects, and present findings to government agencies and major clients. If employment trends hold steady, entering the field of cryogenics may prove to be a beneficial career choice for students pursuing degrees in mechanical or chemical engineering.

Related Occupations

- **Aerospace Engineers:** Aerospace engineers determine the most suitable design and materials for the construction of aircraft.

- **Biomedical Engineers:** Biomedical engineers examine the utility of medical equipment and technology, offering suggestions on possible improvements, rectifying design flaws, and developing new equipment when necessary.

- **Mechanical Engineers:** Mechanical engineers build and improve the design of machines and make mechanical systems more efficient.

- **Food Scientists:** Food scientists study the deterioration and preservation of food items, as well as ways to make processed food healthier and more nutritionally beneficial.

- **Nanosystems Engineers:** Nanosystems engineers research and develop nanotechnology and related systems and tools.

Future Applications

Regardless of industry, most companies face the growing dilemma of how to make cost-efficient products while adhering to the growing body of environmental legislation governing local, state, and national commerce. Green technology is the wave of the future, and cryogenic engineers are at the forefront of the effort to find energy sources that are more ecologically friendly. Efforts to use alternative fuel sources such as frozen hydrogen have met with some success.

Cryogenics will be an important aspect of other industries as well. Despite budget reductions, NASA continues explore space, and cryogenic engineers will play an integral role in researching more efficient technology to facilitate deep-space voyages. In addition, ever-increasing population growth and dispersion across the United States and the world will necessitate improved preservation and refrigeration techniques so that food items can be transported safely to those in need. In these areas and others, the skills of cryogenic engineers will prove essential to further innovation.

—Keith M. Finley, PhD

More Information

Cryogenics and Fluids Branch
Code 552
NASA Goddard Space Flight Center
Greenbelt, MD 20771
istd.gsfc.nasa.gov/cryo

Cryogenic Society of America
218 Lake Street
Oak Park, IL 60302
www.cryogenicsociety.org

Cryogenics Technologies Group
National Institute of Standards and Technology
Mail Stop 638.00
325 Broadway
Boulder, CO 80305
www.cryogenics.nist.gov

Electrical Engineering

FIELDS OF STUDY

Physics; quantum physics; thermodynamics; chemistry; calculus; multivariable calculus; linear algebra; differential equations; statistics; electricity; electronics; computer science; computer programming; computer engineering; digital signal processing; materials science; magnetism; integrated circuit design engineering; biology; mechanical engineering; robotics; optics.

DEFINITION

Electrical engineering is a broad field ranging from the most elemental electrical devices to high-level electronic systems design. An electrical engineer is expected to have a fundamental understanding of electricity and electrical devices as well as be a versatile computer programmer. All of the electronic devices that permeate modern living originate with an electrical engineer. Items such as garage-door openers and smartphones are based on the application of electrical theory. Even the computer tools, fabrication facilities, and math to describe it all is within the purview of the electrical engineer. Within the field there are many specializations. Some focus on high-power analogue devices, while others focus on integrated circuit design or computer systems.

Basic Principles

Electrical engineering is the application of multiple disciplines converging to create simple or complex electrical systems. An electrical system can be as simple as a lightbulb, power supply, or switch, and as complicated as the Internet, including all its hardware and software subcomponents. The spectrum and scale of electrical engineering is extremely diverse. At the atomic scale, electrical engineers can be found studying the electrical properties of electrons through materials.

For example, silicon is an extremely important semiconductive material found in all integrated circuit (IC) devices, and knowing how to manipulate it is extremely important to those who work in microelectronics.

While electrical engineers need a fundamental background in basic electricity, many (if not most) electrical engineers do not deal directly with wires and devices, at least on a daily basis. An important subdiscipline in electrical engineering includes IC design engineering: A team of engineers are tasked with using computer software to design IC circuit schematics. These schematics are then passed through a series of verification steps (also done by electrical engineers) before being assembled. Because computers are ubiquitous, and the reliance on good computer programs to perform complicated operations is so important, electrical engineers are adept computer programmers as well. The steps would be the same in any of the subdisciplines of the field.

Core Concepts

In a typical scenario, an electrical engineer, or a team of electrical engineers, will be tasked with designing an electrical device or system. It could be a computer, the component inside a computer, such as a central processing unit (CPU), a national power grid, an office intranet, a power supply for a jet, or an automobile ignition system. In each case, however, the electrical engineer's grasp on the fundamentals of the field are crucial.

Electricity. For any electrical application to work, it needs electricity. Once a device or system has been identified for assembly, the electrical engineer must know how it uses electricity. A computer will use low voltages for sensitive IC devices and higher ones for fans and disks. Inside the IC, electricity will be used as the edges of clock cycles that determine what its logical values are. A power grid will generate the electricity itself at a power plant, then transmit it at high voltage over a grid of transmission lines.

Electric Power. When it is determined how the device or application will use electricity, the source of that power must also be understood.

Will it be a standard alternating current (AC) power outlet? Or a direct current (DC) battery? To power a computer, the voltage must be stepped down to a lower voltage and converted to DC. To power a jet, the spinning turbines (which run on jet fuel) generate electricity, which can then be converted to DC and power the onboard electrical systems. In some cases, it's possible to design for what happens in the absence of power, such as the battery backup on an alarm clock or an office's backup generator. An interesting case is the hybrid motor of certain cars such as the Toyota Prius—it has both an electromechanical motor and an electric one. Switching the drivetrain seamlessly between the two is quite a feat of electrical and mechanical engineering.

Circuits. If the application under consideration has circuit components, then its circuitry must be designed and tested. To test the design, mock-ups are often built onto breadboards (plastic rows of contacts that allow wiring up a circuit to be done easily and quickly). An oscilloscope and voltmeter can be used to measure the signal and its strength at various nodes. Once the design is verified, the schematic can be sent to a fabricator and mass manufactured onto a circuit board.

Digital Logic. Often, an electrical engineer will not need to build the circuits themselves. Using computer design tools and tailored programming languages, an electrical engineer can create a system using logic blocks, then synthesize the design into a circuit. This is the method used for designing and fabricating application-specific integrated circuits (ASICs) and field-programmable gate arrays (FPGAs).

Digital Signal Processing (DSP). Since digital devices require digital signals, it is up to the electrical engineer to ensure that the correct signal is coming in and going out of the digital circuit block. If the incoming signal is analogue, it must be converted to digital via an analogue-to-digital converter, or if the circuit block can only process so much data at a time, the circuit block must be able to time slice the data into manageable chunks. A good example is an MP3 player: The data must be read from the disk while it is moving, converted to sound at a frequency humans can hear, played back at a normal rate, then converted to an analogue sound signal in the headphones. Each one of those steps involves DSP.

Computer Programming. Many of the steps above can be abstracted out to a computer programming language. For example, in a logical programming language such as Verilog, an electrical engineer can write lines of code that represent the logic. Another program can then convert it into the schematics of an IC block. A popular programming language called SPICE can simulate how a circuit will behave, saving the designer time by verifying the circuit works as expected before it is assembled.

Applications Past and Present

The products of electrical engineering are an integral part of our everyday life. Everything from cell phones and computers to stereos and electric lighting encompass the purview of the field.

For example, a cell phone has at every layer the mark of electrical engineering. An electrical engineer designed the hardware that runs the device. That hardware must be able to interface with the established communication channels designated for use. Thus, a firm knowledge of DSP and radio waves went into its design. The base stations with which the cell phone communicates were designed by electrical engineers. The network that allows them to work in concert is the latest incarnation of a century of study in electromagnetism. The digital logic that allows multiple phone conversations to occur at the same time on the same frequency was crafted by electrical engineers. The whole mobile experience integrates seamlessly into the existing landline grid. Even the preexisting technology (low voltage wire to every home) is an electrical engineering accomplishment—not to mention the power cable that charges it from a standard AC outlet.

One finds the handiwork of electrical engineers in such mundane devices as thermostats to the ubiquitous Internet, where everything from the network cards to the keyboards, screens, and software are crafted by electrical engineers. Electrical engineers are historically involved with electromagnetic devices as well, such as the electrical starter of a car or the turbines of a hydroelectric plant. Many devices that aid artists, such as sound recording and electronic musical instruments, are possible because of electrical engineers.

Below is a sampling of the myriad electrical devices that are designed by electrical engineers.

Computers. Computer hardware and often computer software are designed by electrical engineers. The CPU and other ICs of the computer are the product of hundreds of electrical engineers working together to create ever-faster and smaller devices. Many products can rightfully be considered computers, though they are not often thought of as such. Smartphones, video-game consoles, and even the controllers in modern automobiles are computers, as they all employ a microprocessor. Additionally, the peripherals that are required to interface with a computer have to be designed to work with the computer as well, such as printers, copiers, scanners, and specialty industrial and medical equipment.

Test Equipment. Although these devices are seldom seen by the general public, they are essential to keeping all the other electrical devices in the world working. For example, an oscilloscope can help an electrical engineer test and debug a failing circuit because it can show how various nodes are behaving relative to each other over time. A carpenter might use a wall scanner to find electrical wire, pipes, and studs enclosed behind a wall. A multimeter, which measures voltage, resistance, and current, is handy not just for electrical engineers but also for electricians and hobbyists.

Sound Amplifiers. Car stereos, home theaters, and electric guitars all have one thing in common: They all contain an amplifier. In the past, these have been purely analogue devices, but since the late twentieth century, digital amplifiers have supplanted their analogue brethren due to their ease of operation and size. Audiophiles, however, claim that analogue amplifies sound better.

Power Supplies. These can come in many sizes, both physically and in terms of power. Most people encounter a power supply as a black box plugged into an AC outlet with a cord that powers electrical devices such as a laptop, radio, or television. Inside each is a specially designed power inverter that converts AC power to the required volts and amperes of DC power.

Batteries. Thomas Edison is credited with creating the first portable battery, a rechargeable box that required only water once a week. Batteries are an electrochemical reaction—a realm of chemistry—which demonstrates how far afield electrical engineering can go while remaining firmly grounded in its fundamentals. Battery technology is entering a new renaissance as the charge life is extending and the size is shrinking. Edison first marketed his "A" battery for use in electric cars before they went out of fashion. Electric cars that run on batteries may be making a comeback, and their cousin, the hybrid, runs on both batteries and combustion.

Power Grid. This is one of the oldest accomplishments of electrical engineering. A massive nationwide interdependent network of transmission lines delivers power to every corner of the country. The power is generated at hydroelectric plants, coal plants, nuclear plants, and wind and solar plants. The whole thing works such that if any one section fails, the others can pick up the slack. Wind and solar pose particular challenges to the field, as wind and sunshine do not flow at a constant rate, but the power grid must deliver the same current and voltage at all times of day.

Electric Trains and Buses. Many major cities have some kind of public transportation that involves either an electrified rail, or bus wires, or both. These subways, light rails, and trolleys are an important part of municipal infrastructure, and they are built on many of the same principles as the power grid.

Automobiles. There are many electronic parts in a car. The first to emerge was the electric starter, obviating the hand crank. Once there was a battery in the car to power the starter, engineers came up with all sorts of other uses for it: headlamps, windshield wipers, interior lighting, a radio (and later tape and CD players), and the car alarm, to name a few. The most important electrical component of modern automobiles is the computer-controlled fuel injector. This allows for the right amount of oxygen and fuel to be present in the engine for maximum fuel efficiency (or for maximum horsepower). The recent success of hybrids, and the potentially emerging market of all-electric

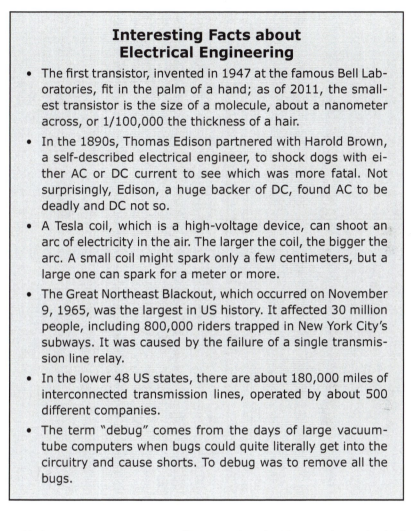

Interesting Facts about Electrical Engineering

- The first transistor, invented in 1947 at the famous Bell Laboratories, fit in the palm of a hand; as of 2011, the smallest transistor is the size of a molecule, about a nanometer across, or 1/100,000 the thickness of a hair.

- In the 1890s, Thomas Edison partnered with Harold Brown, a self-described electrical engineer, to shock dogs with either AC or DC current to see which was more fatal. Not surprisingly, Edison, a huge backer of DC, found AC to be deadly and DC not so.

- A Tesla coil, which is a high-voltage device, can shoot an arc of electricity in the air. The larger the coil, the bigger the arc. A small coil might spark only a few centimeters, but a large one can spark for a meter or more.

- The Great Northeast Blackout, which occurred on November 9, 1965, was the largest in US history. It affected 30 million people, including 800,000 riders trapped in New York City's subways. It was caused by the failure of a single transmission line relay.

- In the lower 48 US states, there are about 180,000 miles of interconnected transmission lines, operated by about 500 different companies.

- The term "debug" comes from the days of large vacuum-tube computers when bugs could quite literally get into the circuitry and cause shorts. To debug was to remove all the bugs.

vehicles, means that there is still more electrical innovation to be had inside a century-old technology.

Medical Devices. Though specifically the domain of biomedical engineering, many, if not most, medical devices are designed by electrical engineers who have entered this subdiscipline. Computed axial tomography (CAT) scanners, x-rays, ultrasound, and magnetic resonance imaging (MRI) machines all rely on electromagnetic and nuclear physics applied in an electrical setting (and controlled by electronics). These devices can be used to look into things other than human bodies as well. Researchers demonstrated that an MRI could determine if a block of cheese had properly aged.

Telecommunications. This used to be an international grid of telephone wires and cables connecting as many corners of the globe where wire could be strung. As of 2011, even the most remote outposts can communicate voice, data, and video thanks to advances in radio technology. The major innovation in this field has been the ability for multiple connections to ride the same signal. The original cell phone technology picked a tiny frequency for each of its users, thus limiting the number of total users to a fixed division in that band. Mobile communication has multiple users on the same frequency, which opens up the band to more users.

Broadcast Television and Radio. These technologies are older but still relevant to the electrical engineer. Radio is as vibrant as ever, and ham radio is even experiencing a mini renaissance. While there may not be much room for innovation, electrical engineers must understand them to maintain them, as well as understand their derivative technologies.

Lighting. Light-emitting diodes (LEDs) are low-power alternatives to incandescent bulbs (the lightbulb that Thomas Edison invented). They are just transistors, but as they have grown smaller and more colors have been added to their spectrum, they have found their way into interior lighting, computer monitors, flashlights, indicator displays, and control panels.

Impact on Industry

New electrical devices are being introduced every day in a quantity too numerous to document. In 2006, consumer electronics alone generated $169 trillion in revenue. Nonetheless, electrical engineering has a strong public research and development component. Increasingly, businesses are partnering with universities to better capitalize on independent research. As of 2011, most IC design is done in the United States, Japan, and Europe, and most of the manufacturing is outsourced to Taiwan and

Singapore. As wind and solar power become more popular, so does the global need for electrical engineers. Spain, Portugal, and Germany lead the European Union in solar panel use and production. In the United States, sunny states such as California give financial incentives to homes and businesses that incorporate solar.

Government Agencies. The United States government funds research in electrical engineering in the forms of grants from organizations such as the Defense Advanced Research Projects Agency (DARPA)—the Internet originated from a Cold War–era DARPA project, when the United States wanted a communications network that would survive a first-strike nuclear assault—and the National Aeronautics and Space Administration (NASA). The National Science Foundation (NSF) indirectly supports research through fellowships. Research can be directed at any of the subdisciplines of the field: different material for transistors or new mathematics for better DSP or unique circuit configuration that optimizes a function. Often, the research is directed at combining disciplines, such as circuits that perform faster DSP. DARPA is interested in security and weapons, such as better digital encryption and spy satellites. Solar power is also a popular area of research. There is a race to increase the performance of photovoltaic devices so that solar power can compete with gas, coal, and petroleum in terms of price per kilowatt hour.

Military. Equipment such as radar, missile guidance systems, and communication equipment depends on advanced electronics. Electrical and electronics engineers design, develop, and test electrical and electronic equipment. They also direct equipment installation and repair. With experience, electrical engineers may advance to senior management positions, such as engineering staff officer, research and development manager, or communications center director.

Business Sector. Careers in the field of electrical engineering are as diverse as its applications. Manufacturing uses electrical engineers to design and program industrial equipment, while telecommunications employs electrical engineers because of their understanding of DSP. Though these companies seem dissimilar—medical devices, smartphones, computers (any device that uses an IC)—they have their

Occupation	Electrical and eletronics engineers
Employment 2010	294,000
Projected Employment 2020	311,600
Change in Number (2010–20)	17,600
Percent Change	6%

Bureau of Labor Statistics, 2012

own staffs of electrical engineers that design, test, fabricate, and retest the devices.

More than half of the electrical engineers employed in the United States are working in electronics—consumer electronics include companies such as Apple, Sony, and Toshiba that make DVD players, video-game consoles, MP3 players, laptops, and computers. More than half of all electrical engineers work in the microchip sector, which uses legions of electrical engineers to design, test, and fabricate ICs on a continually shrinking scale. The majority of the engineering takes place at the constituent component level. Chip manufacturers such as Intel and Advanced Micro Devices (AMD) are household names, but there are a number of other companies producing microchips that find their way into refrigerators, cars, network storage devices, cameras, and home lighting. The FPGA market alone was $2.75 billion, though few end consumers will ever know that they are in everything from photocopiers to cell phone base stations.

In the non-chip sector, there are behemoths such as General Electric, which make everything from lightbulbs to household appliances to jet engines. There are about 500 electric power companies in the contiguous forty-eight states of the United States. Because they are all connected to each other and the grid is aging, smart engineering is required to bring new sources online such as solar and wind. In 2009, the Federal Communications Commission (FCC) issued the National Broadband Plan, the goal of which is to bring broadband Internet access to every United States citizen. Telecommunications companies such as AT&T and cable providers are competing fiercely to deliver ever-faster speeds at lower prices to fulfill this mandate. Electrical engineers are being seen more and more in the role of computer scientists. The course work has been converging since the twentieth century. University electrical engineering and computer science departments may share lecturers between the two disciplines. Companies may use electrical engineers to solve a computer-programming problem in the hopes that the electrical engineer can debug the hardware and software.

Academic Research and Teaching

Electrical engineering requires a diverse breadth of background course work—math, physics, computer science, and electrical theory—allowing for ample opportunity in teaching, including at colleges, vocational schools, and other specialized institutions.

Industry is a primary funder of electrical engineering research at the academic level. Universities that are heavily dependent on industry funding tend to research in areas that are of concern to their donors. For example, Intel, the largest manufacturer of microprocessors, is a sponsor of various University of California electrical engineering departments and in 2011 announced their new three-dimensional transistor. The technology is based on original research first described by the University of California, Berkeley, in 2000 and funded by DARPA.

Occupation	Electrical and electronic engineering technicians
Employment 2010	151,100
Projected Employment 2020	154,000
Change in Number (2010–20)	2,900
Percent Change	2%

*Bureau of Labor Statistics, 2012

Social Context and Future Prospects

Electrical engineering may be the most under-recognized driving force behind modern living. Everything from the electrical revolution to the rise of the personal computer to the Internet and social networking has been initiated by electrical engineers. This field first brought electricity into our homes and then ushered in the age of transistors. Much of the new technology being developed is consumed as software and requires computer programmers. But the power grid, hardware, and Internet that powers it were designed by electrical engineers and maintained by electrical engineers.

As the field continues to diversify and the uses for electricity expands, the need for electrical engineers will grow, as will the demands placed on the knowledge base required to enter the field. Electrical engineers have begun working in the biological sciences, a field they have rarely explored in the past. However, the neurons that comprise the human brain are an electrical system, and it makes sense for both fields to embrace the knowledge acquired in the other.

Other disciplines rely on electrical engineering as the foundation. Robotics, for example, merge mechanical and electrical engineering. As robots move out of manufacturing plants and into our offices and homes, engineers with a strong understanding of the underlying physics are essential. Another related field, biomedical engineering, combines medicine and electrical engineering to produce lifesaving devices such as pacemakers, defibrillators, and CAT scanners. As the population ages, the need for more advanced medical treatments and early detection devices becomes paramount. Green power initiatives will require electrical engineers with strong mechanical engineering and chemistry knowledge. If history is our guide, the next scientific revolution will likely come from electrical engineering.

Further Reading

Adhami, Reza, Peter M. Meenen III, and Dennis Hite. *Fundamental Concepts in Electrical and Computer Engineering with Practical Design Problems.* 2d ed. Boca Raton, FL: Universal, 2005. A well-illustrated guide to the kind of math required to analyze electrical circuits, followed by sections on circuits, digital logic, and DSP.

Davis, L. J. *Fleet Fire: Thomas Edison and the Pioneers of the Electric Revolution.* New York: Arcade, 2003. The stunning story of the pioneer electrical engineers, many self-taught, who ushered in the electric revolution.

Gibilisco, Stan. *Electricity Demystified.* New York: McGraw-Hill, 2005. A primer on electrical circuits and magnetism.

Mayergoyz, I. D., and W. Lawson. *Basic Electric Circuit Theory: A One-Semester Text.* San Diego: Academic Press, 1997. Introductory textbook to the fundamental concepts in electrical engineering. Includes examples and problems.

McNichol, Tom. *AC/DC: The Savage Tale of the First Standards War*. San Francisco: Jossy-Bass, 2006. The riveting story of the personalities in the AC/DC battle of the late nineteenth century, focusing on Thomas Edison and Nicola Tesla.

Shurkin, Joel N. *Broken Genius: The Rise and Fall of William Shockley, Creator of the Electronic Age*. New York: Macmillian, 2006. Biography of the Nobel Prize-winning electrical engineer and father of the Silicon Valley, who had the foresight to capitalize on invention of the transistor but ultimately went down in infamy and ruin.

About the Author: Vincent Jorgensen, BS, graduated from the University of California, Berkeley, with a degree in electrical engineering and computer science in 1999. He spent the next decade designing FPGAs, proving that they work both in simulation and silicon, later transitioning to the emerging cloud-computing field, specializing in cloud infrastructure and how applications communicate and run inside Amazon's Elastic Compute Cloud. He consults for various Silicon Valley startups as an Amazon Web Services (AWS) architect and Web framework designer.

Electrical Engineer 🖋

Earnings (Yearly Median): $85,920 (Bureau of Labor Statistics, 2012)

Employment and Outlook: Slower than average growth (Bureau of Labor Statistics, 2012)

O*NET-SOC Code: 17-2071.00

Related Career Clusters: Arts, Audio/Video Technology & Communications; Information Technology; Manufacturing

Scope of Work

Electrical engineers design electrical equipment and electronics and also test equipment, oversee the manufacture of components, and troubleshoot when problems occur. They work with a wide range of technologies, which may include computer chips, transistors, LEDs, superconductors, fuel cells, and batteries. Electrical engineers play a key role in the design and improvement of innovative technology solutions such as handheld communications devices, cardiac pacemakers, and solar panels.

Essentially, electrical engineers work with electricity as a method of supplying power. Some other applications include power electronics, the control systems that regulate the behavior of other devices; signal processing, in which signals are enhanced for greater understanding; and telecommunications. Electrical engineers who focus on designing electronic equipment are known as electronics engineers.

Education and Coursework

High-school students intending to pursue a career in electrical engineering should study physics and chemistry. Mathematics is equally important, and aspiring electrical engineers should study algebra, geometry, trigonometry, and calculus. Computer-science classes are helpful as well, as they provide a basic understanding of the function of the components that some electrical engineers design and test. Introductory engineering classes, when available, are also a good choice for students interested in entering the field.

Participation in extracurricular activities that are aligned with the principles of the science, technology, engineering, and mathematics (STEM) classes taken can also be beneficial to students. Robotics or science competition clubs and science fairs give high-school students interested in becoming electrical engineers the opportunity to demonstrate their interest and practical knowledge. Tutoring younger students may also help an aspiring electrical engineer reinforce the knowledge gained through academic coursework.

At the undergraduate level, students pursuing a bachelor's degree in electrical engineering will take courses in calculus, linear algebra, statistics, and differential equations. Course work in physics and the field of electromagnetics will also be required. Semiconductor chemistry and discrete-signal analysis, in which noise in electronic systems is encoded and filtered before being transmitted, are also areas of study at the university level.

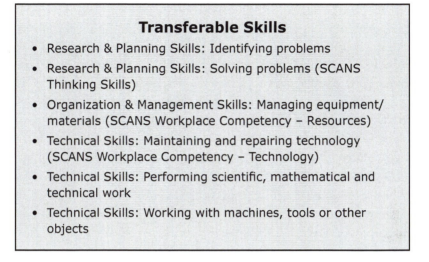

Transferable Skills

- Research & Planning Skills: Identifying problems
- Research & Planning Skills: Solving problems (SCANS Thinking Skills)
- Organization & Management Skills: Managing equipment/ materials (SCANS Workplace Competency – Resources)
- Technical Skills: Maintaining and repairing technology (SCANS Workplace Competency – Technology)
- Technical Skills: Performing scientific, mathematical and technical work
- Technical Skills: Working with machines, tools or other objects

Candidates for an undergraduate electrical-engineering degree typically must also complete coursework in electric circuits, digital logic design, analog and digital electronics, and electromagnetic wave propagation, as well as lab work in fundamental digital circuits and systems. To gain practical experience, students may explore internship opportunities in the field. Such internships allow students to observe the day-to-day responsibilities of electrical engineers. In some cases, undergraduate students may be able to obtain research positions assisting professors or graduate students.

Those pursuing a graduate degree in electrical engineering will complete course work that prepares them for careers in research. Typical areas of research include communications and networking, signal processing, computer engineering, bioelectronics, and systems. Some graduate programs are multidisciplinary and allow students to study multiple branches of engineering or pursue research related to other academic fields.

Career Enhancement and Training

A number of professional associations and societies exist to help electrical engineers network, find jobs, and learn new skills. One of the most prominent of these is the Institute of Electrical and Electronics

Engineers (IEEE), which sponsors conferences and events within the United States and worldwide. These conferences are specific to a sector of the field, such as medicine and biology or vehicle power and propulsion. Local chapters provide ample opportunities for networking and professional education on a regular basis.

The IEEE also publishes a range of technical papers and journals of interest to electrical engineers, with topics ranging from aerospace and electronic systems to wireless communications. The organization's digital library, IEEE Xplore, is available to members by subscription. Student memberships in the IEEE are available to those studying technology or engineering at least part time at an accredited institution.

Some employers require that applicants hold a professional engineer (PE) license; even if not required, this credential may help a candidate further establish his or her qualifications. To obtain a PE license, an engineer must pass the Fundamentals of Engineering (FE) exam after graduating from an engineering program accredited by the Accreditation Board for Engineering and Technology (ABET). He or she must then work as an engineer for a period determined by his or her state of residence before passing the Principles and Practice of Engineering (PE) exam. The PE license is awarded by a state board of registration.

Daily Tasks and Technology

Electrical engineers are involved in the design and testing of electrical or electronic components. They may work on circuit boards and circuits, semiconductors, components for existing technology such as global-positioning satellites (GPS) or heart monitors, or new technology that is in development. Designing a component requires a familiarity with the materials available, the function of the component, and any constraints on price that may be in place. Once the part is designed, the electrical engineer will oversee its manufacture. Testing of the component will also take place to ensure that all requirements are met.

Electrical engineers may also work to design and build systems as part of a team of professionals. In this role, an electrical engineer will take part in meetings, give presentations and briefings, and present reports of findings and progress. The components and systems they design must conform to industry standards and other regulations. Additionally, electrical engineers must be able to work under the envisioned conditions and within the pricing parameters of any given project.

An electrical engineer uses various technological devices and systems in order to design and build components or perform other necessary tasks. A familiarity with electronic filters, inverters, power drive systems, oscilloscopes, and spectrum analyzers is often required, and electrical engineers commonly use computer-aided design (CAD) software when designing complex components such as integrated circuits or complex systems such as electrical grids. Engineers working in certain emerging technologies may design, build, or test very small components and systems that require the use of specialized tools.

Earnings and Employment Outlook

Demand for electrical engineers is expected to grow more slowly than the average for all occupations, increasing by 6 percent between 2010 and 2020. This is due largely to the slow growth or decline in the manufacturing sector of the economy, a major employer of electrical engineers. However, is likely that there will be growth in the area of research and development, as many companies are turning toward new technologies and innovations in existing technologies. There will likely be significant demand for electrical and electronics engineers in the areas of computer-systems design and wireless telecommunications as portable computing devices become more powerful and more widely used. Also, engineering-services firms will need electrical engineers as more companies begin contracting engineering services rather than employing in-house engineers.

Demand for electrical engineers is expected to grow more slowly than the average for all occupations, increasing by 6 percent between 2010 and 2020.

According to the US Bureau of Labor Statistics (BLS), the median annual wage for electrical engineers is well above the median annual wage for all occupations. As a result of the stringent requirements for

A Conversation with Tony Miscio

Job Title: World Wide Operations Manager of Software and Hardware Tools

What was your career path?

My career path was to be a Servo Controls Systems Design Engineer because of the many opportunities available with different companies for this type of engineer.

What are three pieces of advice you would offer someone interested in your profession?

1. There are plenty of sales engineer jobs out there for the engineer/MBA graduates. If you plan on having a family life and marriage, think twice about this type of job. Once into this path you will travel twenty-five days a month all over the world. Sounds exciting for the first few months, but gets very, very old fast. Once in this type of position, it's hard to break this position's stereotype and apply for an inside design or management job. If you're lucky enough to get an inside job you may be caught up in a pending layoff since you will be the new kid to the department.

2. Be careful with grooming your education to the existing highest demand positions. If these positions, i.e. software programmers, have been in demand at all companies for at least a year or two, the companies are already making plans to either farm the work outside or push the major portion of the workload overseas. A US company will never send all of its software work overseas, but they will spend so many dollars of their budget on this task that raises, advancements, and just general growth with the company will be stagnant for you unless you accept a go-between management job between the overseas entity or outside contractor—and there are very few of these types of positions.

3. If you are an introvert and like working by yourself on everything, either begin to change immediately or seek another profession. Engineering has become a

team-type job—everyone is expected to communicate effectively. Your will get the opportunity to carry the ball to the goal line, but not every week, and you better praise your team for their help. Most work alone jobs will go to single outside contractors with years of experience, never a newbie.

What paths for career advancement are available to you?

As an engineer you are considered a problem solver. Spend time at first developing your thinking and observation capabilities. If you have a good, solid mind that can break down multiple complex problems into the component parts, then isolate these problems and effectively communicate them to your management with possible solutions—career advancement will come your way. You will be faced with the decision to take the management or technical path, but I would answer that question as vague as possible until you understand what is available at your company (and that takes six months to a year). If at all possible, remain a generalist; the experts love to talk about their capabilities and will always teach you their specialty.

admission to engineering programs and extensive training required of many engineers, wages will likely continue to be above the median annual wage. The BLS estimates that electrical engineers will be slightly more in demand than electronics engineers; however, average wages for the latter group are slightly higher.

Related Occupations

- **Computer Engineers:** Computer engineers design and test computer chips and a variety of other hardware and software systems.

- **Manufacturing Engineers:** Manufacturing engineers develop equipment for manufacturing products, as well as assembly, production, and quality-control processes.

- **Aerospace Engineers:** Aerospace engineers design and test components for craft that function in the air and in space, including planes, rockets, and satellites.

- **Mechanical Engineers:** Mechanical engineers design, manufacture, maintain, and analyze the performance of mechanical systems.

- **Biomedical Engineers:** Biomedical engineers analyze and design solutions to problems in biology and medicine in order to improve the quality and effectiveness of patient care.

Future Applications

Although the demand for electrical engineers has decreased in some sectors, these workers are expected to continue to play an important role in a number of growing industries. In the telecommunications field, ever-expanding networks and capabilities will require innovation to ensure sufficient capacity at the desired speed. As new means of personal computing develop, engineers will be needed to ensure that the electronics and electrical components within such devices adhere to standards of performance as well as legal and environmental regulations. In the biomedical field, artificial hearts, monitoring equipment, and prosthetics with advanced capabilities will require sophisticated circuitry for reliable performance. Nanotechnology is expected to become a significant subject of research within the biomedical field, and work in this area will require the contribution of electrical engineers skilled in working with very small, complex components and systems.

The increasing public interest in more environmentally friendly technology will likely continue to affect many scientific disciplines, including the field of electrical engineering. Electrical engineers may work to miniaturize components and extend the lives and capabilities of batteries, enabling the technology industry to reduce waste. Similarly, those working with large electrical systems may work to improve the efficiency of power grids and integrate solar panels and other tools for harnessing renewable energy into the existing electrical infrastructure.

—Gina Hagler

More Information

Institute of Electrical and Electronics Engineers
2001 L Street NW
Suite 700
Washington, DC 20036
www.ieee.org

National Society of Professional Engineers
1420 King Street
Alexandria, VA 22314
www.nspe.org

Environmental Physics

FIELDS OF STUDY

Physics; mathematics; computer science; chemistry; biology; biochemistry; geology; geomagnetism; agriculture; mechanics; ecology; atmospheric dynamics; atmospheric chemistry; geodynamics; fluid mechanics; resource management.

DEFINITION

Environmental physics is a multidisciplinary field that investigates the physical principles underlying environmental phenomena and the relationship between the biota (organisms living on the earth) and the nonliving components of the environment. Specifically, environmental physicists attempt to describe environmental processes—such as nutrient or elemental cycling, radiation, and the movement of energy—using the principles of classical physics, including thermodynamics and mechanics. Environmental physics is essential to ongoing efforts to study climate change and is also used widely in energy industry research, meteorology, atmospheric science, hydrology, and the development of green technology.

Basic Principles

Environmental physics grew out of the natural philosophy of the eighteenth and nineteenth centuries, when scientists and philosophers attempted to derive the mathematical relationships underlying environmental phenomena, including weather patterns and tidal movements. Swedish chemist and physicist Svante Arrhenius is one of the fathers of the field, having discovered, in 1896, the physical relationship between greenhouse gases and increases in surface temperature of the earth.

Throughout the twentieth century, physicists made major contributions to the scientific understanding of the environment, coupled with major developments in technology for physical research. Mass spectrometry, a technique used to investigate the relationship between energy and matter, was developed by British physicist Joseph J. Thompson in the 1920s and became an essential technique in physics and chemical research. In the 1930s and 1940s, environmental physicists worked to develop radioisotope dating, which provided scientists with the ability to accurately measure the age of geological specimens. Environmental physics has also been used in the effort to create physical models used to predict the development of global circulation and climate systems. In 1969, Japanese meteorologist Syukuro Manabe used data from atmospheric and oceanic physics to develop the first model of the combined circulation patterns of the ocean and atmosphere.

In the twenty-first century, environmental physics has become a distinct area of research and an important part of environmental science, a field that combines efforts from a variety of related sciences to develop a full scientific understanding of environmental processes. Environmental physics can also be divided into a number of more specific disciplines, including geophysics, which studies the physical principles of the earth's lithosphere, and atmospheric physics, which creates models of physical interactions within the atmosphere. Environmental physics has also been essential to ongoing efforts to develop sustainable energy technology.

Core Concepts

Radiometry. Radiometry is a series of techniques used to measure and study radiation, or the dispersion of energy. Physicists use radiometry to study radioisotopes, which are variations of an atom that are unstable due to the presence or absence of neutrons within their atomic structure. Radioisotopes decay by releasing energized particles in the form of radiation, and thereby transform into more stable isotopes. Decay counting is a technique used in radiometry to measure the distribution and activity of radioisotopes within an environmental sample. Decay counting involves first measuring the number of decays that occur during a certain period of time. This data can then be used to estimate the abundance of certain isotopes.

There are a number of methods used for decay counting, including liquid scintillation counting (LSC) a method that utilizes liquid solvents, like benzene or toluene, to dissolve samples of material containing radioisotopes. These liquids fluoresce—or release visible light—when they come into contact with charged particles. As radioactive decay occurs, releasing alpha and beta particles, light is produced and transmuted into electromagnetic pulses, which can be detected and measured to provide an estimate of the activity and abundance of radioactive material within the sample.

Spectroscopy. Spectroscopy is the study of how radiated energy interacts with matter. There are a variety of techniques used to study spectroscopic principles, including spectrometry, which is a collection of methods used to study the behavior of certain spectrums of energy. A spectrum is the variation within a certain form of energy that can be separated according to measurements of intensity, wavelength, or a variety of other factors. Spectroscopy primarily studies radiated energy in terms of its wavelength.

One of the most important spectrographic techniques in environmental physics is differential optical absorption spectroscopy (DOAS), which is a technique developed by environmental physicists to measure trace gases within a gas sample. A typical DOAS device consists of a chamber containing a gas sample that is subjected to a continuous source of light. Measurements then show how gases in the sample absorb some of the light passed through the sample, thus providing a measurement of the amount of trace gases within the material.

Mass Spectrometry. Mass spectrometry is a series of techniques used to measure the physical composition of a mixture or a sample of material. The basic principle is to separate ions—or charged particles—within a mixture based on their mass and electrical charge ratio and then to use a detector to measure proportions of different ions within the mixture.

Accelerator mass spectrometry (AMS) is one of the major techniques used by environmental chemists and physicists to measure the physical abundance and activity of isotopes in the environment. The basic technique involves using a specialized device to accelerate ions to high speeds, thus increasing the kinetic energy of the sample, before analyzing the sample. Acceleration serves to separate various types of ions from the sample and is useful in attempts to separate and analyze proportions of rare isotopes within a sample. AMS measurement techniques are also used in radioisotope dating.

Eddy Covariance. Eddy covariance is a method used to study turbulence or variation within the layers of the atmosphere. Physicists and meteorologists use eddy covariance to measure the flux—or physical movement over time—of atmospheric components like carbon dioxide, oxygen, and water vapor by comparing the vertical movement of these materials with their horizontal movement through the atmosphere. Measurements are typically achieved through eddy covariance flux towers, which are tall structures equipped with mechanisms used to measure the movement of materials in atmospheric currents, including infrared detectors and kinetic motion detectors.

Eddy covariance is important to meteorology and atmospheric science, helping to develop models of atmospheric movement that help explain meteorological and atmospheric changes over time. Eddy covariance has also been used in the development of oceanographic modeling and technology for weather monitoring used in the agricultural industry. In addition to detection and measurement equipment, eddy covariance also utilizes specialized computer programs to analyze and interpret the results of atmospheric measurements; these computer programs utilize contributions from environmental physicists and computer scientists.

Time-Domain Reflectometry. Time-domain reflectometry (TDR) is a technique used to measure the conductivity of electricity within electrically active systems. The basic technique involves subjecting a soil sample to an electrical charge and measuring conductivity within the soil. The system is advantageous because it measures moisture and salinity in a soil sample in a nondestructive way, thereby preserving the environment. Since the development of environmental TDR, environmental physicists and electrical engineers have been developing new software and sensing equipment to enhance the function of TDR for environmental research. Modern TDR equipment is able to provide highly accurate measurements of soil salinity and water content, which is useful in agricultural and geological research and development.

Ground Penetrating Radar. Ground penetrating radar (GPR) devices emit electromagnetic waves into the earth, which reflect off the surfaces of materials buried within the earth's crust before returning to the surface, where the reflected waves are analyzed. GPR measurements can be used to study the distribution of subterranean water or ice as well as to search for buried fossils and other materials of interest to geoscientists. GPR development is essential to the petroleum industry, where the technique is often used to search for petroleum reservoirs; it is also used in the mining industry to search for deposits of ore and other minerals before drilling into the substrate. Geophysicists use GPR to study a variety of phenomena, including seismic activity and the movement and extent of subterranean water.

Applications Past & Present

Radiometric Dating. Radiometric dating is a technique utilizing the principles of radiometry to determine the age of geological samples by detecting proportions of different isotopes within the sample. Radioactive isotopes decay at specific rates, producing stable isotopes in the process. By measuring the proportion of unstable and stable isotopes within a sample, physicists and geologists can estimate the amount of time that has passed since the sample was formed within the earth. Newly formed rocks and geological formations contain higher levels of radioactive isotopes, which begin to decay as the rock solidifies and cools.

One of the most important methods for radiometric dating is radiocarbon dating, which evolved out of research by American physicist Willard F. Libby in 1949. Carbon-14 is a radioisotope of carbon that decays at a relatively constant rate to produce more stable varieties of carbon. To determine the amount of carbon-14 within a sample, scientists use decay counting techniques including liquid scintillation counting. Radiocarbon dating is useful for analyzing the age of samples of relatively recent origin, dating back to between 55,000 and 65,000 years before the present. In samples older than 65,000 years, radioactive isotopes of carbon are largely absent, having been replaced by stable carbon isotopes.

Uranium-lead radiometric dating is a technique used to estimate the age of older geological samples, and was most notably used to obtain one of the first scientifically accurate estimates regarding the age of the earth. Uranium-lead dating analyzes the proportion of uranium within minerals like zircon compared to the proportion of lead, which is the product of uranium decay.

Climate Modeling. The circulation patterns of air and water responsible for generating the earth's climate are due in part of the transfer of energy between the sun and the materials that make up the planet's environment. General circulation models (GCMs) use complex equations representing physical interactions to create detailed models of circulation patterns in either the oceanic or atmospheric environments. Physicists have also played a role in combining ocean GCMs with atmospheric GCMs to create atmosphere-ocean general circulation models (AOGCMs), which attempt to model the complex physical and energetic relationships between circulation patterns in both the ocean and atmosphere.

Climate modeling is important to meteorology, helping to predict both proximate and long-term developments in weather patterns. Climate models utilize detailed equations to describe the basic thermodynamic relationships and physical interactions that fuel climate change and the development of weather patterns. For instance, to accurately model tropical storm development, climate models must be programmed with the physical laws that govern the formation of storm systems.

Climate Change. Climate change science is an interdisciplinary branch of scientific inquiry that investigates physical, chemical, and biological factors that influence the earth's climate in an effort to predict and model potential future changes in global climate patterns. One of the major issues in climate change science concerns the role of anthropogenic—or human-caused—factors affecting the earth's climate, such as the release of greenhouse gases like carbon dioxide and methane from the burning of fossil fuels. Environmental physics research is used in determining how changes in the levels of greenhouse gases and other pollutants affect circulation patterns that might lead to global changes in climate.

The Intergovernmental Panel on Climate Change (IPCC), a group of scientists and researchers representing sixty countries, was formed by the United Nations in 1988 to coordinate international research on climate change. The IPCC funds and supports a variety of climate research programs around the world and publishes annual reports on the state of the earth's climate and current theories regarding the future of climate change. Environmental physics plays a major role in IPCC research, helping to develop climate and atmospheric models and creating better sensing equipment to detect fluctuations in temperature and gas concentrations.

Wind and Water Power. Modern environmental physics research is often used in the development of sustainable energy technology, including wind and water power systems. Eddy covariance and other measurement systems used to study turbulence are essential in the effort to design machines to capture the kinetic energy of wind currents, which can be used to generate commercial and residential electricity. In the twenty-first century, wind power was used to generate more than 2 percent of the power used around the world and remained a major area of sustainable energy research. Environmental physicists contribute to the industry by helping to design more efficient technology for harvesting wind currents and work with electrical engineers to design systems for storing energy collected from wind farms.

Similarly, environmental physics research plays a role in modeling oceanic tide patterns, which aids in developing tidal and oceanic current energy systems. Utilizing hydroelectric dams, tidal dams, and wave power turbines, engineers capture the kinetic energy of ocean waves and water currents and transition this energy to electricity for commercial applications. Environmental physicists and engineers design equipment to more effectively harness energy from the hydrosphere (all the water of the earth). In the twenty-first century, environmental physics research has been utilized in the development of wave farms, an emerging field of hydropower generation that utilizes special machines to harness continual kinetic motion of waves near the surface of the water and transitions this power into electrical currents through the use of hydraulic pumps. Wave power is currently one of the major areas of research in sustainable energy.

Interesting Facts about Environmental Physics

- French physicist Henri Becquerel accidentally discovered radioactivity when he placed a sample of uranium salts next to photographic plates overnight. When he returned to the laboratory in the morning, the photographic plates had been partially exposed from energy given off by the decaying uranium.

- Time-domain reflectometry (TDR) was a technique developed to help engineers find faults within conducting electrical wires, such as those used in residential and commercial electrical systems. In the 1980s, geophysicists began applying TDR to soil physics research, utilizing the same technology to search for conductivity patterns within the soil.

- The city of Reykjavik, Iceland, is located near a system of shallow volcanic canals, which are harvested to provide heat for the city. More than one quarter of Iceland's energy is produced from geothermal sources, and Reykjavik derives nearly 80 percent of its electricity from converted geothermal energy.

- In 2011, the Pew Trusts organization estimated that investment in the development of green technology had reached approximately $263 billion worldwide, an increase of more than 600 percent since 2011. The European Union was the international leader in terms of green technology investment, with over $99 billion in investment in 2011.

- Roscoe Wind Farm, in Roscoe, Texas, was the world's largest wind power farm in 2011, with more than six hundred wind turbines drawing power to supply thousands of homes. The United States was ranked second in the world in terms of utilizing wind power technology, with only China deriving more of its energy consumption from wind power sources.

Geothermal Energy Development. Geothermal energy is a type of heat energy that emerges from the earth's core, radiating from molten rock (magma) and water heated by the radioactive decay of elements at the core. In some regions, including hot springs and areas near active volcanoes, geothermal energy rises close to the earth's surface and can be used directly to provide heating. Heat arising from these naturally occurring formations can also be captured and utilized through heat pumps to provide heat for distant settlements. In addition, heat captured from geothermal sources can be used to generate electricity by utilizing the kinetic energy of steam to power electrical generators.

Engineered geothermal systems (EGS) use drilling to tap into geothermal sources that lie between three and seven kilometers beneath the earth's surface. The resulting heat is then filtered into a system of reservoirs and used to create steam or heated water, which can be used to generate electricity. Environmental physics research is an important part of the ongoing effort to develop and refine EGS technology, which is expected to provide an important source of sustainable energy in the twenty-first century.

Geologists and geophysicists use ground penetrating radar and other geological exploration techniques to search for areas where geothermal pockets rise close enough to the surface to be useful for energy development. Environmental physicists also help to develop more accurate radar imaging techniques for subterranean exploration and help to develop physical models of convection currents beneath the earth's surface, thereby enhancing efforts to more efficiently harvest geothermal energy.

Impact on Industry

The fastest-growing segment of the environmental sciences is in the field of climate change studies, including climate modeling and atmospheric evaluation. In addition, concern over shrinking supplies of petroleum has created increased demand for alternative and sustainable energy sources. Environmental physicists may find opportunities working for the government or private companies and helping to develop technology for the alternative energy market.

Environmental physics is a highly specialized area of study, drawing specialists from both the environmental sciences and traditional physics research. According to the United States Bureau of Labor Statistics, approximately 89,400 individuals were employed as environmental specialists or scientists in the United States in 2010, and the field was growing slightly faster than average, with 19 percent growth expected by 2020. Only a relatively small percentage of those working as environmental scientists specialized in physics research. The Bureau of Labor Statistics estimated that approximately 18,300 individuals were employed as research physicists, a field that was growing closer to the national average, with 14 percent growth expected between 2010 and 2020.

University Research and Teaching. In 2010, approximately 16 percent of research physicists worked in university research and teaching positions. Many physicists utilize their training in the physical sciences to find postsecondary teaching positions in universities or colleges, where they lead classes on physics and a variety of other scientific fields, including mathematics and general environmental sciences.

Graduate and professional research departments at universities are involved in every facet of environmental physics research. For instance, the Department of Environmental Physics at Kansas State University conducts research into a variety of issues in environmental physics, including the transport of water, salt, and other compounds within the soil, environmental aspects of irrigation and water management, and the potential impacts of agricultural development on the environment. The atmospheric physics research team at the University of Maryland, Baltimore County, works with the National Aeronautics and Space Association (NASA) to conduct research into atmospheric transport of water vapor and gases and conduct ultraviolet, infrared, and visible light measurements of atmospheric gases.

A number of prominent international universities also produce significant research in atmospheric physics. For instance, Germany's University of Heidelberg is one of the world's leading institutions in environmental physics research, with ongoing research projects covering atmospheric and geophysical modeling, physical aspects of climate change, and development of physical measurement technology.

Military. Both the United States Department of Defense and the Armed Forces employ physicists in research positions. Military physicists often participate in atmospheric research, helping to create systems that can

Occupation	Environmental engineers
Employment 2010	51,400
Projected Employment 2020	62,700
Change in Number (2010–20)	11,300
Percent Change	22%

*Bureau of Labor Statistics, 2012

identify developing weather patterns that may affect military operations. Military physicists may also be involved in the development of new military technology, including radar and long-range scanning equipment.

The United States Army Research Office has developed an environmental science research division, which participates in a number of programs involving both atmospheric physics and geophysics research. Among other issues, army environmental scientists are investigating new ways to characterize and analyze terrain to inform military operations. In addition, the army utilizes environmental physics research for programs in habitation, investigating issues regarding the establishment of efficient temporary and permanent military settlements. Habitation research includes developing methods for water purification, and mapping and developing technology for energy storage and allocation, all of which utilize environmental physics research.

Government Agencies. Government agencies employ more than 20 percent of research physicists in the United States. The National Oceanic and Atmospheric Administration (NOAA)—one of the nation's largest institutions supporting atmospheric research and development—employs environmental physicists to study pollution, climate change, and meteorological development. Physicists working for NOAA often participate in efforts to evaluate and measure atmospheric gases and also work on climate modeling and meteorological projects.

NASA's Goddard Institute for Space Studies (GISS) is another prominent government agency that employs research physicists for a variety of projects. The GISS is one of the nation's leading institutions for climate change research and also develops and utilizes climate modeling in research programs. Among a variety of research programs funded by the GISS are programs studying thermodynamics and heat exchange in the atmosphere as well as a number of detailed studies of atmospheric dynamics and pollution.

Private Industry Research and Technology. Privately owned corporations involved in research and technical services account for more than 32 percent of physics research positions in the United States. Privately owned research corporations account for more than half of energy and energy technology research programs in the United States, helping to design energy technology for commercial applications. As the demand for sustainable energy increases—due in part to declining profitability within the petroleum industry and increasing concerns over environmental depletion—the private and commercial development of alternative power is expected to remain one of the nation's fastest growing industries.

Occupation	Environmental engineering technicians
Employment 2010	18,800
Projected Employment 2020	23,400
Change in Number (2010–20)	4,600
Percent Change	24%

*Bureau of Labor Statistics, 2012

For instance, environmental physics is needed in efforts to develop wind, solar, and geothermal energy, and a variety of utility and energy management corporations hire physicists for research and development projects. The Calpine Corporation, headquartered in Newark, Delaware, is one the United States' largest corporations developing power plants for geothermal energy distribution. Another large renewable energy corporation is the Italian multinational company Enel Green Power, which operates extensively in North and South America and works to research, develop, and distribute wind, solar, hydro, and geothermal power for commercial and residential applications.

Social Context and Future Prospects

Climate change research is at the forefront of scientific and political development in the United States and around the world, and this has created increased opportunities for specialists working in the environmental sciences. The environmental sciences industry as a whole is growing 3 to 4 percent faster than the average for all types of occupations in the United States. Much of this development comes from ongoing efforts to create better systems for monitoring environmental fluctuations and for developing green and sustainable energy sources.

Given growing international concern over climate change, atmospheric chemistry, physics, and climatology research has become a major priority in scientific development. Private, university, and government research programs around the world are seeking new ways to monitor greenhouses gases and environmental pollutants; environmental physics plays a major role in this endeavor. One of the most important areas of research concerns the continuing efforts to improve and refine climate models in order to make more precise predictions regarding the future of climate change given current conditions and expected future developments in pollutant levels. Environmental physics research is used both in the design of climate monitoring equipment and directly in the development of computer systems to model climate change on a regional and global scale.

As environmental consciousness has increased, in both the public and private spheres, there have been a variety of new regulatory systems put in place to control pollution, industrial emissions, and waste. The potential for increasingly stringent environmental legislation and restrictions has created a need for private and public research institutions to develop better monitoring and pollution control equipment. Environmental physics research will play an important role in the development of technology used to help meet these guidelines, including strategies for more efficient waste disposal, water purification, soil conservation, and land management.

Further Reading

Dessler, Andrew, and Edward A. Parson. *The Science and Politics of Global Climate Change: A Guide to the Debate*. New York: Cambridge UP, 2010. Print. Introduces the issue of climate change, including atmospheric chemistry and other atmospheric properties research. Also discusses the potential future of research in the area of climate change.

Forinash, Kyle. *Foundations of Environmental Physics*. Washington: Island, 2010. Print. Provides a comprehensive introduction to environmental physics principles governing energy use, storage, and transfer. Focuses on human energy use and the environmental impacts of energy harvesting, development, and waste.

Montieth, John L., and Mike H. Unsworth. *Principles of Environmental Physics*. 3rd ed. Burlington: Academic, 2008. Print. Provides a comprehensive introduction to environmental physics aimed at the undergraduate and graduate audience. Discusses measurement and analysis methods used to research the physical properties of atmospheric, hydrologic, and geological systems with a focus on methods used to research energy transfer in the environment.

National Geophysical Data Center (NGDC). NOAA.gov, 2012. Web. 1 Oct. 2012. Provides information taken from National Oceanic and Atmospheric Administration (NOAA) sponsored research into geophysics. Includes environmental physics research covering geomagnetic and geophysical modeling and information on the physical properties underlying natural hazards and meteorological developments.

Rose, Calvin. *An Introduction to the Environmental Physics of Soil, Water and Watersheds*. New York: Cambridge UP, 2004. Print. Provides an introduction to applications of physics to environmental issues in land management, water management, and agriculture. Also discusses methods used to investigate the physical properties of soil transport and to measure gases, liquids, and other materials in geological samples.

Smith, Claire. *Environmental Physics*. New York: Routledge, 2001. Print. Undergraduate-level introduction to environmental physics providing information on how scientists use physical science principles to investigate and understand environmental issues, including soil conservation, climate change, and weather forecasting.

Wilson, Jim, ed. *NASA Goddard Institute of Space Studies*. USA.gov, 2011. Web. 1 Oct. 2012. Describes a variety of current research programs in environmental sciences and environmental physics. Also contains descriptions of using environmental physics research to develop climate models.

About the Author: Micah L. Issitt (BS) is a professional freelance writer and journalist specializing in writing on the life sciences and sociology. Issitt has written numerous articles covering environmental sciences and the history of environmental science in America.

Environmental Engineer 🖋

Earnings (Yearly Median): $78,740 (Bureau of Labor Statistics, 2012)

Employment and Outlook: Faster than average (Bureau of Labor Statistics, 2012)

O*NET-SOC Code: 17-2081.00

Related Career Clusters: Agriculture, Food & Natural Resources; Government & Public Administration; Health Science; Law, Public Safety, Corrections & Security

Scope of Work

The first documented sewage and aqueduct system, engineered in the third century AD, enabled the Roman Empire to regulate the safety of the city's water sources and provide its residents with a method of effectively removing waste. The Roman aqueduct is credited with providing Rome with enough water to handle its drinking, flushing, and fire-fighting needs, as well as supply its aesthetic fountains.

In the twenty-first century, environmental engineers not only oversee the safety of the world's water and waste systems but also help to combat air pollution, encourage recycling efforts, develop methods for containing and combating hazardous waste, and prescribe ecologically sound development practices. Environmental engineers seek to maintain the safety of the natural world and the health of its inhabitants by crafting engineering solutions for the biological and chemical processes involved in environmental issues.

Education and Coursework

High-school students interested in a degree in environmental engineering should take classes that fulfill the entry requirements of an undergraduate engineering program. The math prerequisites include algebra, geometry, trigonometry, and calculus, while required science classes include biology, chemistry, and physics. In addition, students should take a class in computer science or statistics, as there is a great deal of analysis involved in environmental studies. Students should also take advantage of any environmental or marine science course offered, as these courses provide an introduction to the ecological topics in environmental engineering and include some of the terminology and current issues.

In 2012, there were fifty-nine accredited undergraduate environmental-engineering programs in the United States, often housed within in a more established engineering discipline, such as civil, chemical, or mechanical. A bachelor of science degree is the minimum requirement for entry into the field of environmental engineering. The first two years of study focus on basic engineering and science courses, supplemented with several classes in the social sciences designed to help students understand how societies and individuals work. It is during the last two to three years that the program takes on an environmental focus, with internships and courses in such areas as pollution control, water resources, treatment-plant design, environmental safety, hazardous-waste management, air quality, and hydraulics.

Entry into a master's degree program usually requires an undergraduate degree in environmental engineering from an accredited college. However, programs will often provisionally accept students with an undergraduate degree in math or life sciences if they possess a high enough grade-point average or general GRE (Graduate Record Examinations) score. As the field of environmental engineering becomes more competitive, more employers will be looking for candidates with a master's degree. At the master's level, students will often focus on a specific environmental issue, such as energy technology, carbon management, or climate-change policy.

Students wishing to work as consultants, independent researchers, or college professors must acquire a doctorate, for which they will extensively research and defend a doctoral thesis. A great deal of the doctoral degree is spent outside the classroom in hands-on research.

Career Enhancement and Training

In addition to course work, school-based environmental clubs and local nonprofit conservation organizations provide both volunteer and pay opportunities to students. Through various projects, students can obtain practical experience in many areas of conservation, including recycling, invasive species, wildlife, watersheds, and energy conservation. Journals such as *Chemical & Engineering News* and *Pollution Engineering* provide additional information on current topics and solutions in environmental engineering.

As with most engineering jobs that deal with the public, environmental engineers should acquire a professional engineer (PE) license. In order to achieve this, an engineer must pass the Fundamentals of Engineering (FE) exam at the conclusion of his or her accredited undergraduate degree program, train under a professionally licensed mentor for four years, and then pass the Principles and Practices of Engineering (PE) exam.

In lieu of a master's degree, environmental engineers can also improve their portfolio and expertise through college and online certification programs. Many of these programs require participants to possess an undergraduate degree with a 3.0 grade-point average in their major. Certification programs are offered through many colleges and professional organizations. One example of this is the Leadership in Energy and Environmental Design (LEED) certification, designed to certify engineers as experts in green construction and maintenance.

Professional organizations also offer certification programs, as well as a means of networking for jobs and collaborations. Two popular environmental engineering organizations are the American Academy of Environmental Engineers (AAEE) and the National Registry of Environmental Professionals (NREP).

Daily Tasks and Technology

Environmental engineers are concerned with all aspects of environmental affairs. They help ensure the safety of the air, water, and soil. On the job, environmental engineers can be seen working in various roles. A field engineer may be collecting soil and water samples out in the marshes; an environmental analyst might study air-pollution data

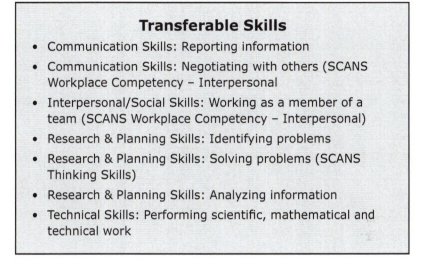

Transferable Skills

- Communication Skills: Reporting information
- Communication Skills: Negotiating with others (SCANS Workplace Competency – Interpersonal
- Interpersonal/Social Skills: Working as a member of a team (SCANS Workplace Competency – Interpersonal)
- Research & Planning Skills: Identifying problems
- Research & Planning Skills: Solving problems (SCANS Thinking Skills)
- Research & Planning Skills: Analyzing information
- Technical Skills: Performing scientific, mathematical and technical work

in a lab; an urban planner may work in an office, helping to ensure that green development codes are enforced; and a legal expert may consult in a court case involving an industrial hazardous waste incident.

Environmental engineers are employed by a number of different businesses, including manufacturing industries, universities, consulting firms, government agencies (at local, state, and federal levels), public-interest groups, private research firms, and international corporations.

Environmental engineers who work for the Environmental Protection Agency (EPA) act as investigators for such events as wildlife death in a local pond. In this instance, in addition to designing a remediation system to remove the hazardous waste, the environmental engineer will try to locate the source of the problem. If the environmental engineer feels the problem may be caused by a manufacturing industry upstream, he or she will tour the plant, review its procedures, and take samples of its wastewater-treatment system. If the problem lies with the manufacturing plant, the environmental engineer can enforce environmental regulations, write up reports, and assist the plant workers in complying with environmental standards.

Environmental engineers use their communication skills in collaborating with scientists, developers, waste technicians, and other engineers in this multidisciplinary field. Their work focuses not only on local problems but on global issues as well, including acid rain, global warming, ozone depletion, and emissions.

Environmental engineers use specialized meters such as mass spectrometers, photometers, and air velocity and temperature monitors. Specialized software programs designed to model groundwater flow include the MIKE product family, developed by the Denmark-based company DHI, and MODFLOW, developed by the US Geological Survey.

Earnings and Employment Outlook

Since the year 2000, the field of environmental engineering has had an excellent employment outlook, boasting more jobs than applicants to fill them. According to the Bureau of Labor Statistics, this profession anticipates a faster-than-average growth rate of 22 percent between 2010 and 2020, with a projected 11,300 new job openings.

According to the Bureau of Labor Statistics, this profession anticipates a faster-than-average growth rate of 22 percent between 2010 and 2020, with a projected 11,300 new job openings.

Though the future of the environmental-engineering field looks bright overall, popular areas of expertise will vary depending on public trends and prevailing government policies. Therefore, environmental engineers need to be adaptable and willing to realign their education as needed; a career path may begin with a focus on wastewater, veer into solid waste, and end with a certification in air pollution.

Close to half of employed environmental engineers work in professional, scientific, and technical-services fields, while approximately 28 percent are hired by federal, state, and local government agencies. Universities, national and international corporations, and self-employed consultants make up the remaining third. Starting salaries for environmental engineers with a bachelor's degree average $47,384 per year, while a senior worker with an advanced degree can earn more than $100,000 per year.

In 2009, the highest-paid environmental engineers worked in fields related to computer systems and design, followed closely by those working in fields related to the federal government. The highest-paying states for environmental engineers in that same year were the District of Columbia, Massachusetts, Virginia, California, and Illinois.

Related Occupations

- **Civil Engineers**: Civil engineers design and oversee large construction projects, including those involved in transportation, water and sewage systems, and buildings.

- **Environmental Engineering Technicians**: Environmental engineering technicians perform hands-on work for environmental engineers, such as collecting samples, performing lab tests, and operating waste-management equipment.

- **Environmental Scientists**: Environmental scientists investigate the causes and potential solutions for environmental hazards, working with data collected from air, food, water, and soil.

- **Hydrologists:** Hydrologists research the properties and qualities of water, as well as its overall cycle in the environment. They are involved in various water projects, including hydroelectric power plants and irrigation systems.

- **Agricultural Engineers:** Agricultural engineers help farmers and industries in addressing their agricultural needs. They specialize in such areas as farm buildings, mechanical and electric power sources, soil and water conservation, and food engineering.

Future Applications

Born out of the environmental movement launched in the 1960s with Rachel Carson's book *Silent Spring* (1962), environmental engineering—previously termed sanitation engineering—is a branch of civil engineering that found its niche in the 1970s push for environmental regulations. Its global focus advanced with the grassroots establishment of Earth Day in 1970 and the United Nations Conference on the Human Environment (Stockholm Conference) in 1972. The future

A Conversation with Jane Madden

Job Title: Senior Vice President with CDM Smith

What was your career path?

When I was young I was captivated by *The Undersea World of Jacques Cousteau* and convinced that I wanted to be a marine biologist so I too could spend my life appreciating the majestic beauty of this hidden world. I entered the University of Vermont as a biology major, but realized after my first year that this was not a perfect fit. Having always excelled in math, I was encouraged to consider engineering. I transferred to civil engineering, and through that curriculum discovered environmental engineering. After graduation, I immediately got a great job with CDM Smith, a consulting, engineering, construction, and operations firm, and have been with the same company for nearly thirty years, protecting the rivers and oceans I love through my work in the design of wastewater treatment facilities.

What are three pieces of advice?

1. Find an occupation that you are passionate about – look for a career, not a job.
2. Work with people you like, with similar core values.
3. Challenge those you work for–question authority; it is these questions that make people think differently, and advance society. Lastly, don't pass up an opportunity when it is offered to you, even though you think you may not be capable–if someone has faith in you, have faith in yourself.

What paths for career advancement are available to you?

The sky is the limit. I have grown up in my current organization starting out as a project engineer, moving to a project manager, then a client manager responsible for sales, and now am responsible for all the public sector work we do in Massachusetts. Since we are a global firm, opportunities exist for me around the world to assist in bringing clean water and sanitation to the global population. With environmental concerns related to greenhouse gas emissions and climate change, the focus of our industry has moved to the water-energy nexus and the vulnerability of communities given rising sea levels and more extreme droughts and rain events. The next step for me is being more involved in policymaking at a state and federal level to ensure that the government is making the right decisions with respect to the environment.

will see an even greater awareness of environmental engineering as drinkable water sources diminish, global climate changes are manifested, and new sustainable energy sources are developed.

The 2015 Millennium Development Goals (MDGs) are a collaborative outreach effort between UNICEF (United Nations Children's Fund) and WHO (World Health Organization) designed to bring safe water sources and sanitation to the world. In their 2012 report, UNICEF/WHO announced that since 1990, they had reduced the amount of people without access to safe drinking water by half. Environmental engineers will be called upon in the effort to continue to meet UNICEF/WHO goals, especially in the field of sanitation.

An increase in both the intensity and the frequency of storms is one of the consequences of global warming, and flooding due to these storms will exceed the current limits of municipal storm drains and wastewater systems. Environmental engineers will be needed to assist in designing these new or modified systems. They will also be integral in addressing ecological issues surrounding future energy sources, including potential groundwater contamination produced by extracting shale gas (called *fracking*) and greenhouse emissions produced by Canada's oil sands reserves.

—*Rose Young*

More Information

American Academy of Environmental Engineers
130 Holiday Court, Suite 100
Annapolis, MD 21401
www.aaee.net

American Society for Engineering Education
1818 N Street NW, Suite 600
Washington, DC 20036
www.asee.org

Environmental and Water Resources Institute
American Society of Civil Engineers
1801 Alexander Bell Drive
Reston, VA 20191-4400
www.asce.org/ewri

Environmental Engineering Division
American Society of Mechanical Engineers
3 Park Avenue
New York, NY 10016-5990
divisions.asme.org/EED

United States Environmental Protection Agency
Ariel Rios Building
1200 Pennsylvania Avenue NW
Washington, DC 20460
www.epa.gov

Fluid Dynamics

FIELDS OF STUDY

Aerodynamics; aeronautical and aerospace studies; aeronautical engineering; applied mathematics; buoyancy; chemical engineering; computational fluid dynamics; computational physics; engineering; gas dynamics; geophysics; heat transfer; high energy physics; hydraulics; hydrodynamics; lubrication theory; magneto-fluids; mathematical physics; mass transfer; mechanical engineering; plasma theory; solid mechanics; rheology; thermodynamics; vector calculus; volcanology; waves and stability.

DEFINITION

Fluids include liquids, gases, and plasmas of all kinds; mathematical equations allow scientists to model different kinds of flows by idealizing fluid itself. It is often accepted in idealized terms that, for mathematical purposes, volume cannot change; a fluid under study has constant density and a force moving through the fluid is constant. Fluid flow is the velocity of a substance in a space-time framework. Fluid dynamics is the complex search for the value of that velocity. Analytical study of fluid dynamics is enriched by applied scientific exploration, and knowledge gained from mathematical efforts to understand idealized fluid flow has many practical uses.

Basic Principles

Isaac Newton's second law of thermodynamics concerns movement and is central to fluid dynamics. Newton's law states that adding together a moving body's mass and acceleration will yield a numerical equivalent for forces pushing that body. Thus, measurable mass, acceleration, and force can be used to learn more about the others. This law of physics provided the foundation on which Leonhard Euler built a theory of fluid dynamics. He developed an equation that tacked velocity to both time and space so that the velocity specified any instant in an electromagnetic flow field. Euler's approach signifies the fluid flow point by point, so that many calculations must be done to understand a whole flow field. From this simple beginning, pressure, density, and other quantities can be calculated. Euler also specified inviscid flow, which uses a theoretical fluid that possesses no friction against itself. The concept of an inviscid flow, which is largely theoretical, has also been useful in basic fluid dynamics for nearly three centuries. Euler further succeeded in using partial differential equations to solve fluid dynamics problems. He published his equations in 1759 and his differentials and algorithms essential to the modern fluid dynamics scientist.

Euler's differentials were improved upon in 1845 by George Stokes. Stokes had been broadening the utility of equations developed by Claude-Louis Navier in 1822, so the resulting equations are known as Navier-Stokes equations. These analyze fluid stress and help to explain many basic problems, such as viscosity changes under temperature variables. A simple example of viscosity change under temperature variable is the way syrup, thick when chilled, thins when heated. However practical the Navier-Stokes equations have been, the full equations have yet to yield analytic solutions. Initially, many subfields of problem-specific equations were worked out for flow fields of different kinds, and the pragmatic aspects of the Navier-Stokes equations were proven. However, as a purely mathematical problem, they remain one of the most important open problems in mathematics today.

Core Concepts

Matter comes in solid, liquid, gas, and plasma states—three out of four of which are fluid. Fluid dynamics studies matter in those states which, in technical terms, have no intrinsic shape and in which elements can move around without affecting the overall properties of the sample. If ice is added to a glass of water, each part of the resulting flow must be understood mathematically, point-by-point, as an instant of space and time, changing place and temperature, but remaining a glass of water.

Values for space and time are therefore highly changeable. For any given velocity, taken as a point moving in a direction at a speed, space and time must be calculated instant by instant. Powerful computer methodology is a dominant force in fluid dynamics and scientists find two approaches helpful. The first is mathematical physics, which creates theories. A mathematical physicist tackles problems in physics and reaches for new mathematical theory. New theories can then be applied to practical problems in such fields as weather, aerodynamics, oilfield technology, and circulatory system biomedics. In the second approach, computational physics takes already known theories and works with them to solve problems. Computational physics is important in fluid dynamics, but applies to many other fields of physics. Clearly, mathematical analysis dominates fluid dynamics; however, physical experimentation remains an unshaken foundation.

Continuum Hypothesis. As with solid matter, when a fluid is studied, it is treated as continuous, even though the molecules within the fluid are distributed in an extremely non-uniform manner. For the sake of study, the fluid is treated as if the molecular structure varies on a smooth basis. This is called the "continuum hypothesis." The continuum hypothesis applies to liquid, gas, and plasma, all of which are subject to fluid dynamics, although in different ways.

Gas and Water. The flow of gas is better understood than the flow of water. Gas can be effectively modeled in a so-called ideal state of free molecules, because in a gas, molecules are spread far and wide. In a liquid, however, every molecule is closer to the next one and subject to force fields of nearby molecules, a phase called "condensed." Accounting for flow in a gas, physicists can depend at times on individual molecular properties. Not so for liquid, where the interplay of closely attached yet mobile groups is highly complex. Another thing that makes the study of fluid dynamics harder for liquid than gas is that water—the most common and widely used liquid—is in many ways different from other fluids. Even though it is a common subject of study, water is not a good representative sample and the fluid dynamics of water cannot always easily translate to other fluids.

Vectors and Tensors. As with basic physics, knowledge of vectors and tensors supplies a fundamental notation for fluid dynamics. A vector is a speed moving in a direction, usually notated with an arrow. It is one-dimensional and, in fluid dynamics, represents a force moving against fluid, such as wind moving over water. It was once believed that wind generated the ocean currents. This is true of surface currents, but the National Aeronautics and Space Administration's (NASA) Aquarius satellite—which has been reading salinity at the surface of the oceans—has aided the understanding that currents are also run from the depths. Deep currents move according to the density of the water, so fluid dynamics physicists notate this with vectors indicating more dense areas of water moving into less dense areas.

Tensors add geometry by mapping additional vectors, grasping three and four dimensions in a closer approximation to reality. Of course, these ocean currents are moving in more than one simple direction, as salinity and temperature also affect water pressure at the depths. The vector and tensor notation, which often differs from problem to problem, can be used to describe material attributes of things in many fields. The fields covered by fluid dynamics encompass much of known reality, ranging from atmospheric physics to electromagnetics to mechanics to medicine—the range goes all the way from the earth's outermost atmospheric plasma layer down to the veins in the human body.

Viscosity. Viscosity is the extent to which a fluid resists flowing, sometimes conceptualized in terms of "internal friction." If the molecules of a flowing substance stick to each other, it makes a highly viscous fluid (wet cement, for example). If flowing molecules stick to each other less, the fluid is less viscous (such as alcohol). An "inviscid" or "ideal" fluid is one with no viscosity—it does not stick to itself. Setting aside superfluids, no such ideal fluid exists in nature, but they have long been mathematically imagined and worked with to some pragmatic end. Euler's eighteenth-century equations were written for inviscid fluids. Long after his equations were proven, physicist Kamerlingh Onnes supercooled helium to the point that some of it turned inviscous. Most pragmatic fluid dynamics are worked around viscous fluids, but some scientists study inviscous fluids and their application. For instance, the inviscous superfluid liquid helium is used in computer cooling, cryogenics, medical technology, offshore oil and gas production, and in many other ways.

Interesting Facts about Fluid Dynamics

- Superfluids were first developed in 1908 by Kamerlingh Onnes, who supercooled helium until a portion of it had zero viscosity. This superfluid has applications in high-energy physics, astrophysics, superconductivity, and superconducting magnets.

- The Clay Mathematics Institute offers a one-million-dollar prize for the individual or team that provides a solution to the Navier-Stokes equations—the equations that describe the motion of fluid substances.

- Australia's Commonwealth Scientific and Industrial Research Organisation (CSIRO) is developing a sensor that would take acoustical fluid pressure readings from within the human body in the proximity of a medical implant, and send signals to a remote device.

- When water is frozen, its ice crystals make a tetrahedral form. At the SLAC labs, scientists have not only found that liquid water also has these tetrahedral clusters, but also that there is another, looser molecular arrangement that coexists that could explain some of water's unusual features.

- Lava flows, mud slides, and glacier flows make fluid dynamics important to geophysics.

Compressibility and Density. Two other important measurable qualities of fluid are its compressibility and density. For the most part, fluids are incompressible, which is to say massive amounts of pressure can only slightly squeeze the volume of, for instance, water. Density is related to compressibility. Pressure on most fluids will not affect their density very much, as long as the temperature remains fairly constant. However, when the heat is turned up a liquid usually expands, changing its density. Expanding fluids are generally less dense than contracting fluids. If temperatures turn down, liquids tend to contract. But fluid dynamics applies also to gas and plasma, and so to grasp the basics of the study, it is important to stabilize some of these many variables. Some scientists begin by assuming a fluid that is incompressible, which has density that varies smoothly if at all, and that is viscous. Once a sample type of such a fluid as this is imagined and assigned numerical signifiers, or procured for the lab, progress can be made in experimentation and theory.

Applications Past and Present

Dynamics. Fluids have mechanical properties that are not necessarily the same as their dynamic properties. Fluid dynamics must be distinguished from fluid mechanics by noting that the study of fluids in motion, or dynamics, is a subfield of fluid mechanics. The central concept of fluid dynamics is a "flow field." A flow field can be seen in anything from wind to lava to blood to laboratory-manufactured polymers. It just has to have a makeup such that its constituent parts shift their positions in relation to one another to a rather large degree under the influence of outside forces. A block of wood struck by a hammer will experience only a small relative rearrangement of its constituent parts; a wooden canoe, on the other hand, skimming over the surface of a lake, will rearrange the constituent parts of the water to a far greater degree. Fluid dynamics seeks the value of velocity, in time and space. A fluid in a state of rest—in a container on a shelf, for example— would not fit into the study of fluid dynamics, but as soon as the container is knocked over, the fluid takes on some velocity, creating a way to calculate any point at any instant in the resulting flow field.

Rheology. Drying concrete, cooling lava, and peanut butter are examples that demonstrate that the boundary between fluid and solid is often complicated. Concrete flows until it sets, becoming one of the most common solids in man-made environments. Lava develops internal solid structures as it cools while still flowing, and peanut butter can melt on a hot day. Rheology is the study of substances like these that participate in flowing, but not fully. Paint, for instance, is fluid until it dries. Rheology is a study of mechanics, not dynamics, but it is important to fluid dynamics because many substances belong in both fields.

Predictability. The purpose of the study of fluid dynamics is to be able to predict situations. As scientists have learned to mathematically predict the physical reactions of fluid masses to force, they have also strengthened their understanding of the many complex motions in fluid; this understanding also sheds light on the many reactions that arise as a result of those motions' interactions with boundary layers and neighboring substances. These studies have practical applications; for instance, the lubrication theory branch of fluid dynamics. Here, the scientist approaches flow fields that have dominant viscous stress. In other words, a good lubricant sticks to itself under stress. Modern machinery is under constant demand to be more efficient, move faster, and withstand ever greater extremes of cold and heat. Therefore, stronger, more viscous lubricants are needed to keep these machines going.

Ships and Airplanes. Two fluids through which people move are water and air. Buoyancy is the force that pushes upward in a fluid. Archimedes described buoyancy in the third century BCE. He said that in the case of water, the weight of water displaced by a sinking object was equal to the force of buoyancy, pushing that object back towards the surface. The principles of buoyancy include the knowledge that the weight of water itself causes more pressure below than above. Divers understand that the increased water pressure at depths is potentially deadly because of its effects on their blood, subjecting them to the dangers of the bends, or decompression sickness. Greater water pressure below causes buoyant materials to seek the lighter pressure above by moving into it. Initially, to build ships, a hands-on understanding of buoyancy was required. Buoyant materials such as inflated sheepskins, bundles of reeds, and pieces of wood have historically been the shipbuilder's materials. Nineteenth-century shipbuilders, aided by growing understanding of the principles of buoyancy, put more and more metal into frames, hulls, and finally whole ships. The ocean is the largest unexplored area on Earth, and knowledge of fluid dynamics is important in constructing the strong, pressure-resistant hulls of today's deep-diving exploratory craft.

Air travel was first made possible by understanding how wings work. In the fluid medium of air, a force known as lift was determined to occur when a thin moving body causes greater pressure in the air underneath it than above it. Just as with buoyancy, the object seeks to move towards the area of less pressure, again in this case upwards. Vortices trail behind the wing, associated with drag forces pulling the wing away from its upward tendency; taming these forces was a big part of the challenge of early flight. Aeronautical scientists Frederick W. Lanchester and Ludwig Prandtl calculated the system of trailing vortices and the drag induced by the wing's movement as flight was being developed. The Lanchester-Prandtl calculations proved useful throughout the era of subsonic flight development and into the twenty-first century. However, supersonic flight and vehicular movement through super-thin atmospheric regions and even into the plasma zone of the upper atmosphere all remain challenges for fluid dynamics scientists.

Medical. Bodily fluids are subject to the study of fluid dynamics since, in a living organism, fluids are in constant motion. The United States Food and Drug Administration (FDA) has a laboratory devoted to the interactions of medical implants and other devices with bodily fluids. Such machinery includes artificial valves in the body, and dialysis pumps outside the body. Fluid dynamics is a life-or-death matter in the medical devices industry, and the FDA uses its Fluid Dynamics Laboratory to regulate and engineer this industry. The situation is complicated by the fact that blood is a fluid, but not an ideal fluid, as are the fluids of pure scientific study. Instead, blood is alive; it has plasma, which is liquid, but suspended in the plasma are all sorts of functioning minute particles, such as blood cells. For medical therapy to work, the exposure of blood to the device must not harm the blood beyond a certain level, nor must blood do damage to the device. For example, blood must not clog filters or stop up a pump by clotting. The time variable is highly sensitive. The FDA Department of Solid and Fluid Mechanics oversees the Fluid Dynamics Laboratory. Much of their scientific research revolves around working out methods for testing and predicting the functionality of various devices that are proposed for the medical market.

Impact on Industry

The wide-ranging presence of fluids in daily life may be surprising to those who feel they live in a solid universe. However, once the earth's atmosphere and oceans are taken into consideration, and human blood, lymph, and other bodily fluids are added, the universe may start to seem more fluid than solid. In between the extremes of the outer atmospheric plasma and blood plasma are many fluids important to modern culture. Crude oil, for example, is a fluid. In addition, natural gas may provide fuel for automobiles in the future. Oilfield technology, including natural gas, is advancing on a daily basis.

Occupation	Hydrologists
Employment 2010	7,600
Projected Employment 2020	9,000
Change in Number (2010–20)	1,400
Percent Change	18%

Bureau of Labor Statistics, 2012

Government Agencies. The United States Department of Energy (DOE) has an Office of Science, which fosters more than one-third of the United States' research into physics. Overseeing the Princeton Plasma Physics Laboratory, the SLAC National Accelerator Laboratory, and several more important research sites, the DOE pursues energy-related knowledge. Part of their work is known as Scientific Discovery through Advanced Computing (SciDAC). This project collects academic research into a journal and has partnerships at universities where the focus is on tera-scale computing. Tera-scale computing whips out calculations by the trillions per second. SciDAC employs computational physicists; one of its fluid-dynamics related challenges is world climate.

Military. In the military, one fluid of interest is the air, and computational modeling of problems in helicopter aeronautics calls for fluid dynamics expertise. At Moffett Federal Airfield in California, the US Army's Aeroflightdynamics Directorate has a program called the High-Performance Computing Institute for Advanced Rotorcraft Modeling and Simulation. Its goal is to improve rotary aircraft for better performance through expert computer modeling. In a more hands-on application, the most basic energy running the United States Air Force is petroleum. Petroleum of course is a fluid, and when it is added to aircraft in flight, the fluid dynamics double. Refueling a plane in flight requires such advanced hoses, valves, nozzles, fittings, filters, adapters, and piping, that a company called Fluid Dynamics subcontracts just this job.

Weather forecasting is a central military interest that relies on fluid dynamics scientists, since the earth's atmosphere is a fluid. For military operations and communication, weather forecasting must be accurate and reliable. Satellites are essential to both weather forecasting and communications. Satellites are also essential to the United States Air Force Academy's Department of Physics, which operates the Space Physics and Atmospheric Research Center (SPARC). Research in the plasma fields of the earth's outer atmosphere is also an area of fluid dynamics. In practical terms, plasma interaction with solar output, which causes solar storms, has detrimental effects on satellites. Atmospheric plasma is studied by cadets and faculty at SPARC, who work across a wide range including theory, computer modeling, advancing observation methods, and building better measurement devices.

University Research and Teaching. At the university level, opportunities for the qualified fluid dynamics scientist to earn a PhD and continue in an academic career are abundant. They can be funded by industrial interests. For example, in 2012 the Illinois Institute of Technology (IIT) Armour College of Engineering runs six laboratories with funding from companies such as Honeywell and Boeing. This suggests that high-quality equipment is available for research into problems of interest to the nation. One of these problems under study at IIT is the dispersion of contaminants, a problem that in general applies to oil spills in water and toxic substances in the air. Like oilfield jobs, the academic scope is international and professors and postdoctoral researchers are in demand at a variety of different institutions, colleges, and universities.

Social Context and Future Prospects

Because materials flow everywhere, there is a broad scope of future prospects for fluid dynamics. Researchers and scholars are needed to examine the field from the minute spaces where capillaries exchange solutes and water across membranes, to the vast plasma storms at the outer atmosphere. Industrial applications for scientists increase as technology develops as well. Consider safety, just one aspect of fluid dynamics that affects daily life. Advances in fluid dynamics can improve the safety of air travel, space travel, medical devices, industrial equipment, and many daily incidents. Computational fluid dynamics (CFD) is of special importance in the field of safety, because CFD programs are used in a number of practical ways. Safety officials use CFD programs in investigations after the fact when a safety incident has occurred, such as an explosion or fire. However, progress is needed in the CFD safety field because current programs fall short when they fail to accurately solve problems in boundary areas, or fail to solve for fluctuations in turbulence that are smaller than the overall picture. Many more detailed programs are needed in the future.

In addition to safety, future work in fluid dynamics will very likely pertain to climate change. Two fluids, the atmosphere and oceans, are the most affected by climate change. The 2012 drought across the American Midwest is one example of a situation that will increase the need for long-term climate forecasting so as to ensure abundant food supplies. Fluid dynamics scientists will be needed to perform basic research and teaching at many levels to help address climate change.

Further Reading

Acheson, D. J. *Elementary Fluid Dynamics*. Oxford: Oxford UP, 1990. Print. A comprehensive overview of fluid dynamics for undergraduate physics students. Discusses applied mathematics in addition to the field's history and applications.

Batchelor, G. K. *An Introduction to Fluid Dynamics*. Cambridge: Cambridge UP, 2000. Print. A reissue of a 1967 introduction to the field that presents information on the theories of fluid mechanics and their mathematic equations.

Moffatt, H. K., and Emily Shuckburgh, eds. *Environmental Hazards: The Fluid Dynamics and Geophysics of Extreme Events*. World Scientific: Singapore, 2011. Print. Includes lectures on subjects such as tsunamis, flooding, and air pollution from perspectives related to geophysics, applied mathematics, and fluid mechanics.

Tritton, D. J. *Physical Fluid Dynamics*. 2nd ed. Oxford: Clarendon, 2003. Print. An overview of fluids in motion that focuses on physics and discusses topics including flow configurations, geophysics, and atmospheric convection.

About the Author: Amanda R. Jones has an MA from Virginia Tech and a PhD in English from the University of Virginia. She has written several articles for EBSCO and published in the *Children's Literature Association Quarterly.*

Hydrologist 🖋

Earnings (Yearly Average): $75,690

Employment and Outlook: Average growth

O*NET-SOC Code: 19-2043.00

Related Career Clusters: Agriculture, Food & Natural Resources; Government & Public Administration; Architecture & Construction

---

Scope of Work

Hydrologists study all facets of the water cycle, from rainfall patterns to the distribution of water through the environment and its eventual return to the atmosphere. Of central importance is the hydrologist's role in ensuring that the earth's population has access to fresh drinking water, a task that has become increasingly challenging as the global population expands. Mixing mathematics and science, hydrologists play a crucial role in any project taking place on or near waterways. Whether building a bridge over a river or planning a subdivision on former pasture land, construction crews must first consult hydrologists to ascertain how such activity will affect local drainage and water quality. All entities, public or private, that do any form of work in which water plays a role will need to retain the services of a hydrologist.

Education and Coursework

Students interested in becoming a hydrologist need to be aware that few institutions of higher learning offer a direct degree in the field. Rather, most universities have concentrations in the discipline as part of a broader environmental science, geology, or engineering program. Although a bachelor of science degree might lead to entry-level employment in the field, an advanced degree is the gateway to broader placement. Students should seek guidance from a faculty member who is either an active hydrologist or connected with active hydrologists in order to acquire field work experience. Many hydrologists conduct research outside the laboratory and must possess a considerable degree of stamina to reach sites in relatively remote locations accessible primarily by foot. A master's degree is preferred by most employers, and for certain posts, such as a university professor or advanced researcher, a doctorate is required. Extensive training in mathematics; the sciences broadly defined, including chemistry, physics, and biology; and computer technology are all expected.

Scholars in the field must also be familiar with a host of other disciplines that intersect with the work of a hydrologist, such as environmental law, local construction ordinances, and an array of other concerns. Admission to graduate programs in the field is very competitive owing to the limited number of existing programs. Scores on the quantitative portion of the Graduate Records Exam (GRE) are carefully scrutinized in the application process. An additional two years on top of the already committed four years of undergraduate training can be expected after high school. During this time, students will gain a more detailed understanding of the discipline and secure critical field experience that will enhance their marketability. Most graduate programs encourage students to develop a broad awareness of and familiarity with the technology that governs hydrologic research. Expertise in computer modeling and mapping are increasingly common criteria for employers, as is familiarity with other research tools such as remote sensing and global positioning equipment.

Career Enhancement and Training

Advanced graduate students are encouraged to join the International Association of Hydrological Sciences, the International Association of Environmental Hydrology, and the American Institute of Hydrology (AIH) for access to the latest research in the field as well as for potential job listings. Membership in such associations remains an essential means of continuing professional education, regardless of the discipline. Associations hold annual conferences that provide excellent networking opportunities, just as they produce scholarly journals and newsletters that keep job seekers informed of openings and the latest technological advances that shape the field. Prudent professionals, regardless of the discipline, recognize the value of membership in professional organizations.

Licensing is required in some states before a hydrologist can practice within its borders. The AIH offers a certification program for its members. State licensing criteria generally consist of a minimum educational attainment or work experience under the guidance of an accredited hydrologist, which is often a prerequisite for taking a licensing exam that tests basic subject knowledge. Periodic renewal of the license is required and certain criminal convictions directly related to employment might preclude future licensing. As with most professions, continuing education, along with the procurement of multiple additional certifications, serves as the only surefire way to ensure advancement and higher compensation.

Daily Tasks and Technology

The daily tasks of a hydrologist are difficult to generalize, as the field is remarkably varied. A hydrologist may study water in the soil, its path to local waterways, or its return to earth in the form of precipitation. In any of these cases, a hydrologist will use complex computer software to record, track, and plot that particular subset of the water cycle he or she is responsible for on a given project. Data collection remains the most critical as well as the most physically demanding component of the job. Data sampling must be done for each individual project, as the circumstances surrounding a given work zone are different and will even change over time. A hydrologist studying the water depth of the Mississippi River to assess the suitability of barge traffic must take new samples rather than rely on old data, owing to a host of mitigating conditions including rainfall patterns and drought conditions. In this sense, the task of scientists in the field is constantly changing, because the environment in which the water cycle unfolds is always evolving. Flooding, for example, is often not the result of heavy local rainfall, but the byproduct of conditions hundreds of miles upriver. Hydrologists must account for factors near and far when modeling flood or erosion conditions. Since scientists cannot be in two places at once, they must rely on electronic sensors to capture water levels and conditions from a distance. Hydrologists who study the suitability of the water

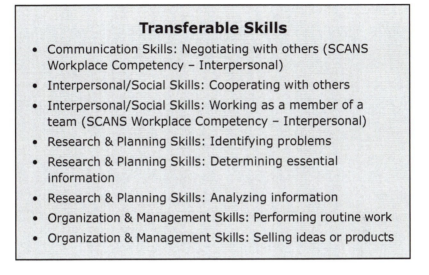

Transferable Skills

- Communication Skills: Negotiating with others (SCANS Workplace Competency – Interpersonal)
- Interpersonal/Social Skills: Cooperating with others
- Interpersonal/Social Skills: Working as a member of a team (SCANS Workplace Competency – Interpersonal)
- Research & Planning Skills: Identifying problems
- Research & Planning Skills: Determining essential information
- Research & Planning Skills: Analyzing information
- Organization & Management Skills: Performing routine work
- Organization & Management Skills: Selling ideas or products

contained in large reservoirs that provide drinking water to metropolitan centers are often required to gather samples in remote, isolated locations. Extensive walking and sample gathering make above-average levels of fitness essential for certain jobs that take place outside the laboratory. After collecting field data, the hydrologist must bring his study samples to the lab for analysis and plug it into computers where the process of mapping and modeling take center stage. A typical day thus may begin in a mountain reservoir and end at a keyboard.

Earnings and Employment Outlook

Few things are certain in forecasting future employment trends, but the field of hydrology offers a future with bright prospects. One of the great dilemmas facing humanity across the globe is securing sufficient clean drinking water. In industrialized nations such as the United States, hydrologists are being called upon to find means of providing water to ever-growing urban and suburban populations as they strain existing supplies. They must also assess the impact of new construction projects on local wells, runoff conditions, and a host of related factors. So long as population growth continues, hydrologists will be called on to provide their expertise. In less industrialized locales, the nature of employment might differ, but the demand for water remains the same. Hydrologists assist drought- and poverty-stricken regions become more effective stewards of the limited resources available to them, just as they offer critical guidance to ensure that local waste runoff does not contaminate water supplies. Water remains a critical component for sustaining human life. Its availability following centuries of waste dumping and mismanagement is as limited today as it has ever been. A bright future exists for hydrologists who offer innovative methods for protecting the globe's most precious resource: water.

The United States Department of Labor estimates that the need for hydrologists over the next twenty years will increase by as much as 18 percent. Population expansion in conjunction with increased concerns regarding pollution will help drive the growth of the profession. As water shortages become more widespread and more acute, it is logical to expect that the financial incentives driving solutions to the crisis will grow as well. Future hydrologists are positioned to make a critical contribution to the world's future while earning ample compensation for their efforts.

Related Occupations

- **Geoscientists:** Geoscientists study all facets of the earth, from its processes to its structure. Water, which covers of 75 percent of the earth's surface, is an essential component of this field.

- **Meteorologists:** Meteorology, the study of weather patterns, often requires an understanding of the evolution of phenomena directly connected to the water cycle. Blizzards, hurricanes, and related weather events are all central to the work performed by hydrologists.

- **Geophysicists:** Geophysicists study the earth using a variety of methods, testing such things as seismic activity. They are often enlisted to assess the suitability of water-related construction projects such as dam or levee building.

- **Geologists:** Geologists examine all aspects of the earth, including the impact of water-driven environmental hazards such as hurricanes and tsunamis.

A Conversation with Robert M. Hordon

Job Title: Physical Geography and Hydrology

What was your career path?

After college graduation, I spent four months at the Naval Officer Candidate School in Newport, RI. This was followed by being stationed for three years at the Naval Weapons Station in Yorktown, VA. My next activity was to enter the graduate program at Columbia University in the Geography Department. My fields of interest included physical geography, hydrology, cartography, fluvial geomorphology, and quantitative methods. After graduating with a MA and PhD, I secured a teaching position at Rutgers University that lasted over forty years.

What are three pieces of advice you would offer someone interested in your profession?

The three major avenues for employment in a field such as hydrology and its many related disciplines would include the private sector (engineering and consulting firms), the government sector at both the federal, state, county, and city level, and the academic sector that ranges from two-year county colleges, to four-year colleges, and graduate schools that are located all over the US with a host of many different types of institutions.

What paths for career advancement are available to you?

Following my recent retirement, I found myself continuing to write book reviews and short articles in some of the publications of the Journal of the American Water Resources Association and Science Books and Films of the American Association for the Advancement of Science. The topics selected were generally technical in nature, and where appropriate, required articles to also include references. In addition, I have also been Treasurer for the American Institute of Hydrology (AIH) and have also been recently asked to become Chairman of the Examination Committee for AIH.

- **Physicists:** Physicists study all aspects of the movement of matter, from subatomic particles on up. Water movement patterns are essential concerns for the physicist as well as the hydrologist.

Future Applications

As the earth's population grows and awareness of the deleterious consequences of human exploitation of the environment expands, the need for more effective stewardship of the earth's limited and fragile resources becomes greater. In many parts of the globe, water rights assume the same priority as human rights do in others. Any future projections regarding population growth must inevitably factor in the availability of water to sustain that growth. Aside from the most obvious manifestations of water in daily life, water is critical to many other basic needs. The cows that provide milk and beef require water to survive, just as their food also requires water. Indeed, few human processes exist independently of one or more aspects of the water cycle.

Despite the necessity of water, it is a resource that remains continually under assault in the modern world. At least in industrialized nations, environmental preservation has become an important social and political issue. At the heart of many efforts to preserve the earth's ecosystem is the drive to keep waterways clean and free of pollutants, while still making those same aquatic environments usable by the humans who rely on them. Hydrologists play the critical role of ensuring that past and present environmental pollution do not prohibit the continued use of water systems. Disasters such as the 2010 BP Deepwater Horizon oil spill in the Gulf of Mexico and other events that highlight the risks associated with fueling and provisioning an ever-expanding populace serve to highlight the importance of balancing the material demands of civilization while at the same time safeguarding the resources that make human life sustainable. Hydrologists will no doubt figure prominently in any future initiatives that require the balancing of population growth, environmental preservation, and natural resource stewardship. Hydrology is a profession that in many ways holds the key to continued human development.

—*Keith M. Finley, PhD*

More Information

American Institute of Hydrology (AIH)
Southern Illinois University Carbondale,
1230 Lincoln Drive Carbondale, IL 62901
www.aihydrology.org

International Association of Environmental Hydrology (IAEH)
2607 Hopeton Drive
San Antonio, TX 78230
www.hydroweb.com

National Ground Water Association
601 Dempsey Road
Westerville, OH 43081
www.ngwa.org/Pages/default.aspx

United States Geological Survey (USGS)
12201 Sunrise Valley Drive
Reston, VA 20192
www.usgs.gov

United States Department of Labor–Bureau of Labor Statistics.
US Department of Labor
200 Constitution Avenue NW
Washington, DC 20210
www.bls.gov/ooh/life-physical-and-social-science/hydrologists.htm

Geophysics

FIELDS OF STUDY

Geology; mineralogy; petrology; structural geology; hydrology; geomorphology; meteoritics; tectonics; carbonate diagenesis; sedimentary cycling; geochronology; stratigraphy; paleoclimatology; sedimentation; chemistry; physics; calculus.

DEFINITION

Geophysics is the branch of geology concerned with the study of the physical characteristics of the earth. This includes the hydrosphere and the atmosphere. It also includes the physical processes acting upon, above, and within the earth and its relationship to the rest of the universe. Included in geophysics are the fields of seismology, the study of earthquakes; volcanology, the study of volcanoes; meteorology, the study of climate and weather; and oceanography, the study of the oceans. The study of seismology and volcanology can lead to the ability to better predict the occurrence of earthquakes and volcanic eruptions. The study of meteorology contributes to an understanding of climate change, along with enhanced capabilities in the forecasting of catastrophic weather events.

Basic Principles

Geophysics is the study of the earth using quantitative physical methods. It examines the physics of the earth and the environment on and surrounding the planet. To gain an understanding of these relationships, geophysicists study a number of phenomena that include gravitational fields, magnetic fields, the hydrological cycle, fluid dynamics at work in the oceans, seismology, the ionosphere and magnetosphere, and solar-terrestrial relations.

Humans have been studying phenomena such as the magnetic field, earthquakes, volcanoes, and violent weather for centuries. The study of geophysics as a formal discipline originated in the nineteenth century, during the time when science was being used as a tool to add to understanding in many disciplines; there were, however, discoveries that came before the 1800s. Notably, there was William Gilbert's work *De Magnete, Magneticisque Corporibus, et de Magno Magnete Tellure* (1600; *On the Loadstone and Magnetic Bodies, and on That Great Magnet the Earth*, 1893), in which he put forth the theory that compasses point north because the earth is magnetic. Sir Isaac Newton published his *Philosophiæ Naturalis Principia Mathematica* in 1687. In this work, Newton laid the groundwork for classical mechanics and gravitation. He also offered explanations for such geophysical phenomena as the tides.

The water cycle first came into discussion as a result of the work of notable scientists such as Vitruvius, Leonardo da Vinci, and Bernard Palissy. Several others studied rainfall averages and other related measures of precipitation. Daniel Bernoulli's work with pressure and Henri Pitot's work with the Pitot tube took place in the eighteenth century. The first textbook on oceanography was published in 1855.

The twentieth century was a time of rapid discovery in the field of geophysics. Plate-tectonic theory was developed, and significant discoveries about the ocean were made through the use of acoustic measurements of sea depth and large-scale computer simulations. During the International Geophysical Year (IGY), an international science collaboration that took place in 1957 and 1958, many advances were made regarding auroras, cosmic rays, gravity, oceanography, seismology, and other related areas.

With a demand for petroleum exploration in the 1920s, the principles of geophysics were put to practical, industrial use. As a result, mining and groundwater geophysics improved. An understanding of the instability of specific soil and site areas was also gained.

Core Concepts

Mineral Physics. Mineral physics is the study of the material properties of minerals, particularly at the extremely high temperature and pressures found at the center of the earth. While material properties have been under investigation for quite some time, the conditions within the earth's crust have proven difficult to replicate until the past century. Massive hydraulic presses could deliver enormous pressures and, when paired with furnaces, could replicate a wide range of temperature pressure conditions. The advent of diamond anvil presses in the 1950s greatly simplified matters, as they could be made far smaller and efficient. Some models can even fit in cryostats, which are chambers designed for low-temperature measurements. The data gathered from these experiments allows researchers to better understand what conditions are like inside the earth and other celestial bodies. This field is also important in many other areas, such as when studying groundwater and the oceans.

Fluid Mechanics. Fluid mechanics is the study of flows of gas, liquid, and plasma and their interactions with force. It is very useful when studying ocean currents and cycles, as well as when examining weather. Fluid mechanics often yields patterns such as Rossby waves, which govern weather patterns in the atmosphere and are tied to thermocline waves in the oceans. The flow of the lithosphere can also be examined through fluid mechanics. In addition to the flows of the depths, the earth's mantle also acts as a fluid over long time periods; when examined, it yields data on postglacial rebound and isostasy, the latter of which is the equilibrium that keeps the tectonic plates floating.

Heat Transfer. Heat transfer, also called heat flow, is a concept critical for understanding the earth. Heat flows often take the form of giant convection cycles, which govern the movements of the oceans, the weather, and even plate tectonics. These trends are essential for the functioning of the climate and environment, with oceanic currents being of particular interest. All of the water in the oceans circulates, not only between oceans, but also between the different layers of the ocean. Major upper-level currents include the Gulf Stream, the East Australian Current, and the Australian Circumpolar Current. Water is separated into layers by temperature differences; the boundary between the layers is called the thermocline. The whole system is referred to as thermohaline circulation, and it not only raises nutrients from the seabed (which is why polar seas have so much biodiversity) but also keeps the climate in balance. Given the recent awareness of climate shift, a better understanding of the importance and functioning of the thermohaline conveyor is vital. Historically, observation of all of these patterns, weather and oceanic, has been difficult. In the twenty-first century, satellite observation has greatly simplified data collection.

Seismology and Vibrations. Though seismographs have existed since second-century China, it was not until recently that the field of seismology came into its own. With the invention of better equipment and continuous recorders in the twentieth century, scientists have been able to map the earth's core through seismological data. They can determine the densities of the layers of the inner earth by collecting seismic data from large earthquakes in a variety of locations and examining the geographical spread of the sites where vibrations can be detected, as the angles at which those vibrations travel change by refraction depending on the earth's composition. Understanding the reaction of various materials to earthquakes also helps ensure safer building practices.

Electromagnetism. An understanding of the mechanics that govern the earth's magnetic field is essential to the study of electromagnetism. The planet's magnetic field, which protects it from cosmic rays that could harm life, reverses every few hundred thousand years. Scientists can date material such as the oceanic crust by looking for records of this reversal in stone. Electromagnetism is also used in analyzing lightning and other phenomena of electric discharge. This is possible because, due to cosmic rays, the earth's atmosphere has a net positive charge, which makes its way down into the earth by various mechanisms and back up during lightning. It has been recently discovered that there is more to lightning than the discharge from cloud to ground; upper-atmosphere phenomena known as sprites and elves (from the acronym ELVES, for *e*missions of *l*ight and *v*ery low-frequency perturbations due to *e*lectromagnetic pulse *s*ources) are also generated. Terrestrial electromagnetism can also generate interference in signaling equipment. By understanding the earth's response to electromagnetism, researchers can use it to survey for useful materials. A common system that does this is called transient electromagnetics. The system induces a charge in the earth and measures the time it takes to disperse. This data gives an indication of the sort of materials that can be found there.

Radioactivity. Knowledge of radioactivity is useful in geophysics. It is important for understanding the earth's heating system, as nearly 80 percent of the earth's internal heating is thought to come from radioactive decay. Equally, because half-lives are predictable, they can be used to establish the age of rocks; this has allowed us to build a picture of Earth's history.

Applications Past and Present

Construction. Knowledge of geophysics is useful in construction applications because it gives those involved a method for determining the stability of the land they are building on. It is important to understand the likelihood of seismic activity when selecting a project site, whether that project involves homes, commercial real estate, roads, or other structures. Geophysics is the field of science that gives those in the construction industry the tools they need to assess the effect of stress on the soil and rock involved. It is also possible for a very large project, such as a dam or reservoir, to introduce seismic activity where none was present before, or to intensify any such preexisting activity. This is called induced seismicity and has occurred several times when large dams have been built.

Another important application of geophysics within construction is safety. This can take the shape of building codes that are designed to make structures more earthquake resistant. Because sand liquefies when shaken, it is especially important in areas with significant seismic activity to have building codes that lessen the impact of that activity on structures. For instance, geophysics can be used to help determine the best building materials and methods for compacting the earth.

In fact, building codes actually emerged from earthquakes and state responses to them. Building codes and earthquake engineering can be traced back to the 1755 earthquake that nearly leveled Lisbon, the capital of the Portuguese Empire, and shocked Europe. On November 1 of that year, a massive earthquake struck in the ocean off the southwest

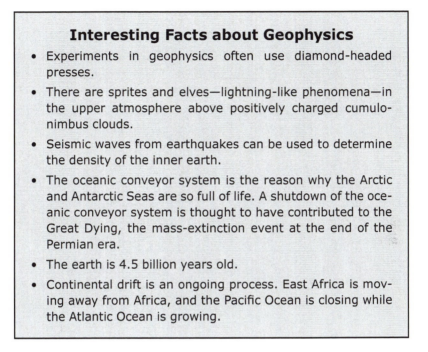

Interesting Facts about Geophysics

- Experiments in geophysics often use diamond-headed presses.
- There are sprites and elves—lightning-like phenomena—in the upper atmosphere above positively charged cumulonimbus clouds.
- Seismic waves from earthquakes can be used to determine the density of the inner earth.
- The oceanic conveyor system is the reason why the Arctic and Antarctic Seas are so full of life. A shutdown of the oceanic conveyor system is thought to have contributed to the Great Dying, the mass-extinction event at the end of the Permian era.
- The earth is 4.5 billion years old.
- Continental drift is an ongoing process. East Africa is moving away from Africa, and the Pacific Ocean is closing while the Atlantic Ocean is growing.

coast of Portugal. Much of Lisbon was destroyed by the earthquake and accompanying tsunami. The king and his prime minister, the Marquess of Pombal, survived, and the king immediately tasked his minister with reconstruction. To this end, the prime minister sent surveys around the countryside that asked such questions as whether water levels in wells had fluctuated, if animals had behaved strangely, and how many and what types of buildings had been destroyed. This survey allowed the earthquake to be reconstructed with great detail.

Back in the ruins of Lisbon, the king and the prime minister decided to level the ruined sections of Lisbon and completely rebuild. The peasantry was pressed into service and strict discipline was kept. As a result, there were no mass famines or epidemics, and Lisbon was cleared within a few months. To keep the city safe from future earthquakes, several innovative ideas were implemented. Scale models of buildings were made and soldiers were ordered to march around them to test their safety. These designs made use of an interior wooden frame that would shake but not collapse, presaging modern techniques. To get everyone rehoused as quickly as possible, the buildings were designed to use prefabricated units, a new idea at the time. To prevent massive fires like those seen after the earthquake, fire walls were included in designs. An even greater challenge was found in reconstructing the district of Baixa. The district, by the water, had been built on unstable ground. To circumvent this problem, wooden poles were buried beneath the area so as to stabilize the soil. Similar techniques are used to this day in areas where soil liquefaction is a concern.

The earthquake also had a massive affect on European philosophy and science. People decided that the earthquake must have had a natural cause, and in the spirit of the age, they set forth to figure out what that reason was. This launched the scientific quest to study earthquakes as a natural phenomenon. The Lisbon earthquake thus initiated the scientific study of earthquakes and also marked the first policies designed to improve survival.

Geothermal Power. Geothermal power is an application of geophysics that results in the generation of power that can be used to power the electric grid. Iceland is a country that has successfully integrated geothermal power into its grid. The benefit of using geothermal power is that it is a renewable energy source that produces little to no pollution and has no significant environmental impact.

Mining. Geophysics is especially important to the mining industry, where workers are regularly sent thousands of feet beneath the ground. An understanding of seismic activity and the likelihood of such activity is vital to their safety, as well as to the structural integrity of the tunnels. The principles of geophysics are used both to determine the integrity of the tunnel structure and to help pinpoint the types of minerals being sought.

Mineral exploration has always been a time-consuming processing, historically requiring panning for samples, but with geophysical techniques, the process has become swifter and more precise. Often it begins by looking at the sort of rock present in an area and then applying ore-genesis theories to determine what is likely to be found there. Geophysicists can then use readings of local magnetic and gravitational anomalies to identify areas of interest. Satellite images in other spectra can further refine the areas of interest. An understanding of what makes up minerals, gleaned from geophysics, has allowed sampling efforts to progress, meaning that chemical samples can suggest likely ores. For example, arsenic and antimony tend to accompany gold, so if tree buds or soil samples have high concentrations of these, there may be gold deposits nearby. The mineral is then located, typically by drilling. Often this is done by drilling on a set grid in order to determine the size of the deposit. This process results in less time and money being wasted on the exploration of areas that do not contain the desired minerals.

Climatology. Geophysics is used by those studying weather patterns and climate over time. Scientists can use sea sediment to identify climate changes that occurred over long periods of time. Fossil records can also be used for this purpose. By examining historical patterns and satellite data and incorporating them into predictive models, scientists can predict climate cycles such as El Niño that have an impact on weather and agriculture. In the case of climate change, an understanding of these cycles is even more important, as knowing what happens as they change will greatly aid in mitigating their negative effects. Climatological data also aids in fields such as agriculture and construction. By using climate models, climatologists can help farmers plan what crops to grow; and in the far north, where much of the ground was once permafrost but is now melting, they can give builders information about what ground conditions to expect and take into account.

Oceanography. The study of oceanic currents leads to a greater understanding of their effect on the biosphere. It also leads to an understanding of the way nutrients and other materials circulate through the oceans. Deep-sea currents carry the water throughout the oceans and up into the polar seas. This causes massive blooms of algae that attract other organisms to come and feed. This is why life is abundant in the polar seas. These algal blooms are an essential part of the ecosystem and the health of myriad ocean species, including humpback whales, penguins, puffins, seals, and polar bears. It is feared that if the oceanic conveyor system were to shut down, it would lead to deep-sea anoxia and a disruption of the nutrient cycle, which in turn would lead to an excessive proliferation of algal blooms across the surface. This would cause the demise of most ocean life and cause hydrogen sulfide to build up in the oceans and eventually be released into the atmosphere, making the air unbreathable for land-based species. This is thought to have happened at the end of the Permian period, 250 million years ago. Such events are an extreme case, but an understanding of them is needed as, at present, oceanic anoxia is on the rise. Equally, knowledge of the flows of the seas aids in understanding how ecosystems come into being and are sustained. In addition to the scientific benefit, this also is useful for keeping fish populations sustained for fishing operations.

Impact on Industry

Meteorology. One of the largest impacts of geophysics in everyday life is in the area of weather prediction. Though commonplace and often taken for granted, weather prediction helps save lives and money. It helps keep flying safe, as planes can avoid storms. Meteorology in conjunction with climate also helps utility companies, allowing them to estimate the amount of power needed for heating and cooling on any given day and prepare the grid accordingly. Perhaps nowhere is it more useful than in agriculture, where warning of storms and frost can save entire crops, resulting in larger crop yields. Equally, management of aquifers is another important task that geophysicists can help with, since these underground sources of drinking water often take years to replenish and can benefit from active management in areas with high use.

Mineral Prospecting. Mineral prospecting is also a major industrial beneficiary of geophysics. Geophysics allows companies to locate valuable resources such as oil, coal, iron, aluminum, and a variety of other minerals more efficiently and economically than ever before. Understanding how the earth works also aids in the extraction of these resources in as cheap, safe, and environmentally friendly a manner as possible. It can also make mines safer for those who work in them.

United States Geological Survey. The United States Geological Survey (USGS) manages aquifers and the mineral resources of the United

States, and geophysics plays a pivotal role in their ability to do so. By utilizing the techniques employed in the search for minerals and the identification of aquifers, they are able to better study and manage the landscapes of the United States and its natural resources.

Occupation	Geoscientists
Employment 2010	33,800
Projected Employment 2020	40,100
Change in Number (2010–20)	7,100
Percent Change	21%

Bureau of Labor Statistics, 2012

Environmental Protection Agency. The Environmental Protection Agency (EPA) uses the principles of geophysics to safeguard the environment. An example of this is their work at the Love Canal site at Niagara Falls, where a toxic-waste dump caused a public-health emergency in the 1970s. Geophysicists discovered that toxic waste was seeping into the groundwater and soil of a small community. With this knowledge, they were able to devise a plan to halt this contamination. The experience at the Love Canal led to protocols that are used today to protect populations from toxic hazards.

Military. An understanding of mineral resources is needed for making plans during war, as there is a high probability of trade, and thus manufacturing, being disrupted. Many countries keep reserves of strategic materials so as to continue production should war break out. The United States, for example, has a sixty-day reserve of petroleum. Other ways the military makes use of geophysics is with construction of large bunkers, such as North American Defense Command (NORAD) at the Cheyenne Mountain Air Force Station, which was built inside a mountain during the Cold War so as to survive a potential nuclear strike.

Academic Research. Most universities have geophysics departments, and active work is being done across the field, ranging from climate work to mineral physics and investigations into electromagnetic phenomena.

Social Context and Future Prospects

Geophysics will be critical to resolving the problem of peak oil. Oil is, on the human time scale, a finite and nonrenewable resource. Thus, there is a maximum that can be extracted both in total and at any one time. Peak oil is the point at which oil production is maximized; after that, oil production will shrink and prices will rise. It is currently estimated that most of the cheapest oil has already been found and that the world is approaching peak oil. Managing peak oil requires a combination of effective global action and new technologies to make most of the remaining resources.

Future prospects for the application of geophysics are boundless. Geothermal construction, hydroelectric power, the prospect of geo-engineering, and someday perhaps even terraforming other worlds leaves much to look forward to.

Further Reading

Gadallah, Mamdouh R., and Ray L. Fisher. *Exploration Geophysics*. Berlin: Springer, 2008. Print. Covers the acquisition of two-dimensional and three-dimensional seismic data and the ways in which this data is interpreted and used.

Kirsch, Reinhard. *Groundwater Geophysics: A Tool for Hydrogeology.* Berlin: Springer, 2008. Print. Describes the use of geophysics in the delineation and detection of groundwater resources.

Lowrie, William. *Fundamentals of Geophysics*. Cambridge: Cambridge UP, 2007. Print. Explores the fundamental principles of geophysics. Designed as an introductory text for geoscience undergraduates.

Milsom, John, and Asger Eriksen. *Field Geophysics*. Hoboken: Wiley, 2011. Print. Provides practical information to those working on small-scale surveys. Includes an update on the use of global positioning systems (GPS) and a section on seismic surface waves, borehole geophysics, and towed-array systems.

Reynolds, John M. *An Introduction to Applied and Environmental Geophysics*. Chichester: Wiley, 2010. Includes mineral and hydrocarbon exploration, with an emphasis on the use of geophysics in civil engineering. Also covers environmental and groundwater investigations.

About the Author: Gina Hagler writes about science and technology. Her book about applied fluid dynamics, *Modeling Ships and Space Craft: The Science and Art of Mastering the Oceans and Sky*, was published in the fall of 2012.

Oceanographer 🖋

Earnings (Yearly Median): $82,500 (Bureau of Labor Statistics, 2012)

Employment and Outlook: Faster than average growth (Bureau of Labor Statistics, 2012)

O*NET-SOC Code: 19-2042.00

Related Career Clusters: Agriculture, Food & Natural Resources; Government & Public Administration; Health Science

---

Scope of Work

Oceanographers utilize an interdisciplinary approach to study the interaction between the geological, physical, chemical, and biological aspects of the world's oceans. The geological division is involved in mapping ocean floors, conducting sedimentation analysis for oil and mineral deposits, and examining the effects of plate tectonics in forming ocean basins. Physical oceanography describes the effects of water properties on wave actions, tides, currents, weather, climate, and shoreline processes. It also records the transmission properties of light and sound in the ocean. Chemical oceanographers analyze the chemical composition of ocean water, exploring the toxic effects of pollutants on marine ecosystems and investigating potential desalination processes for drinking sources. The biological division researches specific marine species and their global distribution, food web interactions, threats to ecosystems, and sustainable ocean food harvesting methods. In addition, an emerging biotechnology branch examines the potential of marine organisms as human biomedical and industrial resources.

Education and Coursework

Students should start preparing in high school by taking courses that provide a solid foundation in math and science, while not neglecting the need for strong communication and computer skills. In the area

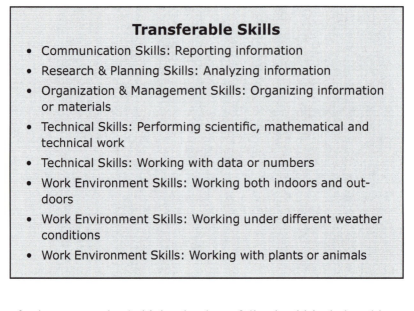

Transferable Skills

- Communication Skills: Reporting information
- Research & Planning Skills: Analyzing information
- Organization & Management Skills: Organizing information or materials
- Technical Skills: Performing scientific, mathematical and technical work
- Technical Skills: Working with data or numbers
- Work Environment Skills: Working both indoors and outdoors
- Work Environment Skills: Working under different weather conditions
- Work Environment Skills: Working with plants or animals

of science, a student's high school portfolio should include subjects such as biology, chemistry, physics, and earth science. Advisable math courses include algebra, trigonometry, statistics, and calculus. Outside of the classroom, students are encouraged to participate in local aquatic-oriented volunteer programs or summer camps. In addition, any shipboard or scuba diving experience would be an added bonus for future field research.

Entry-level positions in oceanography usually require a bachelor's degree, which affords a student employment as a laboratory assistant or technician. Undergraduate programs specific to marine biology and oceanography are on the rise, growing from approximately twenty to twenty-five in 1986 and to over sixty in 2010. However, oceanographers have historically entered the field through master's or doctoral programs, after having completed undergraduate degrees in biology, geology, physics, zoology, chemistry, or engineering. Those applying to a focused marine science or oceanography bachelor's program are encouraged to ensure that it has a strong life-science foundation. In response to this need, many undergraduate degrees offer a double-major program, combining marine science with a basic science such as biology, chemistry, geology, physics, or computer science.

A bachelor's degree program generally includes physics, statistics, geology, chemistry, biology, and basic oceanography courses, with several in the student's intended area of marine specialization. In addition to classroom course work, oceanography programs also include a great deal of laboratory work and field research, some involving time spent on extended trips at sea.

In order to advance to a management position, it is necessary to obtain a master's degree. Master's programs usually involve a large portion of field and laboratory work. In light of this, it is important to investigate the research being carried out in any program of interest.

For an upper-level research or administrative position, students will need to pursue a doctoral degree in oceanography. Graduate programs in oceanography are highly competitive and programs look for students who have a degree that emphasizes a core science such as physics, chemistry, biology, or geology or that features some other interdisciplinary focus, such as social science or engineering.

Career Enhancement and Training

Networking should begin as early as the junior or senior year of undergraduate work. Interested students should volunteer in a research lab at the university where they are studying, at a local marine facility, or with a nonprofit organization, such as the National Audubon Society.

There are many scholarships, internships, and fellowships available through such organizations as the National Oceanic and Atmospheric Administration (NOAA) and the Association for the Sciences of Limnology and Oceanography (ASLO). In addition, a number of universities offer summer research programs.

Membership in professional associations and organizations is an ideal way to network and stay abreast of current research and funding opportunities; established associations include the Oceanography Society (TOS), ASLO, and the American Fisheries Society (AFS).

Certification for oceanographers is still under discussion. In 2006, the Marine Advanced Technology Education (MATE) investigated the prospect of implementing a certification program for oceanographic professions (CPOP) and decided it was unnecessary at the time. However, certification as a scuba diver is an advantage for many oceanography positions.

Daily Tasks and Technology

Given the multidisciplinary approach to the field of oceanography, it is difficult to detail the average day of an oceanographer. Field research could involve traveling on a fishing vessel and tagging large mammals on a three-month ocean project, or a day out on a smaller watercraft collecting microscopic bacteria samples. Oceanographers' work can take them from the warm waters of the Caribbean to Arctic icecaps. They might venture to the depths of the ocean in a deep-sea submersible, scuba dive at the continental shelf, or skim phytoplankton off the ocean's surface.

Although field research is a component of many oceanographer job profiles, a great deal of the job, as with most sciences, is spent using computers to analyze and graph data, conducting library research, writing grants and papers, and participating in scientific meetings. Oceanographers working for a university will often have the additional duty of teaching and supervising students.

Oceanography fieldwork can be physically demanding and is often hampered by weather constraints. It is also intellectually demanding, as it requires data analysis, creative technical problem solving, and the ability to adapt to and master new modeling software programs.

Approximately 50 percent of oceanographers can be seen working for government and state agencies, while 40 percent work in university settings. The remaining 10 percent work in private industries such as oil and mining companies. They are also often asked to work alongside policy makers and social scientists in an effort to help maintain the ocean's natural resources, as well as in industrial firms developing specialized marine equipment.

Oceanographers utilize state-of-the-art marine technology and data-collection systems. Several examples of such technology include remote-sensing satellite-tracking instruments; weather-tracking buoys; conductivity, temperature, and density (CTD) instrument profilers; bathymetry sonar equipment; and deep-sea remotely operated vehicles (ROV).

Earnings and Employment Outlook

The demand for oceanographers is expected to grow faster than average compared to other occupations, with a 21 percent increase between 2010 and 2020. However, some disciplines of oceanography will likely fare better than others. While competition will be steep in the marine biology area, the new branches of biotechnology and molecular biology may provide expansion opportunities as companies turn to the ocean for new medications, industrial resources, and revelations in molecular genetics. The most competitive candidates in oceanography will be those who have a combined degree in oceanography and general science or engineering.

The demand for oceanographers is expected to grow faster than average compared to other occupations, with a 21 percent increase from between 2010 and 2020.

A bachelor's degree is the minimum requirement for work in the marine sciences. Moving up from a technician or assistant post usually involves a master's degree, while employment as an independent researcher necessitates a doctoral degree.

In 2006, the average salary for an entry-level geoscientist, which includes geologists, geophysicists, and oceanographers, was $50,460, while experienced oceanographers earned an average of $99,690. However, salary levels can vary from higher to lower within the profession, based on location within the United States (Texas versus Florida), area of discipline (chemical, physical, and engineering branches versus biological branches), and employer (private industry versus state agencies).

Coastal development has recently increased, and with this growth comes public concern for the resulting environmental impact. To this end, governments, local environmental agencies, and environmental consulting firms will be employing more oceanographers to help with planning,

A Conversation with Paul P. Sipiera

Job Title: Adjunct Curator of Meteorites—Field Museum of Natural History (Chicago, Illinois) President and CEO of the Planetary Studies Foundation (Galena, Ill.)

What was your career path?

After graduating high school, my career path was uncertain. It was not until my junior year in college that I realized that I could actually make a career out of my love for astronomy and earth science. It became clear that I could reach that goal by teaching at the college level; this would give me the opportunity to share my knowledge and love of science with others and to pursue my own research interests during the summer months. After graduating with a bachelor's degree, I continued on with my education and was awarded a master's degree in earth science and a PhD in natural science. My thirty-five-year career teaching geology and astronomy gave me the opportunity to travel the world studying meteorites and even stand at the South Pole three times. My career turned out to be more fulfilling than I could have ever imagined.

What are three pieces of advice you would offer someone interested in your profession?

My profession as a planetary geologist is a very challenging career since it is highly competitive with limited job opportunities. I was fortunate to find an alternative teaching career that would support my family and me, and allow me to conduct my own independent research. My three pieces of advice:
1. Set yourself a realistic goal and stay focused on it until you achieve that goal.
2. Don't be discouraged by outside influences such as a bad economy and reports of high unemployment—good qualified people always find good jobs.
3. Education and job experience always pays off, and always look for alternative situations to reach your goal.

> **What paths for career advancement are available to you?**
>
> I am a retired college professor with thirty-five years of experience behind me with a very good pension, the benefits of hard work and dedication to my profession. As retirement closed the "teaching door" for me it opened another "door of opportunity," one that allows me to conduct my research at a world-renown museum. I now have the job I always dreamed of some thirty-five years ago, so you never know when your dreams might come true. Patience is still a virtue.

coastal zone management, environmental impact studies, and public awareness campaigns.

Related Occupations

- **Geophysicists:** Geophysicists use the principles of physics to research the earth's interior, focusing on its gravitational, magnetic, and electric fields.

- **Ocean Engineers:** Ocean engineers use their technological expertise to design tools and equipment specific to the needs of various marine research projects and ocean environments.

- **Hydrologists:** Hydrologists focus on the water cycle and its interaction with the environment. They chart water's movement and properties, examining its quality and availability, as well as the feasibility of irrigation systems and hydroelectric power plants.

- **Marine Policy Specialists:** Marine policy specialists establish safe fishing and marine resource guidelines and policies. Their combined oceanic and social-science backgrounds enable them to present sustainable ocean proposals to businesses and politicians.

- **Marine Archaeologists:** Marine archaeologists systematically explore the ocean depths in order to locate and study artifacts from previous cultures and shipwrecks.

Future Applications

The ocean covers over 70 percent of the earth's surface, yet only 5 percent of it has been explored. However, with new technological advancements, scientists are beginning to map and view these remote parts of the ocean. As the world population increases, there will be an increased need for food, natural resources, and health products. NOAA's Fisheries Service Centers have been expanding research of environmentally sound aquaculture methods in an effort to increase food supplies. Private industries will continue to fund biotechnology research in hopes of discovering more medicinal applications. A multiagency project is already underway mapping the continental shelf in the Arctic in an effort to lay claim to the natural resources and wildlife underlying the melting polar caps.

Attempts to deal with global issues will at times involve international efforts, such as that seen in the 2000–2010 Census of Marine Life, which comprised 80 nations and 2,700 scientists. The census study identified over six thousand new species.

Another factor that will promote future jobs within the field of oceanography is the increased concern for global climate change and rising ocean levels. There are already reports that the sea level of the Atlantic Ocean is rising faster than originally anticipated. This may result in an increased need for oceanic engineers and marine policy specialists.

—Rose Young

More Information

American Fisheries Society
5410 Grosvenor Lane
Bethesda, MD 20814
www.fisheries.org

Association for the Sciences of Limnology and Oceanography
5400 Bosque Boulevard, Suite 680
Waco, TX 76710-4446
www.aslo.org

MarineBio
PO Box 235273
Encinitas, CA 92023
www.marinebio.org

Marine Technology Society
1100 H Street NW, Suite LL-100
Washington, DC 20005
www.mtsociety.org

National Oceanic and Atmospheric Administration
Communications and Education Division
NOAA's National Ocean Service
SSMC4, Room 13317
1305 East-West Highway
Silver Spring, MD 20910
oceanservice.noaa.gov

The Oceanography Society
PO Box 1931
Rockville, MD 20849-1931
www.tos.org

Nanotechnology

FIELDS OF STUDY

Agriculture; artificial intelligence; bioinformatics; biomedical nanotechnology; business; chemical engineering; chemistry; computational nanotechnology; electronics; engineering; environmental studies; mathematics; mechanical engineering; medicine; molecular biology; microelectromechanical systems; molecular scale manufacturing; nanobiotechnology; nanoelectronics; nanofabrication; molecular nanoscience; molecular nanotechnology; nanomedicines; pharmacy; physics; toxicology.

DEFINITION

Nanotechnology is dedicated to the study and manipulation of structures at the extremely small nano level. The technology focuses on how particles of a substance at a nanoscale behave differently from particles at a larger scale. Nanotechnology explores how those differences can benefit applications in a variety of fields. In medicine, nanomaterials can be used to deliver drugs to targeted areas of the body that need treatment. Environmental scientists can use nanoparticles to target and eliminate pollutants in the water and air. Microprocessors and consumer products will also benefit from the use of nanotechnology, as components and their associated products become exponentially smaller.

Basic Principles

Nanotechnology is the science that deals with the study and manipulation of structures at the nano level. At the nano level, things are measured in nanometers, or one billionth of a meter (10^{-9}). The symbol for nanometers is *nm*. Nanoparticles can be produced using a process known as top-down nanofabrication, which starts with a larger quantity of material and removes portions to create the nano-sized material.

Another method being developed is bottom-up nanofabrication, in which nanoparticles will create themselves when the necessary materials are placed in contact with one another.

Nanotechnology is based upon the discovery that materials behave differently at the nano scale, less than 100 nm in size, than they do at a slightly larger scale. For instance, gold is classified as an inert material because it neither corrodes nor tarnishes. However, at the nano level, gold will oxidize in carbon monoxide. It will also appear as colors other than the yellow for which it is known.

Nanotechnology is not simply about working with materials like gold at the nano level. It is about taking advantage of these differences at the nanoscale to create markers and other new structures that are of use in a wide variety of medical and other applications.

Core Concepts

Basic Tools. Nanoscale materials can be created for specific purposes, but there also exists natural nanoscale material, such as smoke from fire. To create nanoscale material and to be able to work with it requires specialized tools and technology. One essential piece of equipment is an electron microscope. Electron microscopy makes use of electrons, rather than light, to view objects. Because these microscopes have to get the electrons moving, and because they need several thousand volts of electricity, they are often quite large.

One type of electron microscope, the scanning electron microscope (SEM), requires a metallic sample. If the sample is not metallic, it is coated with gold. The SEM can give an accurate image with good resolution at sizes as small as a few nanometers.

For smaller objects or closer viewing, a transmission electron microscope (TEM) is more appropriate. With a TEM, the electrons pass through the object. To accomplish this, the sample has to be very thin, and preparing the sample is time consuming. The TEM also has greater power needs than the SEM, so the SEM is used in most cases, reserving the TEM for times when a resolution of a few tenths of a nanometer is absolutely necessary.

The atomic force microscope (AFM) is a third type of electron microscope that is designed to give a clear image of the surface of a sample. This microscope uses a laser to scan across the surface. The result is an image that shows the surface of the object, making visible its peaks and valleys.

Moving the actual atoms around is an important part of creating nanoscale materials for specific purposes. Another type of electron microscope, the scanning tunneling microscope (STM), not only images the surface of a material in the same way as the AFM, but the tip of the probe, which is typically made up of a single atom, can also be used to pass an electrical current to the sample. This charge lessens the space between the probe and the sample. As the probe moves across the sample, the atoms nearest the charged atom move with it. In this way, individual atoms can be moved to a desired location in a process known as quantum mechanical tunneling.

Molecular assemblers and nanorobots are two other potential tools. The assemblers would use specialized tips to form bonds with materials that would make specific types of materials easier to move. Nanorobots might someday move through a person's bloodstream or through the atmosphere, equipped with nanoscale processors and other materials that enable them to perform specific functions.

Bottom-Up Nanofabrication. Bottom-up nanofabrication is one approach to nanomanufacturing. This process builds a specific nanostructure or material by combining components of atomic and molecular scale. Creating a structure this way is time consuming, so scientists are working to create nanoscale materials that will spontaneously join to assemble a desired structure without physical manipulation.

Top-Down Nanofabrication. Top-down nanofabrication is a process in which a larger amount of material is used at the start. The desired nanomaterial is created by removing, or carving away, the material that is not needed. This is less time consuming than bottom-up nanofabrication, but it produces considerable waste.

Specialized Processes. To facilitate the manufacture of nanoscale materials, a number of specialized processes are used. These include nanoimprint lithography, in which nanoscale features are stamped or printed onto a surface; atomic layer epitaxy, in which a layer that is only one atom thick is deposited on a surface; and dip-pen lithography, in which the tip of an atomic force microscope writes on a surface after being dipped into a chemical.

Applications Past and Present

Smart Materials. Smart materials are materials that react in ways appropriate to the stimulus or situation they encounter. Combining smart materials with nanoscale materials would, for example, enable scientists to create drugs that would respond when encountering specific viruses or diseases. They could also be used to signal problems with other systems, like nuclear power generators or pollution levels.

Sensors. The difference between a smart material and a sensor is that the smart material will generate a response to the situation encountered and the sensor will generate an alarm or signal that there is something that requires attention. The capacity to incorporate sensors at a nanoscale will greatly enhance the ability of engineers and manufacturers to create structures and products with a feedback loop that is not cumbersome. Nanoscale materials can easily be incorporated into the product.

Medical Uses. The potential uses for nanoscale materials in the field of medicine are of particular interest to researchers. Theoretically, nanorobots could be programmed to perform functions that would eliminate the possibility of infection at a wound site. They could also speed healing. Smart materials could be designed to dispense medication in appropriate doses when a virus or bacteria is encountered. Sensors could be used to alert physicians to the first stages of malignancy. There is great potential for nanomaterials to meet the needs of aging populations without intrusive surgeries that would require lengthy recovery and rehabilitation.

Energy Production and Efficiency. Nanomaterials also hold promise for energy applications. With nanostructures, components of heating and cooling systems can be tailored to control temperatures with greater efficiency. This can be accomplished by engineering the materials so that some types of atoms, such as oxygen, can pass through, but others, such as mold or moisture, cannot. With this level of control,

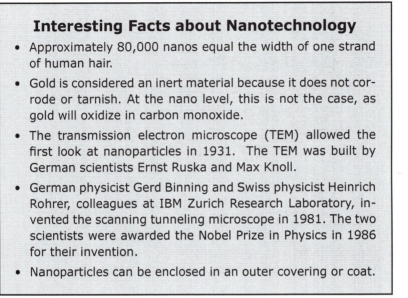

Interesting Facts about Nanotechnology

- Approximately 80,000 nanos equal the width of one strand of human hair.
- Gold is considered an inert material because it does not corrode or tarnish. At the nano level, this is not the case, as gold will oxidize in carbon monoxide.
- The transmission electron microscope (TEM) allowed the first look at nanoparticles in 1931. The TEM was built by German scientists Ernst Ruska and Max Knoll.
- German physicist Gerd Binning and Swiss physicist Heinrich Rohrer, colleagues at IBM Zurich Research Laboratory, invented the scanning tunneling microscope in 1981. The two scientists were awarded the Nobel Prize in Physics in 1986 for their invention.
- Nanoparticles can be enclosed in an outer covering or coat.

living conditions can be designed to meet the specific needs of different categories of residents.

Extending the life of batteries and prolonging their charge has been the subject of decades of research. With nanoparticles, researchers at Rutgers University and Bell Labs have been able to better separate the chemical components of batteries, resulting in longer battery life. With further nanoscale research, it may be possible to alter the internal composition of batteries to achieve even greater performance.

Light-emitting diode (LED) technology uses 90 percent less energy than conventional, non-LED lighting. It also generates less heat than traditional metal-filament light bulbs. Nanomanufacture would make it possible to create a new generation of efficient LED lighting products.

Electronics. Moore's law states that transistor density on integrated circuits doubles about every two years. With the advent of nanotechnology, the rate of miniaturization has the potential to double at a much greater rate. This miniaturization will profoundly affect the computer industry. Computers will become lighter and smaller as nanoparticles are used to increase everything from screen resolution to battery life while reducing the size of essential internal components, such as capacitors.

Impact on Industry

The job outlook for those individuals involved with nanotechnology is strong. According to National Science Foundation estimates, the United States will need eight hundred thousand to 1 million nanotechnologists in the next decade. Similarly, the outlook for nanosystems engineers is also bright, and is expected to experience rapid growth—an employment increase of 29 percent or more—through 2020, according to the United States Bureau of Labor Statistics.

Private Industry. Nanotechnology will have a profound impact on the private sector as individuals and private companies work to develop ideas and products they can patent and produce. For example, major corporations are investigating the use of nanoparticles such as carbon nanotubes to strengthen the materials used in the components that make up cars and airplanes. Further, reducing the size of components to nanoscale will mean that the internal circuits of a computer will be etched on a surface too small to be seen by the naked eye. With circuit boards and other components reduced in size, finished products will be similarly reduced in scale.

Industries such as the automotive industry, which must have products of a certain size to function, also will take advantage of nanoparticles and materials. Their use will result in components that weigh less and are stronger because of the manufacturing use of structures such as the carbon nanotube.

The use of lighter coatings of materials on the components of vehicles destined for space will result in significantly lighter loads and reduced fuel requirements. Even space suits will be improved by the use of nanoparticles in their manufacture, as layers of bulky material are replaced with trimmer fabrics providing the same or better protection.

In the medical field, experimentation is already under way to deliver medication to tumors in places that are not readily accessible through conventional means. Researchers are also experimenting with coatings to protect tissue as medication moves through the human body and with markers to guide medication to the proper treatment site.

Nanotechnology is already a technology with broad applications for the business community. Commercialization of research findings is a priority. The funding from the commercialization will pay for future research as consumers take advantage of the positive effects of nanotechnology. Because nanotechnology is rising to prominence during the information age, which includes the Internet and web, research findings and writings are readily available. Another factor advancing progress in this field is the global reach of research and information dissemination.

Government Agencies and Military. In 2000, the United States National Nanotechnology Initiative (NNI) was founded with the mandate to coordinate federal nanotech research and development. According to the NNI, by 2012, at least fifteen government agencies had specific budgets for the research and development of nanotechnology. The initiative is also involved in setting standards for nanotechnology and is legislating for policies and regulations for this new branch of science. Great growth in the creation of improved products using nanoparticles has taken place since the initiative's founding in 2000. For example, the creation of smaller and smaller components—which reduces all aspects of manufacture, from the amount of materials needed to the cost of shipping the finished product—is driving the use of nanoscale materials in the manufacturing sector. Furthermore, the ability to target delivery of treatments to areas of the body needing those treatments is spurring research in the medical field. In 2012, the federal budget provided approximately $2.1 billion in funding for the NNI.

According to the NNI, there are four unique categorizations, called generations, regarding the development of nanotechnology, and as of 2012, research still remained in the very first generation. As research moves beyond this first phase, it is likely that military applications will be the next emerging technology from this field.

Academic Research and Teaching. Universities around the world have shown a strong interest in nanotechnology. Many universities have affiliated research institutes and programs, such as the University of California, Los Angeles, which promotes nanotechnology research collaboration through the California NanoSystems Institute (CNSI).

Alliances are being formed to create solutions to problems such as air and water pollution. One such application under development is the use of nanostructures to create products that will clean oil spills before widespread damage is done to wildlife and their habitats.

Occupation	Engineers, all other
Employment 2010	156,500
Projected Employment 2020	166,800
Change in Number (2010–20)	10,300
Percent Change	7%

Bureau of Labor Statistics, 2012

Many colleges and universities have nanosystems engineering departments that offer opportunities for teaching. Because such specialized positions as nanotechnologists require a degree in a science or engineering discipline, there is also ample opportunity for teaching within those disciplines.

Social Context and Future Prospects

Engineering and architecture, the health-care industry, and the manufacturing industry are just a few of the career fields that will be touched by advances in nanotechnology and its applications. Nanoscale materials will result in stronger, lighter materials that can be created specifically for their functions. This will result in lighter, more durable airplanes, ships, spacecraft, and other vehicles. Nanotechnology will also be a factor in the selection of materials used by civil engineers for roads, bridges, and dams. Architects will have a new range of materials available as they design homes and commercial buildings.

Professionals in the health industry, from personal trainers to surgeons, will feel the effect of advances in nanotechnology. From the use of nanomaterials to speed patient recovery to the use of nanostructures in prosthetics and related aids, nanotechnology will change current practices at a rapid pace.

In manufacturing, advances in the use of nanotechnology will result in stronger materials of lighter weight that are better suited for their purpose. Products that now must be of a certain size to accommodate internal components will not have this constraint in the future. In a move analogous to the switch from televisions with cathode-ray tubes to those using liquid-crystal or plasma displays, advances in the production of nanocomponents will alter design constraints on a variety of products.

Further Reading

Drexler, K. Eric. *Engines of Creation 2.0: The Coming Era of Nanotechnology.* Updated ed. *WOWIO.* WOWIO, 2007. Web. 9 Oct. 2012. An updated edition of the 1986 work that introduced the possibilities and theoretical foundations of nanotechnology. Available in e-book format only.

Ratner, Daniel, and Mark A. Ratner. *Nanotechnology and Homeland Security: New Weapons for New Wars.* Upper Saddle River: Prentice, 2004. Print. Discusses the potential applications of nanotechnology in fighting terrorism.

Ratner, Mark A., and Daniel Ratner. *Nanotechnology: A Gentle Introduction to the Next Big Idea.* Upper Saddle River: Prentice, 2003. Print. An introduction to how nanotechnology works and the industry surrounding it.

About the Author: Gina Hagler writes about science and technology. She is the author of numerous science books, including *Modeling Ships and Space Craft: The Science and Art of Mastering the Oceans and Sky* (2012).

Nanosystems Engineer 🖋

Earnings (Yearly Median): $90,580 (O*NET On-Line, 2012)

Employment and Outlook: Slower than average growth (O*NET OnLine, 2012)

O*NET-SOC Code: 17-2199.09

Related Career Cluster(s): Manufacturing; Health Science; Transportation, Distribution & Logistics; Government & Public Administration

Scope of Work

Nanosystems engineers work in developmental laboratories, universities, private engineering companies, and the federal government. They work with material on the nanoscale, that is, matter that is typically between one and one hundred nanometers. One nanometer (nm) is equivalent to one billionth of a meter, small enough to measure the diameter of atomic particles.

Unlike mechanical engineers, who work on a macroscale, nanosystems engineers study matter at the molecular level and use nanoparticles to create technology and mechanisms that benefit society. A number of industries and products benefit from nanotechnology, including medicine, electronic devices, computer software, agriculture, green energy, and consumer goods.

In addition to conducting experiments with nanoscale materials in a laboratory setting, nanosystems engineers constantly research the properties of molecular material and invent new applications for nanotechnology. They evaluate experiments, write reports, and collaborate with other engineers and scientists to solve complex problems. Nanosystems engineers work from the bottom up, exploring the structure of molecular material and how it interacts with other molecules and then using that material to build and enhance the performance of larger technologies.

Education and Coursework

A nanosystems engineer must have a bachelor's degree in nanosystems engineering, chemical engineering, or bioengineering. A degree in a related field, such as materials science, is also acceptable. Hands-on laboratory experience with nanoparticles in a laboratory class, an internship, or as a research assistant is necessary during the course of an engineer's education.

A nanosystems engineer's four-year undergraduate education is an amalgam of chemistry, biology, technology, physics, and engineering courses, including organic chemistry, engineering physics, particle physics, molecular biology, and advanced engineering, as well as classes in computer labs. There are master's and PhD programs in nanosystems engineering and other engineering disciplines, and most employers prefer entry-level candidates with an advanced degree. An

---

Transferable Skills

- Communication Skills: Speaking effectively (SCANS Basic Skill)
- Interpersonal/Social Skills: Working as a member of a team (SCANS Workplace Competency – Interpersonal)
- Research & Planning Skills: Solving problems (SCANS Thinking Skills)
- Organization & Management Skills: Managing equipment/materials (SCANS Workplace Competency – Resources)
- Technical Skills: Using technology to process information (SCANS Workplace Competency – Information)
- Work Environment Skills: Working in a laboratory setting

---

engineering school may offer a five-year joint bachelor's and master's program; a master's degree on its own can typically be completed by a full-time student in two years.

Having a master's degree augments an applicant's resume and may potentially increase an engineer's salary. A master's degree offers students specialized laboratory experience and the opportunity to produce a professional research thesis or project (a master's thesis or dissertation) that contributes to the field of nanosystems engineering. An advanced engineering degree may also require business and management courses in order to prepare graduates for managerial positions. Enrolling in a master's or PhD program can also help individuals establish valuable connections within the engineering profession.

Career Enhancement and Training

In all US states, engineers need to be licensed if they offer services to the public, although licensing requirements vary by state. Under US law, it is illegal to start an engineering company without a professional license. Private companies who employ engineers may also require them to have a license. Though some private companies may waive this requirement, they may still offer bonuses and salary increases to employees who are licensed.

There are three primary steps to earning a professional engineering license: a candidate must have a bachelor's degree, pass two comprehensive exams given and scored by the National Council of Examiners for Engineering and Surveying (NCEES), and complete four years of engineering experience under the supervision of a professional engineer. The first NCEES exam is called the Fundamentals of Engineering exam (FE). After passing this exam, a candidate can take the NCEES Principles and Practice of Engineering (PE) exam, which evaluates an engineer's knowledge and skills in a specific concentration. An individual will have earned his or her license and be officially considered a professional engineer (PE) upon passing this examination.

Continuing education is an important aspect of a nanosystems engineer's career. They are obligated to take additional courses and read the current literature on advancements in the industry. Nanosystems engineers are often employed by the federal government to create military technology and defense systems, in which case they need both an engineering license and a high security clearance.

Joining a professional engineering society or organization is a great way to network with other professionals and learn more about the engineering industry. The International Association of Nanotechnology (IANT), for instance, offers meetings and networking opportunities for nanosystems engineers and other professionals involved in the development of nanotechnology around the world. In addition to making connecting with other professionals, these gatherings are a great opportunity to learn more about current research and innovations from world-renowned scientists. Being a member of the IANT is a beneficial addition to a résumé, as it shows potential employers an applicant's dedication to the field of nanotechnology.

Daily Tasks and Technology

The majority of a nanosystems engineer's time is spent examining molecular material and designing prototypes and three-dimensional simulations of this material using computer software. They conduct experiments and write reports evaluating nanoparticles and the efficiency of new nanotechnology, recording any progress or setbacks. From the results of these experiments, engineers develop nanodevices and nanomaterials and explore ways nanotechnology can be used for other applications.

Nanosystems engineers have several important tasks outside of the laboratory. After a product is completed, for example, an engineer may demonstrate to the consumer how the product works and explain the mechanisms involved. Writing proposals to secure grant money is usually necessary in order to fund experiments and the production of technology.

Nanotechnology is becoming a more important component in green technology. Engineers are researching ways molecular material can reduce the carbon footprint of energy sources. In solar photovoltaic electricity (or solar power), nanotechnology is being used to create more cost-effective solar cells. In fuel cells, nanosystems engineers are developing platinum nanoparticles to produce hydrogen, therefore decreasing cost. Engineers have also developed silicon nanowires to enhance the efficiency of batteries for electronic devices.

Nanosystems engineers use a variety of tools and technology. A scanning electron microscope (SEM), for example, is a microscope that uses electrons to view molecular material. The SEM is also capable of looking beneath the surface of a material and revealing its composition and other properties, such as conductivity. Spectrometers and spectroscopes are instruments used to measure properties of materials, such as electromagnetic waves, which include light, gamma rays, and other forms of radiation. Engineers also use an electron beam (e-beam) evaporator to heat material with electron beams, causing evaporation. The evaporation process occurs in a vacuum chamber, allowing engineers to acquire a gaseous material from the substance and learn more about its composition.

In addition, nanosystems engineers use basic desktop-computer technology for word processing and spreadsheet creation. More advanced software, such as computer-aided design (CAD) software, is used to create prototypes of molecular substances.

Earnings and Employment Outlook

The demand for nanosystems engineers is expected to grow more slowly than average—between 3 and 9 percent—through 2020. The demand for nanotechnology, however, is gradually increasing as engineers discover new mechanisms to benefit medicine, agriculture, green energy, electronic devices, and a number of other applications.

The demand for nanosystems engineers is expected to grow more slowly than average—between 3 and 9 percent—through 2020. The demand for nanotechnology, however, is gradually increasing.

Engineers and scientists believe nanotechnology is still in its early stages, not unlike computers in the 1960s, and will become more significant in the near future. It is estimated that by 2015, the profit from nanotechnology will exceed $1 trillion. Future employment for nanosystems engineers therefore looks promising, as this industry continues grow.

According to information accessed from Recruiter.com in 2012, the average salary for nanosystems engineers was between $64,000 and $96,000. Salaries vary by employer, with nanosystems engineers working for the federal government and in the private sector earning the most and those employed by state or local governments earning the least. Average annual salaries also varied by state: the District of Columbia had the highest at $116,420, and Nebraska the lowest with $57,580.

Related Occupations

- **Chemical Engineers:** Chemical engineers design chemical-based manufacturing processes and oversee the use of chemicals in industrial production.

- **Materials Scientists:** Materials scientists study the structures and properties of natural or man-made substances. They devise new combinations of and uses for existing materials and invent new materials for use in products and applications.

- **Biological Engineers:** Biological engineers use the principles of biology and molecular biology to solve problems and create applications for living organisms.

A Conversation with Trina Vian

Job Title: Associate Technical Staff

What was your career path?

My career path was quite non-traditional and began with an enlistment in the United States Navy. With the assistance of an ROTC scholarship, I received a BA degree in physics followed by a Navy tour as a meteorologist. After an honorable discharge, I went back to school and earned an MS degree in mechanical engineering. I have been employed as a research engineer with an emphasis in aerosol science ever since.

What are three pieces of advice you would offer someone interested in your profession?

1. Establish a strong foundation in math and science; these steps allow greater flexibility in career choice or subsequent career change as interests evolve.
2. Become proficient in a programming language; even if not required later, the ability to reduce a large problem down to its smaller constituents is a valuable and widely-applicable skill
3. Strive to define and maintain a healthy work-life balance

What paths for career advancement are available to you?

Although my organization has a relatively flat management structure, it is possible to advance technically or managerially through different channels. Promotions tend to be rare though as the recipient needs to remain competitive in the new group.

- **Biophysicists:** Biophysicists study the physical properties of living organisms, including processes such as metabolism, heredity, and reproduction.

Future Applications

Nanosystems engineering is a relatively young science, but scientists agree that the possibilities for nanotechnology are innumerable. Many industries and products will benefit from nanotechnology in the up-coming decades. In medicine, for instance, nanosystems engineers are currently experimenting with nanoparticles capable of injecting che-motherapy directly into cancer cells, thereby decreasing harmful side effects. Nanoparticles may also be capable of directly attacking and destroying viruses in the human body. Every sector of the medical field could potentially benefit; artificial organs may be created, and genetic therapies may be designed to prevent disease before it occurs. Even treatments that are capable of reversing the aging process are within nanotechnology's reach.

Nanosystems engineers could potentially develop advanced ro-bots and machines that were once only conceivable in science fiction books. Robots, for example, could use nanotechnology to perform in-tricate surgical procedures. Nanoparticles may allow computer chips to become more powerful and reach incredibly small sizes. Connec-tions between the human brain and electronic devices—moveable prosthetic arms and legs, for instance—could be created with nano-technology interfaces.

Nanosystems engineers could help solve the global-warming crisis and the need for green energy. Nanotechnology could aid in the dis-covery of cheaper and cleaner energy alternatives to expensive fossil fuels. For instance, nanosystems engineers are exploring ways to con-vert sunlight into methane, and they are close to developing technol-ogy capable of deriving hydrogen fuel by splitting water molecules.

—Daniel Castaldy

More Information

Institute of Nanotechnology
Strathclyde University Incubator
Graham Hills Building
50 Richmond Street
Glasgow G1 1XP Scotland
www.nano.org.uk

International Nanotechnology and Society Network
Arizona State University
Consortium for Science, Policy & Outcomes
PO Box 874401
Tempe, AZ 85287-4401
www.nanoandsociety.com

National Nanotechnology Initiative
4201 Wilson Boulevard
Stafford II Room 405
Arlington, VA 22230
www.nano.gov

Sustainable Nanotechnology Organization
www.susnano.org

Nuclear Medicine

FIELDS OF STUDY

Medicine; biology; radiation biology; physics; chemistry; radiopharmacy; computer science; mathematics; diagnostic studies.

DEFINITION

Nuclear medicine is a subspecialty in the medical profession in which radioactive matter is employed to diagnose and treat diseases. Unlike traditional methods for examining inside the human body, radioactive diagnostic scans enable doctors to assess both the structure and function of internal organs by tracing the path of radiopharmaceuticals throughout the body. Nuclear techniques often afford doctors the opportunity to catch and treat potentially harmful developments much sooner than traditional methods.

Basic Principles

Nuclear medicine involves placing a small amount of radioactive material inside of a patient and then using special cameras to create images of the body that, in turn, facilitate a more accurate diagnosis. Patients receive a low dose of radiopharmaceuticals that can be swallowed, inhaled as a gas, or injected, depending on the nature of the procedure. Individual radiopharmaceuticals are attracted to specific organs and tissues of the body. The radioactive matter used to diagnose the thyroid, for example, is not the same as the one employed when examining the liver. Following the infusion of radiation, special cameras take pictures of the body that capture the location of radiopharmaceuticals by tracing the radioactivity they emit. The data and images gathered by the camera are then relayed to computers. From there, trained nuclear physicians have insight into the function and health of organs, bones, tissues, and other components of the body. Before the widespread availability of nuclear procedures, doctors could, at best, catch a glimpse of the appearance of internal body structures with existing technology.

Nuclear medicine also encompasses the deployment of radiation to destroy damaged or diseased cells to prevent them from spreading. Following the same logic that informs the use of radioactive particles in the diagnostic end of the medical practice, it is becoming increasingly common to utilize the same principle to treat diseased portions of the body with the appropriate radionuclides (a type of radioactive atom, also called radioisotopes).

Of critical concern in any nuclear procedure is the risk associated with it. Although every precaution is taken and the amount of radiation a patient is exposed to is carefully controlled by federal guidelines, the health risks involved are not insignificant. Exposure to radiation, even at low levels, increases the risk of cancer. Most individuals who undergo a nuclear medical procedure will experience no deleterious effects, although a small number will, because radiation affects different people in different ways. However statistically insignificant a link between the ingestion of radioactive matter and cancer, it still represents a troubling concern. Central to the success of any participant in the field of nuclear medicine is the ability to convey to patients that the procedure they are about to undergo will not harm them—that the radiation they will be exposed to is comparable to the level of radiation they face in their everyday life.

Core Concepts

Deploying Radiopharmaceuticals. Nuclear medicine is a dynamic field that offers an array of diagnostic tools using radioactivity to detect internal abnormalities. Some nuclear tests offer a two-dimensional image, while others provide a three-dimensional perspective. Most generate a more detailed glance at a specific organ rather than capturing a generalized image of the mass in question along with everything else around it, as earlier technology afforded. Radionuclides, atoms with an unstable nucleus, are the radiopharmaceuticals used in nuclear medicine. The most commonly used compound is technetium-99m, which accounts for the overwhelming percentage of nuclear examinations performed in the world, owing to its emission of easily recognized gamma radiation that limits patient exposure to potentially carcinogenic compounds. In nature, unstable atoms attempt to return to a state of stability by shedding protons and neutrons. When used in the context of nuclear medicine, radionuclides will join to a compound generally found in the specific part of the body under investigation, and "tag" along with it to that location. Along the way, the radioactive material will emit tracer radiation that is captured by a camera, yielding important data for nuclear physicians.

Fashioning Usable Radionuclides. Finding a suitable radionuclide is one of the more difficult challenges in nuclear medicine. To be usable, these nuclides must emit enough radiation to be captured by available equipment, yet contain a short enough half-life to disappear shortly after the medical procedure is completed. Producing radionuclides is undertaken in a limited number of specialized labs. Transporting the finished product to the nuclear medicine facility can lead to degradation of the radioactive matter if the process takes too long. Since the most valuable radionuclides are also ones with the shortest half-life, time is an important factor. Many facilities purchase longer-lived radionuclides that remain viable even after an extended time in transit so that they may harvest the radioactive decay and utilize it as a radiopharmaceutical. Cyclotrons or particle accelerators are often used to irradiate a radionuclide with a long half-life in order to harvest a shorter lived product useful in nuclear imaging procedures. Many of the radionuclides used in 2012 have such short half-lives that their creation and administration to the patient must take place right away. Highly skilled nuclear professionals must be on hand to produce the radionuclides necessary for procedures with the assorted kits and generators currently available. A mistake, even a seemingly small one, can at best fail to yield the digital images needed to make a diagnosis or, at worst, kill the patient. Utmost care and rigorous testing of any nuclear substance that will be placed in a human body always takes priority.

Imaging Technology. During the course of a positron emission tomography (PET) exam—the most common nuclear procedure—a healthy body will handle introduced radioactive matter in a predictable way. A diseased or sick body will yield more erratic patterns. PET tests provide accurate detail on critical factors that can help a doctor make a diagnosis concerning the functioning of a patient's vital organs. Most PET tests are done in conjunction with a CT (computed tomography) scan, which further increases the predictive ability of the attending physician. Superimposing the results of both tests offers a more detailed picture than if the exams were performed separately. Blood flow, sugar metabolism, and oxygen intake are a few of the myriad functions that this test can measure.

Patients are encouraged not to eat at least six hours before the exam, as the natural digestion process may yield false results. Punctuality is also critical in the administration of the test, owing to the brief half-life of the radiopharmaceuticals employed. Upon intravenous administration of most radionuclides, patients must wait approximately one hour for the tracer to reach its target in the body. At this point a patient is placed in the PET-CT scanner and told to remain absolutely still. Any movement, fidgeting, or readjustment on the patient's part can throw off the results of the high-tech machinery. The testing and scanning process typically takes between thirty minutes to an hour. Other nuclear exams in which the same general principles apply include the single photon emission computed tomography (SPECT) test, which is most commonly prescribed for neurological disorders, and assorted cardiovascular and bone imaging exams.

Professionals in the Field. In general, nuclear medicine practices are most efficient at detecting cancer, ascertaining the effectiveness of cancer treatment, determining the relative health of the heart, and in evaluating the brain and its function. Specialized gamma cameras are used in these procedures to capture a wide variety of images that form a dataset that can then be interpreted by a nuclear medicine specialist. More advanced procedures offer a three-dimensional image that a doctor can rotate, reverse, and even dissect from a computer. The result of such technology is a more nuanced understanding of the problem plaguing the patient, arrived at in a noninvasive manner. Nuclear medical technicians will study, read, and interpret the results, which are then forwarded to a patient's primary physician. Should the nuclear medical scan prove negative or inconclusive, the attending physician can rule out many of the most common maladies suffered by individuals. Different avenues must be pursued, and nuclear imaging can offer clues about where next to investigate. For those whose tests come back with signs of abnormalities, additional tests are likely needed before an aggressive treatment regimen commences.

Radiation Treatment. In some cases, radionuclide therapy is prescribed to treat certain medical problems. Specific radioactive isotopes relevant to the type of treatment required are injected into a diseased patient's bloodstream. As in the imaging process, the radiopharmaceutical employed tags along with a compound to a specific location—most typically the thyroid gland—where it can destroy cancerous growths in a circumscribed location without damaging healthy surrounding tissue.

Applications Past and Present

Emergence of Nuclear Medicine. Although some might trace the advent of nuclear medicine to the late nineteenth century and Henri Becquerel and Marie Curie, most regard the profession as a mid-twentieth-century phenomenon. To be sure, modern nuclear science owes its birth to the pioneering work of Becquerel, who first noted the appearance of rays emanating from uranium, and to Curie, who coined the term "radioactivity" to define those rays; but the first medical application of radioactive material dates to nearly fifty years later. Starting in 1943, Samuel M. Seidlin, the chief endocrinologist at New York City's Montefiore Hospital, began treating a thyroid cancer patient with an "atomic cocktail" consisting of I-131, or radioiodine, which resulted in the destruction of the cancer cells. Seidlin's research represented a significant departure from previous experiments, which were limited to the use of animals rather than humans, and which commonly employed more aggressive radioactive materials. As early as the 1910s, some in the scientific community had recognized the value of radiation in the treatment of illness, but research experiments in the field tended to avoid imperiling human subjects. For those who risked such experimentation, death most often followed radiation injections. The success of Seidlin's treatment prompted him and his associates to expand their research on patients with similar thyroid conditions. Most of these efforts were successful and led to a series of seminal articles in leading medical journals. The age of nuclear medicine had begun.

Improving Diagnostic Tools. During the 1950s, the radioactive isotope I-131 went from being a treatment for thyroid cancer to becoming a valuable tool in efforts to determine the functioning of the gland in the body. Scientists were beginning to understand the tracer value of radioactive matter and started turning this knowledge into a diagnostic tool. As knowledge of the pathways covered by radioactive materials in the body expanded, so too did the ability to create images from the emission of radioactivity. Machines such as scintillation detectors, positron detectors, and eventually cameras capable of recording tracers within the body began to emerge. Electrical engineer Hal Anger, in particular, spent much of the 1950s undertaking pioneering research to create a top-quality medical imaging system. It was his scintillation camera that many consider a critical step toward more advanced PET and SPECT systems.

Creating a Profession. Coinciding with this era of discovery and advancement was even greater research on other radioactive materials that might also serve as tracers in the body. In 1954, the Society of Nuclear Medicine was formed, and its publication, the *Journal of Nuclear Medicine*, first produced in the 1960s, became central to the growing intellectual exchange among those who worked in the field. Also in the 1960s, a machine capable of producing technetium-99m was introduced. This artificial substance today serves as the most-utilized radionuclide in the nuclear medicine field. Cyclotrons and other machines for creating artificial isotopes hit the market shortly thereafter, based on the design specifications pioneered by Ernest Lawrence in the 1930s. Discovery in the field yielded newer and more improved methods of turning the data yielded by radionuclide tracers into usable information. In the early 1960s, David Kuhl pioneered research in photon emission tomography that served as the true beginning of modern PET and SPECT technology.

Official Recognition. At the start of the 1970s, the field of nuclear medicine had come a long way from the crude experimentation of Seidlin and others. Most of the major organs of the body could now be

Interesting Facts about Nuclear Medicine

- In the United States, approximately sixteen million nuclear-medicine-related procedures are performed annually. Out of this number, almost half are exams related to the heart. These procedures are painless and are capable of detecting internal bodily abnormalities long before other technologies.

- Patients receive about as much radiation from a nuclear procedure as they do from receiving an x-ray. Most people are unaware that they are exposed to radiation every day. It is in the soil, in color television sets, even in smoke detectors. In their day-to-day lives people are exposed annually to more radiation than is received in a nuclear imaging exam. Nuclear exams are both safe and carefully regulated.

- The National Research Universal reactor at Chalk River Laboratories in Ontario, Canada, is one of the world's largest producers of industrial and medical radioisotopes. It is rivaled in production only by the High-Flux Reactor in the Dutch city of Petten.

- The most commonly used radiopharmaceutical in nuclear procedures is technetium-99m. It is estimated that nearly 80 percent of all nuclear diagnostic exams are performed with this radionuclide, which was discovered in 1937.

- The Society of Nuclear Medicine and Molecular Imaging asserts that worldwide there are approximately 4,000 board-certified nuclear physicians and over 15,000 certified technicians in the field.

studied through the use of select radiopharmaceuticals that emitted recordable tracers. In 1971, the American Medical Association (AMA) officially recognized nuclear medicine as a specialty within the profession. With AMA recognition came the critical legitimacy that the subfield needed. One year later, the American Board of Nuclear Medicine was formed. It serves as the primary certifying body for nuclear medicine in the United States. The remainder of the decade and the one that followed brought with them the creation of new radionuclides as well as improvements in imaging technology that produced more detailed and robust pictures of the human body. Radiopharmaceuticals came into production that revealed both heart disease as well as cancer, further broadening the scope of this ever-expanding field of science. Cancer cells could now be discovered before they became observable by older technology, thereby greatly improving a patient's chances for survival.

PET-CT Scan. By the late 1990s, nuclear medicine benefitted from the creation of machines that joined existing CT and PET technology in a single process. The new combined exam not only saved patients time, it also gave doctors the opportunity to assess the structure and the function of the human body and its major organs at the same time—a development that increased the accuracy of medical diagnoses. The dawn of the twenty-first century brought renewed efforts to produce medical equipment capable of diagnosing medical problems even earlier than existing technology.

Molecular Imaging. In 2012, scientists and inventors are drawn to the concept of molecular imaging that will enable health care practitioners to understand and treat the basic molecular pathways. Molecular imaging has the potential of granting doctors the ability to uncover abnormalities before they develop into full-blown illnesses and give them options for treatment as it uncovers the biology of disease development. Current scans and exams provide physicians with information regarding the end result of molecular disturbances. So important does the Society of Nuclear Medicine view this new development that it altered its name to include the phrase "and Molecular Imaging."

Safety Concerns. Millions throughout the world undergo nuclear medical procedures each year. The safety track record of these exams remains impressive, as does the large number of test options currently available. Most of the major problems that plague the human body can now be diagnosed sooner and more accurately because of nuclear procedures. Scientists and engineers are busy searching for even more efficient techniques to revolutionize once again the field of medicine as pioneers in the mid-twentieth century did when they first began experimenting with radiation. Technological improvements in the field of computers and graphic design only brighten the future of nuclear medicine.

Impact on Industry

The practice of nuclear medicine remains largely confined to wealthy industrialized nations. It is a field, however, that continues to grow both in terms of the number of applications it has and the number of people it employs. The impact of the profession on the economy and on quality of life remains high, and employment prospects for those practicing nuclear medicine are robust.

Government Agencies. In the early days of America's nuclear weapons program, many government agencies funded clandestine experiments to test the effects of radiation on men, women, and even children. Today, the government has renounced this practice and disavows the use of humans for such purposes. The Nuclear Regulatory Commission (NRC) carefully controls the nature and extent of radioactive materials available at any time in the United States. In the wake of the September 11, 2001, terrorist attacks, regulatory agencies have increased their scrutiny of radioactive materials. While ensuring national security, the NRC also provides guidelines to ensure that patients do not receive too much radiation exposure, and it oversees the proper disposal of nuclear medical waste so that it poses as small a threat to the environment as possible.

Military. The United States military, like other components of the government, was once involved in experiments designed to test the impact of radiation on the human body. Such tests were designed more to see what would actually happen than to diagnose or treat illness. In the twenty-first century, the military, which possesses a massive Cold War–era nuclear arsenal, stays out of funding nuclear research for anything but military purposes.

University Research and Teaching. Many of the most significant advances in the field of nuclear medicine have come through the efforts of those working at the nation's large research universities. Resource pooling in terms of technology, finances, and availability of skilled professionals enables scientists and engineers to bring to bear

Occupation	Nuclear medicine technologists
Employment 2010	21,900
Projected Employment 2020	22,900
Change in Number (2010–20)	1,000
Percent Change	19%

Bureau of Labor Statistics, 2012

the manifold items needed for high-level research and discovery.

Private Industry. In the field of medical science, private firms are often at the forefront of advances. Profit drives product research and development in most fields, and the medical profession is no different. Intense competition exists to create the next great advance in imaging technology that will save lives and enrich patent holders of the design. Companies such as GE Healthcare, Siemens, and Hitachi all struggle to gain a greater market share in a field where demand for innovation is great but in which the number of potential buyers is exceedingly small.

Social Context and Future Prospects

In the twentieth century scientists learned to harness nuclear power to cause great devastation, just as they began unlocking its ability to expand and sustain life. As nuclear weapons were increasingly viewed with trepidation, advances in the field of nuclear medicine were, by contrast, heralded for their diagnostic accuracy and early warning capabilities. Technological advances in the field of computers and tomography have made the images produced in nuclear procedures crisper and more precise than ever before, just as the creation of new radionuclides expands the reach of the field. Everything from organ health and function to cancer screening and cardiovascular vitality are now detectable through one of the many nuclear screens currently available. Molecular imaging serves as the next great advance for practitioners of nuclear medicine. It promises to revolutionize patient treatment and care.

Despite great advances made in the field, the technology necessary for its use, the scarcity of resources needed for its implementation, and the staggering cost of its principal tools makes nuclear medicine a viable option only in the most developed countries. Access to the equipment is often not available in poorer nations, save for those items donated by charity; repairs and replacement parts are also expensive and difficult to secure, often making a donation

Occupation	Nuclear technicians
Employment 2010	7,100
Projected Employment 2020	8,200
Change in Number (2010–20)	1,000
Percent Change	14%

Bureau of Labor Statistics, 2012

short-sighted. Many poor nations where quality of life, environmental laws, and other factors necessary for a healthy populace are substandard could benefit from the predictive strength of nuclear medicine. Those born in nations bypassed by prosperity—and who are more likely to suffer from a host of health problems owing to poor nutrition and lack of medical care in general—are forced to do so without the types of procedures that could extend and enhance their lives. Making health care procedures such as those in nuclear medicine affordable to those from less developed regions is an important ethical issue in the twenty-first century. It requires more than just sending talented and idealistic youth to such regions: It demands a commitment of the best and brightest as well as wealth and resources.

A major concern with nuclear medicine remains its safety for both patients and the environment. Despite millions of nuclear procedures performed annually, there remains a lingering fear, especially in places such as the United States, that radiation in any form will cause cancer. Widely publicized incidents such as the 1979 partial meltdown at the Three Mile Island nuclear plant in Pennsylvania turned American support against nuclear power and raised concerns about exposure to any form of radiation. A careful examination of literature from the nation's leading medical centers underscores just how important assuaging fears of radiation exposure is for Americans. Though exposure to radiation through such procedures as a PET scan is negligible, there is still widespread concern regarding the disposal of that waste as well as of the security of the radioactive material in the nation's hospitals and research facilities.

Further Reading

Malley, Marjorie C. *Radioactivity: A History of a Mysterious Science*. New York: Oxford UP, 2011. Print. An accessible study of the evolution of nuclear technology from a global perspective. This work offers a detailed rendering of the many discoveries in the field.

Meggitt, Geoff. *Taming the Rays: A History of Radiation and Protection*. Raleigh: Lulu Enterprises, 2010. Print. Focuses on the promise and especially the fears surrounding the use of radiation in medicine. It explores why those fears first existed and points to why trepidation concerning nuclear medicine continues.

Shackett, Pete. *Nuclear Medicine Technology: Procedures and Quick Reference*. 2nd ed. New York: Lippincott, 2008. Print. Although designed for practitioners in the field, this work offers an excellent synopsis of the myriad nuclear imaging procedures currently available, just as it highlights the most frequently used radiopharmaceuticals. It also provides lessons on how to assuage patient fears on the risks versus the benefits of choosing a nuclear procedure.

Shuler, James Mannie. *Understanding Radiation Science: Basic Nuclear and Health Physics*. Boca Raton: Universal, 2006. Print. Straightforward rendering of nuclear medicine geared toward a nonscientific audience that commences with a discussion of the nature of the atom and progresses to an analysis of its manifold uses.

Stephens, Martha. *The Treatment: The Story of Those Who Died in the Cincinnati Radiation Tests*. Durham: Duke UP, 2002. Print. Tragic tale of cancer patients who hoped that radiation might cure them of their ailment. Instead, military officials intervened and placed them in an experiment in which, unbeknownst to the afflicted, they received enormous amounts of radiation.

About the Author: Keith M. Finley, PhD, is an instructor of history and the assistant director of the Center for Southeast Louisiana Studies at Southeastern Louisiana University. He has written extensively on twentieth-century American politics, society, and ecology, including the 2010 D. B. Hardeman Prize for *Delaying the Dream: Southern Senators and the Fight Against Civil Rights, 1938–1965*. Finley has also cowritten two award-winning documentary films on coastal erosion and environmental degradation in south Louisiana.

Nuclear Medicine Technologist

Earnings (Yearly Average): $69,450 (Bureau of Labor Statistics, 2011)

Employment and Outlook: Average growth (Bureau of Labor Statistics, 2010)

O*NET-SOC Code: 29-2033.00

Related Career Clusters: Health Science; Manufacturing; Transportation, Distribution & Logistics

Scope of Work

Nuclear medicine technologists work in hospitals, imaging clinics, public health centers, research institutes, and other healthcare facilities. They administer radioactive materials known as radiopharmaceuticals to patients, scan patients' bodies, and diagnose a variety of medical conditions, including cancer, heart disease, neurological disorders, and bone injuries. Unlike the anatomy-based practice of diagnostic radiology, nuclear medicine examines the function of organs and detects concealed abnormalities, such as malignant tumors.

After using computers and equipment to process and enhance images generated from scans, technologists analyze these images and look for areas with higher or lower concentrations of radiation, which can indicate abnormalities in organs or sections of the body. For instance, a scan can reveal whether blood is flowing correctly through the heart, if a bone is healing correctly, or if an organ or part of the body is functioning properly. Nuclear medicine technologists closely monitor radioactive drugs and ensure the safety of their patients, preventing dangerous reactions or overexposure to radiation.

Education and Coursework

At a minimum, a nuclear medicine technologist must hold a certificate or an associate's degree, preferably in nuclear technology or one of the biological sciences. Bachelor's degree programs in nuclear medicine are also available at some institutions. In order to be successful in this occupation, an individual must possess a strong aptitude for math and science. A technologist's education consists of courses in algebra, chemistry, biology, anatomy, physiology, physics, and computer technology, as well as more advanced classes in radioactive medicine and radiation safety. A technologist must have strong interpersonal, technical, and organizational skills. He or she must also be fastidious and detail oriented, as carefully following instructions and accurately measuring radioactive drugs are imperative.

Due to the constant growth of the field and advancements in nuclear medicine technology, technologists must pursue further education and training throughout their careers. In addition to providing an understanding of new technology and techniques, additional training and education may open up a variety of career paths in the healthcare industry, allowing some technologists to advance to positions in fields such as hospital administration, research, or physician assisting.

A number of organizations provide support and educational opportunities to nuclear medicine technologists. The Society of Nuclear Medicine and Nuclear Imaging is a nonprofit organization composed of nuclear imaging professionals. The society's mission is to promote awareness of nuclear medicine technology and its benefits and support the advancement and education of professionals in the field. The Radiological Society of North America, an international society, similarly provides education and networking opportunities for nuclear medicine professionals.

Career Enhancement and Training

Certification and licensing requirements vary among states and employers, but a certificate is often required. Certification is earned through a national agency, such as the Nuclear Medicine Technology Certification Board, and includes a comprehensive exam. An individual who does not hold a degree in nuclear medicine technology may be required to attain four or more years of clinical experience under a physician or nuclear medicine professional prior to applying for certification. Some technologists may pursue specialty certification in a procedure such as magnetic resonance imaging (MRI), positron

> ## Transferable Skills
>
> - Communication Skills: Reporting information
> - Interpersonal/Social Skills: Providing support to others
> - Research & Planning Skills: Analyzing information
> - Organization & Management Skills: Managing equipment/ materials (SCANS Workplace Competency – Resources)
> - Technical Skills: Using technology to process information (SCANS Workplace Competency – Information)
> - Work Environment Skills: Working in a medical setting

emission tomography (PET), or computed tomography (CT). Being specialized in a procedure may enhance a technologist's marketability in the healthcare industry and potentially increase his or her salary.

More than half of US states require nuclear medicine technologists to be licensed. In order to obtain a license, an individual must typically hold a degree, complete a period of clinical service, and pass a comprehensive exam. License requirements vary by state: New York, for instance, requires that licensed technologists complete a set number of continuing education credits each year. Connecticut only licenses individuals working in radiography and radiation therapy, while states such as Ohio also license technologists working in the fields of nuclear medicine, radiology, and fusion imaging. Some employers require national certification.

Daily Tasks and Technology

Nuclear medicine technologists work in high-tech healthcare environments and operate computers and equipment on a daily basis. They are responsible for maintaining the technology used in scans and preventing harmful radiation exposure and adverse reactions in patients. After preparing and measuring the appropriate amount of radioactive drugs needed for a procedure and administering the drugs to the patient, a technologist scans the patient's body, monitors the radiation levels, records the results, and produces images on radioactive film or on a computer. The technologist then uses these images to pinpoint abnormalities and diagnose medical conditions.

Various technology is used in radiation treatments. Gamma cameras, for example, are used to capture and produce images of radiation in the body. Single photon emission computed tomography (SPECT) uses a gamma camera to generate three-dimensional images of the body. Positron emission tomography (PET) does not use a gamma camera and instead captures radiation with rings of detectors within a scanner.

In addition to using technology, a large part of a nuclear medicine technologist's job is working closely with patients. Technologists are responsible for explaining procedures, obtaining medical history, alleviating any anxiety over the procedure, and responding to any questions or concerns. This level of patient care requires compassion and strong interpersonal skills.

Earnings and Employment Outlook

The demand for nuclear medicine technologists is expected to experience average growth between 2010 and 2020. Nuclear imaging technology is advancing and becoming a more important tool in medicine, particularly in the area of cancer detection. Such technology makes it possible to identify conditions early on, thus increasing the likelihood that treatment will be successful. In many cases, early detection saves lives, allowing medical professionals to identify and treat cancer before it spreads to other areas of the body.

The demand for nuclear medicine technologists is expected to experience average growth between 2010 and 2020.

As the population increases, there will be a greater demand for medical professionals. The proliferation of heart disease and cancer in the United States is also increasing the demand for nuclear medicine technologists, who play a vital role in diagnosing these conditions. The employment outlook is strongest in states with a large number of nuclear reactors, such as Pennsylvania and New York, and in states with an abundance of hospitals and healthcare facilities, such as Massachusetts.

Annual wages for nuclear medicine technologists vary based on a number of factors, including industry of employment. According to the US Bureau of Labor Statistics, technologists working in physicians' offices and specialty hospitals are paid higher wages, on average, than those working in general hospitals and medical laboratories. However, employment in the former industries is relatively low.

Related Occupations

- **Radiologic Technologists:** Radiologic technologists use x-rays and other imaging techniques to diagnoses diseases.

- **Cardiovascular Technologists:** Cardiovascular technologists use imaging equipment to diagnose cardiac conditions such as heart disease and blood clots.

- **Diagnostic Medical Sonographers:** Diagnostic medical sonographers use imaging equipment based on sound waves to obtain images and diagnose patients.

- **Radiation Therapists:** Radiation therapists use radiation treatments to treat cancer in patients

- **Medical Assistants:** Medical assistants assist physicians with examining patients and may prepare samples or perform basic tests.

Future Applications

As nuclear medicine technologies and applications develop further, it is expected that technologists will continue to play an important part in the diagnosis and prevention of medical conditions. Nuclear medicine may be used to track biochemical changes and help explain the mechanism of certain diseases and how they develop in the body. The technology may also allow researchers to observe structural changes in the brain and study the link between such changes and human behavior.

New equipment used in nuclear medicine may be sensitive enough to detect abnormalities before they develop into actual diseases.

Advancements in nuclear technology are also expected to allow scientists to test the efficacy of prescription drugs and how they act on the body. This will likely speed up the mandatory drug-testing process, allowing new drugs to be approved faster. Scientists may also be able to enhance the efficiency of drugs by learning how they are absorbed into the human body, which will help determine the most effective dose needed for a drug to reach its full potential.

Despite these advancements, the field of nuclear medicine technology is expected to face some challenges. The lack of nuclear reactor facilities in many states inhibits the development of radionuclides used in radiopharmaceuticals, in turn likely hindering the growth of the industry. In addition, disputes regarding the adequacy of existing training and licensing procedures may affect the quality and quantity of nuclear medicine technologists in certain parts of the country.

—Daniel Castaldy

More Information

American Board of Science in Nuclear Medicine
3000 Spout Run Parkway
D-401
Arlington, VA 22201
www.snm.org/absnm

American Registry of Radiologic Technologists
1255 Northland Drive
St. Paul, MN 55120
www.arrt.org

Nuclear Medicine Technology Certification Board
3558 Habersham at Northlake
Building I
Tucker, GA 30084
www.nmtcb.org

Radiological Society of North America
820 Jorie Boulevard
Oak Brook, IL 60523
www.rsna.org

Society of Nuclear Medicine and Molecular Imaging
1850 Samuel Morse Drive
Reston, VA 20190
www.snm.org

Nuclear Physics

FIELDS OF STUDY

Particle physics; calculus; algebra; statistics; optics; condensed matter physics; astronomy; astrophysics; computer science; geometry; acoustics; atomic/molecular physics; health/medicine; theoretical physics; mathematical physics.

DEFINITION

Nuclear physicists are scientists who analyze the energy generated within cells' nuclei and how this energy may be applied in the modern world. The field began in the early twentieth century as part of weapons research, culminating in nuclear bombs. However, nuclear physics also led to the establishment of alternatives to coal and other sources of energy. In 2012, nuclear physics is used to treat diseases such as cancer, determine the age of items uncovered in archaeological digs, and change the properties of solids to use them as semiconductors □ an invaluable tool in engineering. Scientists continue to find applications for the products of nuclear-physics research.

Basic Principles

Nuclear physics owes its roots to the 1896 discovery by Henri Becquerel of radiation emanating from phosphorescent (glowing) uranium salts. Marie and Pierre Curie continued Becquerel's research, finding more radioactive elements and coining the term *radioactivity*. Over time, many more naturally radioactive substances were discovered. During this period, greater attention was paid to the nature of radioactivity, with scientists tracing the radiation to atoms within the nuclei of cells. By the 1930s, it became apparent to scientists that radiation in many materials was increased, or "excited," when exposed to light and other forms of energy. This concept, nuclear fission, became the launching point for the development of nuclear weapons.

Although there were military application for nuclear physics in the 1930s, over the course of the Cold War, nuclear physics also saw applications as a source of energy. Nuclear energy has since become a major source of power throughout the industrialized world, and it is increasingly being applied in developing nations as well. This knowledge has also been applied elsewhere, largely in the field of health care, where nuclear medicine is being used for treatment of cancer and other ailments.

Development in the field of nuclear physics is reliant on the particle accelerator, a large piece of technology that uses electronic or electromagnetic fields to speed subatomic particles and have them collide with other particles. The resulting high-energy rays (x-rays and gamma rays) are then cataloged and analyzed by nuclear physicists. This research helps them understand the nature of nuclear energy and its place within the natural and industrialized worlds.

Core Concepts

Nuclear physicists analyze the energy produced by natural and engineered nuclear reactions, as well as the effects those reactions have on their respective environments. They research the atomic forces that cause radiation, creating models and developing theories about how subatomic particles are structured and reorganized during nuclear reactions. Nuclear physicists use the data they uncover during their research to draft scholarly papers and other literature, along with models that can be used as the basis for further research. Engineers, scientists, and others have applied the work of nuclear physicists to the development of medicine, weapons, energy systems, and other technologies.

Subparticles. The central focus of a nuclear physicist is the subatomic particle. The basic premise on which nuclear physics operates is the notion that within the nucleus of any atom exists a group of charged particles. There is a vast array of such particles, including protons, neutrons, electrons, quarks, and photons. Some of these particles are researched in earthbound substances, such as rocks and other compounds, while other subatomic particles radiate from space-based sources.

When charged, these particles come into contact with one another, or collide, causing a reaction. Such reactions can change the composition of the substance in which the interaction occurs. The reaction also triggers a release of energy in the form of radiation. Nuclear physicists analyze these reactions to better understand their nature and the implications for the world.

Technology. One of the ways nuclear physicists detect and quantify nuclear radiation and reactions is through the use of a frequency analyzer. This device works on the principle that radiation may be detected in the form of sound waves. The analyzer's microphone picks up the sound, and the device converts it into voltage and organizes the samples with numerical values. These samples are then analyzed for their frequencies and intensities.

Another set of devices used to analyze nuclear samples uses light rather than sound. Spectrometers, for example, operate on the basis that each atom emits its own wavelength of light. Spectrometers emit light beams at a sample and then analyze the responding emissions from the atoms within that sample. Nuclear physicists also use lasers, targeting a sample and calculating its emissions as well.

Still another vital tool utilized by nuclear physicists is a particle accelerator. These complex devices use electromagnetic fields to accelerate a stream of subatomic particles, such as protons and electrons, as they travel through a sealed chamber. Nuclear physicists then study the energy that is released when these charged particles collide with each other. Particle accelerators appear in many different configurations and sizes. Some, like those used in hospitals and medical-research facilities, are mobile and can fit in a single room. Others, like the Large Hadron Collider (LHC) in Switzerland, are considerably larger, requiring much greater space and facilities. These devices—also known as "atom smashers"—may be circular in configuration (cyclotrons) or operate on a straight line (linear accelerators).

Semiconductors. Nuclear physicists frequently use semiconductors as the basis for their experiments. There are three general types of materials in the natural world—those that allow for energy to be transmitted through them (conductors), those that resist such charges (insulators), and semiconductors, which resist some charges and allow others. Nuclear physicists may use a particle accelerator to run a stream of charged particles through a semiconductor. The resulting reaction can dramatically change the chemical-electric composition of that substance. By infusing different ions into a semiconductor, a process called doping, scientists can alter its structure and, therefore, its uses. One well-known semiconductor, for example, is the element silicon, which has many different applications after the doping process is applied, including the development of jewels and computer chips.

Computer Software. Nuclear physicists must compile a great deal of data from their experiments, collating it into manageable components in order to analyze it and generate reports. Relevant computer systems and software are essential for this purpose. Scientists rely on analytical and scientific software capable of collating the information collected into easily accessed components. Among the types of scientific software available are the three-dimensional Opera suite and specialized databases. Additionally, nuclear physicists rely on high-definition graphic imaging and modeling systems like Adobe Photoshop, the GNU Image Manipulation Program, and computer-aided design (CAD) software, such as Autodesk's AutoCAD suite.

Research Projects and Presentations. Nuclear physicists do not develop nuclear technologies, but the theories they introduce and the discoveries they make lay the groundwork for such innovations. These hypotheses and revelations are presented in scholarly articles, papers, and books. Nuclear physicists are generally expected to have or be on track to receive a doctorate, and their dissertations often takes several years' worth of research, gathered while working at a particle-accelerator facility or in another scientific venue. The dissertation serves as a nuclear physicist's resume after receiving a doctorate.

Following graduation, nuclear physicists must produce many more scholarly works throughout their careers. They publish such pieces in scientific periodicals like the *Journal of Nuclear Physics* and the *American Journal of Physics*. Frequently, they are called upon to present their findings at nuclear physics–oriented conferences, where they may give a formal presentation on the paper in question. A large number of nuclear physicists are also university professors, presenting their theories—as well as the theories of their peers and other scientists, past and present—to aspiring nuclear physicists at the undergraduate and graduate levels.

Applications Past and Present

Although one of the first applications of nuclear physics was the creation of the atomic bomb, nuclear physicists have discovered a vast array of other applications for the discipline. Among these applications, many of which are presently being developed for the future, are nuclear energy, nuclear weapons, nuclear medicine, and archaeology.

Energy Sources. One of the most common applications for nuclear physics is in the field of energy. Nuclear energy entails the use of the radioactive isotope known as uranium-235, chosen because its atoms are easily split. This material is mined and converted into rods, which are bundled and placed into a tank of water in a nuclear reactor. The rods are then showered with neutrons, causing the atoms in the rods to split, a reaction called fission. The nuclear reaction generates a great deal of heat, which causes the water to convert to steam, which is then run through turbines. The turbines convert the steam into electricity, which is then transferred onto the grid for consumption. Once the rods in the chamber are spent, special control rods of a neutron-absorbing material are placed in the water to absorb the excess neutrons.

Nuclear energy has long been embraced as a more efficient alternative to coal, gas, and other types of energy production, generating larger volumes of energy. However, there are risks involved with nuclear energy, including the storage of the spent uranium and control rods after use and the concern that nuclear power plants, if breached, could cause devastation to the surrounding populations. The disasters at the Three Mile Island and Chernobyl facilities during the late twentieth century proved the existence of such dangers, as did the Fukushima Daiichi nuclear facilities in Japan following the 2011 earthquake and tsunami. Nuclear physicists continue to research ways to ensure safe fission reactions at these facilities, as well as study ways to better detect radiation in order to prevent more such incidents.

Nuclear energy is not applied solely to public grids. It is commonly used on naval vessels such as submarines and aircraft carriers. These ships use smaller reactors than those at nuclear power plants, but the

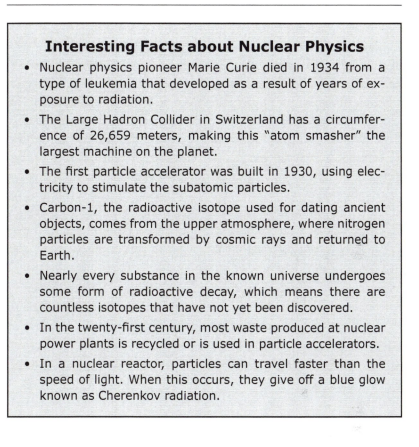

Interesting Facts about Nuclear Physics

- Nuclear physics pioneer Marie Curie died in 1934 from a type of leukemia that developed as a result of years of exposure to radiation.
- The Large Hadron Collider in Switzerland has a circumference of 26,659 meters, making this "atom smasher" the largest machine on the planet.
- The first particle accelerator was built in 1930, using electricity to stimulate the subatomic particles.
- Carbon-1, the radioactive isotope used for dating ancient objects, comes from the upper atmosphere, where nitrogen particles are transformed by cosmic rays and returned to Earth.
- Nearly every substance in the known universe undergoes some form of radioactive decay, which means there are countless isotopes that have not yet been discovered.
- In the twenty-first century, most waste produced at nuclear power plants is recycled or is used in particle accelerators.
- In a nuclear reactor, particles can travel faster than the speed of light. When this occurs, they give off a blue glow known as Cherenkov radiation.

same approach is used. Nuclear physicists are also exploring the effects of nuclear-fission reactions in space, research that could lead to nuclear-powered spacecraft in the future.

Weapons. The atom bombs that devastated the Japanese cities of Hiroshima and Nagasaki in 1945 were the products of years of research in nuclear physics. Atom bombs function by nuclear fission. They contained radioactive uranium surrounded by dynamite; when the dynamite is detonated, the force of the explosion compresses the already-unstable uranium, causing its neutrons to release great quantities of energy during a chain reaction. This chain reaction is capable of destroying an entire city.

The capability for destruction contained within those two bombs was considerably smaller than that of the missiles developed thereafter, as nuclear research continued at breakneck speed during the Cold War. The atom bomb's successors—hydrogen and thermonuclear weapons—were based on physics research performed not on fission but on fusion. Such weapons comprise a core of unstable isotopes (elements with added nuclei) of hydrogen surrounded by smaller atom bombs and encased in radioactive plutonium. When detonated, the bombs' explosive force causes the isotopes to compress violently, forming new nuclei and releasing tremendous amounts of energy. Meanwhile, the atom bombs also cause a fission reaction, adding to the weapon's destructive capability.

The Cold War was driven in part by a race to build and position nuclear weapons, but leaders worked to avoid any confrontation that might warrant their use. Ultimately, the United States and the Soviet Union began dismantling their respective nuclear arsenals. However, other nations, as well as global terrorist organizations, are pursuing nuclear weapons of their own in the twenty-first century. Although some nations are also developing missiles that could carry a nuclear warhead, terrorists would rather build smaller weapons that can be smuggled into target areas. These weapons could be generate a fission or fusion reaction, but on a much smaller scale. Their purpose is often not to destroy buildings but to contaminate the target area with large volumes of radiation. Such a weapon is known as a dirty bomb, and nuclear physicists' knowledge of radiation and nuclear science is proving useful in the detection of this post-Cold War form of nuclear warfare. They are working with engineers and others to research the types of radiation that are emitted by active nuclear weapons, thereby helping government agents track stolen bombs and bomb components before they can put people in harm's way.

Medicine. The study of radiation through nuclear physics has had a great impact on the field of medicine. One of the earliest examples of this is the x-ray machine. This device emits x-rays through a person; the interference detected by the machine provides a detailed image of organs, bones, and other structures. X-ray machines have been improved with the introduction of computer-aided tomography (CAT), which combines x-ray devices with computer-signal-processing technologies, providing images of internal organs and bones without obstruction from other body parts.

The growing field of nuclear medicine has evolved beyond the x-ray machine to include nuclear magnetic resonance (NMR). This technology uses a principle of nuclear physics that states that every human body contains diverse quantities of atoms containing radiation-emitting particles known as radionuclides. These subatomic particles vary in volume based on the chemical composition of the structure in which they are found. Medical professionals use a magnetic resonance scanner to detect the radiation emitted by these particles, providing a three-dimensional image of internal organs and structures without the need for an x-ray scan. Scientists are hopeful that this innovation will enable medical professionals to detect diseases much earlier than before. Research on NMR continues to evolve as more radioactive isotopes and their subatomic particles are discovered.

In addition to medical scanning, nuclear physics has directly aided the treatment of diseases such as cancer. Medical professionals can target cancerous cells with a particle beam, which leaves noncancerous cells intact. The infusion of this radiation destabilizes the cellular structure and triggers a chain reaction that carries over into the other cells that make up the tumor. This application of nuclear physics to medicine continues to evolve, not just in terms of combating different types of cancer, but in terms of treating other diseases (such as Alzheimer's disease) as well.

Archaeology. Archaeologists are concerned with studying civilizations, peoples, and events in human history in order to understand how humanity has developed over the millennia. An important aspect of this pursuit is archaeologists' ability to determine the dates of origin of the artifacts they uncover. Nuclear physics is contributing greatly to this aspect of archaeology.

Central to how nuclear physics is applied to archaeological dating is the notion that radiation is the energy emitted by an object that is decaying to the point at which it becomes stable. Scientists use this principle to analyze certain types of radioactive isotopes as they decay toward that point of stability. For example, they may analyze the presence of the isotope carbon-14 in a body unearthed at a dig site. Based on the length of time it would take for carbon-14 to decay to half of its original volume—its half-life, a constant figure of 5,730 years—researchers can effectively gauge the age of that body.

This field of carbon dating has proven invaluable to the field of archaeology. Scientists continue to analyze other radioactive subparticle emissions contained within living and dead organisms, as well as other objects. As this nuclear physics–based research continues to evolve, it is anticipated that archaeologists will in the future be able to better pinpoint the ages of invaluable historical finds.

Impact on Industry

Nuclear Weapons and Weapons Research. One of the most important innovations introduced in the early twentieth century was based on nuclear physics. The atom bomb, and later the hydrogen and thermonuclear bombs, quickly changed the face of modern warfare, giving the American military and its allies the ability to virtually wipe entire cities from existence. The Soviet Union's subsequent development of this weapon gave rise to the Cold War, which would drive international politics for decades, until its ultimate conclusion in the early 1990s.

Other nations have since developed their own nuclear weapons programs, while still others are presently pursuing such devices, as well as the missiles that can deliver them to their targets. The presence of nuclear weapons in India, Pakistan, and China, along with the purported development of nuclear-weapons programs in Iran and North Korea, threatened the stability of the regions in which these countries are located. Government military agencies such as the Pentagon in the United States have played a major role in developing nuclear weapons and weapons-detection technologies, but they are not alone; intergovernmental organizations such as the North Atlantic Treaty Organization (NATO) and the United Nations are also among the institutions thus affected by the weapons applications of nuclear physics. The US military and civilian and government organizations do work related to nuclear physics as well.

The US military continues to research and develop technologies based on the principles of nuclear physics. Although treaties signed with other nations prohibit the future production of nuclear weapons, the military's pursuit of technologies capable of detecting nuclear devices and materials remains a major endeavor.

Other agencies and institutions within the United States government play a role in monitoring the development and operation of nuclear weapons and materials, including the Nuclear Regulatory Commission and the Department of Homeland Security. The Lawrence Livermore National Laboratory, a federally funded research facility, also does research in this arena.

Medicine and Health Care. In addition to military infrastructures, nuclear physics plays a role in the pursuit of medical advances. Nuclear medicine has been seen as an effective tool in detecting and combating cancer; based on this, scientists are exploring its use in the treatment of other illnesses as well. In the United States, government and quasi-government agencies like the National Institutes of Health (NIH) and the Centers for Disease Control and Prevention (CDC) have been involved in this research, as have universities across the country. Outside of the public sector, pharmaceutical companies and manufacturers of medical technology have also been influenced by breakthroughs in nuclear physics and their applications in the health-care arena. Within the government, the NIH, based in Bethesda, Maryland, has long been a leading institution in researching innovative medical practices and technologies. The CDC, based in Atlanta, Georgia, is dedicated to tracking and treating major health issues and conditions.

Many major American hospitals and universities work in conjunction with one another in researching medical applications for nuclear physics. Among some of the leading institutions in this arena are the University of Pennsylvania School of Medicine in Philadelphia; the Mayo Clinic in Rochester, Minnesota; and Harvard Medical School in Boston, Massachusetts.

Many pharmaceutical and medical-technology manufacturers are developing new products based on the work of nuclear physicists. Among these private corporations are the Novartis Institutes for

Occupation	Nuclear technicians
Employment 2010	7,100
Projected Employment 2020	8,100
Change in Number (2010–20)	1,000
Percent Change	14%

Bureau of Labor Statistics, 2012

Biomedical Research, Millennium Pharmaceuticals, and the Merck Research Laboratories.

Nuclear Energy. The energy produced from fission reactions remains one of the most common nonmilitary applications of nuclear physics. Today, government agencies, private and university research facilities, and energy companies all play a role in the continued research of nuclear energy. These institutions and business organizations are committed to making nuclear energy more efficient and safe as both an alternative and a complementary energy source.

The United States government is responsible for generating guidelines and regulations that ensure that the energy generated through nuclear-fission principles is safe and efficient. Among the agencies involved are the Nuclear Regulatory Commission, the Environmental Protection Agency, and the Department of Energy.

In light of the enormous potentials of nuclear power as an alternative energy source, many universities and private research facilities are exploring and experimenting using the principles of nuclear physics. This research leads to safer plants, more efficient energy generation, and safer disposal of spent rods and semiconductors. Among the organizations involved in research in this arena are the University of Michigan, Stanford University, and the Massachusetts Institute of Technology.

Archaeology . A growing application of nuclear physics is dating archaeological finds. Those engaged in research in this arena are primarily based in universities, combining the disciplines of archaeology, physics, and engineering. However, a great deal of research is being conducted by museums as well, such as the Smithsonian Institute.

Social Context and Future Prospects

Nuclear physics has contributed greatly to modern civilization, presenting to the world a form of energy that, once understood, improved the lives of many. However, the applications of nuclear physics, particularly the development of nuclear weapons, have also had a profound and negative impact on society, beginning with the first detonation of such weapons during World War II and extending for decades during the Cold War. Even one of its most widespread benefits—nuclear energy—has generated mixed social returns: the efficiency and output associated with well-maintained nuclear power plants have been offset in the minds of many by the terrifying events surrounding the Three

Occupation	Physicists
Employment 2010	18,300
Projected Employment 2020	20,900
Change in Number (2010–20)	2,600
Percent Change	14%

Bureau of Labor Statistics, 2012

Mile Island, Chernobyl, and Fukushima facilities, the last of which was created by the combination of a major earthquake and a tsunami in 2011.

Despite the mixed benefits and risks associated with nuclear energy, continued exploration of the world of nuclear physics will continue. Researchers have only discovered a small percentage of the presumed nuclides and isotopes that exist, and they are actively pursuing the discovery of new subatomic particles and their respective elements. New supercollider facilities, such as the LHC in Switzerland, are being used for a wide range of experiments on the dynamics of subatomic particles, including research into quarks—subatomic particles containing a fraction of the electrical charges held by other such particles—and space-based dark matter. Furthermore, many scientists are exploring new approaches to studying particle collisions, potentially leading to the discovery of new types of particles and more information about how these particles interact.

Further Reading

Bern, Zvi, Lance J. Dixon, and David A. Kosower. "Loops, Trees and the Search for New Physics." *Scientific American* 306.5 (2012): 35–41. Print. Reports that many nuclear physicists are seeing traditional research techniques as outdated and exploring new approaches that make research less complex and convoluted.

Feller, W. B., et al. "Microchannel Plate Special Nuclear Materials Sensor." *Nuclear Instruments & Methods in Physics Research* 652.1 (2011): 25–28. Print. Reviews nuclear-physics research that is enabling the development of new technologies that detect nuclear materials.

Jamieson, Valerie, and Richard Webb. "There's a Particle for That." *New Scientist* 17 Mar. 2012: 32–36. Print. Discusses the subatomic particles that have already been discovered in nuclear physics, as well as the wide range of other such particles that are still being explored theoretically, including dark matter and quarks.

Suzuki, Y. "Recent Developments in Nuclear Cluster Physics." *International Journal of Modern Physics* 20.4 (2011): 753–58. Print. Discusses the value of analyzing subatomic particles in clusters and how this cluster approach can reveal new facts about subparticle interactions.

Walker, Phil. "The Atomic Nucleus." *New Scientist* 1 Oct. 2011: 1–8. Print. Reviews the nature of the nucleus and how radioactive decay is examined. Also discusses the many applications of nuclear physics, including radiocarbon dating, medical science, and energy production.

About the Author: Michael P. Auerbach has over nineteen years of professional experience in public policy and administration, business and economic development, and political science. He is a 1993 graduate of Wittenberg University and a 1999 graduate of the Boston College Graduate School of Arts and Sciences. He is a veteran of state and federal government, having worked for seven years in the Massachusetts legislature and four years as a federal government contractor. He has written on a wide range of topics, including the environment, health care, international relations, and history.

Nuclear Monitoring Technician 🖋

Earnings (Yearly Median): $68,090 (Bureau of Labor Statistics, 2012)

Employment and Outlook: About as fast as average (Bureau of Labor Statistics, 2012)

O*NET-SOC Code: 19-4051.02

Related Career Clusters: Government & Public Administration; Health Science; Manufacturing; Transportation, Distribution & Logistics

Scope of Work

Nuclear monitoring technicians work in nuclear power plants, waste-management facilities, laboratories, and other facilities that use radiation or contain radioactive material. In addition to assisting engineers with production and research in nuclear power plants, nuclear technicians are responsible for monitoring and evaluating radiation levels to assess the performance of the plant and ensure the safety of personnel. They operate equipment and chemical instruments for collecting and testing radioactive samples. Another important responsibility is teaching personnel safety procedures, including how to wear protective suits and protocols in the case of an emergency. In laboratories, nuclear monitoring technicians assist physicists and scientists in the production of nuclear technology, such as fuel cells, reactors, and medications, and conduct experiments and research. Nuclear technicians oversee the disposal of radioactive waste in waste-management treatment facilities.

Education and Coursework

Nuclear monitoring technicians are not required to hold a bachelor's degree, but they do need either an associate's degree in nuclear science and technology from an accredited community college or a vocational certificate from a technical school. Mandatory course work includes foundation classes in math and science and specialized courses in nuclear radiation and equipment operation.

After completing their education, technicians begin training in nuclear plants under the supervision of professional nuclear technicians. Their training consists of learning both the safety procedures and the operation of chemical instruments and machines. Due to the complexity of nuclear equipment and the importance of grasping safety procedures, training may take up to two years to complete, depending on

---

Transferable Skills

- Communication Skills - Speaking effectively (SCANS Basic Skill)
- Interpersonal/Social Skills - Teaching others (SCANS Workplace Competency – Interpersonal)
- Research & Planning Skills - Solving problems (SCANS Thinking Skills)
- Organization & Management Skills - Managing equipment/materials (SCANS Workplace Competency – Resources)
- Technical Skills - Using technology to process information (SCANS Workplace Competency – Information)
- Work Environment Skills - Working in a dangerous setting

---

the facility's requirements. Training for nuclear technicians, however, does not end after two years; the rapid growth of nuclear science and technology requires constant training and further education throughout a technician's career.

Nuclear monitoring technicians may choose to undergo additional instruction and transition into more advanced operational positions. After working in a plant for some time, it is not uncommon for a technician to pursue a bachelor's degree in nuclear engineering. A two-year associate's degree in nuclear science will have fulfilled some of the foundation courses required for a bachelor's degree; therefore, it is possible to finish in less than four years as a full-time student. It is also possible to work in a plant full time and attend school part time, and an employer may help fund further education. Experience working in a nuclear plant is excellent and valuable preparation for a successful career as a nuclear engineer or even as a nuclear physicist, which requires a doctorate in physics.

There are a number of societies and organizations nuclear technicians can join to keep up with and promote the education and awareness of nuclear technology. The American Nuclear Society, for example, is a nonprofit organization dedicated to promoting the advancement of nuclear science. The World Nuclear Association is an organization that connects working professionals and educates them on the expeditious growth of the nuclear industry. These organizations are also committed to promoting public awareness of nuclear science and its benefits.

Career Enhancement and Training

A license is not required to be a nuclear technician; however, in order to be successful in this occupation, candidates need to possess strong critical-thinking, mathematical, interpersonal, problem-solving, and monitoring skills. They need to be proficient in the basic principles and laws of physics as well as the structure and workings of subatomic particles. Experience with chemistry—specifically, knowledge of chemical properties and their interactions with other chemicals, the unique structures of chemicals, and safe procedures for disposing of chemical substances—is also required.

In addition to formal education, many facilities require two or more years of training in a plant before an applicant is considered for a position. Networking is an important tool for finding a job as a nuclear technician. Joining a professional society or organization, such as the American Nuclear Society, can help a candidate make valuable connections with working professionals in the nuclear industry and may lead to a job. Institutions offering associate's degrees in nuclear science and technology often have valuable connections with power plants, laboratories, and waste-management facilities. Many programs offer co-ops and internship opportunities.

Daily Tasks and Technology

Most nuclear technicians work standard eight-hour shifts, but working irregular hours and night shifts is not uncommon in order to monitor equipment and ensure the safety and efficiency of the plant. Some technicians will have to work or be on call for weekends and holidays.

A nuclear technician's daily tasks fall into two categories: safety and technical. A technician's safety responsibilities include monitoring levels of radiation to protect against overexposure, checking employees for high levels of radiation, instructing personnel in safety procedures and how to wear protective clothing, informing supervisors of abnormal radiation levels, orchestrating evacuations in the case of an emergency, inspecting equipment and machinery for safety, and disposing of hazardous waste. Their technical duties include installing equipment to collect and test radiation samples, operating chemical instruments, inputting and organizing data on computers, maneuvering machinery to transport material and install equipment, monitoring and processing chemical samples, conducting research, and developing chemical solutions.

Nuclear technicians use a variety of tools and technology. A dosimeter, for instance, is a measuring device used to evaluate an individual's radiation level. A gamma counter is a machine that measures radiation, similar to dosimeters, but is also used in researching and developing radioactive compounds. Spectrometers and spectroscopes are instruments used to measure electromagnetic waves, including light, gamma rays, x-rays, and other forms of radiation.

Nuclear technicians use basic desktop computers for word processing, spreadsheet creation, and e-mail. They also operate more complex computer software, such as gamma waste assay systems (GWAS) and radiological assessment display and control systems (RADACS).

Earnings and Employment Outlook

The demand for nuclear monitoring technicians is on the rise and expected to grow as fast as average through 2020. Nuclear energy is efficient, is environmentally safe, and costs less over time than coal and other carbon-based fossil fuels. There is, therefore, an escalating demand for nuclear power plants, though the potential for nuclear accidents is a barrier preventing the extensive spread of nuclear energy. However, the threat of global warming and the call for green energy and a decrease in toxic greenhouse gases is supplanting the fear of dangerous nuclear meltdowns, which are very rare due to advancements in safety and technology. Additional plants are being constructed, increasing the prospects for nuclear monitoring technicians.

According to information accessed from Salary.com in 2012, the average hourly wage for entry-level nuclear engineers, including nuclear monitors, was $65,420. Starting incomes at the lowest end of the scale averaged $56,697 per year, while those at the highest end of the scale averaged $78,605 per year.

The demand for nuclear monitoring technicians is on the rise and expected to grow as fast as average through 2020.

The demand for nuclear energy is expected to increase the need for nuclear technicians. In October 2011, the Nuclear Regulatory Commission reported that it had received twenty-three applications to build thirty-seven new nuclear power reactor units between 2007 and 2016. President Barack Obama announced a goal to decrease carbon emissions by 80 percent by the year 2050 and a push toward green energy, including wind, solar, geothermal, and nuclear energy. Wages for nuclear technicians are expected to increase concurrently with the rise of nuclear plants in the upcoming decades.

Related Occupations

- **Health and Safety Engineers:** Health and safety engineers maintain facilities and machinery and ensure the safety of personnel within a work setting.

- **Nuclear Engineers:** Nuclear engineers develop the instruments and systems needed to produce nuclear energy.

- **Physicists and Astronomers:** Physicists and astronomers develop technology and conduct research by studying the universe, space, and matter.

- **Nuclear Medicine Technologists:** Nuclear medicine technologists are health-care workers who scan images of the body using radioactive drugs.

- **Power Plant Operators and Distributors:** Power plant operators and distributors operate the systems and technology that generate energy in a power plant.

Future Applications

Only 17 percent of the world's electricity is currently generated by nuclear power, with the United States deriving approximately 20 percent of its own energy from nuclear plants. Nuclear power's lack of a carbon footprint makes it an appealing source of energy in a time of concern over global warming, and it is expected to eventually produce well above 20 percent of the world's electricity.

Controversy over nuclear power arose on March 11, 2011, when a tsunami and a powerful earthquake damaged the Fukushima Daiichi plant in Japan, one of the largest nuclear plants in the world. The plant sustained considerable damage and suffered a nuclear leak. Due to high levels of radiation, a twenty-kilometer evacuation zone was established around the now-disabled plant.

The Fukushima Daiichi plant is the second in history to reach a severity level of 7 on the International and Radiological Event Scale (INES), which rates nuclear accidents on a scale from level 1 anomalies to level 7 major accidents. The only other level 7 accident was the 1986 Chernobyl nuclear disaster. The accident at the Chernobyl plant in what is now Ukraine released a dangerous amount of radioactive material into the atmosphere. It is believed to be the most catastrophic nuclear accident in history, having killed thirty people due to overexposure and subsequent acute radiation illness.

Despite new safety precautions and technology, fear of nuclear accidents is a negative for the nuclear industry and has inhibited its growth. The potential dangers are also a burden for nuclear monitoring technicians, who are in the midst of radioactive substances. More importantly, nuclear monitoring technicians are responsible for ensuring the safety of personnel and preventing a catastrophic accident. The push for carbon-free energy is a positive sign for the future development of nuclear power plants and the increase in employment for nuclear monitoring technicians.

—*Daniel Castaldy*

More Information

American Nuclear Society
555 North Kensington Avenue
La Grange Park, IL 60526
www.new.ans.org

European Nuclear Society
Rue Belliard 65
B-1040 Brussels
Belgium
www.euronuclear.org

International Atomic Energy Agency
Vienna International Centre
PO Box 100
A-1400 Vienna
Austria
www.iaea.org

MIT Industrial Performance Center
292 Main Street (Building E38-104)
Cambridge, MA 02142-1014
web.mit.edu/ipc

World Nuclear Association
22a St. James's Square
London SW1Y 4JH
United Kingdom
www.world-nuclear.org

Optics

FIELDS OF STUDY

Astronomy; geometrical optics; ophthalmology; optometry; photography; physical optics; physics; quantum optics; quantum physics.

DEFINITION

Optics is the study of light. It includes the description of light properties that involve refraction, reflection, diffraction, interference, and polarization of electromagnetic waves. Most commonly, the word "light" refers to the visible wavelengths of the electromagnetic spectrum, which is between 400 and 700 nanometers (nm). Lasers use wavelengths that vary from the ultraviolet (100 nm to 400 nm) through the visible spectrum into the infrared spectrum (greater than 700 nm). Optics can be used to understand and study mirrors, optical instruments such as telescopes and microscopes, vision, and lasers used in industry and medicine.

Basic Principles

Optics is the area of physics that involves the study of electromagnetic waves in the visible-light spectrum between 400 and 700 nm. Optics principles also apply to lasers, which are used in industry and medicine. Each laser has a specific wavelength. There are lasers that use wavelengths in the 100-to-400-nm range, others that use a wavelength in the visible spectrum, and some that use wavelengths in the infrared spectrum (greater than 700 nm).

Light behaves as both a wave and a particle. This duality has resulted in the division of optics into physical optics, which describes the wave properties of light; geometric optics, which uses rays to model light behavior; and quantum optics, which deals with the particle properties of light. Optics uses these theories to describe the behavior of light in the form of refraction, reflection, interference, polarization, and diffraction.

When light and matter interact, photons are absorbed or released. Photons are a specific amount of energy described as the sum of Planck's constant h (6.626 × 10^{-34}) and the wavelength of the light. The formula to describe the energy of photons is $E = hf$. Photons have a constant speed in a vacuum. The speed of light (c) is approximately 186,000 miles per second. The constant speed of light in a vacuum is an important concept in astronomy. The speed of light is used in the measurement of astronomic distances in the unit of light-years, or the distance light travels in a year (about 5.9 trillion miles).

Core Concepts

Physical Optics. Physical optics is the science of understanding the physical properties of light. Light behaves as both a particle and a wave. According to the wave theory, light waves behave similarly to waves in water. As light moves through the air the electric field increases, decreases, and then reverses direction. Light waves generate an electric field perpendicular to the direction the light is traveling and a magnetic field that is perpendicular both to the direction the light is traveling and to the electric field.

Interference and coherence refer to the interactions between light rays. Both interference and coherence are often discussed in the context of a single wavelength or a narrow band of wavelengths from a light source. Interference can result either in an increased intensity of light or a reduction of intensity to zero. The optical phenomenon of interference is used in the creation of antireflective films.

Coherence occurs when light is passed through a narrow slit. This produces waves that are in phase with the waves exactly lined up or waves that are out of phase but have a constant relationship with one another. Coherence is an important element to the light emitted by lasers and allows for improved focusing properties necessary to laser applications.

Polarization involves passing light waves through a filter that allows only wavelengths of a certain orientation to pass. For example, polarized sunglasses allow only vertical rays to pass and stop the horizontal rays, such as light reflected from water or pavement. In this way, polarized sunglasses can reduce glare.

Diffraction causes light waves to change direction as light encounters a small opening or obstruction. Diffraction becomes a problem for optical systems of less than 2.5 millimeters (mm) for visible light. Telescopes overcome the diffraction effect by using a larger aperture; however, for very large-diameter telescope, the resolution is then limited due to atmospheric conditions. Space telescopes such as the Hubble are unaffected by these conditions as they are operating in a vacuum.

Scattering occurs when light rays encounter irregularities in their path such as dust in the air. The increased scattering of blue light due to particles in the air is responsible for the blue color of the sky.

Illumination is the quantitative measurement of light. The watt is the measurement unit of light power. Light can also be measured in terms of the luminance of light as it encounters the eye. Units of luminance include lumens and candela.

The photoelectric effect that supports the particle theory of light was discovered by German physicist Heinrich Rudolph Hertz in 1887. In 1905, Albert Einstein proposed that light exists in particles called photons, which he called the quantum theory of light. When light waves hit a metallic surface, electrons are emitted. This effect is used in the generation of solar power.

Geometric Optics. Geometric optics describes optical behavior in the form of rays. In most ordinary situations the ray can accurately describe the movement of light as it travels through various media, such as glass, air, and as it is reflected from a surface such as a mirror.

Geometric optics can describe the basics of photography. The simplest way to make an image of an object is to use a pinhole to produce an inverted image. When lenses and mirrors are added to the pinhole, a refined image can be produced.

Reflection is another optical situation where geometric optics applies. Reflections from plane (flat) mirrors, convex mirrors, and concave mirrors can all be described using ray diagrams. A plane mirror creates a virtual image behind the mirror. The image is considered virtual because the light is not coming from the image but only appears to because of the direction of the reflected rays. A convex mirror can create a real image in front of the lens or a virtual image behind the lens depending on where the object is located. If an object is past the focal point of the convex mirror then the image is real and located in front of the mirror. If the object is between the focal point and the convex mirror then the image is virtual and located behind the mirror. A convex lens will create a virtual image. Geometric optics involves ray diagrams that will allow the determination of image size (magnification or minification), location of the image, and if it is real or virtual.

Refraction of light happens when light passes between two different substances, such as air and glass or air and water. Snell's law expresses refraction of light as a mathematic formula. One form of Snell's law is: $ni \sin \theta i = nt \sin \theta t$ where ni is the refractive index of the incident medium, θi is the angle of incidence, nt is the refractive index of the refracted medium, and θ_t is the angle of transmission. This formula, along with its variations, can be used to describe light behavior in nature and in various applications such as manufacturing corrective lenses. Refraction also occurs as light travels from the air into the eye and as it moves through the various structures inside the eye to produce vision.

Magnification or minification can be a product of refraction and reflection. Geometric optics can be applied to both microscopes and telescopes, which use lenses and mirrors for magnification and minification.

Quantum Optics. Quantum optics is a division of physics that comes from the application of mathematical models of quantum mechanics to the dual wave and particle nature of light. This area of optics has applications in meteorology, telecommunications, and other industries.

Applications Past and Present

Optics dates back to ancient times. The 3,000-year-old Nimrud lens is crafted from natural crystal, and it may have been used for magnification or to start fires. Early academics such as Euclid in 300 B.C.E. theorized that rays came out of the eyes in order to produce vision. Greek astronomer Claudius Ptolemy later described angles in refraction. In the thirteenth century, English philosopher Roger Bacon suggested that the speed of light was constant and that lenses might be used to correct defective vision.

By the seventeenth century, telescopes and microscopes were being developed by scientists such as Hans Lippershey, Johannes Kepler, and Galileo Galilei. During this time, Dutch astronomer Willebrord Snellius formulated the law of refraction to describe the behavior of light traveling between different media, such as from air to water. This is known as Snell's law, or the Snell-Descartes law, although it was previously described in 984 by Persian physicist Ibn Sahl.

Sir Isaac Newton was one of the most famous scientists to put forward the particle theory of light. Dutch scientist Christiaan Huygens was a contemporary of Newton's and an advocate of the wave theory of light. This debate between wave theory and particle theory continued into the nineteenth century. French physicist Augustin-Jean Fresnel was influential in the acceptance of the wave theory through his experiments in interference and diffraction.

The wave versus particle debate continued into the twentieth century. The wave theory of light described many optical phenomena; however, some findings, such as the emission of electrons when light strikes metal, can be explained only using a particle theory. In the early twentieth century, German physicists Max Planck and Albert Einstein described the energy released when light strikes matter as photons with the development of the formula $E = hv$, which states that the photon energy equals the sum of the wavelength and Planck's constant.

By the early twenty-first century, it was generally accepted that both the wave and the particle theories are correct in describing optical events. For some optical situations light behaves as a wave and for others the particle theory is needed to explain the situation. Quantum physics tries to explain the wave-particle duality, and it is possible that future work will unify the wave and particle theories of light.

Photography. Cameras and color photography were refined over the twentieth century; however, the biggest revolution in photography has been digital imaging. By the early twenty-first century, digital cameras had virtually replaced standard film. Digital photography takes

Interesting Facts about Optics

- English surgeon Sir Harold Ridley decided on polymethyl-methacrylate (PMMA) as suitable material for intraocular lens implants after observing Royal Air Force pilots with pieces of the PMMA airplane canopy in their eyes after accidents. He noticed that this material was not rejected in the eye, and it was used for subsequent decades to implant lenses after cataract surgery.

- The first images received from the Hubble Space Telescope in 1990 were blurry because of spherical aberrations caused by a flaw the size of one-fiftieth of a sheet of paper in the focusing mirror. NASA scientists designed a series of small mirrors that were installed by a team of astronauts in 1993 to overcome this flaw. The subsequent Hubble images were free from the aberration and had the excellent resolution expected from a space-based telescope.

- The stereo images produced by the Mars Pathfinder's cameras functioned similarly to stereo vision produced by binocular vision in humans. Two sets of cameras produced individual images that were fused used prisms. The successor to the Pathfinder is NASA's Opportunity, which is still sending images from Mars.

- Geckos' eyes have 350 times more sensitivity to color in dim light than human eyes.

- Newer-generation excimer laser systems used for vision-correction surgery have the capacity to measure and correct higher-order optical aberrations of the human eye. Iris recognition with a rotational adjustment is also available on some lasers.

- The different colors of the northern lights are created when solar energy in the form of solar flares enter Earth's magnetic sphere and collide with atmospheric gases. These collisions cause the gases to emit light. Collisions with oxygen will tend to cause a red color, while nitrogen or helium will produce blue or green colors.

advantage of the photoelectric effect described more than a century ago by Heinrich Rudolph Hertz.

Vision Care and Vision Science. The advances in optics that have changed industry have also been applied to correcting people's vision. In 1949, English surgeon Sir Harold Ridley implanted the first intraocular lens following a cataract surgery. Before the intraocular lens was developed, a patient who had cataracts removed would have to wear very thick eyeglasses in order to have useful vision. As a result of advances in the ability to manufacture and use lightweight materials and an understanding of the optics of vision, surgeons and patients now have the choice to implant multifocal lenses, which can give the patient freedom from glasses. Similarly, advances in the ability to shape materials to achieve specific optical properties have led to advances in contact, bifocal, and progressive lenses, and to artificial corneal implants.

Perhaps the most widely known advancement since the 1990s is laser vision correction. With the advancement in lasers it was discovered that the excimer laser, a form of laser using ultraviolet light, emits a wavelength that is very specific to the clear corneal layer on the front of the eye. This type of laser is able to evaporate the specific corneal tissue to reshape the front of the eye precisely and improve uncorrected vision. More recently, devices to measure the wave-front aberrations from a human eye have been developed. It is now possible to use these measurements to refine laser vision corrections to produce better vision results.

Lasers. The term "laser" derives from the acronym for "light amplification by stimulated emission of radiation." The possibility of lasers was postulated by Albert Einstein, and a microwave laser was developed in the 1950s. Some credit American physicist Gordon Gould with the invention of the first laser using light; however, the ruby laser invented by American physicist Theodore Maiman in 1960 is considered to be the first laser to use light.

Lasers have since been developed using a wide range of wavelengths, from the ultraviolet spectrum to visible light and into the infrared spectrum. In order to generate laser emissions, an energy source is used to excite atoms in the active medium, which then emits a particular wavelength of light. The active medium can be a gas or solid. This light is then amplified to increase coherence. Lasers emit monochromatic light that is a single wavelength or a narrow spectrum of wavelengths. Some lasers also use polarizing filters to refine the beam characteristics further.

Since 1960, dozens of types of lasers have been developed and put to use in wide-ranging applications. From the laser pointer, which uses helium and neon, to medical and industrial lasers, the applications span all areas of industry. Lasers are used for measuring, cutting, shaping, cauterizing, printing, and numerous other applications. It is a remarkable revolution in the use of light for industrial applications.

Impact on Industry

A career in an optics field can be as varied as the applications, and the impact immeasurable. An interest in optics might lead to a career in physics, astronomy, meteorology, vision care, or photography.

Fiber Optic Industries. The reflective properties of light include the property of some materials to have total internal reflection. For specific materials of a certain size and with specific optical properties, a light ray will continue to propagate through the material via internal reflection without the light exiting the material. This feature of reflected light was investigated during the twentieth century, and was used in the invention of fiber optics by Corning scientists in 1970. By the mid-1970s, fiber optics was used to transmit telephone and computer communications. Millions of miles of fiber-optic cable are used worldwide, most notably in the telecommunications industry, and fiber optics is present in the defense, engineering, data storage, cable, and medical industries.

Vision and Vision Science. There is a vast network of health care professionals and industries that study and measure vision and vision problems as well as correct vision. Optometrists measure vision and refractive errors in order to prescribe corrective spectacles and contact lenses. Ophthalmologists are medical doctors who specialize in eye health and vision care. Some ophthalmologists specialize in vision-correction surgery, which uses lasers to reduce the need for glasses or contact lenses. In order to perform vision-correction surgeries, there are a number of optical instruments that may be used to perform vision-correction surgeries, including wave-front mapping analyzers

The industries that support optometry and ophthalmology practices include laser manufacturers, optical diagnostic instruments manufacturers, and lens manufacturers. Lenses are used for diagnosis of vision problems as well as for vision correction. Development of new lens technology in academic institutions and industry is ongoing, including multifocal lens implants and other vision-correction technologies.

Academic Research and Teaching. Many areas of research, including astronomy and medicine, use optical instruments and optics theory in the investigation of natural phenomena. In astronomy, distances between planets and galaxies are measured using the characteristics of light traveling through space and expressed as light-years. Meteorological optics is a branch of atmospheric physics that uses optics theory to investigate atmospheric events. Both telescopes and microscopes are optimized using optical principles. Many branches of medical research use optical instruments in the investigations of biological systems.

Medicine and Other Industries. Lasers have become commonplace in medicine, from skin-resurfacing and vision-correction procedures to the use of carbon-dioxide lasers in general surgery. There is an industry sector that is dedicated to the manufacture and development of vision-correction and diagnostic lenses and tools. Optics is an important part of the telecommunications industry, which uses fiber optics to transmit images and information. Photography, from the manufacture of cameras and lenses to their use by photographers, involves applied optics. Lasers are also used for precision manufacturing of a variety of products.

Government Agencies and Military. The Hubble Space Telescope, launched by the National Aeronautics and Space Administration (NASA) in 1990, demonstrates the amazing progress in land- and space-based astronomy that has been made possible through the study of optics. Hubble has generated a large amount of data since its launch and is proposed to function until 2011. The success of the Hubble is in part because of the fact that as a space-based telescope it is not subject to optical interference from the atmosphere. The successor to the Hubble is the James Webb Space Telescope, which is scheduled to launch in 2014.

Optics applications and photonics are also present in the military, where emerging technology in this field is paramount. The military employs both photonics engineers and photonics technicians.

Occupation	Engineers, all other
Employment 2010	156,500
Projected Employment 2020	166,800
Change in Number (2010–20)	10,300
Percent Change	7%

Bureau of Labor Statistics, 2012

Social Context and Future Prospects

The advancements in optics theory and application have changed the fabric of life in industrialized countries, from the way people communicate to how the universe is understood. It is almost impossible to imagine what future advances will occur in optics, since the last fifty years has brought profound changes in the fields of photography, medicine, astronomy, manufacturing, and a number of other fields.

As wireless technology advances, it seems possible that this technology may replace some of the millions of miles of fiber-optic telecommunications cables that currently exist. Because of their reliability, fiber optics will continue to be used for the foreseeable future. Existing lasers will continue to be to optimized, and most likely new lasers will be developed. With the launch of the James Webb Space Telescope in 2014, the understanding of the solar system and space will be further advanced.

Refinements in optical systems will aid in research in a variety of fields. For example, oceanographers already apply optics theory to the study of low-light organisms and to the development of techniques for conducting research in low light. Improved optical systems will likely have a positive impact on this and other research.

Quantum computers using photonic circuits are a possible future development in the field of optics. A quantum computer that takes advantage of the photoelectric effect may be able to increase the capacity of computation over conventional computers. Optics and photonics may also be applied to chemical sensing imaging through adverse atmospheric conditions, and solid-state lighting.

Some scientists have commented that the wave and particle theories of light are perhaps a temporary solution to the true understanding of light behavior. The area of quantum optics is dedicated to furthering the understanding of this duality of light. It is possible that in the future a more unified theory will lead to applications of optics and the use of light energy in ways that have not yet been imagined.

Further Reading

American Academy of Ophthalmology. *Clinical Optics*. San Francisco: American Academy of Ophthalmology, 2006. This volume of the American Academy of Ophthalmology basic science course covers the fundamental concepts of optics as it relates to lenses, refraction, and reflection. It also covers the basic optics of the human eye and the fundamental principles of lasers.

Meschede, Dieter. *Optics, Light, and Lasers: The Practical Approach to Modern Aspects of Photonics and Laser Physics*. 2d ed. Weinheim, Germany: Wiley-VCH, 2007. An undergraduate text that explains modern lasers and photonics using the fundamentals of optics theory. It includes chapters on everyday optics such as the human eye and telescopes as well as chapters on quantum optics.

Pedrotti, Frank L., Leno M. Pedrotti, and Leno S. Pedrotti. *Introduction to Optics*. 3d ed. Upper Saddle River, NJ: Prentice Hall, 2007. Intended for the physics undergraduate and includes chapters on basic optics including wave optics, geometric optics, and modern optics.

Siciliano, Antonio. *Optics Problems and Solutions*. Singapore: World Scientific, 2006. Geared to physics and engineering undergraduates, this text includes chapters on basic optics with problems that can be used by students to improve understanding of optical concepts.

Tipler, Paul A., and Gene Mosca. *Physics for Scientists and Engineers*. 6th ed. New York: Freeman, 2008. A staple for introductory university physics courses for many years. Chapters cover basic physics concepts including optics and the dual wave and particle nature of light.

Wolfe, William J. *Optics Made Clear: The Nature of Light and How We Use It*. Bellingham, WA: SPIE, 2007. Contains basic optics chapters followed by a large number of chapters about applied optics, including industrial and environmental topics; may appeal both to students and general readers interested in this topic.

About the Author: Ellen E. Anderson Penno, BS, MS, MD, FRCSC, Dip ABO, received a bachelor of science degree from Carleton College and an MS and MD from the University of Minnesota. She completed an ophthalmology residency at the Mayo Clinic in Rochester, Minnesota, and a refractive surgery/research fellowship at the Gimbel Eye Center in Calgary, Alberta. She has worked for more than a decade in refractive surgery. Her numerous publications include articles, book chapters, a book, and two surgical textbooks.

Photonics Engineer 📝

Earnings (Yearly Average): $73,000 (SPIE, 2012)

Employment and Outlook: Slower than average growth (Bureau of Labor Statistics, 2010)

O*NET-SOC Code: 17-2199.07

Related Career Clusters: Arts, Audio/Video Technology & Communications; Information Technology; Manufacturing

Scope of Work

Photonics engineers harness light and use it in a variety of applications. Some engineers use it as a means to transmit packets of information across vast distances at increasingly high speeds. Others develop the lasers used in LASIK eye surgery and optical diagnostics, allowing doctors to correct vision or identify internal medical issues. Photonics engineers are also responsible for the development of many high-tech consumer products such as digital cameras and high-definition televisions.

The word "photonics" comes from "photon," the elementary particle that gives light its dual wave-particle nature. Photonics as a field of study developed in the mid-twentieth century, beginning with the invention of the laser in 1960. The science revolutionized the telecommunications industry with the advent of fiber-optic information transmission in the 1970s. Within decades, laser-powered fiber-optic cables became able to transmit information in the form of light through strands of glass as thin as human hair.

Education and Coursework

An entry-level photonics position requires a bachelor's degree in a relevant engineering discipline. Many universities with robust science programs offer a photonics specialization within a broader major. Some schools, such as Boston University, have dedicated photonics centers and curricula. The typical coursework for a four-year degree in electrical engineering, mechanical engineering, or engineering science lends itself well to a future in photonics. Any aspiring engineer should be well versed in computer-assisted design and manufacturing.

Most photonics workers start off as lab assistants to more experienced engineers. From there, it is possible to advance to management, research, and principal positions, dependent on an engineer's strengths. Upper-level positions in lasers and fiber optics typically require an advanced degree, which can be attained through a university graduate engineering program or from a dedicated photonics and optics college. The University of Central Florida in Orlando operates one such specialized graduate school, the College of Optics and Photonics. The program is renowned within the industry and encompasses three research branches—the Center for Research and Education in Optics and Lasers, the Townes Laser Institute, and the Florida Photonics Center for Excellence.

Career Enhancement and Training

Membership in a professional organization can provide photonics engineers with numerous opportunities for career enhancement and additional training. Founded in 1955 as the Society of Photographic Instrumentation Engineers but now known solely by its acronym, SPIE is the leading international trade group for photonic and optical research and technology. SPIE works to advance light-based technology through industry collaboration, exhibitions, grants, and continuing education. Membership in SPIE provides engineers with invaluable networking opportunities and connections throughout all sectors of the field.

> ## Transferable Skills
>
> - Organization & Management Skills: Managing equipment/materials (SCANS Workplace Competency – Resources)
> - Interpersonal/Social Skills: Working as a member of a team (SCANS Workplace Competency – Interpersonal)
> - Interpersonal/Social Skills: Demonstrating leadership (SCANS Workplace Competency – Interpersonal)
> - Technical Skills: Using technology to process information (SCANS Workplace Competency – Information)
> - Technical Skills: Applying technology to a task (SCANS Workplace Competency – Technology)
> - Technical Skills: Working with data or numbers

Recruitment and job-placement services are available for those looking to break into the photonics industry. Some recruitment firms offer contingency recruitment, temporary placement, and referral services and work with high-profile clients, including military contractors developing ground, air, and marine laser, infrared, and night vision systems.

Daily Tasks and Technology

The daily tasks and necessary technical abilities of photonics engineers are as varied as the applications of the science. A large subset of photonics engineers are employed in telecommunications, working with fiber-optic cables and other optical information systems. Fiber-optic cables are insulated clusters of glass strands that transmit light signals. Various technologies, from telephone systems to cable television, use fiber-optic lines to send pieces of digital information.

The optical fiber medium of information relay came into popular use due to the speeds at which signals could be sent long distances with minimal signal decay. In a fiber-optic system, a transmitter produces and encodes information as an optical signal and sends the information to its intended target via optical fibers. Signal loss inevitably occurs along the way, so optical regenerators are intermittently positioned along the fiber-optic cable to recharge the signal. An optical regenerator uses lasers to amplify weakened incoming signals, retaining their characteristics and sending them on with renewed strength. At the end of the cable is an optical receiver that decodes and converts the light signal into an electrical one to be sent to the receiving computer, phone, television, or other device. Photonics engineers may be responsible for designing, manufacturing, and maintaining the equipment used at every stage of the fiber-optic transmission process.

Some photonics engineers may design and develop laser systems used in manufacturing or in medicine. Lasers are used for a wide variety of medical procedures, including surgeries and cancer treatment, and the demand for new applications is always rising. When used correctly, clinical lasers can treat conditions with minimal discomfort, no risk of infection or scarring, and limited side effects.

Earnings and Employment Outlook

Photonics engineering positions are available in a diverse array of fields. The telecommunications, medical, and information management industries are perhaps the most visible options for a job-seeking photonics engineer, but entertainment, mining, and public administration also offer positions with high earning potential. According to a survey carried out by SPIE in 2012, the median salary for photonics engineers varies significantly among industries. The SPIE report found that engineers working in the aerospace industry earn the highest median wage. Geographical location and private-sector employment also contribute to higher salary levels.

According to the US Bureau of Labor Statistics, job growth within the electronic engineering field—a category that includes photonics—is expected to increase at a slower-than-average rate between 2010 and 2020.

According to the US Bureau of Labor Statistics, job growth within the electronic engineering field—a category that includes photonics—is expected to increase at a slower-than-average rate between 2010 and 2020. This is due in large part to a widespread decline in the manufacturing sector. However, the rapid pace of technological development will drive demand for research and development positions within the photonics industry. As more consumer goods begin using photonics-related components such as fiber-optic systems, an increase in manufacturing positions could occur.

Related Occupations

- **Electrical Engineers:** Electrical engineers study electricity, electromagnetism, and their applications in infrastructure, telecommunications, signal processing, and other fields.

- **Aerospace Engineers:** Aerospace engineers design and construct aircraft, spacecraft, and related technology such as rockets and satellites.

- **Nuclear Engineers:** Nuclear engineers study and apply subatomic physics, using the fission and fusion of atomic nuclei to various ends.

- **Materials Scientists:** Materials scientists develop metals, ceramics, polymers, and composites for use by other engineers in the design and construction of machinery, consumer goods, and other products.

- **Laser Technicians:** Laser technicians operate laser technology for a variety of purposes, typically in the medical field.

Future Applications

The sheer versatility of light as a means of information management suggests that the field of photonics engineering will continue to expand as new applications develop. Such applications may include mapping through the use of LIDAR (Light Detection and Ranging). Immediately following Hurricane Isaac in the summer of 2012, scientists from the US Geological Survey used terrestrial LIDAR to map a three-dimensional model of storm damage. Terrestrial LIDAR collects topographic data from ground level by bouncing laser pulses off surfaces and measuring the time it takes for the reflected beam to return. LIDAR scanners can produce models accurate down to the millimeter and could prove useful in assessing the damage from natural disasters and developing future strategies for handling them.

In keeping with the prevailing trend in technology development, many photonics engineers will likely continue to look for ways to make the systems they design smaller. The Massachusetts Institute of Technology opened its Microphotonics Center in 2000 to research ways of miniaturizing optical communication components for use in smaller and higher-functioning computing and telecommunication systems. Data routers equipped with microphotonic components would eliminate electronic bottlenecks, allowing for a smoother flow of information and increased network speed.

—*Steve Miller*

More Information

IEEE Photonics Society
445 Hoes Lane
Piscataway, NJ 08855
www.photonicssociety.org

Optical Society of America
2010 Massachusetts Avenue NW
Washington, DC 20036
www.osa.org

SPIE
PO Box 10
Bellingham, WA 98227
www.spie.org

Quantum Physics

Physics; mathematics; chemistry.

DEFINITION

Quantum physics is a science on the atomic and subatomic scales. Much of the field involves advanced mathematics, as this is the tool best able to represent the behavior of the universe. Though its conclusions are often counterintuitive because activities on such small scales are dramatically different from those on a larger scale, quantum physics has proven remarkably accurate and adept at explaining various previously inexplicable phenomena. Each advance in quantum physics brings scientists a better understanding of the fundamental workings of the cosmos. Fields under active research include quantum field theory, which explains how particles work, and string theory, which is one proposed theory of everything.

Basic Principles

Research in quantum physics began in the early twentieth century when physicists encountered problems that they could not model with classical physics. One of these problems was the production of blackbody radiation, the process by which objects glow when heated. In 1900, Max Planck theorized that the energy output is quantized, that is, occurs in discrete steps. This theory was soon applied to photons and electrons themselves, demonstrating that particles can only have energies at specific levels and not at points in between, and electrons can exist only at certain points around an atom and cannot exist in between those points.

Another major innovation in quantum physics was the realization of wave-particle duality, by which all particles have properties of both particles and waves. A good example of this realization is the double-slit experiment. If researchers throw electrons or photons at a target with sufficiently good aim, they will hit the exact same spot every time. However, if pieces of material with two slits are placed between the thrower and the target, rather than doing as one might expect and passing through one slit (or colliding with the material), the thrown particle will pass through both slits and crash into itself. This action is visible because the particle scatters across the target in a pattern identical to the sort that occurs when waves interfere. The results of this experiment give rise to the wave function, a mathematical formulation of the probability of the location and behavior of a particle. When the particle must be at one point, the wave function collapses and acts as a particle.

Core Concepts

Quantum physics also makes extensive use of principles from several specialized areas of physics, especially theoretical physics, as well as advanced mathematics.

Field theory. Fields are the basic schema for understanding particles in particle physics. In quantum field theory, particles are regarded as excitations of an underlying field, so that electrons are excitations of the universal electron field, for example. A field is a set of properties for points in space-time. These properties can be directions and strengths of force, probabilities of particles existing, or something such as temperature. Quantum field theory makes much use of a concept in differential geometry called a spinor field; such fields have a number of special properties suited to modeling the properties and behaviors of particles.

Electromagnetism. Electromagnetism is at the heart of many of the principles, historical developments, and experimental methodologies of quantum physics. It is one of the four fundamental forces of the universe, which unify as energy increases. Electromagnetism is transmitted by electromagnetic waves that can also be described as particles called photons. Visible light is an electromagnetic wave, and the speed at which it travels is the upper boundary for the rate at which massive objects can travel. This velocity is a result of the permeability and permittivity of the vacuum, properties of which govern the behavior of magnetic and electric fields.

Quantum theory arose during investigation of electromagnetism, and electromagnetism is one of the primary tools used in quantum physics. Particle accelerators, which hurl particles at one another to see what is produced by the collision (typically more fundamental bits of the universe), use technologies that utilize electromagnetism to accelerate, aim, and detect the events in the accelerator. Electromagnetic systems allow for particle detection, and with each new topic of research, new systems are devised.

Advanced Mathematics. In order to model, quantify, and predict the complex and random behaviors of reality, scientists often use advanced mathematics, ranging from multivariable and multidimensional calculus to non-Euclidian geometry and complex numbers. The use of these mathematical forms stems from the fact that fields predominate in quantum physics and one must often account for the effects of multiple variables at one time. Also, because space-time is not really three-dimensional, physicists need a system that goes beyond the limits of Euclidean space.

Euclid based his geometry on five postulates. Typically, the fifth postulate, which states that parallel lines never intersect, is the one most often disregarded in quantum physics; assuming that such lines can intersect allows one to better analyze certain situations. Also, some fields, such as string theory, operate in many additional dimensions, and reality is often tied to obscure mathematical patterns. For example, the strong nuclear force is well modeled with the gamma function, a mathematical curiosity from the eighteenth century. In addition, when dealing with the probabilistic nature of reality, a strong understanding of probability is useful.

Quantum Mechanics—Uncertainty Principle. There is a maximum limit to the information that can be known about anything. For example, one can know, to a good degree of certainty, the velocity of a particle; however, the more data one has on the velocity, the less one can have on another property, such as location. Thus, it is possible to know exactly how fast the particle is traveling but have no idea where it is. This is because of the wave nature of reality. Fourier transforms, which are a means of translating wave motion, do not mesh cleanly with classical frequencies and their motions.

Quantum Mechanics—Superposition. Superposition underlies much of the apparent strangeness in quantum physics. Basically, it is the ability of an object to be in several states at once. Thus, wave-particle duality is a form of superposition, but it is typically discussed in terms of a particle whose wave function could evolve in several ways. A popular example of superposition is Erwin Schrödinger's thought experiment about the cat in the box, commonly referred to as Schrödinger's cat. In Schrödinger's hypothetical scenario, a cat is sealed in a box with some food and water. The box also contains a tiny bit of radioactive material and a device that will kill the cat if the material decays and releases radioactivity. At any given moment, since radioactive decay is probabilistic, the cat can be considered both alive and dead at the same time. The analogy breaks down here because the cat becomes one or the other when one looks in the box, while a particle in superposition really is "alive" and "dead" at the same time. This property is thought to have applications in quantum computing.

Quantum Mechanics—Entanglement. Entanglement is a situation in which two objects share superposition. It is a nonlocal property, meaning that it is not dependent upon distance. When the superposition collapses, regardless of the distance, both objects will manifest the same property. A possible analogy would be a set of dice that always roll the same number as each other, even when one die is in Las Vegas and the other is in New York.

Quantum Mechanics—Tunneling. Tunneling is a phenomenon by which particles can skip a region difficult to pass through. An electron may not be able to go through a barrier, but its probability wave can; as such, the electron "hops over" the barrier. This process surfaces in a variety of areas, including electronics and fusion. It is also thought that scent may rely on this process.

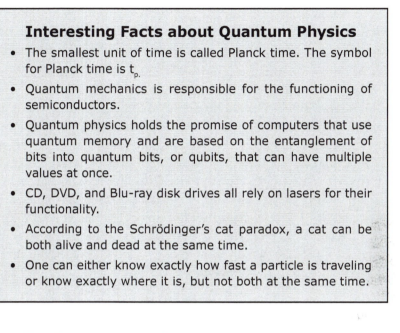

Applications Past and Present

Semiconductors. When electronics was first being developed at the beginning of the twentieth century, vacuum tubes were essential for signal processing, switching, and amplification. These devices allowed for the radio boom of the 1920s and enabled the development of early computers. Unfortunately, vacuum tubes are energy intensive and burn out easily, reflecting their similarity to incandescent bulbs. The vacuum tube works by exciting electrons by running a current through a filament. The electrons then jump off the filament and onto a collector, providing a current. The current can be modulated by the voltage and used for amplification and switching purposes.

Semiconductors have the same function and operation as vacuum tubes, but they can be made far smaller and require less power. Because they do not require heating, they are also more energy efficient. The reduction in size has allowed the miniaturization of electronics, which spurred the information revolution.

Semiconductors function through the manipulation of an atomic lattice. Charge is carried either by a hole, which is a lack of electrons, or by free electrons. This effect is produced by doping the semiconductor with small amounts of either an electron acceptor or a donor. As an example, a silicon chip may be doped with an acceptor such as aluminum. When the silicon is introduced into the crystal lattice, it has one fewer electron than a standard bond for silicon, allowing it to accept an electron and, thus, produce a mobile hole that can be passed along the semiconductor. The hole functions as a mobile positive charge. This is called a p-type semiconductor.

Doping with a donor produces an n-type semiconductor, which is achieved by introducing an atom that is capable of providing an extra electron. When using silicon as the base, phosphorus works as an electron donor, which allows electrons to carry charge. Quantum physics is used to understand the functioning of the lattice because the interactions of the electrons and the crystal lattice are best described in terms of quantum mechanics.

Lasers. Lasers are found in all sorts of technology. CD, DVD, and Blu-ray disk drives all rely on lasers, as do barcode scanners, and lasers play a significant role in many other fields as well. To understand how they work, one must first understand how atoms work. At the center of an atom lies the nucleus, which is positively charged. At discrete points away from the nucleus, there are regions where it is possible and probable for electrons to exist. These regions are called energy levels. When electrons gain energy, they enter an excited state and jump to a higher level. When they return to their original level, the ground state, they reemit energy in the form of a photon.

Lasers work by exciting electrons so they jump an energy level and release photons when they return to the ground state. In a laser, the process does not stop at this juncture. Because of an external electromagnetic field, a dipole is formed. Then the photon is reabsorbed, exciting the electron so that it produces two photons of less power than the first. This happens at a constant frequency, shared across the medium, meaning that the resultant electrons are in phase with one other.

The light of a laser is produced by a process called *pumping*. It is then amplified, typically by use of a mirrored chamber, at one end of which the mirror is partially transparent. This process allows some of the light to escape after amplification. Amplification can occur because the light is at the same wavelength and, because of the shared frequency of emission, is in phase. A more detailed explanation, as well as the ability to design a better laser, requires calculations using quantum physics. Lasers are also often used as a dependable source of photons in experiments.

Electronics. The field of electronics uses much from quantum physics, including the semiconductor. Additionally, quantum effects are used in the production of new components. As electronic devices continue to shrink, future designers will have to be mindful of the quantum nature of materials. In addition to these uses, some of the more exotic tenets of quantum physics hold potential for future development. It is hoped that tunneling can lead to more efficient solar panels and devices, while mastery of entanglement could possibly produce nonlocal communications devices, theoretically allowing circumvention of the light-speed barrier.

Computing. A major projected use for quantum physics is in computing, with a new type of computer called a quantum computer. Computers are simply ways of encoding, storing, and manipulating data. In fact, they do not even need to be electronic; the first Turing machine was designed in the nineteenth century and used gears. Modern computers work by encoding data in binary. What this means is that a switch in the computer is at either a high or a low state. These states are quantized, meaning that a bit (short for *binary digit*) must be one or the other; there is no middle. Operations are strings of bits that tell the processor what memory to access and what to do with it. Fundamentally, the operations are logical operators given solid form by the nature of the machine into which they are constructed; a computer is a device that carries out these mathematical operations. The idea is that there is a minimal set of operators that should allow a computer to compute any calculation through proper use of operators and recursion. As long as a computer can perform this function, it is described as *Turing complete*.

Computers need not be binary. One prospect is the development of a new type of computer that uses quantum-entangled bits, meaning that rather than being either on or off, they could be both. Ways of implementing this include measuring polarization of photons (left, right, or both left and right) and counting the number of electrons (0, 1, or both 0 and 1). Quantum bits, or *qubits*, would allow for much greater computational power. One can entangle multiple qubits and keep entire chunks of memory in superposition, allowing them to hold multiple values. Also, since quantum teleportation has been demonstrated with data, implementation of this technology will prove useful. Quantum computing will yield higher computational power and stronger security at introduction.

Quantum Biology. The nascent field of quantum biology studies the ways life-forms make use of quantum physics. It is thought that the smelling mechanism uses quantum tunneling and that bird navigation relies in part on quantum phenomena. Also, photosynthesis seems to rely on quantum tunneling for its high efficacy. Future advances in biomedical technology will no doubt also use quantum physics.

Computational Chemistry. Much of computational chemistry employs quantum mechanics when simulating chemical reactions, as quantum effects are significant on the scale at which the reactions occur. This is useful for making drugs and catalysts.

Impact on Industry

Quantum physics is used primarily in research and development work. As a result, there are applications being developed that use the field as background to a variety of purposes in the civil and military arenas. Quantum physics is most used in electrical-engineering projects, especially projects that include semiconductors. It is also used in nuclear-fusion research, which, though a bit farther from implementation than other technologies, will provide a source of clean energy.

Laser research is another prominent field in which quantum physics plays a part. New modes of light production and modulation are under active investigation because lasers are ubiquitous in modern industry and technology. New innovations in laser technology center on increasing output and decreasing size. Lasers also have peripheral applications in fields such as chemical engineering, where they are useful for molecule design in computational chemistry.

Most of the applications of quantum physics use quantum phenomena already present in an object. For example, quantum teleportation cannot yet be used to increase the efficiency of solar panels because solar panels do not yet have entangled memory banks. The next wave of expansion will involve direct use of quantum phenomena.

Quantum computing and much of the other technology mentioned make use of exotic phenomena. Much of the work is being done at universities and by the military and will enter consumer research in the near future. The industry associated with these technologies will be immense. The associated increase in computing power due to quantum computing alone will lead to many significant advances.

Occupation	Physicists
Employment 2010	18,300
Projected Employment 2020	20,900
Change in Number (2010–20)	2,600
Percent Change	14%

Bureau of Labor Statistics, 2012

Electronics Manufacturing. The introduction of the transistor in the 1950s changed the way technology is used by allowing electronics to be made much smaller, thus leading to widespread modern computer usage. Quantum physics continues to be important in the process of making better and smaller transistors. Although the impact of transistors has been revolutionary, there is still much room for development.

Cybersecurity. One of many fields that will benefit from advances in quantum computing is cybersecurity. This emerging field aims to keep information and computers safe. Computer hacking is a weapon that can be used to disrupt government and corporate operations, and protecting sensitive networks, equipment, and data is a top priority for both governments and businesses. Quantum computing offers the potential to vastly increase the range of possibilities.

Academic Research. Most dedicated research into quantum physics is done through universities. University research tends to focus on particle physics, which utilizes theoretical mathematics.

Government-Funded Laboratories. Many governments sponsor research in the field of quantum physics. One such government-sponsored research initiative is being conducted by the European Organization for Nuclear Research, better known as CERN, which is home to the Large Hadron Collider (LHC), the largest particle collider yet constructed. Research into entirely new areas is possible because the size of the collider allows for high-energy collisions. Fermi National Accelerator Laboratory, better known as Fermilab, is home to the largest particle accelerator in the United States. Its research also takes advantage of entirely new areas of study as a result of the large size of the collider.

Social Context and Future Prospects

Quantum physics allows for a greater understanding of the universe at its smallest scales, the analysis of what constitutes it, and the discovery of better ways to construct at miniscule levels. With the rise of nanotechnology, quantum physics could reveal better means of working with tiny materials and machines. Also, research into managing quantum phenomena could allow for more efficient electronics. There has been much benefit from the field in terms of practical technology. Lasers, semiconductors, and many more devices rely on quantum mechanics. There is room to expand research and many ways to develop new technologies.

Furthermore, the world of physics research is full of possibilities. CERN's LHC has opened an array of new avenues of investigation. One of the more exciting discoveries is the possible confirmation of the Higgs boson, the particle that, if it exists, provides the explanation for why objects have mass. Research into the existence of this particle will lead to further investigation.

Quantum physics is one of the best ways to find out about the true nature of the universe. Humans are only beginning to glimpse the deeper levels of reality. Quantum physicists are starting to ponder questions once considered to be in the realm of metaphysics. Research into quantum physics will soon investigate such questions as the nature of time and existence, the origins of the cosmos, and the existence of other universes.

Further Reading

Demtröder, Wolfgang. *Atoms, Molecules, and Photons: An Introduction to Atomic, Molecular, and Quantum Physics*. 2nd ed. London: Springer, 2010. Provides an introduction to atomic and molecular physics and explains the present model of atoms and molecules. Introduces quantum physics and the wave model of particles.

Einstein, Albert, and Leopold Infeld. *The Evolution of Physics: From Early Concepts to Relativity and Quanta*. New York: Simon, 1938. Written by Infeld, based on his discussions with Einstein. Addresses the development of physics and the ideas and theories in use.

Feynman, Richard P., Robert B. Leighton, and Matthew L. Sands. *The Feynman Lectures on Physics*. Reading: Addison, 1963. Contains the lectures Nobel Prize winner Richard P. Feynman gave to his freshmen and sophomore students at Caltech in the 1960s. Covers mechanics, electromagnetism, and quantum mechanics.

Le Bellac, Michel. *Quantum Physics*. Cambridge: Cambridge UP, 2006. Uses algebra and symmetry principles to teach the fundamentals of quantum physics. Includes discussions of one-dimensional potentials, angular momentum, and scattering theory.

Peskin, Michael Edward, and Daniel V. Schroeder. *An Introduction to Quantum Field Theory*. Reading: Addison, 1995. Targets graduate physics students. Covers relativistic quantum mechanics, quantum electrodynamics, and Feynman diagrams. Also includes a discussion of the physical principles underlying elementary particle physics.

Zelevinsky, Vladimir. *Quantum Physics*. Weinheim: Wiley, 2011. Two-volume set with a focus on problem solving. Presents fundamental knowledge before moving into applications. Contains a full modern graduate course in quantum physics.

About the Author: Gina Hagler writes about science and technology. She is the author of numerous science books, including *Modeling Ships and Space Craft: The Science and Art of Mastering the Oceans and Sky* (2012).

Quantum Physicist

Earnings (Yearly Median): $105,430 per year (Bureau of Labor Statistics, 2012)

Employment and Outlook: Average growth (Bureau of Labor Statistics, 2012)

O*NET-SOC Code: 19-2012.00

> **Related Career Clusters**: Government & Public Administration; Education & Training; Information Technology

Scope of Work

The field of quantum physics is broad in scope—ranging from quantum optics to studies in unified field theory, more commonly known as the elusive "theory of everything"—and quantum physicists perform a variety of tasks in both theoretical and experimental capacities. A majority of quantum physicists work in academia as researchers or professors. Others are employed by the government, and a small number of quantum physicists are employed by private companies to develop new technologies based on the behavior of subatomic particles.

Experimental quantum physicists observe and analyze physical effects on subatomic particles. For example, physicists at CERN (the European Organization for Nuclear Research) record data produced by the Large Hadron Collider (LHC) in Geneva, Switzerland. The LHC is the world's largest particle accelerator.

Theoretical quantum physicists seek to reconcile existing theories with observations and data. They also suggest new theories that they hope can be proven through experimentation.

Education and Coursework

Knowledge of the quantum universe and the behavior of subatomic particles is constantly evolving and is sometimes in dispute among theorists. For this reason, research in the field is closely tied to academia; it could even be said that the education of a quantum physicist, which begins in high school and officially ends with postdoctoral research, is never truly over.

Aspiring quantum physicists should study general physics and mathematics in high school. The American Physical Society (APS) recommends courses in pre-algebra, algebra, advanced algebra, and precalculus. For undergraduate students, the APS suggests a strong foundation in a variety of mathematics and science courses, augmented by courses in communication, science writing, and education for

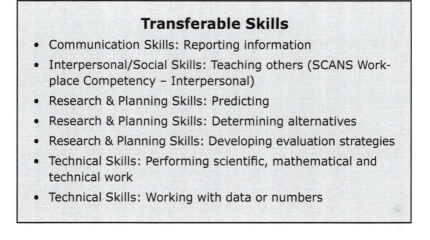

those who want to teach. Most colleges offer a major in general physics, though students interested in theoretical quantum physics should be equally versed in mathematics.

Specializations such as quantum physics come through research opportunities. The APS recommends getting involved with research as early as possible, even if the research is outside of a student's chosen area of specialization. Undergraduate research experience is a valuable asset in the graduate-school admissions process and teaches real-world skills such as deadline management, problem solving, and improvisation. The APS lists internship opportunities for graduate as well as undergraduate students.

Graduate studies, both master's and doctoral, in quantum physics are research based and offer advanced studies in specialized branches of quantum physics, including cosmology, energy research, field theory, quantum chromodynamics, quantum computing, quantum gravity, and string theory. As many of the world's leading quantum physicists work in academia, graduate students can expect to be on the cutting edge of the field. For example, a popular postdoctoral area of research for theoretical quantum physicists is string theory, an evolving and complex theory that seeks to relate Albert Einstein's general theory of relativity to quantum mechanics. String theory posits that elementary particles are vibrating "strings" of energy. For experimental quantum physicists, quantum entanglement, which will one day be used to encrypt messages and build ultrafast computers, is a rich new field of research.

After graduate school, quantum physicists usually participate in two to three years of postdoctoral research. Students can expect to spend at least five to seven years total completing both their doctoral and postdoctoral work.

Career Enhancement and Training

Quantum physics, which deals with the behaviors of subatomic particles, is vitally important to a greater understanding of the known universe and to the development of new technologies. Advancements in the field are beneficial to a number of other areas, which is why much of the research performed by quantum physicists is funded by collaborations among governments, universities, and private companies.

Collaboration among quantum physicists is equally important, from analyzing and verifying data to developing new theories and advancing old ones. Thus, opportunities for sharing and publishing work are vital to the career of a quantum physicist. The Internet has significantly broadened the playing field in this respect. In addition, working physicists attend meetings and conferences to share their work with other physicists from around the world. Very few quantum physicists work completely independently of their peers or a university or research institution, though some, including a number of theorists who oppose string theory, have argued that the politics of association and funding have stifled creativity in the field and popularized stale arguments.

Networking is also an important part of any physicist's career. Quantum physicists can apply for membership with a number of professional organizations, including the APS, the American Association for the Advancement of Science (AAAS), and the American Association of Physics Teachers (AAPT).

Daily Tasks and Technology

Theoretical quantum physicists often work in academia, teaching physics courses to undergraduate or graduate students. Physicists who are also teachers or full-time professors must balance education and independent research, which may include analyzing complex mathematical systems and creating theoretical models as well as writing grant proposals and scholarly articles.

The twenty-first-century development of many new technologies has made it possible to test a number of theories for the first time, and with incredible precision. The LHC, which began operations in 2008, allows physicists at CERN to recreate and observe how matter behaved in the fraction of a second after the big bang. CERN and the LHC project employ a number of quantum physicists in capacities related to the technical operation of the collider and the constant stream of data it produces.

The LHC is an underground, 16.5-mile circular tunnel inside which technicians accelerate beams of particles from opposite directions. When the beams collide, new particles are created. The LHC's greatest achievement to date came in 2012, when CERN was able to provide experimental proof of the Higgs boson particle, an important puzzle piece of theoretical quantum physics. Technologies like the LHC have allowed for more collaboration between experimental quantum physicists and theoretical quantum physicists than ever before.

Some private companies, like the computer company IBM, employ quantum physicists to develop new technologies with their engineers. In the past, quantum physicists have often been at the technological forefront; the twentieth century saw the advent of transistors, atomic clocks, and lasers, all due to the work of quantum physicists.

Earnings and Employment Outlook

The growth rate for jobs in physics and astronomy, which are grouped together by the Bureau of Labor Statistics, is on par with that of similar fields, though the demand for newer and faster technology is high. In 2012, the *New York Times* reported that IBM was working with quantum physicists to create a working quantum computer in the near future. A computer that could process information in accordance with the strange laws that govern quantum mechanics could solve a number of equations simultaneously, computing, perhaps in seconds, calculations that would take a computer of today nearly 14 billion years to solve.

The growth rate for jobs in physics and astronomy, which are grouped together by the Bureau of Labor Statistics, is on par with that of similar fields, though the demand for newer and faster technology is high.

Physicists are well paid, with a median salary of $106,370 in 2010, but are required to have a PhD and postdoctoral experience in quantum mechanics and particle physics. The research of most quantum physicists is funded by the government, universities, and research institutions. A decline in public funding is expected to be offset by growing funds from private companies like IBM.

Related Occupations

- **Mathematicians**: Theoretical mathematicians create and expand theories in high-level mathematics. Their work can be can be used to advance technologies in physics and engineering. Mathematicians working in applied mathematics analyze data in a particular industry, such as transportation or finance.

- **Nuclear Engineers:** Nuclear engineers apply principles of nuclear science to a variety of industries. They also design, operate, and monitor nuclear power plants.

- **Electronics Engineers:** Electronics engineers design a wide range of electronic devices, including global positioning systems (GPS), computer software, and broadcasting equipment.

- **Computer and Information Research Scientists:** Computer and information research scientists look for new ways to improve existing computer technology and write new software. Specializations within the field include hardware architecture and robotics.

- **Biophysicists:** Research in biophysics can be applied to the development of new drugs, genetically engineered foods, and biofuels. Biophysicists often work with scientists in other fields, including chemistry and engineering.

Future Applications

Quantum physicists are developing new technologies, including quantum computers, based on a phenomenon known as quantum entanglement. Quantum entanglement describes the relationship between two separate particles that control each other over vast distances. The relationship between the two, sometimes different, particles is such that if a particular change occurs in one particle, the same change occurs instantaneously in the other. Physicists hope to exploit this behavior to transmit and encrypt information. They refer to this endeavor as quantum teleportation because the information does not travel through space and, therefore, cannot be hacked. Though the technology does not yet exist, scientists were able to transmit photons a record distance of eighty-eight miles in 2012.

The Joint Quantum Institute, a collaboration between the University of Maryland and the National Institute of Standards and Technology (NIST), has undertaken studies in quantum tunneling. Another strange phenomenon exclusive to quantum mechanics, quantum tunneling occurs when a particle passes through or surmounts a barrier that, according to the laws of the natural world, it should not be able to. Scientists are able to measure such phenomena with greater accuracy than ever before, and they hope the data will lead to real-world applications.

—*Molly Hagan*

More Information

American Physical Society
1 Physics Ellipse
College Park, MD 20740
www.aps.org

CERN (European Organization for Nuclear Research)
CERN CH-1211
Genève 23
Switzerland
public.web.cern.ch

Joint Quantum Institute
Room 2207
Computer and Space Sciences Building
University of Maryland
College Park, MD 20742
jqi.umd.edu

National Institute of Standards and Technology
100 Bureau Drive, Stop 1070
Gaithersburg, MD 20899
www.nist.gov

Society of Physics Students
1 Physics Ellipse
College Park, MD 20740
www.spsnational.org

Solid Mechanics

FIELDS OF STUDY

Applied mathematics; applied science; biology; biomechanics; biomedical engineering; calculus; chemistry; computational mechanics; engineering (aerospace, civil, manufacturing, materials, mechanical, structural); geology; geomechanics; geometry; materials science; mathematics; microelectronics; nanotechnology; physics; physiology; rheology; seismology; statics; tectonophysics

DEFINITION

Solid mechanics is the study and testing of a solid material and structure as it reacts to outside influences such as force and temperature. Its practical applications include testing the load and stress limits of structures such as roofs and airplanes and structural materials such as pine and carbon composites. Solid mechanics uses applications that require an understanding of mathematics, computer algorithms, and the laws of physics. Successfully predicting the reaction of a material to a variety of physical stresses addresses safety, economic, and practical concerns. The principles of solid mechanics are used across many branches of engineering.

Basic Principles

The theories and applications of solid mechanics have been practiced for centuries, with basic principles of engineering and mechanics first explained by the ancient Greeks. Greek mathematician Archimedes (ca. 287–ca. 212 B.C.E.), for instance, developed the law of the lever, which explains mechanical force and stress. Fifteenth-century Italian artist and architect Leonardo da Vinci designed mechanisms made of beams and then identified stress distribution across a beam's section (deformation). Sixteenth-century Italian mathematician Galileo Galilei tested beams to their breaking point (failure). These discoveries and elucidations allowed early builders to know, among other things, the amount of stress materials could withstand before bending or breaking and subsequently compromising the structure being built. Today, advances in the study of solid mechanics have made calculating either the mass of a planet or the properties of a nanoparticle solvable tasks.

The field of solid mechanics still tests solids for stress, deformation, and failure by using a combination of physical testing and mathematics to predict the interactions of matter and force. An additional distinction is now made, however, between statics (the study of objects that are motionless) and dynamics (those that are in motion). Additionally, if the shape of a solid is changed through stress or deformation and the solid returns to its original shape, it is considered elastic. If it remains changed, it is considered plastic.

Additionally, some materials show characteristics that are both solid and fluid, and these are studied in the related field of rheology. Rheology studies material that is primarily in a liquid state, but material that is plastic in nature is also studied. Solid mechanics and its sibling fluid mechanics are known together as "continuum mechanics," which studies the physical properties of both solids and fluids using mathematical objects and values. However, as solid matter studies delve deeper into micro- and nanotechnology, new mathematical models are constantly needed and being developed.

Core Concepts

The field of solid mechanics began as a branch of mathematics and did not become a branch of engineering until the mid-twentieth century. However, its principles and subspecialties have existed for centuries.

Early Discoveries and Applications of Solid Mechanics. Seventeenth-century English physicist and mathematician Isaac Newton developed three laws of motion that shaped the field of classical mechanics by explaining the relationship between forces applied to a material and the resulting motion caused by those forces. However, his laws did not take into consideration the motion of rigid bodies (solid material that does not change shape or size when force is applied) or of deformable bodies (solid material that undergoes a temporary or a permanent change in shape when force is applied). German mathematician

Leonard Euler extended Newton's laws in 1750 by applying calculus equations in order to include rigid and deformable material in the laws of motion.

Robert Hooke, a late-seventeenth-century mechanician, studied the behavior of metal springs and made important progress in the subfield of elasticity. He discovered Hooke's law, which explains that force and deformation are related in a linear way: The amount of deformation of an object is in direct proportion to the deforming force, and when the force is removed, the object returns to its original shape and size.

In the nineteenth century, French mathematician Augustin Louis Cauchy developed the present-day mathematical theory of elasticity by studying the effect of pressure on a flat surface. Through this work he introduced the concepts of stress and strain into the theory of elasticity.

Force and Stress. Solid mechanics is concerned with the study of material as it is affected by external force that may or may not cause it to undergo a change in its position or shape. Stress is the measure of the effect (such as twisting, bending, compressing, or stretching) that the external force has on an object or material.

Force can bear on a solid in a "normal" (or perpendicular) direction, or it can bear "in shear." Shear stress occurs when force is applied at an angle, and materials that don't support shear stress are generally considered fluids. When shear stress causes an object to twist, the resulting condition is called torsion.

Deformation (Strain), Elasticity, and Plasticity. Deformation, often referred to as strain, is the change in shape, size, or temperature of an object as a result of force being applied to it. Strain measures any internal or external change in the material and informs the mechanician how and where the solid object is changing as it accumulates stress. Applied force or temperature can lead to temporary or permanent deformation of an object or can cause structural failure, which is the complete loss of the material's ability to support a load.

Elasticity is the ability of some materials to return to their original shape and size after external force or temperature is removed. Hooke's law explains the linear elasticity of most springs: Until a certain level of force is exhibited, the extension of the spring (its deformation) is in direct proportion to the load (or the force) applied to it. The muscles around the heart obey Hooke's law, as do spring-operated weighing machines. Structural analysts and engineers use mathematical equations to determine the linear elasticity of material in order to determine load capacity.

Plasticity, on the other hand, is a material's inability to return to its original size or shape once an applied force is removed. Plasticity is also referred to as nonlinear elasticity and is seen, for example, when metal is bent using force or high temperature.

Fracture, Creep, and Failure. Fractures are cracks in material when force or temperature is applied. Analytical solid mechanics uses mathematics and knowledge of stress and strain of a material to determine the level of force the material can withstand before fracturing. Fracturing occurs suddenly and often results in the failure of a material or object to perform as it was designed. Creep, on the other hand, is the gradual and permanent deformation of a material as a result of stress. It is time dependent, and the speed with which creep occurs is determined by the weight of the force or the temperature that is applied. Creep may or may not result in failure.

Mechanical Engineering. Mechanical engineering and applied mathematics are two subfields of solid mechanics involved in the construction and efficiency of engines, turbines, and motorized vehicles. With modern levels of engine performance, extreme stress and strain are variables for consideration, and engineers must understand and predict potential areas of stress, fracture, creep, strain, and deformation for each piece of the equipment.

Materials Science. Primary areas of research in materials science include energy storage and composite materials design. A relatively new solar energy technology is the development of thin-film photovoltaic cells, whereby any building surface that faces the sun can use strips of thin-film cells to convert solar energy into electricity. Material scientists and engineers also study the change in properties of materials whose dimensions approach nanometers (billionths of a meter).

Microelectronics and Nanotechnology. The use of solid mechanics in microelectronics and nanotechnology involves creating

Interesting Facts about Solid Mechanics

- In 2010, Walt Disney World's Epcot theme park opened the exhibit "Take a Nanooze Break," which allows visitors to view and manipulate molecules and nanoscale versions of everyday items.

- The Atomic Force Microscope lets us see at nanoscale, and the Scanning Tunneling Microscope allows scientists to view and manipulate objects smaller than 100 billionths of a meter.

- Augustin-Louis Cauchy, who developed the modern theory of elasticity, has more mathematical concepts and theorems named for him than any other mathematician to date.

- Living cells have a cytoskeleton, their own kind of outside surface, which is a composite material. Its makeup includes polymers and proteins, and it can be lab-tested for stress.

- As of 2008, over three hundred companies in over twenty countries produced products that contained nanomaterials.

- The "dimples" on golf balls allow them to travel farther than a smooth ball would. The indentations reduce the amount of drag caused by the air.

- Polycrystalline materials "grow" when a material rapidly moves from fluid to solid. It starts to solidify at many points, and the solid crystals move out from these points. Then the solid areas intersect along random boundaries that scatter light.

- John Deere builds body panels for tractors and combines that are polymeric plastics manufactured from the soybeans that the tractors planted and that the combines harvested.

- Gibson guitar company has put microprocessors in its latest guitar.

- The ancient Greek philosopher Aristotle wrote the first book on biomechanics, *De Motu Animalium* (On the Movement of Animals).

custom-designed miniature electronic equipment for industry, manufacturing, academics, and the military, among other areas. "Packaging" microchips, microcircuits, and other devices, along with connecting them for better performance, involves consideration of material stress, strain, creep, and failure rates in order to keep up with the current demand for product and technological developments.

Nanotechnology, which merges sciences such as physics, chemistry, biology, and solid materials, involves the study and use of new nanoscale materials that are far lighter and stronger than old ones. These materials must be analyzed from a solid mechanics point of view for their use in, for example, medical devices and drugs, which has generated public concern. US government agencies such as the Occupational Safety and Health Administration (OSHA), the Food and Drug Administration (FDA), and the Environmental Protection Agency (EPA) have also voiced concern about the invasiveness and potential for unintended consequences of nanotechnology in medicine.

Applications Past and Present

Geomechanics. Geomechanics is the study of the behavior of the earth's soil and rock and how they react to fractures, strains, and stresses. Expertise in solid mechanics and knowledge of its related equipment and testing procedures is crucial to being better able to predict earthquakes, developing cleaner and safer methods of extracting oil from the ground, and to devising new technologies in building increasingly tall structures.

Cultural Infrastructure. In the most basic sense, builders throughout history who attached a roof to a structure depended on solid mechanics. Materials science has its roots in the stonemasonry and ceiling management technology that advanced during the age of medieval cathedrals, especially with the addition of flying buttresses, which allowed ceilings of unprecedented height to be constructed. When steel was added to buildings in the nineteenth century, engineers and designers incorporated knowledge of statics, dynamics, and applied mathematics. Rectangular-shaped skyscrapers have been replace by curving steel shapes with specially engineered glass in shell-type planes. Mechanicians and engineers employed solid mechanics' technology in order to be able to predict the thermal and wind stresses the glass could withstand as well as the potential effects of the building's strain as it expands and contracts with extreme temperatures or shifts in the wind.

Biomedical Engineering or Biomechanics. Biological organisms combine fluid dynamics and solid matter, as body fluids flow within a solid muscular, skeletal structure. Cells have cytoskeletons, and a cell shape, its "geometry," affects its life and death. Using nanotechnology, a cell's cytoskeleton can be stress-tested and mathematically analyzed. Biomedical engineering is profoundly affected by advances in solid mechanics. Prosthetic science, for example, has created metal "bones" that are made of carbon-fiber composites, which are lighter and more maneuverable than ever before.

Manufacturing Engineering. Hermann Staudinger, a German chemist, proved the existence of macromolecules and subsequently won the 1953 Nobel Prize in Chemistry. Polymers are a kind of macromolecule composed of many similar units of molecules strung together. If one were to knit a scarf, for example, then knit another scarf onto the end of the first and a third onto the end of the second and so on, one would have an analogous design—a very long scarf made of scarves. Solid mechanicians engineer new polymers and design the machines and other processes used to make them. Polymers have certain qualities that make them useful, such an ability to "stick" together. Naturally occurring cellulose polymers form wood by bonding together to make trees strong. Manufactured polymers have been used in plastics for many years in beverage bottles, garbage bags, and clothing such as raincoats. But new uses continually arise. Polyurethane, Teflon, and Dacron are well known for their uses in wood preservation, frying pan coatings, and cloth, but all three materials are also used in the manufacture of artificial heart valves.

Manufacturing engineering is also concerned with formulating new metals and testing them for fracture and deformation as well as for thermal stress and strain. Engineers also predict a material's potential as a structural component and then determine the effective applications of the material. Polycrystalline substances that are used in solar cells and composites that are used in aerospace and military applications are solids that undergo the constant need for upgraded technology in order to allow them to perform efficiently and economically.

Impact on Industry

Solid mechanics has many subfields, such as engineering, geomechanics, biomechanics, and computational mechanics. Materials science, especially the fields of biomedical and electronic engineering with the development of nanoscience and nanotechnology, is a rapidly growing area where a background and education in solid mechanics would prove extremely useful. The Bureau of Labor Statistics reported that in 2010, there were 262,800 open positions for civil engineers and projected that the job outlook for biomedical engineers through 2020 would prove to be faster than the national average for all occupations.

Military. The study of materials and how they react to force, stress, and temperature are important to defense technology and advanced weaponry. The B-2 Stealth bomber is coated in a carbon composite called AHFM that allows it to avoid radar detection and was designed by experts in materials science. Rotors on Australia's attack helicopter the Eurocopter Tiger are made of a fiber plastic composite that increases the helicopter's ability to stay in the air under fire. Similarly, body and tank armor are now made of a high-tech, classified material that is much more effective at stopping incoming fire.

There are many who believe, however, that the next age in military defense will be more focused on robots than on materials development. Getting the soldier out of the tank and behind a remote operating device, as in drone surveillance and firepower delivery, may be the way microelectronics, materials science, and robotics contribute uniquely to modern warfare. For example, modern shorelines are subject to piracy, terrorism, and smuggling, and new applications for solid mechanics are being developed to address these threats. One such project, in development since 2005, aims position an array of sensors in the water along shallow coasts. Approaching dangers would be picked up and targeted by fleets of unmanned underwater vehicles (UUV's) that are linked to manned submarines.

University Research and Teaching. Many top-ranked US research universities such as California Tech, Cornell University, Virginia Tech, and the University of Texas at Austin have solid mechanics programs at both the undergraduate and graduate levels. Some second-tier universities, such as the University of New Mexico, have faculty with specializations in solid mechanics, which helps an undergraduate foster the access to a career path in the field.

Occupation	Physicists
Employment 2010	18,300
Projected Employment 2020	20,900
Change in Number (2010–20)	2,600
Percent Change	14%

Bureau of Labor Statistics, 2012

Government Agencies. The need for solid mechanicians is also seen in US government agencies. The National Aeronautics and Space Administration (NASA), for example, has sent robots to Mars to explore the surface as well as the interior of the planet, and satellites are used for worldwide communications, military intelligence, and climatic studies. Groups such as the Drug Enforcement Agency (DEA) and the Border Patrol rely on modern guns with machined parts made by robots and formed with designed metals and plastics. The Food and Drug Administration (FDA) protects and encourages public health. It supervises and regulates the manufacture and distribution of not only food, but also tobacco, prescription and over-the-counter medication, dietary supplements and vitamins, and cosmetics. Microtesting supplements has become a $23 billion industry, and scientists with the FDA have begun testing cosmetics for nanoparticles, which pose potential serious health risks.

Social Context and Future Prospects

Research into solid mechanics has changed a great many aspects of modern society. With the help of microelectronics, long-distance communication, once limited to land-line phones in homes and offices or the postal service, now happens through cell phones, which take phone conversations almost anywhere. Email has replaced conventional mail as a social form and has permitted far more frequent and informal letter writing than ever before. Computers, run by the silicon-based microchip, have increased work time and efficiency in offices and schools.

Advances in tectonophysics and seismology are bringing us closer to realistic and reliable earthquake prediction, raising hopes of saving countless lives and dollars. The manufacture of composite materials has made airplanes lighter and armor stronger, which serves to better protect soldiers. Additionally, progress in materials science has given those who do survive battle but who have lost limbs access to better prosthetics than ever before. In the pharmaceutical field, new products include nanoparticles that deliver products more effectively to the body, thereby increasing survival rates in cancer patients. Cosmetics, where nanoparticles build better sunscreen and deliver lipids more effectively to thirsty skin, raise hopes for anti-aging products that will literally change the face of future elders. Nanoparticles are proving to be controversial, however, as their long-term effect on the body are unknown.

Further Reading

Adhami, Reza, Peter M. Meenen III, and Dennis Hite. *Fundamental Concepts in Electrical and Computer Engineering with Practical Design Problems*. 2nd ed. Boca Raton: Universal, 2005. Print. A well-illustrated guide to the kind of math required to analyze electrical circuits, followed by sections on circuits, digital logic, and DSP.

Arteaga, Robert R. *The Building of the Arch*. 10th ed. St. Louis: Jefferson National Parks Association, 2002. Print. Describes, with illustrations, how the Gateway Arch in St. Louis, Missouri, was built up from both sides and came together at the top.

Davidson, Frank Paul, and Kathleen Lusk-Brooke, comps. *Building the World: An Encyclopedia of the Great Engineering Projects in History*. Westport, CT: Greenwood, 2006. Print. Examines more than forty major engineering projects, from the Roman aqueducts to the tunnel under the English Channel.

Finn, John Michael. *Classical Mechanics*. Sudbury: Jones, 2009. Print. Comprehensive introduction to the study of classical and applied mechanics, suitable for advanced students of physics and mathematics. Contains sections on statistical dynamics and fluid mechanics.

Goldfarb, Daniel. *Biophysics Demystified*. Maidenhead, England: McGraw-Hill, 2010. Print. Examines anatomical, cellular, and subcellular biophysics as well as tools and techniques used in the field. Designed as a self-teaching tool, this work contains ample examples, illustrations, and quizzes.

National Geographic Society. *The Builders: Marvels of Engineering*. Washington, DC: National Geographic Society, 1992. Print. Documents some of the most ambitious civil engineering projects, including roads, canals, bridges, railroads, skyscrapers, sports arenas, and exposition halls. Discussion and excellent illustrations are included for each project.

Shurkin, Joel N. *Broken Genius: The Rise and Fall of William Shockley, Creator of the Electronic Age*. New York: Macmillan, 2006. Print. Biography of the Nobel Prize–winning electrical engineer and father of the Silicon Valley, who had the foresight to capitalize on his invention of the transistor but ultimately went down in infamy and ruin.

About the Author: Amanda R. Jones has a master of arts degree from Virginia Tech and a doctorate in English from the University of Virginia. She has written several articles for EBSCO and has published in the *Children's Literature Association Quarterly.*

Materials Physicist 🖋

Earnings (Yearly Average): $84,600 (O*NET, 2012)

Employment and Outlook: Average (O*NET, 2012)

O*NET-SOC Code: 19-2032.00

Related Career Clusters: Government & Public Administration; Health Science; Manufacturing; Transportation, Distribution & Logistics

Scope of Work

Materials physicists work in laboratories, private companies, the high-tech industry, research institutions, and for the federal government. Materials physicists combine the field of physics with the principles of chemistry and engineering. They research and analyze the structure and behavior of metals, ceramics, composites, and other materials.

Materials physicists work from the bottom up: they analyze the chemical properties and physical aspects of materials at the microscopic level and use this knowledge to apply these materials to macro-level products and technologies.

Due to the large research component of this occupation, much of a material physicist's time is spent experimenting and analyzing material in a laboratory. From these experiments, they record and analyze their findings and use this information to create products that benefit society. The materials produced by materials physicists include prosthetic arms and legs, hard drives, computer software, semiconductors, and everyday consumer goods such as sunscreen.

Education and Coursework

A bachelor's degree in physics is the basic requirement for this occupation, but an advanced degree is needed for research positions. A bachelor's degree will qualify for assistant and technician positions in a materials physics laboratory. A master's degree will qualify for developmental positions in private laboratories and, in some cases, research positions, but this usually only applies to candidates with over ten years of laboratory experience. A PhD is strongly preferred over a master's degree in this profession.

A PhD program in physics takes five to seven years to complete, and a master's degree in materials physics or a related field (e.g., theoretical physics) is often a prerequisite. It is not uncommon for universities to offer a joint master's and PhD program. The University of South Florida, for example, offers a dual MS degree and PhD in physics. PhD programs in materials physic are highly competitive, and a candidate must have an excellent academic record and laboratory experience either in an academic setting or an internship. An applicant must score high on the GRE and the subject test in physics (PGRE). Many doctorate programs look for applicants who have published work and contributed their knowledge to the field.

A candidate for a PhD program in materials science must possess superior mathematical, analytical, problem-solving, interpersonal, and critical-thinking skills. A PhD program in physics consists of coursework in mathematics, physics, and chemistry—quantum mechanics,

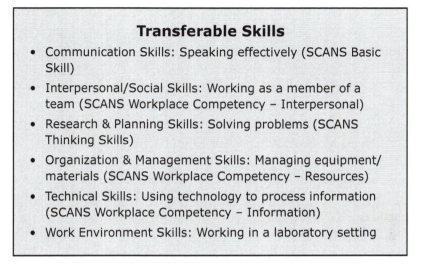

Transferable Skills

- Communication Skills: Speaking effectively (SCANS Basic Skill)
- Interpersonal/Social Skills: Working as a member of a team (SCANS Workplace Competency – Interpersonal)
- Research & Planning Skills: Solving problems (SCANS Thinking Skills)
- Organization & Management Skills: Managing equipment/materials (SCANS Workplace Competency – Resources)
- Technical Skills: Using technology to process information (SCANS Workplace Competency – Information)
- Work Environment Skills: Working in a laboratory setting

statistical and mathematical physics, organic, inorganic, and physical chemistry. Courses in computer technology and advanced laboratory classes are also required. In order to earn a PhD, a candidate must pass a comprehensive exam, complete a dissertation (a thesis that presents the results of original research), and successfully defend the dissertation in front of a doctoral committee.

After successfully defending the dissertation and earning a PhD, a materials physicist often pursues postdoctoral research. It is not uncommon for an employer to require a candidate for a research position to have extensive experience in a research laboratory. This mandatory research experience can be accomplished as a postdoctoral candidate. During the course of postdoctoral research, physicists work under the supervision of senior scientists for approximately two to three years.

Career Enhancement and Training

A materials physicist does not need a license. If the scientist works for the federal government, however, he or she may need a high security clearance if involved in developing confidential defense system technology. Training for a materials physicist includes completing research in a physics laboratory, which is often accomplished during postdoctoral research. A postdoc lasts approximately two to three years, wherein a physicist is supervised by a team of professionals. After a year of supervision, a postdoc candidate often performs independent research and prepares for a subsequent career as an independent researcher. Most materials physicists will concentrate their research on a particular material—such as steel, plastic, or ceramic—and specialize in creating and enhancing products using this material.

Having a membership to a professional organization for physicists provides many benefits. The American Physical Society (APS) is an organization that connects over fifty thousand professionals. The American Institute of Physics (AIP) is known for hosting networking opportunities and exhibitions for physicists and other scientists involved in the physics industry. Students also benefit from this organization's one-year free trial membership, which allows them to meet and network with professionals and learn more about new innovations in the field. Having a membership with AIP is also a great addition to a résumé—it shows a potential employer or a PhD admissions committee an applicant's commitment to his or her chosen field.

Daily Tasks and Technology

The daily tasks of materials physicists fall into two categories: laboratory and office work. In the lab, material physicists study the chemical structure and behavior of materials and create simulations of these materials using advanced computer software. From the study of the chemical composition of materials, they invent new technology and enhance existing products—from cars, computer chips, plastic, and ceramics to golf clubs and other consumer goods. A materials physicist oversees a team of technicians and assistants in a laboratory through the research and production process. In order for a product to be approved, a materials physicist must test the safety and effectiveness of a technology and meet strict governmental safety standards.

After a product is completed and approved for production, materials physicists oversee the training of personnel in operating the technology and explain the mechanisms and materials involved. They may also supervise the production of these products in a factory or other industrial facility. Additionally, these scientists write reports summarizing and analyzing the results of experiments with the intent of publishing their findings in a scholarly journal, a magazine, and other academic publications. It is not uncommon for materials physicists to work as professors in colleges and universities.

Materials physicists use a variety of technology in the laboratory. An electron microscope, for instance, emits a beam of electrons to generate extremely close-up images of a material. Another technique employed is x-ray scattering, in which x-rays are focused on a material and reveal its unique structure and chemical makeup. Neutron diffraction (or neutron scattering) is another technique used to examine the atomic structure of a material. A materials physicist examines the electromagnetic waves of a material—the light, gamma rays, x-rays, and other forms of radiation—with spectrometers and spectroscopes.

Earnings and Employment Outlook

The demand for materials physicists is expected to grow as fast as average through 2020. According to information obtained from O*Net in 2012, the average yearly salary for a materials scientist is $84,600. The Bureau of Labor Statistics reports that salaries of materials scientists ranged, in 2010, from less than $45,810 annually to more than $130,070 annually.

The need for materials physicists is steadily increasing due to the importance of inventing new products and enhancing existing products in the areas of medical technology, electronic devices, computer software, and a number of other products. Scientists believe materials physics will grow concurrently with the rapid growth of science and technology in the twenty-first century; it is, in other words, ultimately the materials within a product that create advanced technology. The importance of materials in the development of future technologies, therefore, will call for an increase in materials physicists. The popularity of materials physics is also due to its uniting a wide range of scientific disciplines, from chemistry and engineering to polymer science and biophysics.

Related Occupations

- **Nanosystems Engineer:** Nanosystems engineers work with material on the nanoscale and develop technology from the study of nanoparticles.

A Conversation with Edward N. Clarke

Job Title: Occasional Distinguished Lecturer and Visiting Lecturer; Volunteer

What was your career path?

Undergraduate engineering degree from Brown University; Service in the US Navy during and after World War II; graduate degrees in applied physics and engineering science from, Harvard University: PhD in physics from Brown University. Then, I worked as a physicist in semiconductor surfaces, semiconductor crystal growing, and transistor technologies for the Sylvania Electric Co. Then, cofounder of Sperry Rand semiconductor division and head of research and development, followed by cofounder, director, and vice president of operations for National Semiconductor Corp. Then, in order, I became the Associate Dean of the Faculty, Director of Research, Associate Dean of Graduate Studies, Founder of the Center for Solar Electrification (semiconductor solar PV), and Professor of engineering and science, at the Worcester Polytechnic Institute (WPI).

What are three pieces of advice you would offer someone interested in your profession?

1. Retain mobility and be willing to use one's skills wherever they are needed.
2. Do not become too comfortable and secure. Move on to find new challenges.
3. Stay young with variety in one's life and a healthy use of the out-of-doors.

What paths for career advancement are available to you?

I have continued lecturing and advising others during retirement. I have taken courses in Atomic Force Microscopy and in Astrophysics when I was beyond age eighty. I continue to read and learn subjects that were new or did not even exist during my younger years. I am eighty-seven years of age.

- **Chemical Engineer:** Chemical engineers design manufacturing plants and oversee the chemicals used in production.

- **Chemist/Materials Scientist:** Chemists and materials scientists study the properties of chemical substances and develop new technology.

- **Mechanical Engineer:** Mechanical engineers design mechanical systems, such as machines and tools, with the use of physics and materials science.

- **Civil Engineer:** Civil engineers oversee the design and configuration of roads, bridges, and other large natural and physical construction projects.

Future Applications

The future of materials physics is expected to impact a wide range of products and industries. NASA physicists and engineers, for example, are researching and manufacturing materials that will produce armor for spacecraft that will be capable of repairing themselves after sustaining damage. In medicine, materials are being developed that will impact tissue engineering—cornea tissue rejuvenation, for example—and enhance the efficiency of implantable structures such as artificial heart valves and orthopedic implants.

The Defense Advanced Research Projects Agency (DARPA) has funded the research of materials that will enhance the power of radar and wireless communication devices. They are also working on using advanced materials to increase the amount of data that communication systems can transmit.

The National Academy of Engineering (NAE) emphasizes the importance of material physics and science in overcoming some of the major challenges of the twenty-first century, including global warning, the growing need for renewable energy, and the need for clean water. The future of green energy will depend upon the discovery and application of materials that will allow green energy sources—fuel cells and photovoltaic cells (solar power)—to perform at an optimal and cost-effective level.

Materials physics will not only apply to green energy, but also to the construction of energy-efficient homes, buildings, and vehicles. In the transportation industry, materials physicists and scientists will work on creating biodegradable and environmentally safe packaging materials that will be capable of distributing food and water to the world's growing population.

—Daniel Castaldy

More Information

American Institute of Physics
One Physics Ellipse
College Park, MD 20740
www.aip.org

Brookhaven National Laboratory
P.O. Box 5000
Upton, NY 11973
www.bnl.gov

European Physical Society
6 rues des Frères Lumière
68200 Mulhouse
France
www.eps.org

Graduate Study at FSU Physics
Florida State University
315 Keen Building
Tallahassee, FL 32306
www.physics.fsu.edu

Institute of Physics
76 Portland Place
London W1B 1 NT
UK
www.iop.org

Systems Engineering

FIELDS OF STUDY

Mathematics; computer science; business management; industrial engineering; performance engineering; organizational studies; software programming.

DEFINITION

Systems engineering is the field of engineering that deals with the manner in which complex and interdisciplinary engineering projects can be organized, designed, and managed. It focuses on coordination of separate teams, logistics, life-cycle maintenance, automation, and other ways of working with large projects. It does this through development of processes and design paradigms as well as interfacing parts of the project. Systems engineering often straddles the line between technical and human-centered disciplines, with business, organizational studies, and project management on one end and various disciplines of engineering on the other. Developed as a means to manage the massive projects of the Cold War–era Department of Defense (DOD) and the National Aeronautics and Space Administration (NASA) in the United States, systems-engineering paradigms have since become critical to diverse disciplines, particularly software development.

Basic Principles

Systems engineering developed from a need to coordinate large-scale projects involving not only a variety of engineering work but different organizations and groups as well. The term is first recorded as being used at Bell Laboratories for use on large projects, mostly work in support of the Allied war effort during World War II. Among other tasks, Bell statisticians helped in ammunition and materials sampling. The methodology was soon picked up by the DOD and NASA. The DOD found systems engineering useful because it allowed them to coordinate the new defense projects needed during the Cold War. Since secrecy was often important, those in charge found the ability to break a task down into components a useful part of systems engineering.

By determining the critical components and sequences for successful outcomes, those managing the projects found that they could increase the effectiveness of defense programs. Projects such as President Dwight D. Eisenhower's interstate highway construction, the establishment of Strategic Air Command, and various intelligence programs all benefited from systems engineering because people with expertise in the technology could interface directly with those who needed the systems. They could then discuss the practical goals and desired outcomes of the project. The engineers could devise an abstract framework so as to meet goals. In addition, the DOD could find better ways to organize their own groups to meet emergent threats.

The American space program was also an ideal candidate for systems engineering. Not only the rockets but also the infrastructure and methodology were designed from the ground up. After President John F. Kennedy's 1961 declaration of intent to go to the moon, the space program became dedicated to producing a moon-capable system. Thus NASA designed a process that would develop the technology in a timely and efficient manner by determining what components were likely critical and devising a way to test as many of these features as possible.

Systems engineering has spread across many fields since the 1960s, and in the twenty-first century, many projects begin by outlining goals and developing systems and teams to accomplish them. This is a particularly common practice in software development. Systems engineers view their problems holistically and look at how the parts fit together, then divide the workload into manageable chunks with clear goals. This is accompanied by analyzing the project to find which steps depend on others and prioritizing those on which others depend in what is called the *critical path*.

Core Concepts

Abstraction. In order to prioritize and decide upon its goals, a systems engineer must be able to look at the abstract of the situation. For example, a systems engineer must be able to see commonalities between different portions and tasks so as to group them. Also, the ability to temporarily ignore unimportant details and view the project as many interrelated tasks while visualizing the relationships between those tasks is fundamental to the process that allows systems engineering to work. The challenge is to decide which things to simplify, but often these are self-evident upon inspection of the project. Abstractions of the project can also aid in tasks such as prioritization, where a designer may look at the task and see what the trade-offs would be for any given change or development. An example of this is often seen in computer programming, where data transactions are abstracted to the data structure. A data structure is the way in which the data is organized; it is the relationship between one datum and another, be it linear or an ever-expanding tree. Once the processes have been abstracted, a systems engineer can devise functions to accomplish these goals in the abstract, and then pass in the specifics.

Holistic View. A holistic view of the project is also necessary to good results in systems engineering, because every component must fit together and no part can be viewed in isolation. Considering how the end product fits together is essential to successful completion of the goals. The process by which the product is designed is itself designed and must be optimized and changed as needed. By recognizing the design process as designed, systems engineers can ensure that they are achieving optimal results and setting useful goals. Through awareness of these facts and a good view of how the whole project fits together, systems engineers can spot the best ways to interface and prioritize the project and its subprojects.

Models. When dealing with complex and often abstract systems, it is often imperative to have some type of model. Not simply useful for the engineers who use them to keep track of their place in the larger picture, models also serve as invaluable tools for communicating with the client to better ensure that the project is turning out as desired and get feedback as the work progresses.

There are many varieties of models. Graphic representations are very common and often include flow charts, which can model things ranging from outcomes of a project to the workings of a computer program to failure modes and emergency systems. Other models are simpler, such as equations, graphs, and charts. Models are useful in design as well, as they can be used for testing. Models can also be more abstract, such as the waterfall design paradigm, an approach to development. The power in these sorts of models is that they give everyone a way of organizing their tasks within a shared framework.

Often, models will have a standardized methodology, so that they can be shared across projects and participants will be familiar with the layout. One such standardization is Unified Modeling Language, or UML. Unified Modeling Language is built for use in software design. This system aids in the identification of logical groupings of components, processes, and agents in those transactions and in the development of reusable software.

System. For something so critical, it may surprise many to find that there is no single agreed-upon definition of a system. Fundamentally, a system is a set of elements that achieves a goal. The looseness of this definition allows it to be adapted to a specific problem set. This also allows for the system to be enlarged and shrunk as the project progresses, while retaining the understanding that the designers are part of the process as well

Complexity. An understanding of the complexity of the project is critical to successful systems engineering. This comes up in the hierarchy of the project as critical components are identified and prioritized, thus motivating the development of better systems, algorithms, and analytical tools to handle the complexity of a given system, such as a space station.

Effectiveness. Effectiveness is the rubric by which the success of the project is judged. It can include a series of objectives that must be optimized overall. Because of this, a project that accomplishes one of its objectives very well but the rest very poorly might be less effective than one that is mediocre across all objectives. Objectives are things that can be measured objectively and are benchmarks for progress and success. A very common objective is cost, which is often a deciding factor on the systems that can be implemented and motivates many tradeoffs. While ideally a system could use the best components for all

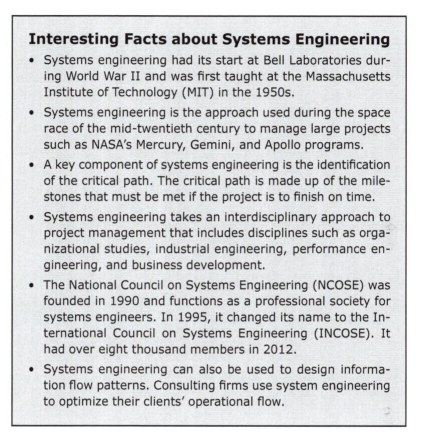

Interesting Facts about Systems Engineering

- Systems engineering had its start at Bell Laboratories during World War II and was first taught at the Massachusetts Institute of Technology (MIT) in the 1950s.

- Systems engineering is the approach used during the space race of the mid-twentieth century to manage large projects such as NASA's Mercury, Gemini, and Apollo programs.

- A key component of systems engineering is the identification of the critical path. The critical path is made up of the milestones that must be met if the project is to finish on time.

- Systems engineering takes an interdisciplinary approach to project management that includes disciplines such as organizational studies, industrial engineering, performance engineering, and business development.

- The National Council on Systems Engineering (NCOSE) was founded in 1990 and functions as a professional society for systems engineers. In 1995, it changed its name to the International Council on Systems Engineering (INCOSE). It had over eight thousand members in 2012.

- Systems engineering can also be used to design information flow patterns. Consulting firms use system engineering to optimize their clients' operational flow.

of its parts, such items are often expensive. This forces the engineer to decide which segments of the project require the best available performance and which do not.

Applications Past and Present

Apollo Program. There are few better examples of systems engineering than NASA's Apollo program. The project emerged out of a Cold War rivalry between the United States and the Soviet Union. Both powers were attempting to assert dominance through superiority in space technology. The Soviets sent the first human into space in 1961. Shortly afterward, President Kennedy declared the American intention of going to the moon before the end of the decade. Thus NASA's problem was more than simply designing a new spaceship to get to the moon, as it may have appeared at first glance. Instead, they had to first get people into space and devise ways for them to live under those conditions for the mission's duration; NASA also had to land astronauts safely on the moon and let them take off again, all while designing new rockets to supply power. Engineers needed to assess what the surface of the moon was like and devise new systems to support the rockets and astronauts. The entire American space program during that period became a test bed for developing the technologies and systems required to get to the moon. NASA engineers designed a process by which to develop the technology in a timely and efficiently manner by first determining what components were likely critical and then devising a way to test as many of these features as possible.

They began with the Mercury space program in the late 1950s, which simply aimed to get astronauts into space. Once this goal was achieved, engineers began collecting data on what happened to people during space travel. The next step was Project Gemini, a program intended to test the engineers' ability to design systems such as airlocks and accommodations for multi-person crews and long-duration flights. Other tasks included docking in space. Once these systems were designed and tested, the work then shifted to the Apollo program, which developed the lunar technology. Simultaneously, automated satellites were designed and sent to find good landing sites on the moon. The successful integration of several successive and simultaneous programs over nearly a decade allowed the Americans to land two people on the moon in 1969. Since the end of the Apollo program and the reduction in American space-oriented ambition, NASA has needed to become more flexible in their approach.

Defense Industry. With the need in the defense industry to coordinate complex projects across multiple agencies and organizations to obtain optimal results, systems engineering is immensely important to ensure that work is carried out as efficiently as possible. This is not simply for large-scale physical installations, such as the radar network for the North American Aerospace Defense Command (NORAD), but also for intelligence and intelligence-distribution systems. Before the development of the paradigm, there was often conflict between agencies, which reduced effectiveness. The DOD benefited greatly from people outside the agency providing new perspectives and setting up better systems to allow those agencies to interact. Thus, systems engineering not only designs a system, for example a spy satellite, but also designs the context for said system, for instance a way for the Central Intelligence Agency (CIA), US Army, US Navy, and National Security Agency (NSA) to share data from that satellite. Systems engineers would also maintain this satellite in situations where, for instance, the Navy is willing to support ground stations but not fund repair missions. Thus, systems engineering designs a product and the use for that product. It is widely used throughout the military-industrial complex.

A good example of systems engineering that occurred before formalization of the field was the Manhattan Project. In order to develop nuclear weapons before Germany during World War II, the United States initiated a massive covert engineering project called the Manhattan Project. In order to make an atomic bomb, researchers first had to develop the materials for it. This required the establishment and operation of uranium-production facilities and particle accelerators for testing, as well as the procurement of facilities to test and build the bomb itself. Equally important was the need to recruit and house physicists, engineers, and laborers—even the custodial staff—in total secrecy. The need for clandestine operations caused the project to be split into many components, a good exercise in abstraction and complexity management. To ensure the success of the project in the shortest possible time, several promising approaches were used, in the hope that at least one would succeed. In support of the Manhattan Project, as part of the greater atomic war effort, missions were organized to gather data on and sabotage the German bomb project. The resulting seamless integration of science, industry, intelligence service, and international military operations is a good example of systems engineering.

Industry. The systems-engineering paradigm has spread from the military, government, and Bell Laboratories to all parts of industry. While industry does not have multiple agencies with overlapping goals to sort out, many contemporary projects are multifaceted and combine many disciplines. A good example might be the manufacture of a car. Not only must the structure of the car be designed, but the frame and the engine must work together to create an acceptable gas mileage. If the frame is too heavy, then the gas mileage will be poor, but if the frame is not strong enough, the car will be unsafe. If a certain engine is used, the car will be too expensive, but if that engine is not used, it will not be efficient. Such considerations go into the decision-making process as tradeoffs. A successful and effective product will balance all of these pressures adequately.

Equally, when designing a car, a manufacturer may choose to use certain parts because they are already in production and will make procurement and maintenance easier. A systems engineer may optimize the assembly-line procedure for a new part or alter the supply chain to simplify matters. In the twenty-first century, computer technology is near universal, so computerized control systems are also often put into cars. A systems engineer will need to get an idea of how the software fits in and what it should do. Other considerations may include where to construct the car, whether it is simpler to ship it from Japan or if it is more efficient to build a new factory in America to produce the cars. Specialists in specific fields will provide the data for many of these tasks and decisions. By coordinating all of these activities, a systems engineer can deliver an optimal product.

Software Design. Software projects often use ideas from systems engineering because most programming projects have a plethora of possible solutions. These solutions are often worked on in segments by different people, yet they must seamlessly integrate internally and be compatible with a variety of external systems. This integration is typically accomplished by a process called encapsulation, wherein each piece of the program functions as its own unit, with specified inputs and outputs. The code thus functions as a black box, where data is placed inside and the proper outputs are received without having to look into the box at all. By stacking these boxes together and sharing the list of specifications, engineers know that a piece of code, written by one person for one project, will work with code written for a wholly different project.

In fact, the object-oriented design paradigm of computer-programming languages is structured around systems-engineering ideals. In a good program, the general flow can easily be followed and the data is stored in a manner that is readily accessible when it is needed. Data is kept in discrete sections where it can be called upon by central and universal processes; the particulars are typically handled by the code surrounding those specific sections. For example, a database program would have sorting functions that work on all things that could be put in the database, but the specific types of things—whether they are, dogs, cats, or robots—would have functions specific to them. These might be things such as determining breed or seeing if it a robot has been

Occupation	Engineers, all other
Employment 2010	156,500
Projected Employment 2020	166,800
Change in Number (2010–20)	10,300
Percent Change	7%

Bureau of Labor Statistics, 2012

charged today. Many object-oriented languages have data constructs such as interfaces, which list out a set of functions that are implemented by the code. In general, the systemic approach allows code to be easy to work with and easy to maintain.

Impact on Industry

Systems engineering has had a tremendous impact on industry. All industries with large projects are able to take advantage of the systems-engineering methodology to plan and manage multidisciplinary projects. This is of great importance when taking into consideration the cost in dollars and working hours for such large-scale undertakings. With the use of a systems-engineering approach, a project manager can not only identify the critical path from the start but also define the function of future departments and operational groups. Identifying the critical path allows industries to avoid waste by focusing their resources on the tasks that must happen if the project is to be completed on time. This qualitative approach to resource allocation avoids duplication of efforts and interdisciplinary bickering that would otherwise result in wasted effort and funds. Once the critical path is identified, there is no point in arguing that resources should be allocated to other tasks that are less vital.

The ability to plan and manage large projects with efficiency has reduced the cost of large undertakings for all areas of industry. It has also given consultants who work on large-scale projects a common vocabulary and methodology, enabling the consultants for the various entities to integrate their work products effectively and resulting in a substantial savings for their company clients.

Social Context and Future Development

The paradigm of systems engineering has dramatically changed a variety of fields and is the new model of integration for large-scale projects. In a world that is increasingly interdisciplinary, the ability to integrate information and make clear goals across a project is critical. With the rise of ubiquitous computing, even the most prosaic projects make use of coding; new materials give new options for formerly simple tasks. These and many other changes to the way we work mean that unification of information will be invaluable.

Systems engineering has already overseen some of the largest projects in the twentieth and twenty-first centuries, including the Apollo program and the optimization of work flow in many industries. Because programming is actually abstract data manipulation, it is a good example of systems-engineering principles. Since the design of a program is usually arbitrary—a problem can often be solved in multiple, equally efficient ways—constraints from the client and adaptability typically dominate. Projects often involve many programmers, each working on a different section. The qualities that make for good code on the individual scale are used to coordinate mass effort. This is because even the simplest projects tend to involve multiple pieces to keep them simple at the abstract level. A programmer might put code for data manipulation in one place and the interface in another. This, of course, necessitates a means for sharing, which is accomplished though variables that can then be used by other people to add to the project. This use of systemic thinking is easily applicable to any type of project. A recent trend has been the rise of consulting firms that provide systemic analysis for their clients. As humans engage in increasingly ambitious projects, designing not only the technology but also the process around the technology will lead to better results.

Further Reading

Blanchard, Benjamin S., and W. J. Fabrycky. *Systems Engineering and Analysis*. Boston: Prentice, 2011. Print. Focuses on the design and engineering of human-made systems and systems analysis. Concentrates on the use of systems engineering to identify what an entity is to do before determining what the entities are.

Buede, Dennis M. *The Engineering Design of Systems: Models and Methods*. Hoboken: Wiley, 2009. Print. Provides a reference to the methods for systems engineering that are in use today. Uses a model-based approach to introduce methods and models used in actual practice.

Kerzner, Harold. *Project Management: A Systems Approach to Planning, Scheduling, and Controlling*. Hoboken: Wiley, 2009. Print. Often referred to as "the Bible" of project management. Aligns with the latest release of the Project Management Institute's Project Management Body of Knowledge.

Rouse, William B., and Andrew P. Sage. *Handbook of Systems Engineering and Management*. Hoboken: Wiley, 2009. Print. Focuses on the engineering and management techniques for systems design, with emphasis on information technology and software-intensive systems involving human and organizational elements.

Zhang, Mingjun, and Ning Xi. *Nanomedicine: A Systems Engineering Approach*. Singapore: Pan Stanford, 2009. Print. Provides a detailed look at nanomedicine from a systems-engineering perspective.

About the Author: Gina Hagler writes about science and technology. Her book about applied fluid dynamics, *Modeling Ships and Space Craft: The Science and Art of Mastering the Oceans and Sky*, was published in 2012.

Robotics Engineer

Earnings (Yearly Median): $90,580 (O*NET On-Line, 2011)

Employment and Outlook: Slower than average growth (O*NET OnLine, 2011)

O*NET-SOC Code: 17-2199.08

Related Career Clusters: Architecture & Construction; Information Technology; Manufacturing

Scope of Work

Robotics engineers research, design, and construct robots for a variety of tasks in industry and manufacturing. In the late twentieth and early twenty-first centuries, they have applied their trade to space research and exploration, medicine, agriculture, mining, and the military. Service robots perform jobs that humans cannot, either because the jobs are too dangerous (the Gemini-Scout mine rescue robot) or too distant (NASA's *Curiosity* rover on Mars). Some companies, like Amazon.com, are even looking to use robots in their warehouses to perform stocking and assembly-line work that is currently performed by unskilled laborers.

Robotics engineers oversee the construction of a robot from design blueprint to operation, performing tests throughout in order to measure the robot's effectiveness. Engineers need to be able to think creatively in order to develop robots that can accomplish a growing number of tasks, but they must also be comfortable with the complex mathematics required to construct a working robot. Robotics engineers use a variety of tools, including computers, drafting software, and hand tools, to complete their work.

Education and Coursework

Aspiring robotics engineers are encouraged to take advanced courses in mathematics, computer science, and physics in high school. Secondary schools typically do not offer courses in robotics, but there are several robotics competitions available to high school and even middle school students. VEX Robotics Design System and the Technology Student Association (TSA) sponsor a competition for middle and high school students, and the nonprofit group FIRST (For Inspiration and Recognition of Science and Technology) sponsors several robotics competitions for young people ages six through eighteen.

Robotics engineers must hold a bachelor's degree in robotics engineering or a related field, such as electronic or mechanical engineering. Although it is more common for colleges to offer majors in the latter two fields, many colleges also offer individual courses in robotics. Industrial engineering, electrical engineering, manufacturing engineering, and computer science are also applicable. The Accreditation Board for Engineering and Technology (ABET) is the organization that accredits

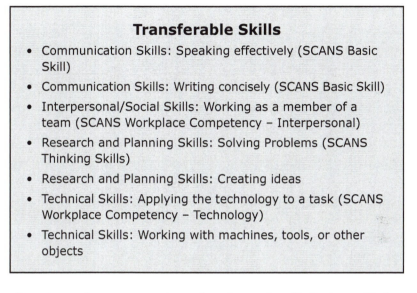

Transferable Skills

- Communication Skills: Speaking effectively (SCANS Basic Skill)
- Communication Skills: Writing concisely (SCANS Basic Skill)
- Interpersonal/Social Skills: Working as a member of a team (SCANS Workplace Competency – Interpersonal)
- Research and Planning Skills: Solving Problems (SCANS Thinking Skills)
- Research and Planning Skills: Creating ideas
- Technical Skills: Applying the technology to a task (SCANS Workplace Competency – Technology)
- Technical Skills: Working with machines, tools, or other objects

all postsecondary programs in engineering and applied science. Undergraduate students studying robotics will most likely focus primarily on technical aspects such as mechanical systems, electric circuits, and automation controls. Robotics engineers who graduate with a bachelor's degree are eligible to become technicians and machine controllers.

Some robotics engineers pursue a master's degree in order to further their career or earn a higher salary. Worcester Polytechnic Institute (WPI) in Massachusetts is the first postsecondary school in the United States to offer all three major degrees (bachelor's, master's, and PhD) in robotics engineering. The majority of students working toward their master's degree will use computers to learn higher-level design techniques and will take courses in computer and engineering theory.

As with most scientific fields, research is an important component of a degree in robotics engineering. At WPI, for example, graduate professors and robotics professionals research and teach specialized branches of the field, including artificial intelligence (or human-robot interactions), biomechanics, robot kinematics and dynamics, and sensors and manipulation. Many of the robotics engineers who graduate with a master's degree opt for careers in robotics design. Those who choose to pursue a doctorate will continue to research relevant topics in robotics. They typically choose careers in research or academic capacities.

Career Enhancement and Training

Robotics engineers are usually required to obtain a license before entering the field. After graduating from an ABET-accredited program, or during a student's last year of school, candidates for licensure are required to take the Fundamentals of Engineering (FE) exam, administered by the National Council of Examiners for Engineering and Surveying (NCEES) in conjunction with individual state licensing boards.

In order to be certified as a professional engineer (PE), robotics engineers must gain at least four years of work experience in the field and then pass the Principles and Practice of Engineering (PE) exam. The PE exam is also administered by NCEES and tests an engineer's abilities in his or her own field. There is no exam for robotics, but other PE exam focus areas include electrical engineering and electronics, control systems, industrial engineering, mechanical systems and materials, and software. Both the FE and the PE exams are eight hours long and comprise both a morning and an afternoon session. The PE exam is "open book," meaning that test takers are allowed to bring reference materials. The FE exam is not open book. Robotics engineers must continue to earn education credits to maintain their engineering license.

Daily Tasks and Technology

Robotics engineers work in a number of capacities and use a variety of technologies to complete day-to-day tasks. Two computer systems, computer-aided design (CAD) and computer-aided manufacturing (CAM), are integral to the design and manufacture of robots and robotic systems and the manufacture of goods. CAD is a complex system, and many institutions offer an associate's degree in computer-aided design and drafting.

CAM has revolutionized the manufacturing industry. The program allows industrial tools, such as milling or welding machines, to be controlled by computers. Since in the mid-twentieth century, manufacturing companies using CAM have evolved to become highly automated, thus allowing for greater precision and consistency of output.

Robotics engineers work in a variety of settings, including industrial plants and computer laboratories. Communication and written skills are essential assets because robotics engineers usually work in teams.

Like most careers in engineering, robotics engineering requires a mind that is both mathematical and creative. Engineers and designers must have the imagination to envision automated systems that can perform the same tasks as humans and the technical and computation skills necessary to bring those visions to life.

Earnings and Employment Outlook

Regardless of specialty, a robotics engineer's annual salary is significantly higher than the national average. Despite the projected slower-than-average growth rate for careers in fields closely related to robotics engineering, an increasing number of colleges and universities are offering courses in robotics as the commercial appeal of automation and robotics systems increases, and the potential for job growth in the field is promising. In March 2012, the *New York Times* reported that Amazon.com had purchased Kiva Systems, a robot-manufacturing company, for $775 million. Amazon hopes to use the Kiva robots to stock their warehouses alongside, and in some cases instead of, human workers. Also in 2012, the newspaper reported that the Pentagon had teamed up with the robotic design firm Boston Dynamics to build a robot prototype that could "run" at a pace of eighteen miles per hour and would be used in battle situations.

> **Despite the projected slower-than-average growth rate for careers in fields closely related to robotics engineering, an increasing number of colleges and universities are offering courses in robotics as the commercial appeal of automation and robotics systems increases, and the potential for job growth in the field is promising.**

Though debate outside of the field of robotics has focused on issues surrounding the need for employment for workers replaced by robots, one thing is certain: an increased demand for automation and robotic systems can only mean more work for robotics engineers.

Related Occupations

- **Aerospace Engineers:** An aerospace engineer may create new technologies for either aircraft or spacecraft.

- **Computer Hardware Engineers:** Computer hardware engineers oversee the production of faster and more efficient computer technologies, and they design new software and test computer equipment.

- **Biomedical Engineers:** Biomedical engineers design devices or products specifically for medicine. This includes artificial organs as well as computer software for x-ray machines.

- **Electricians:** Electricians often work independently to design, install, and repair electrical systems in residential and industrial settings.

- **Mechanical Engineers:** Mechanical engineering is a broad field that oversees the development of mechanical devices such as tools, engines, and machines from the initial design of the device to its construction.

Future Applications

Sandia National Laboratories of Albuquerque, New Mexico, announced in 2011 that its robotics engineers had developed a robot that could aid first responders in mining accidents. Named the Gemini-Scout mine rescue robot, it is designed to move through obstacles such as fallen rubble and water and is equipped with a thermal camera to locate survivors and carbon monoxide sensors to alert rescuers to potential dangers.

In 2012, NASA successfully landed the *Curiosity* rover on the planet Mars. The rover uses a customized version of a navigation software called Field D*, developed by robotics engineers from the Robotics Institute at Carnegie Mellon University in Pittsburgh. The software maps the rover's course as it makes its way over new terrain. *Curiosity* can then retrace a route or program a new one autonomously.

In many ways, the future of robotics is tied to the future of industry and exploration. The online retailer Amazon.com is responsible for shipping thousands of products across the globe and uses robots to meet its incredible demand. Other companies will no doubt soon follow suit. Some have pointed to increased interest in automation as the first step toward a future in which humans will be irrelevant and easily replaced by machines. Others argue that behind every efficient robot or automated system is a team of human robotics engineers, and that it is thanks to the robots developed by those engineers that humans can achieve a number of things that they would otherwise be incapable of doing.

—*Molly Hagan*

More Information

Accreditation Board for Engineering and Technology
111 Market Place, Suite 1050
Baltimore, MD 21202
www.abet.org

FIRST
200 Bedford Street
Manchester, NH 03101
www.usfirst.org

IEEE Robotics and Automation Society
www.ieee-ras.org

International Federation of Robotics
Lyoner Strasse 18
60528 Frankfurt am Main
Germany
www.ifr.org

National Robotics Engineering Center
Carnegie Mellon University Robotics Institute
10 Fortieth Street
Pittsburgh, PA 15201
www.rec.ri.cmu.edu

Thermodynamics

FIELDS OF STUDY

Physics; mathematics; chemistry; biology; fluid dynamics and mechanics; biochemistry; cell biology; molecular biology; engineering; bioengineering; computer science; astronomy; mechanical engineering; thermal-fluid engineering; molecular chemistry; atmospheric science; geophysics; environmental physics; environmental chemistry; materials science; astrophysics; energy engineering.

DEFINITION

Thermodynamics is a foundational branch of the physical sciences that seeks to understand, describe, and explain the relationship between energy and work and the transfer of energy between systems. Thermodynamic principles apply to the energetic relationships of all physical systems, from the entire universe to subatomic particle interactions. Thermodynamics research is used in experimental and applied physics and engineering and is involved in the design and operation of a variety of electrical and mechanical systems.

Basic Principles

The earliest roots of thermodynamics research can be found in the natural philosophy of the ancient Greeks and in the work of early scientists like Galileo Galilei (1564–1642), who developed one of the first scientific theories of temperature. The modern science of thermodynamics hinges on the four laws of thermodynamics. Developed between the mid-nineteenth and mid-twentieth centuries, these laws laid the foundation for the development of thermodynamics as a field of modern physics research.

The four laws of thermodynamics describe the fundamental relationships between matter and energy and define the concepts of temperature, heat, energy, and entropy. These concepts hinge on the thermodynamic concept of work, which can be broadly defined as a system's capacity to exchange energy with another system. As a star decays, for instance, it does work by exchanging its energy with surrounding planets and with the vacuum of space.

The zeroth law of thermodynamics was the last of the four laws to be formally defined, but it is referred to as the "zeroth" because it is the most fundamental of the four concepts. German physicist Arnold Sommerfeld (1868–1951) formally defined the law in 1951, though a number of other physicists theorized the existence of the zeroth law in previous work. The zeroth law defines thermodynamic equilibrium as a state in which the exchange of energy and heat between systems is equal in both directions and in which both systems have the same temperature. The zeroth law then states that if two systems are in thermodynamic equilibrium with a third system, they are also in equilibrium with each other.

French physicist Nicolas Sadi Carnot (1796–1832) is sometimes called the father of thermodynamics for his pioneering research into heat exchange, which led to his development of the Carnot cycle in an 1824 publication, often cited as the first attempt to describe the second law of thermodynamics. The formal definitions of the first and second laws are attributed to the research of British physicist William Thompson Kelvin (1824–1907) and German physicist Rudolf Clausius (1822–88), who described these laws in the 1850s.

The first law defines the principle of conservation of energy with regard to thermodynamic systems. The law states that energy within a closed system can never be created or destroyed, but merely transitions from one form of energy to another. This law also states that the amount of work done by a system is equal to the amount of energy available to that system.

The second law defines the concept of entropy, which is a property of energetic systems that refers to the degree to which a system has become dissipated or homogenized. On the particle level, entropy is a state in which particles are evenly dispersed and mixed such that no new changes can take place. On a larger scale, entropy is a state at which all of the heat or potential energy of a system has dissipated, leaving the system without sufficient energy to complete any additional work. The second law states that entropy always remains constant or increases, but that it can never decrease. The increase of entropy is considered one of the fundamental laws of the universe and plays an important role in theoretical models of the universe developed by physicists.

The third law, which defines the relationship between entropy and temperature, was formulated by German chemist Walther Nernst (1864–1941) in the first decade of the 1900s. The third law states that entropy reaches its maximum when the temperature of a system reaches absolute zero, at which point there is no heat and no potential energy within the system.

Throughout the twentieth century, physicists and chemists used these thermodynamic principles to investigate a variety of scientific issues, from the design of energy-utilizing machines to the transfer of energy within the earth's environment. Thermodynamics research involves both tracking the transfer of heat between entire systems and the study of particle interactions at the subatomic level. By the twenty-first century, thermodynamics had been divided into a number of more specific subdisciplines, including chemical, molecular, statistical, cosmological, and biothermodynamics.

Core Concepts

Branches of Research. The study of thermodynamics can be divided into several distinct, but related, fields of inquiry. Classical thermodynamics is the study of thermodynamic principles as they apply to entire systems, which may include biological systems or engineering applications. This is the most general field of thermodynamics research and led to the development of the other, more specific fields. Statistical thermodynamics, also called statistical mechanics, is the study of thermodynamics as it applies to the behavior of individual atoms or molecules. Statistical thermodynamics research often involves the study of subatomic interactions between particles. Chemical thermodynamics is the study of energetic relationships within chemical systems. Generally, chemical thermodynamics research involves studying the energy of a chemical system before and after reactions to measure the transfer of the energy that occurs during chemical reactions. Computational thermodynamics is a branch of research that combines the study of entropy and energy transfer with mathematic calculations of kinetics. Computational thermodynamics can be used to create modeling systems that apply to chemical and statistical thermodynamics research.

Thermometers. Thermometers are devices used to measure the temperature of a system, utilizing either a chemical or physical reaction to map temperature changes against a relative scale. Bulb thermometers rely on the principle that the volume of a liquid increases in concert with increasing temperature. As the liquid within the bulb is heated, its volume increases and it expands, causing some of the liquid to rise. This provides a way to correlate increases in liquid volume with temperature values. Infrared, or laser thermometers, utilize a different principle to gauge temperature. These thermometers measure the radiation emitted by an object or sample area and correlate the emissions with calculations of the average rate of heat emitted from the object or material in question. Laser thermometers can be used to measure the temperature of distant objects, while bulb thermometers must be in contact with the sample to record an accurate measurement.

Calorimetry. Calorimetry is the process of measuring the heat or energy produced by a system during reactions or other types of physical activities. A calorimeter measures the output products of reactions, including heat or various gases, and correlates these energetic byproducts with the relative amount of energy needed to fuel a particular reaction. One common application of calorimetry is to measure energy usage in biological systems. For instance, colorimeters can measure the gas output of the human body during or after a period of exercise or activity; this information can then help calculate the amount of energy used to complete the activity. Calorimetry is also used in chemical thermodynamics to measure the energy released during certain chemical reactions and then create thermodynamic models that display the various energy inputs and outputs of a chemical system.

Spectroscopy. Spectroscopy is a series of measurement techniques aimed at understanding how matter interacts with various types of radiant energy. There are a variety of techniques utilized in spectroscopy, including spectrometry, which is the study of energy spectrums. Spectroscopy is an important tool in physics and chemical research, as it allows scientists to investigate the molecular and atomic structure of substances as well as to measure a variety of energetic properties. Variable temperature infrared spectroscopy (VTIR), a measurement technique invented in the twenty-first century, investigates the temperature range of interactions between solids and gases. The resulting data is then used to develop a thermodynamic profile of these interactions.

Thermodynamic Reservoirs. One of the most important concepts in thermodynamics research is the thermodynamic reservoir, a hypothetical environment that is large or insulated enough that it can supply or absorb heat without undergoing a change in temperature. For instance, an ocean can be considered a thermal reservoir because it is large enough to absorb heat from the thermodynamic systems operating within it, without undergoing a significant change in overall temperature. Reservoirs that supply heat to a system are called sources, whereas reservoirs that absorb heat are called sinks. The definition of sources and sinks defines the limits of investigation for thermodynamic measurements and thereby aids scientists in formulating thermodynamic experiments. Thermodynamic models, such as those created to model atmospheric dynamics, rely on this definition to track the energy entering and exiting the system under investigation.

Applications Past and Present

Steam Power. Carnot made his breakthrough on the Carnot cycle—considered the most efficient heat engine cycle—while attempting to improve the efficiency of steam engine technology. In the early twenty-first century, most of the energy produced for commercial applications has come from burning fossil fuels to produce steam, which is then used to fuel the production of electricity. A steam engine is a device that harnesses the kinetic energy present in steam as it rises relative to the surrounding air; it then uses this energy to produce work.

Mechanical and electrical engineers utilize thermodynamics research to create more efficient machines for harvesting steam energy. In a generalized model of the steam engine, a chamber containing

Interesting Facts about Thermodynamics

- Galileo Galilei is credited with inventing the first thermometer in 1593. Galilei's instrument did not measure temperature in degrees, but rather simply indicated whether a liquid sample was getting warmer or cooler based on the expansion of liquid within the device.

- The calorie is a unit of energy based on the amount of energy required to raise the temperature of a fixed quantity of water by one degree Celsius. The calorie was developed in 1824 by physicist Nicolas Clément, but was later replaced by the joule, an SI unit. The calorie is still used as a unit of food energy and is used in nutritional calculations.

- A barometer estimates pressure by measuring fluctuations in the volume of liquid contained within a vessel. Measurements of pressure are important in thermodynamics research, because the difference in pressure between two reservoirs plays a role in determining the potential movement of molecules and atoms. Italian inventor Evangelista Torricelli is credited with creating the first barometer in the 1640s.

- Thermoelectric materials are materials developed to translate differences in temperature into electrical potential that can be used to power the operation of a device. Engineers use thermoelectric switches in the development of solar powered machines.

- Theoretical physicists used thermodynamics research to formulate the «heat death theory» regarding the ultimate fate of the universe. According to this theory, entropy in the universe will continue to increase until there is no free energy remaining, ultimately leading to the extinction of all life and energetic processes active in the universe.

burning coal or natural gas is connected to a reservoir containing water. The heat from the combustion of the fossil fuels is transferred to the water, causing the water to transition into water vapor, or steam. Steam from the reservoir then rises through a chamber where it is used to power the rotation of rotors. Thus, the mechanical energy of the steam is transferred to electrical energy through a generator. While steam power is one of the oldest forms of energy generators, the steam engine is still used around the world and researchers continue to devise ways to increase the efficiency of the basic steam engine design.

Internal Combustion Engine. The internal combustion engine is familiar around the world because of its common usage in automobiles and other powered vehicles. The most common type of combustion engine found in automobiles utilizes a four-stroke cycle, which refers to the stages in the revolution of the engine. The principles of heat exchange, energy transfer, and entropy are all demonstrated by the operation of a combustion engine, which translates the energy released from chemical reactions into mechanical energy; this energy then powers the rotation of gears that can be used for a variety of applications. In the process, a certain amount of energy is "lost" as heat released in exhaust, thereby contributing to the overall increase in entropy.

In a four-stroke engine, the first stroke, referred to as the intake stroke, draws oxygen and vaporized fuel into a chamber. The second stroke compresses the mixture of oxygen and fuel, increasing both temperature and pressure within the mixture. The third stroke brings the mixture into contact with an ignition source, generally a spark from a spark plug in a modern automotive engine. This ignites the gases, causing an explosion of heat and mechanical energy, which is transferred to a device that moves other parts of the engine, thus powering the motion of the machine. The fourth stroke releases spent gases as exhaust and brings the piston back into the starting position for the beginning of a new cycle.

Reaction Engines. A reaction engine uses the force produced during the combustion of fuel directly to achieve propulsion. This type of engine relies on Newton's third law of motion, which states that for any reaction, there is an equal and opposite reaction. Applied to propulsion, the principle explains why the force produced by the combustion of fuel can cause an object, such as a rocket or jet, to move in the opposing direction. Reaction engine design is based on thermodynamics research that calculates the relationship between combustion energy output and the work needed to achieve various levels of propulsion.

Jet engines utilize a cycle of air suction and compression coupled with an ignition source that ignites a mixture of air and vaporized fuel. The result is a controlled explosion that forces ignited gases through one end of the engine. This force creates a vacuum that helps to draw additional vaporized fuel and oxygen into the engine while simultaneously producing mechanical force that propels the jet through the air. The suction and airflow produced by the engine can also be used to power a secondary system that translates mechanical energy, within the flow of air, to electrical energy that can be used to power electrical systems within a rocket or jet-powered vehicle.

Refrigeration. Home refrigerators depend on principles of heat and energy transfer that have been developed through thermodynamics research. Heat has a natural tendency to move from warmer regions to cooler regions, according to the laws of thermodynamics, thus dispersing heat evenly within the environment. Refrigeration processes are used to reverse the natural spread of heat by using a heat pump to transfer heat from cooler environments to warmer environments. Heat transfer is a major field of ongoing research in thermodynamics and is closely linked to the development of new refrigeration technology.

Most common refrigerators function according to a vapor-compression cycle, utilizing a chemical liquid called a refrigerant. The liquid is introduced to the cycle as a vapor, generally at low pressure. The vapor travels through a compressor, where it pressurized and superheated; it then travels through a series of coils known as a condenser, which help to condense the vapor to a liquid state through exposure to lower temperatures. The liquid is forced through a compartment into a low-pressure environment, causing the liquid to evaporate explosively, with a sudden decrease in pressure. This process draws heat from the environment, cooling the surrounding air to below the ambient room temperature. The cooled air is then blown, with a fan, into the refrigerator compartment.

Climate Change Research. Climate change research is one of the most active applications of thermodynamics research. Patterns governing climate change rely on thermodynamic phenomena such as energy cycling and heat transfer. A variety of research projects have been underway to study the various thermodynamic properties of cosmic and atmospheric systems.

Thermodynamics research is used to study the influx of solar radiation and the principles that govern the escape of solar energy into space. For instance, investigation of the thermal properties of different gases helps evaluate which gases are most likely to increase the amount of radiant heat retained in the lower atmosphere. Climate modeling is one of most active fields of climate research, which uses thermodynamic data to create precise models of the energy inputs, outputs, and transfers important to climate patterns. Atmospheric chemists and physicists therefore rely on thermodynamic data in modeling the dynamic changes present in atmospheric systems.

Renewable Energy Technology. Since global supplies of petroleum are in decline, private companies and government research organizations have been investing in new methods of generating energy, including solar, wind, geothermal, water, and wave power technologies. Thermodynamics research constitutes an important facet of renewable and green energy development by helping to evaluate energy generating machines in terms of efficiency and waste.

Electrical and mechanical engineers utilize calculations based on thermodynamics to create systems for measuring the energy inputs and outputs of various electrical generators, including the turbines used to harvest wind energy. Geophysicists also use thermodynamic equations to design systems that efficiently capture and transfer energy from geothermal sources for heating and for the generation of electricity. Renewable energy development has increased around the world by more than 5 percent annually since 1990, leading to increased demand for more efficient alternative energy technologies.

Impact on Industry

Increasing demand for alternative and renewable energy sources is likely to create more opportunities for physicists with backgrounds in thermodynamics research over the coming decades. The renewable energy industry was one of the fastest growing facets of physics research in the 2000s and involves contributions from university, government, and private research organizations.

According to the Bureau of Labor Statistics (BLS), approximately 18,300 individuals in the United States were employed in research physics positions in 2011, only a small number of whom worked as thermodynamics specialists. The research physics field was growing at a rate of 14 percent annually, which was slightly higher than the 11 percent average for all occupations in the United States.

University Research and Teaching. Approximately 16 percent of research physicists worked in university research and teaching positions in 2011. Princeton University is one of a number of US universities that employs specialists who conduct thermodynamics research. The university's Department of Thermodynamics and Statistical Mechanics conducts research focusing on computational materials science, a field that investigates emerging materials used in a variety of engineering projects including metals and alloys, as well as materials used for energy generation and conduction. Thermodynamics specialists at the University of Ghent, in Belgium, conduct research in applied thermodynamics and heat transfer. Among a variety of applications, thermodynamics research at Ghent is conducted for the design of new refrigeration and heating systems that utilize cutting-edge technology to maximize efficiency and decrease waste.

Military. Both the US Department of Defense and the US Armed Forces employ physicists in research positions. The US Army Research Office, for instance, utilizes thermodynamics research in projects designed to enable mobile army units to tap into alternative power sources—such as wind and geothermal energy—for habitation, the establishment of temporary and permanent military settlements. The US Army Corps of Engineers also funds thermodynamics research programs for a variety of applications. In 2000, the Corps of Engineers conducted research to investigate the phenomenon of frost heave, which causes the buckling of soil in areas where moisture freezes below the surface. This information is used to inform engineers working on building and settlement projects in areas subject to intense freezing during part of the year.

Occupation	Engineers, all other
Employment 2010	156,500
Projected Employment 2020	166,800
Change in Number (2010–20)	10,300
Percent Change	7%

Bureau of Labor Statistics, 2012

The US Air Force (USAF) utilizes thermodynamics research in the design of rocket and jet propulsion systems. The development of engines with more efficient combustion systems can be applied to military applications, such as the design of more fuel-efficient or accurate missile systems. These improved combustion systems can also be used in commercial applications, such as the improvement of engines for commercial airlines.

Government Agencies. Government agencies employ more than 20 percent of research physicists in the United States. Organizations like the National Oceanic and Atmospheric Administration (NOAA) employ thermodynamics specialists to work on a variety of projects for designing climate monitoring and prediction technology. This research is used in climate change studies and also helps to refine and improve national and international meteorological systems.

NASA, the National Aeronautics and Space Administration, is another government agency involved in thermodynamics research, especially in regard to the development of rocket propulsion systems. Thermodynamics research is also utilized in studies of atmospheric gases, both on the earth and on other planets. Thermodynamics scientists research the dispersion and generation of radiation within space to understand the energetic relationships between the earth and other planets in the solar system. Additionally, thermodynamic data is used to investigate the atmospheres of distant planets in efforts to search for planets that might sustain life.

Private Industry Research and Technology. Privately-owned research organizations and corporations account for 32 percent of employment in the research physics field. The automotive and petroleum industries employ thermodynamics specialists to investigate energy flow and efficiency in engine design. This data helps to inform the next generation of engines used to power automobiles and to generate commercial power.

Thermodynamics specialists are also involved in the development of renewable and alternative energy technology. In 2011, most of the renewable energy produced in the United States and other countries was produced by systems designed and engineered by private research and development companies. The multinational corporation Enel Green Power is one of many corporations participating in thermodynamics and engineering research used to develop current and future energy systems. Enel Green Power employs physicists and engineers to work on research and development projects for solar, geothermal, wind, and water power systems.

Social Context and Future Prospects

In the twenty-first century, thermodynamics specialists have been helping to design new and innovative materials to enhance engineering projects. The field of smart materials research is an emerging, multidisciplinary effort to create plastics, fabrics, metals, and other materials with integrated systems that make them responsive to various stimuli. Examples include fabrics that respond to changes in pressure by altering shape, and metals containing integrated electronic systems capable of reacting to a variety of environmental conditions.

Growing global concern regarding climate change and the state of the environment has created opportunities for atmospheric and environmental scientists in a variety of fields. As mentioned earlier, thermodynamics research is utilized in a variety of environmental applications, including climate modeling, temperature measurement, and meteorological monitoring and measurement systems. In addition, thermodynamics specialists assist in developing the next generation of machines and computer systems to be used in the production of green and renewable technology. For instance, thermodynamic data is essential in the design of lighting systems that are more efficient, thereby helping to conserve electricity. In the coming decades, thermodynamics specialists and other physicists will play an increasingly important role in dictating the future of energy use as the petroleum industry continues to experience reductions in supply and profitability.

Further Reading

Atkins, Peter W. *The Laws of Thermodynamics: A Very Short Introduction*. New York: Oxford UP, 2010. Print. Nonmathematical introduction to the four laws of thermodynamics. Uses practical examples to illustrate thermodynamic principles in nature and in human culture.

Haddad, Wassim M., VijaySekhar Chellaboina, and Sergey G. Nersesov. *Thermodynamics: A Dynamical Systems Approach*. Princeton: Princeton UP, 2005. Print. Introduction to the mathematical and physical science foundations of thermodynamics, written for undergraduate students of the physical sciences.

Haynie, Donald Templeton. *Biological Thermodynamics*. 2nd ed. New York: Cambridge UP, 2008. Print. Overview of thermodynamic principles and research methods as they apply to the study of biology and the life sciences. Contains a discussion of the four laws, with examples found in biological form and function.

North, Gerald R., and Tatiana L. Erukhimova. *Atmospheric Thermodynamics: Elementary Physics and Chemistry*. New York: Cambridge UP, 2009. Print. Discussion of thermodynamics and physics as applied to the atmospheric sciences. Contains a discussion of thermodynamics in climate modeling and in the context of climate change research.

Turns, Stephen R. *Thermodynamics: Concepts and Applications*. New York: Cambridge UP, 2006. Print. General introduction to thermodynamics and applications to engineering development. Presents a variety of examples of technical and practical applications of thermodynamic principles.

About the Author: Micah L. Issitt, BS, is a professional freelance writer and journalist who specializes in the life sciences and sociology. Issitt has written numerous articles covering the environmental sciences and the history of environmental science in America.

Thermodynamics Engineer

Earnings (Yearly Average): $97, 480 (Bureau of Labor Statistics, 2012)

Employment and Outlook: Average growth (Bureau of Labor Statistics, 2012)

O*NET-SOC Code: 17-2011.00

Related Career Clusters: Manufacturing; Health Science; Architecture & Construction; Transportation, Distribution & Logistics

Scope of Work

Thermodynamics is a scientific discipline that deals with the relationship between heat and mechanical energy. Thermodynamics engineers apply their knowledge of the properties of heat transfer, distribution, and conversion to a vast array of industrial pursuits. Automobiles, airplanes, refrigerators, air conditioning systems, automated production lines—all utilize thermodynamics at one point or another during manufacturing, installation, and use.

As with most scientific fields, thermodynamics is in a state of constant change. A great many engineers work in research positions, developing new technologies for the military and green marketplace, while contributing to the academic exploration of thermodynamics by writing papers and collaborating on studies.

The majority of thermodynamics engineers work in the aerospace industry, designing and testing aircraft and spacecraft components. The principles of thermodynamics, however, can be applied to nearly every mechanical process. Internal combustion engines, for example, function effectively thanks to the laws of thermodynamics and their applications.

Education and Coursework

Students interested in pursuing thermodynamics should establish a strong foundation in mathematics—specifically algebra and trigonometry—during high school. Advanced placement courses in physics, chemistry, calculus, and biology are available and provide students with a basis for college-level study. Students should also engage in extracurricular activities and clubs involving chemistry.

Entry level thermodynamics positions require at least a bachelor's degree in chemical, mechanical, environmental, civil, or aerospace engineering. Colleges and universities do not generally offer

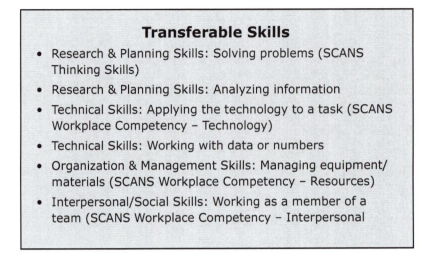

undergraduate degrees in thermodynamics engineering. However, because thermodynamics is a set of scientific principles rather than a stand-alone discipline, curricula of many courses of scientific study are likely to spend time on the laws and potential applications of thermodynamics. An advanced degree in a relevant field is highly recommended, and many thermodynamics engineers enter doctoral programs after working in the field for several years.

Career Enhancement and Training

Registration as a professional engineer is required for most engineering positions. It is especially important for thermodynamics engineers to obtain certification given the frequency with which their work overlaps with the military and mass transportation sectors. In the United States, a bachelor's degree from an engineering program accredited by the Accreditation Board for Engineering and Technology is required to take the Fundamentals of Engineering exam. Following the completion of the exam, a prospective engineer must acquire four years of professional experience under the supervision of a certified engineer. Upon completion of this period, one may take the Professional Engineer exam to become a registered professional engineer.

Thermodynamics engineers should continually monitor industry trends and emerging technologies so as to remain competitive in their field. A thermodynamics engineer working in aerospace, for example, can become a member of SAE International or another professional aerospace organization, to receive publications informing them of developments in the field. Membership in a trade group will also provide engineers with the opportunity to attend workshops and seminars to build their professional network and keep their knowledge current.

Daily Tasks and Technology

The principles of thermodynamics play a part in nearly every scientific discipline. Thermodynamics engineers, therefore, perform a wide variety of tasks over a broad array of fields. For example, thermodynamics engineers are employed in automobile engine manufacturing, power plant systems management, HVAC and refrigeration, geothermal energy, and the design and building of structures such as skyscrapers and bridges.

The aerospace industry, however, is one of the biggest employers of thermodynamics engineers. Their skills are utilized throughout the design, manufacture, and testing of airplane and spacecraft components. In aerospace work, thermodynamics engineers are tasked with drafting conceptual designs of aerospace products, overseeing certain aspects of the manufacturing process, and testing the finished product. Interdepartmental communication and cross-discipline research and collaboration are a frequent component of the thermodynamics engineer's job.

Airplane and spacecraft parts are required to endure exceptional amounts of stress. Thermodynamics engineers use computer assisted drafting and other design software to develop digital models to predict environmental effects on craft components. They also perform the physical tests necessary to ensure the quality and structural integrity of aerospace products.

Earnings and Employment Outlook

Specific salary information for thermodynamics engineers is not available due to the wide range of fields in which they are employed.

However, earnings statistics for the top fields that utilize thermodynamics are available. According to the US Bureau of Labor Statistics Occupational Outlook Handbook, aerospace engineers made a median wage of $97,480 in 2010. A study conducted by *Aviation Week* found that entry-level aerospace engineers have an average salary of $61,379.

Mechanical engineering—a career that requires extensive knowledge of the intricacies and application of thermodynamic principles—paid a median wage of $78,160 in 2010, according to the BLS. Mechanical engineers use thermodynamics in the processing of materials, the automation and control of manufacturing systems, and the design and development of machinery.

According to the Bureau of Labor Statistics, employment of aerospace engineers is expected to grow 5 percent between 2010 and 2020. This rate is slower than average for all the occupations tracked by the BLS. While engineers will be in demand for military sector jobs developing more environmentally efficient aircraft, a general slump in manufacturing will negatively contribute to aerospace employment growth.

Employment of mechanical engineers is also expected to grow at a slower than average rate, jumping 9 percent between 2010 and 2020, according to the BLS. Demand for mechanical engineers will remain relatively constant in industries developing the next generation of labor-saving and green machinery. Still, the overall decline in manufacturing production will have a negative impact on the employment of mechanical engineers.

Related Occupations

- **Aerospace Stress Engineer:** Aerospace stress engineers study the effects of environmental stress on aircraft, missiles, and spacecraft, looking for ways to mitigate its negative impact.

- **Civil Engineer:** Civil engineers plan, design, and oversee the construction and maintenance of such structures and facilities as roads, railroads, bridges, dams, power plants, and water and sewage systems.

- **Electrical Engineer:** Electrical engineers research, design, and develop electrical equipment, components, and systems for use in any number of applications.

- **Marine Engineer:** Marine engineers design, develop, and install ship machinery and equipment, including propulsion and power supply systems.

- **Industrial Engineer:** Industrial engineers develop, test, and evaluate systems for managing production processes.

Future Applications

The US Department of Labor's Occupational Information Network (O*NET), lists aerospace engineering as a "green enhanced skills occupation," meaning the aerospace industry is undergoing significant change as the result of green technology and institutional awareness of environmental impact. This environmental focus is not confined to aerospace, however. Many other industries that employ thermodynamics engineers are also making the shift toward greener practices and technology.

The mass transportation industry in particular is developing products and manufacturing methods that reduce pollution and increase efficiency. Propulsion systems that make use of alternative energy sources, such as solar and electric power, will likely replace fossil fuel burning engines as resources are depleted and the push to end dependence on oil becomes stronger. Thermodynamics engineers will be in demand to develop the machinery required to manage and utilize such alternative energy sources.

More Information

SAE International
400 Commonwealth Drive
Warrendale, PA 15096
www.sae.org

Aerospace Industries Association
1000 Wilson Boulevard, Suite 1700
Arlington, VA 22209
www.aia-aerospace.org

American Institute of Aeronautics and Astronautics
1801 Alexander Bell Drive, Suite 500
Reston, VA 20191
www.aiaa.org

National Society of Professional Engineers
1420 King Street
Alexandria, VA 22314
www.nspe.org

Appendixes

General Bibliography

Adhami, Reza, Peter M. Meenen III, and Dennis Hite. *Fundamental Concepts in Electrical and Computer Engineering with Practical Design Problems*. 2nd ed. Boca Raton: Universal, 2005. Print. A well-illustrated guide to the kind of math required to analyze electrical circuits, followed by sections on circuits, digital logic, and DSP.

American Academy of Ophthalmology. *Clinical Optics*. San Francisco: American Academy of Ophthalmology, 2006. This volume of the American Academy of Ophthalmology basic science course covers the fundamental concepts of optics as it relates to lenses, refraction, and reflection. It also covers the basic optics of the human eye and the fundamental principles of lasers.

Anderson, John D., Jr. *Introduction to Flight*. 5th ed. New York: McGraw-Hill, 2005. This popular textbook, setting developments in a historical context, is derived from the author's tenure at the Smithsonian Air and Space Museum.

Atkins, Peter W. *The Laws of Thermodynamics: A Very Short Introduction*. New York: Oxford UP, 2010. Print. Nonmathematical introduction to the four laws of thermodynamics. Uses practical examples to illustrate thermodynamic principles in nature and in human culture.

"Atomic and Molecular Physics." *JILA: CU Boulder and NIST*. JILA, 17 May 2010. Web. 3 Oct. 2012. Presents state-of-the-art research in atomic and molecular physics at JILA, a highly respected research center. Includes descriptions of current research topics and their importance.

Bass, Henry E., and William J. Cavanaugh, eds. *ASA at Seventy-Five*. Melville, NY: Acoustical Society of America, 2004. An overview of the history, progress, and future possibilities for each of the fifteen major subdivisions of acoustics as defined by the Acoustical Society of America.

Bekey, Ivan. *Advanced Space System Concepts and Technologies, 2010–2030+*. Reston, VA: American Institute of Aeronautics and Astronautics, 2003. Summaries of various advanced concepts and logical arguments used to explore their feasibility.

Bern, Zvi, Lance J. Dixon, and David A. Kosower. "Loops, Trees and the Search for New Physics." *Scientific American* 306.5 (2012): 35–41. Print. Reports that many nuclear physicists are seeing traditional research techniques as outdated and exploring new approaches that make research less complex and convoluted.

Blanchard, Benjamin S., and W. J. Fabrycky. *Systems Engineering and Analysis*. Boston: Prentice, 2011. Print. Focuses on the design and engineering of human-made systems and systems analysis. Concentrates on the use of systems engineering to identify what an entity is to do before determining what the entities are.

Buede, Dennis M. *The Engineering Design of Systems: Models and Methods*. Hoboken: Wiley, 2009. Print. Provides a reference to the methods for systems engineering that are in use today. Uses a model-based approach to introduce methods and models used in actual practice.

Carroll, Bradley, and Dale Ostlie. *An Introduction to Modern Astrophysics.* 2nd ed. San Francisco: Pearson, 2007. Comprehensive and accessible for readers with interest in and basic understanding of astronomy and physics. Covers tools of astronomy, the nature of stars, the solar system, galaxies, and cosmology.

Claycomb, James R., and Jonathan Quoc P. Tran. *Introductory Biophysics: Perspectives on the Living State.* Sudbury: Jones, 2011. Print. A textbook that considers life in relation to the universe. Relates biophysics to many other fields and subjects, including fractal geometry, chaos systems, biomagnetism, bioenergetics, and nerve conduction. Contains a compact disc that allows computer simulation of biophysical phenomena.

"Condensed Matter News." *Phys.org.* Phys.org, 2012. Web. 26 Sept. 2012. Online magazine of condensed matter studies that offers articles for students, interested lay readers, and professionals.

Davidson, Frank Paul, and Kathleen Lusk-Brooke, comps. *Building the World: An Encyclopedia of the Great Engineering Projects in History.* Westport, CT: Greenwood, 2006. Examines more than forty major engineering projects from the Roman aqueducts to the tunnel across the English Channel.

Davis, L. J. *Fleet Fire: Thomas Edison and the Pioneers of the Electric Revolution.* New York: Arcade, 2003. The stunning story of the pioneer electrical engineers, many self-taught, who ushered in the electric revolution.

Demtröder, Wolfgang. *Atoms, Molecules, and Photons: An Introduction to Atomic, Molecular, and Quantum Physics.* 2nd ed. London: Springer, 2010. Provides an introduction to atomic and molecular physics and explains the present model of atoms and molecules. Introduces quantum physics and the wave model of particles.

Design Engineering Technical Committee. *AIAA Aerospace Design Engineers Guide.* 5th ed. Reston, VA: American Institute of Aeronautics and Astronautics, 2003. A concise book of formulae and numbers that aerospace engineers use frequently or need for reference.

Dessler, Andrew E., and Edward A. Parson. *The Science and Politics of Global Climate Change: A Guide to the Debate.* New York: Cambridge UP, 2010. Print. Introduction to the issue of climate change, including atmospheric chemistry and other atmospheric properties research. Also discusses the potential future of research in the area of climate change.

Drexler, K. Eric. *Engines of Creation 2.0: The Coming Era of Nanotechnology.* Updated ed. WOWIO. WOWIO, 2007. Web. 9 Oct. 2012. An updated edition of the 1986 work that introduced the possibilities and theoretical foundations of nanotechnology. Available in e-book format only.

Everest, F. Alton, and Ken C. Pohlmann. *Master Handbook of Acoustics.* 5th ed. New York: McGraw-Hill, 2009. A revision of a classic reference work designed for those who desire accurate information on a level accessible to the layperson with limited technical ability.

Feller, W. B., et al. "Microchannel Plate Special Nuclear Materials Sensor." *Nuclear Instruments & Methods in Physics Research* 652.1 (2011): 25–28. Print. Reviews nuclear-physics research that is enabling the development of new technologies that detect nuclear materials.

Finn, John Michael. *Classical Mechanics*. Sudbury: Jones, 2009. Comprehensive introduction to the study of classical and applied mechanics, suitable for advanced students of physics and mathematics. Contains sections on statistical dynamics and fluid mechanics.

Ford, Kenneth W. *The Quantum World: Quantum Physics for Everyone*. Cambridge: Harvard UP, 2005. Print. Presents the history and basic concepts of quantum mechanics to a general audience, thereby introducing the reader to the landscape of atomic and molecular physics.

Forinash, Kyle. *Foundations of Environmental Physics*. Washington: Island, 2010. Print. Provides a comprehensive introduction to environmental physics principles governing energy use, storage, and transfer. Focuses on human energy use and the environmental impacts of energy harvesting, development, and waste.

Frederick, John E. *Principles of Atmospheric Science*. Sudbury, MA: Jones & Bartlett, 2008. Print. Introductory text describing the various fields of atmospheric sciences, including atmospheric chemistry, atmospheric physics, and climatology. Describes techniques and research methods utilized in modern climate and atmospheric research.

Gadallah, Mamdouh R., and Ray L. Fisher. *Exploration Geophysics*. Berlin: Springer, 2008. Print. Covers the acquisition of two-dimensional and three-dimensional seismic data and the ways in which this data is interpreted and used.

Gibilisco, Stan. *Electricity Demystified*. New York: McGraw-Hill, 2005. A primer on electrical circuits and magnetism.

Glaser, Roland. *Biophysics*. 5th ed. New York: Springer, 2005. Print. Contains numerous chapters on the molecular structure, kinetics, energetics, and dynamics of biological systems. Also looks at the physical environment, with chapters on the biophysics of hearing and the biological effects of electromagnetic fields.

Goldfarb, Daniel. *Biophysics Demystified*. Maidenhead: McGraw, 2010. Print. Examines anatomical, cellular, and subcellular biophysics, as well as tools and techniques used in the field. Designed as a self-teaching tool.

Haddad, Wassim M., VijaySekhar Chellaboina, and Sergey G. Nersesov. *Thermodynamics: A Dynamical Systems Approach*. Princeton: Princeton UP, 2005. Print. Introduction to the mathematical and physical science foundations of thermodynamics, written for undergraduate students of the physical sciences.

Hawking, Stephen, and Roger Penrose. *The Nature of Space and Time*. Princeton: Princeton UP, 2010. Overview of contemporary issues in cosmology, including reconciling classical and quantum physics in astrophysics to understand the structure and organization of the universe. Illustrated.

Hayes, Allyson E., ed. *Cryogenics: Theory, Processes and Applications*. Hauppauge: Nova Science, 2010. Details global research on cryogenics and applications such as genetic engineering and cryopreservation.

Haynie, Donald Templeton. *Biological Thermodynamics*. 2nd ed. New York: Cambridge UP, 2008. Print. Overview of thermodynamic principles and research methods as they apply to the study of biology and the life sciences. Contains a discussion of the four laws, with examples found in biological form and function.

Herman, Irving P. *Physics of the Human Body*. New York: Springer, 2007. Print. Analyzes how physical concepts apply to human body functions.

Irwin, Judith. *Astrophysics: Decoding the Cosmos*. Hoboken: Wiley, 2007. Description of the processes by which astrophysics captures and analyzes signals received through a variety of observational means. Looks at how astrophysics works on a practical level.

Jamieson, Valerie, and Richard Webb. "There's a Particle for That." *New Scientist* 17 Mar. 2012: 32–36. Print. Discusses the subatomic particles that have already been discovered in nuclear physics, as well as the wide range of other such particles that are still being explored theoretically, including dark matter and quarks.

Jenkins, Dennis R. *X-15: Extending the Frontiers of Flight*. NASA SP-2007-562. Washington, DC: US Government Printing Office, 2007. Contains various copies of original data sheets, memos, and pictures from the days when the X-15 research vehicle was developed and flown.

Jha, A. R. *Cryogenic Technology and Applications*. Burlington: Elsevier, 2006. Deals with most aspects of cryogenics and cryogenic engineering, including historical development and various laws, such as heat transfer, that make cryogenics possible.

Kaneko, K. *Life: An Introduction to Complex Systems Biology*. New York: Springer, 2006. Print. Provides an introduction to the field of systems biology, focusing on complex systems.

Kerzner, Harold. *Project Management: A Systems Approach to Planning, Scheduling, and Controlling*. Hoboken: Wiley, 2009. Print. Often referred to as "the Bible" of project management. Aligns with the latest release of the Project Management Institute's Project Management Body of Knowledge.

Kibble, Tom W. B., and Frank H. Berkshire. *Classical Mechanics*. 5th ed. River Edge: World Scientific, 2004. Detailed overview of classical mechanics that introduces Newton's laws of motion, relativity theory, and basic types of motion, with information regarding applications to biology and engineering.

Kirsch, Reinhard. *Groundwater Geophysics: A Tool for Hydrogeology*. Berlin: Springer, 2008. Print. Describes the use of geophysics in the delineation and detection of groundwater resources.

Le Bellac, Michel. *Quantum Physics*. Cambridge: Cambridge UP, 2006. Uses algebra and symmetry principles to teach the fundamentals of quantum physics. Includes discussions of one-dimensional potentials, angular momentum, and scattering theory.

LeBlanc, Francis. *An Introduction to Stellar Astrophysics*. Hoboken: Wiley, 2010. Useful survey of an essential aspect of astrophysics; ranges from introduction of basic concepts to stellar formation and evolution. Includes exercises and appendix of tables.

Lowrie, William. *Fundamentals of Geophysics*. Cambridge: Cambridge UP, 2007. Print. Explores the fundamental principles of geophysics. Designed as an introductory text for geoscience undergraduates.

Malley, Marjorie C. *Radioactivity: A History of a Mysterious Science*. New York: Oxford UP, 2011. Print. An accessible study of the evolution of nuclear technology from a global perspective. This work offers a detailed rendering of the many discoveries in the field.

McCall, Martin. *Classical Mechanics: From Newton to Einstein; A Modern Introduction*. New York: Wiley, 2011. Written for undergraduate students of the physical sciences. Presents the history and basic principles of classical mechanics, including applied mechanics research, plus the basics of relativity theory as it applies to celestial mechanics.

McNichol, Tom. *AC/DC: The Savage Tale of the First Standards War*. San Francisco: Jossy-Bass, 2006. The riveting story of the personalities in the AC/DC battle of the late nineteenth century, focusing on Thomas Edison and Nicola Tesla.

Meggitt, Geoff. *Taming the Rays: A History of Radiation and Protection*. Raleigh: Lulu Enterprises, 2010. Print. Focuses on the promise and especially the fears surrounding the use of radiation in medicine. It explores why those fears first existed and points to why trepidation concerning nuclear medicine continues.

Meschede, Dieter. *Optics, Light, and Lasers: The Practical Approach to Modern Aspects of Photonics and Laser Physics*. 2d ed. Weinheim, Germany: Wiley-VCH, 2007. An undergraduate text that explains modern lasers and photonics using the fundamentals of optics theory. It includes chapters on everyday optics such as the human eye and telescopes as well as chapters on quantum optics.

Mészáros, Péter. *The High Energy Universe*. New York: Cambridge UP, 2010. Survey of contemporary issues in high-energy astrophysics and cosmology, with chapters ranging from building blocks and the dynamics of the universe to gamma rays, gravitational waves, cosmic rays, neutrinos, and the quest for dark matter. Requires some knowledge in physics.

Milsom, John, and Asger Eriksen. *Field Geophysics*. Hoboken: Wiley, 2011. Print. Provides practical information to those working on small-scale surveys. Includes an update on the use of global positioning systems (GPS) and a section on seismic surface waves, borehole geophysics, and towed-array systems.

Moffatt, H. K., and Emily Shuckburgh, eds. *Environmental Hazards: The Fluid Dynamics and Geophysics of Extreme Events*. World Scientific: Singapore, 2011. Print. Includes lectures on subjects such as tsunamis, flooding, and air pollution from perspectives related to geophysics, applied mathematics, and fluid mechanics.

Montieth, John L., and Mike H. Unsworth. *Principles of Environmental Physics*. 3rd ed. Burlington: Academic, 2008. Print. Provides a comprehensive introduction to environmental physics aimed at the undergraduate and graduate audience. Discusses measurement and analysis methods used to research the physical properties of atmospheric, hydrologic, and geological systems with a focus on methods used to research energy transfer in the environment.

Morin, David. *Introduction to Classical Mechanics: With Problems and Solutions*. New York: Cambridge UP, 2008. Introductory text to mechanics written for undergraduate students that provides a guide to solving and interpreting differential equations for classical mechanics problems.

NASA Goddard Institute for Space Studies. National Aeronautics and Space Administration, 2012. Web. 21 Aug. 2012. Describes a variety of current research programs in the environmental sciences, physics, and atmospheric chemistry. Also contains descriptions of using atmospheric physics in the study of climate change and global warming.

National Geophysical Data Center (*NGDC*). NOAA.gov, 2012. Web. 1 Oct. 2012. Provides information taken from National Oceanic and Atmospheric Administration (NOAA) sponsored research into geophysics. Includes environmental physics research covering geomagnetic and geophysical modeling and information on the physical properties underlying natural hazards and meteorological developments.

Neffe, Jürgen. *Einstein: A Biography*. Baltimore: Johns Hopkins UP, 2009. Print. Puts Einstein's scientific accomplishments in the context of his personal life, painting a vivid picture of both.

North, Gerald R., and Tatiana L. Erukhimova. *Atmospheric Thermodynamics: Elementary Physics and Chemistry*. New York: Cambridge UP, 2009. Print. Discussion of thermodynamics and physics as applied to the atmospheric sciences. Contains a discussion of thermodynamics in climate modeling and in the context of climate change research.

Pedrotti, Frank L., Leno M. Pedrotti, and Leno S. Pedrotti. *Introduction to Optics*. 3d ed. Upper Saddle River, NJ: Prentice Hall, 2007. Intended for the physics undergraduate and includes chapters on basic optics including wave optics, geometric optics, and modern optics.

Peebles, Curtis. *Road to Mach 10: Lessons Learned from the X-43A Flight Research Program*. Reston, VA: American Institute of Aeronautics and Astronautics, 2008. A contemporary experimental flight-test program description.

Phillips, Anthony C. *Introduction to Quantum Mechanics*. New York: Wiley, 2003. Basic introduction to quantum mechanics that discusses the types of problems researched by quantum-mechanics specialists and discusses the theoretical implications of quantum theory.

Ratner, Daniel, and Mark A. Ratner. *Nanotechnology and Homeland Security: New Weapons for New Wars*. Upper Saddle River: Prentice, 2004. Print. Discusses the potential applications of nanotechnology in fighting terrorism.

Ratner, Mark A., and Daniel Ratner. *Nanotechnology: A Gentle Introduction to the Next Big Idea*. Upper Saddle River: Prentice, 2003. Print. An introduction to how nanotechnology works and the industry surrounding it.

Reynolds, John M. *An Introduction to Applied and Environmental Geophysics*. Chichester: Wiley, 2010. Includes mineral and hydrocarbon exploration, with an emphasis on the use of geophysics in civil engineering. Also covers environmental and groundwater investigations.

Rose, Calvin. *An Introduction to the Environmental Physics of Soil, Water and Watersheds*. New York: Cambridge UP, 2004. Print. Provides an introduction to applications of physics to environmental issues in land management, water management, and agriculture. Also discusses methods used to investigate the physical properties of soil transport and to measure gases, liquids, and other materials in geological samples.

Rossing, Thomas, and Neville Fletcher. *Principles of Vibration and Sound*. 2d ed. New York: Springer-Verlag, 2004. A basic introduction to the physics of sound and vibration.

Rouse, William B., and Andrew P. Sage. *Handbook of Systems Engineering and Management*. Hoboken: Wiley, 2009. Print. Focuses on the engineering and management techniques for systems design, with emphasis on information technology and software-intensive systems involving human and organizational elements.

Rumsey, Francis, and Tim McCormick. *Sound and Recording: An Introduction*. 5th ed. Boston: Elsevier/Focal Press, 2004. Presents basic information on the principles of sound, sound perception, and audio technology and systems.

Schwadron, Terry. "Hot Sounds from a Cold Trumpet? Cryogenic Theory Falls Flat." *New York Times*. New York Times, 18 Nov. 2003. Web. 9 Oct. 2012. Explains how two Tufts University researchers studied cryogenic freezing of trumpets and determined the cold did not improve the sound.

Shackett, Pete. *Nuclear Medicine Technology: Procedures and Quick Reference*. 2nd ed. New York: Lippincott, 2008. Print. Although designed for practitioners in the field, this work offers an excellent synopsis of the myriad nuclear imaging procedures currently available, just as it highlights the most frequently used radiopharmaceuticals. It also provides lessons on how to assuage patient fears on the risks versus the benefits of choosing a nuclear procedure.

Shuler, James Mannie. *Understanding Radiation Science: Basic Nuclear and Health Physics*. Boca Raton: Universal, 2006. Print. Straightforward rendering of nuclear medicine geared toward a nonscientific audience that commences with a discussion of the nature of the atom and progresses to an analysis of its manifold uses.

Shurkin, Joel N. *Broken Genius: The Rise and Fall of William Shockley, Creator of the Electronic Age*. New York: Macmillan, 2006. Print. Biography of the Nobel Prize–winning electrical engineer and father of the Silicon Valley, who had the foresight to capitalize on his invention of the transistor but ultimately went down in infamy and ruin.

Siciliano, Antonio. *Optics Problems and Solutions*. Singapore: World Scientific, 2006. Geared to physics and engineering undergraduates, this text includes chapters on basic optics with problems that can be used by students to improve understanding of optical concepts.

Spencer, Roy. *Global Warming*. Roy Spencer, 2012. Web. 23 Aug. 2012. Spencer, a climatologist, used to work for NASA. His website offers alternative ideas to the common view that global warming is caused by human activity.

Strong, William J., and George R. Plitnik. *Music, Speech, Audio.* 3d ed. Provo, UT: Brigham Young University Academic, 2007. A comprehensive text, written for the layperson, which covers vibration, the ear and hearing, noise, architectural acoustics, speech, musical instruments, and sound recording and reproduction.

Suzuki, Y. "Recent Developments in Nuclear Cluster Physics." *International Journal of Modern Physics* 20.4 (2011): 753–58. Print. Discusses the value of analyzing subatomic particles in clusters and how this cluster approach can reveal new facts about subparticle interactions.

Svanberg, Sune. *Atomic and Molecular Spectroscopy: Basic Aspects and Practical Applications.* 4th ed. Berlin: Springer, 2004. Print. Describes the many ways that light is used to study atoms and molecules.

Tipler, Paul A., and Gene Mosca. *Physics for Scientists and Engineers.* 6th ed. New York: Freeman, 2008. A staple for introductory university physics courses for many years. Chapters cover basic physics concepts including optics and the dual wave and particle nature of light.

Tritton, D. J. *Physical Fluid Dynamics.* 2nd ed. Oxford: Clarendon, 2003. Print. An overview of fluids in motion that focuses on physics and discusses topics including flow configurations, geophysics, and atmospheric convection.

Turns, Stephen R. *Thermodynamics: Concepts and Applications.* New York: Cambridge UP, 2006. Print. General introduction to thermodynamics and applications to engineering development. Presents a variety of examples of technical and practical applications of thermodynamic principles.

Ventura, Gugliemo, and Lara Risegari. *The Art of Cryogenics: Low-Temperature Experimental Techniques.* Burlington: Elsevier, 2008. Comprehensive discussion of various aspects of cryogenics, from heat transfer and thermal isolation to cryoliquids and instrumentation for cryogenics.

Walker, Phil. "The Atomic Nucleus." *New Scientist* 1 Oct. 2011: 1–8. Print. Reviews the nature of the nucleus and how radioactive decay is examined. Also discusses the many applications of nuclear physics, including radiocarbon dating, medical science, and energy production.

Weingardt, Richard G. *Engineering Legends: Great American Civil Engineers: Thirty-Two Profiles of Inspiration and Achievement.* Reston, VA: American Society of Civil Engineers, 2005. Looks at the lives of civil engineers who were environmental experts, transportation trendsetters, builders of bridges, structural trailblazers, and daring innovators.

Wilson, Jim, ed. *NASA Goddard Institute of Space Studies.* USA.gov, 2011. Web. 1 Oct. 2012. Describes a variety of current research programs in environmental sciences and environmental physics. Also contains descriptions of using environmental physics research to develop climate models.

Wolfe, William J. *Optics Made Clear: The Nature of Light and How We Use It.* Bellingham, WA: SPIE, 2007. Contains basic optics chapters followed by a large number of chapters about applied optics, including industrial and environmental topics; may appeal both to students and general readers interested in this topic.

Zelevinsky, Vladimir. *Quantum Physics*. Weinheim: Wiley, 2011. Two-volume set with a focus on problem solving. Presents fundamental knowledge before moving into applications. Contains a full modern graduate course in quantum physics.

Zhang, Mingjun, and Ning Xi. *Nanomedicine: A Systems Engineering Approach*. Singapore: Pan Stanford, 2009. Print. Provides a detailed look at nanomedicine from a systems-engineering perspective.

Detailed STEM Undergraduate Majors

Computer majors

- Computer and information systems
- Computer programming and data processing
- Computer science
- Information sciences
- Computer administration management and security
- Computer networking and telecommunications

Math majors

- Mathematics
- Applied mathematics
- Statistics and decision science
- Mathematics and computer science

Engineering majors

- General engineering
- Aerospace engineering
- Biological engineering
- Architectural engineering
- Biomedical engineering
- Chemical engineering
- Civil engineering
- Computer engineering
- Electrical engineering
- Engineering mechanics physics and science
- Environmental engineering

- Geological and geophysical engineering
- Industrial and manufacturing engineering
- Materials engineering and materials science
- Mechanical engineering
- Metallurgical engineering
- Mining and mineral engineering
- Naval architecture and marine engineering
- Nuclear engineering
- Petroleum engineering
- Miscellaneous engineering
- Engineering technologies
- Engineering and industrial management
- Electrical engineering technology
- Industrial production technologies
- Mechanical engineering related technologies
- Miscellaneous engineering technologies
- Military technologies

Physical and life science majors

- Animal sciences
- Food science
- Plant science and agronomy
- Soil science
- Environmental science
- Biology
- Biochemical sciences
- Botany
- Molecular biology

- Ecology
- Genetics
- Microbiology
- Pharmacology
- Physiology
- Zoology
- Miscellaneous biology
- Nutrition sciences
- Neuroscience
- Cognitive science and biopsychology
- Physical sciences
- Astronomy and astrophysics
- Atmospheric sciences and meteorology
- Chemistry
- Geology and earth science
- Geosciences
- Oceanography
- Physics
- Nuclear, industrial radiology, and biological technologies

Source: US Department of Commerce, Economics and Statistics Administration

Colleges to Consider

The following resource provides a list of the most highly selective four-year colleges in the United States for pursuing and attaining a bachelor's degree in physics. This list was built using a college search tool provided by EBSCO Career Guidance System, a staple for guidance counselors and students that offers a centralized location to work together on career guidance. The list was constructed using the following select criteria:

- **Type of School:** 4 year
- **Average Cost:** Over $30,000
- **Selectivity:** Highly Selective (Minimum requirements: Graduated in top 40 percent of class; B to B+ average; SAT score between 1100–1199 or ACT score between 27–28)
- **Major:** Physics, General

*Designates those undergraduate tuition costs that are comprehensive and include room and board and possibly other fees.

Agnes Scott College
Decatur, GA
Enrollment: 871
Tuition (2012–13): $43,476*
agnesscott.edu

Amherst College
Amherst, MA
Enrollment: 1791
Tuition (2012–13): $44,610*
amherst.edu

Barnard College
New York, NY
Enrollment: 2,445
Tuition (2012–13): $41,850
barnard.edu

Bates College
Lewiston, ME
Enrollment: 1,769
Tuition (2011–12): $55,300*
bates.edu

Boston College
Chestnut Hill, MA
Enrollment: 9,088
Tuition (2012–13): $43,140
bc.edu

Bowdoin College
Brunswick, ME
Enrollment: 1,778
Tuition (2012–13): $43,676
bowdoin.edu

Brown University
Providence, RI
Enrollment: 6,380
Tuition (2011–12): $41,328
brown.edu

Bryn Mawr College
Bryn Mawr, PA
Enrollment: 1,313
Tuition (2012–13): $41,260
brynmawr.edu

Bucknell University
Lewisburg, PA
Enrollment: 3,554
Tuition (2012–13): $45,132
bucknell.edu

California Institute of Technology
Pasadena, CA
Enrollment: 978
Tuition (2012–13): $38,085
caltech.edu

University of California—Berkley
Berkley, CA
Enrollment 36,142
Tuition (2012–13): $14,985.50 (residents); $37,863.50 (nonresidents)
berkeley.edu

Carleton College
Northfield, MN
Enrollment: 1,991
Tuition (2012–13): $44,184
carleton.edu

Carnegie Mellon University
Pittsburg, PA
Enrollment: 6,281
Tuition (2012–13): $44,880
cmu.edu

Case Western Reserve University
Cleveland, OH
Enrollment: 4,016
Tuition (2012–13): $40,120
case.edu

Colby College
Waterville, ME
Enrollment: 1,815
Tuition (2012–13): $55,700*
colby.edu

Colgate University
Hamilton, NY
Enrollment: 2,947
Tuition (2012–13): $44,330
colgate.edu

Columbia University
New York, NY
Enrollment: 6,027
Tuition (2012–13): $45,028
columbia.edu

Connecticut College
New London, CT
Enrollment: 1,896
Tuition (2012–13): $56,790
conncoll.edu

Cornell University
Ithaca, NY
Enrollment: 14,167
Tuition (2012–13): $43,185
cornell.edu

Dartmouth College
Hanover, NH
Enrollment: 4,194
Tuition (2012–13): $43,782
dartmouth.edu

Davidson College
Davidson, NC
Enrollment: 1,756
Tuition (2012–13): $40,809
davidson.edu

Duke University
Durham, NC
Enrollment: 6,680
Tuition (2012–13): $42,308
duke.edu

Emory University
Atlanta, GA
Enrollment: 5,500
Tuition (2011–12): $40,600
emory.edu

Furman University
Greenville, SC
Enrollment: 2,825
Tuition (2012–13): $41,152
furman.edu

Georgetown University
Washington, DC
Enrollment: 7,590
Tuition (2013): $42,360
georgetown.edu

Grinnell College
Grinnell, IA
Enrollment: 1,692
Tuition (2012–13): $41,004
grinnell.edu

Hamilton College
Clinton, NY
Enrollment: 1,864
Tuition (2012–13): $43,910
hamilton.edu

Harvard College
Cambridge, MA
Enrollment: 6,676
Tuition (2012–13): $54,496*
college.harvard.edu

Harvey Mudd College
Claremont, CA
Enrollment: 777
Tuition (2012–13): $44,159
hmc.edu

Haverford College
Haverford, PA
Enrollment: 1,198
Tuition (2012–13): $43,310
haverford.edu

Hendrix College
Conway, AR
Enrollment: 1,415
Tuition (2012–13): $35,900
hendrix.edu

The Johns Hopkins University
Baltimore, MD
Enrollment: 5,066
Tuition (2011–12): $42,280
jhu.edu

Lafayette College
Easton, PA
Enrollment: 2,478
Tuition (2012–13): $41,920
lafayette.edu

Lawrence University
Appleton, WI
Enrollment: 1,496
Tuition (2012–13): $39,732
lawrence.edu

Macalester College
St. Paul, MN
Enrollment: 2,005
Tuition (2012–13): $43,472
macalester.edu

**Massachusetts Institute of
    Technology**
Cambridge, MA
Enrollment: 4,384
Tuition (2011–12): $40,732
mit.edu

Middlebury College
Middlebury, VT
Enrollment: 2,507
Tuition (2012–13): $55,570*
middlebury.edu

Mount Sinai School of Medicine
New York, NY
Enrollment: 606
Tuition (2012–13): $41,238
mssm.edu

New York University
New York, NY
Enrollment: 22,280
Tuition (2012–13): $43,204
nyu.edu

Northwestern University
Evanston, IL
Enrollment: 9,466
Tuition (2012–13): $43,380
northwestern.edu

Oberlin College
Oberlin, OH
Enrollment: 2,959
Tuition (2012–13): $44,512
oberlin.edu

Princeton University
Princeton, NJ
Enrollment: 5,249
Tuition (2012–13): $54,780*
princeton.edu

Reed College
Portland, OR
Enrollment: 6,676
Tuition (2012–13): $44,200
reed.edu

Rensselaer Polytechnic Institute
Troy, NY
Enrollment: 5,322
Tuition (2012–13): $43,350
rpi.edu

Rice University
Houston, TX
Enrollment: 3,708
Tuition (2011–2012): $34,900
rice.edu

**Rose-Hulman Institute of
    Technology**
Terre Haute, IN
Enrollment: 1,895
Tuition (2012–13): $38,313
rose-hulman.edu

Scripps College
Claremont, CA
Enrollment: 966
Tuition (2012–13): $43,406
scrippscollege.edu

Southwestern University
Georgetown, TX
Enrollment: 1,347
Tuition (2012–13): $34,410
southwestern.edu

Stanford University
Stanford, CA
Enrollment: 6,988
Tuition (2012–13): $41,250
stanford.edu

Stevens Institute of Technology
Hoboken, NJ
Enrollment: 2,427
Tuition (2012–13): $41,670
stevens.edu

Swarthmore College
Swarthmore, PA
Enrollment: 1,545
Tuition (2012–13): $42,744
swarthmore.edu

Trinity University
San Antonio, TX
Enrollment: 2,431
Tuition (2012–13): $46,274*
trinity.edu

Tufts University
Medford, MA
Enrollment: 5,194
Tuition (2012–13): $43,688
tufts.edu

Tulane University
New Orleans, LA
Enrollment: 8,338
Tuition (2012–13): $45,240
tulane.edu

The University of Chicago
Chicago, IL
Enrollment: 6,676
Tuition (2012–13): $43,581
uchicago.edu

University of Notre Dame
Notre Dame, IN
Enrollment: 6,676
Tuition (2012–13): $42,971
nd.edu

University of Pennsylvania
Philadelphia, PA
Enrollment: 9,779
Tuition (2012–13): $39,088
upenn.edu

University of Richmond
Richmond, VA
Enrollment: 3,000
Tuition (2012–13): $44,210
richmond.edu

University of Rochester
Rochester, NY
Enrollment: 6,676
Tuition (2012–13): $42,890
rochester.edu

University of Southern California
Los Angeles, CA
Enrollment: 17,414
Tuition (2012): $42,162
usc.edu

University of Tulsa
Tulsa, OK
Enrollment: 3,004
Tuition (2012–13): $32,410
utulsa.edu

Vassar College
Poughkeepsie, NY
Enrollment: 2,386
Tuition (2012–13): $45,580
vassar.edu

Wake Forest University
Winston-Salem, NC
Enrollment: 4,775
Tuition (2012–13): $39,190
wfu.edu

Washington and Lee University
Lexington, VA
Enrollment: 1,793
Tuition (2012–13): $42,425
wlu.edu

Washington University in St. Louis
St. Louis, MO
Enrollment: 7,329
Tuition (2012–13): $42,500
wustl.edu

Wellesley College
Wellesley, MA
Enrollment: 2,502
Tuition (2012–13): $41,824
wellesley.edu

Wesleyan University
Middletown, CT
Enrollment: 2,882
Tuition (2012–13): $45,358
wesleyan.edu

Wheaton College
Wheaton, IL
Enrollment: 2,433
Tuition (2012–13): $43,480
wheaton.edu

Whitman College
Walla Walla, WA
Enrollment: 1,598
Tuition (2012–13): $41,790
whitman.edu

Williams College
Williamstown, MA
Enrollment: 2,053
Tuition (2012–13): $44,660
williams.edu

Wofford College
Spartanburg, SC
Enrollment: 1,536
Tuition (2012–13): $34,555
wofford.edu

Worcester Polytechnic Institute
Worcester, MA
Enrollment: 3,849
Tuition (2012–13): $40,790
wpi.edu

Yale University
New Haven, CT
Enrollment: 5,349
Tuition (2012–13): $58,600*
yale.edu

Career Guidance Portals

This resource presents some of the more comprehensive career-oriented portals maintained by preeminent and influential societies and organizations representing chemists, physicists, and other scientists and science-related workers. Selections go beyond those websites offering a simple job board to include those portals that offer additional career resources and job-seeking tools.

Note: The following sites were visited by editors in 2012. Because URLs frequently change, the accuracy of these addresses cannot be guaranteed; however, long-standing sites, such as those of national organizations and government agencies, generally maintain links when sites are moved or updated.

The American Astronomical Society
www.aas.org
The American Astronomical Society is the major organization for professional astronomers in North America. The Job Register page is organized according to different positions in the field, including faculty, pre-doctoral, post-doctoral, and science management positions. The AAS hosts a Career Center during each of its winter meetings, giving job seekers the opportunity to meet with employers. The AAS site also offers tips for employers, suggesting successful recruitment and hiring practices.

The American Institute of Aeronautics and Astronautics
www.aiaa.org
The AIAA Career Center displays comprehensive information regarding careers and recruiting in the aerospace industry. Apart from the basic job seeker and employers boards, the AIAA offers a Myers-Briggs personality test to help job seekers understand themselves and their personal skills and challenges. The Aerospace Career Handbook provides information about a variety of industry divisions within the aerospace industry, the types of jobs that are available, what young professionals can anticipate in those positions, and how young professionals can make the most of opportunities during their college years.

Salary information is provided here also. The Career Coach 2.0 page contains podcasts detailing timely and relevant career advice. The Professional Career Time Line includes a checklist that allows users to set goals and plan for success during every phase of their professional career.

The American Meteorological Society

www.ametsoc.org

The career center from the American Meteorological Society supplies information about careers in the atmospheric and related sciences. Apart from the job board and resume postings, the site provides a career guide that provides educational guidance, career opportunities and hiring organization lists, methods to enhance credentials, and tips for getting a job. There is also a listing of schools in the atmospheric and related sciences, as well as intern opportunities, scholarships, and fellowships.

American Physics Society

www.aps.org

The APS's Careers in Physics section presents a wide-ranging career portal. The Physics Jobs section displays helpful information for those seeking jobs as well as those organizations seeking employees. The Becoming a Physicist page presents information for interested physicists of all levels, supplying information for what interested parties can do to enhance their own careers immediately. The career guidance page displays information regarding professional development, webinars, tools for career advisors, and additional career resources. The Statistical Data tab contains graphs produced by the American Institute of Physics Statistical Research Center, which publishes and analyzes data on education and employment in physics. These figures display graphics relating to employment sectors, fields of employment, starting salaries, and the value of a bachelor's degree. The Careers in Physics page also has information relating to upcoming job events such as the APS Division of Plasma Physics Job Fair. The Physics InSight slide shows inform students about careers and opportunities in physics.

The American Society of Civil Engineers

www.asce.org

The Career Connections page offered by the American Society of Civil Engineers presents basic job search tools such as a job-listing database, resume tips, e-mail alerts, as well as an income and salary survey which displays salary information from over 20,000 engineers. It is designed to show the most accurate pay information for engineering professionals in multiple fields of study. The career development page helps to answer questions such as where you want your career to be in ten years, how to reach goals or learn certain skills. The Career Paths in Civil Engineering brochure displays various career paths to follow, with practical and specific tips for career advancement. The ASCE also offers mentoring programs to those beginning their careers in engineering.

The American Society of Mechanical Engineers

www.asme.org

The American Society of Mechanical Engineers' career development page displays information for those in all stages of their professional careers. There are different pages for teachers, managers, and students. Each page offers a podcast or reading resources, as well as career advice regarding management positions, what to do in a down economy, and other advice. Information regarding future career-related conferences and proceedings is displayed as well, along with associations related to the field of mechanical engineering.

The Biophysical Society

www.biophysics.org

The Biophysical Society's career page displays information for those curious about biological processes and biophysics in general. The Careers in Biophysics booklet gives readers a glance into the world of biophysics and the Biophysicist in Profile page helps prospective members to learn about the careers of other society members—both their backgrounds and how they progressed in their careers. Opportunities to connect with members around the world through the Mentor Board are available, offering users career guidance and networking.

Cryogenic Society of America
www.cryogenicsociety.org/
The Cryogenic Society of America's careers page presents a representative list of universities and other educational institutes offering research programs in cryogenics, as well as the Cryogenics Job Registry where interested job seekers can browse through job postings in the cryogenic fields in academic or research institutions, national laboratories, government, and other related businesses. Cryo Central, a cryogenic information resource page, provides links to career-related information, such as cryogenic applications in pest control, processing, surgery, and astronomy.

Institute of Electrical and Electronics Engineers
www.ieee.org
The Institute of Electrical and Electronics Engineers (IEEE) site offers a wide range of resources geared toward learning, career improvement, and employment options within the engineering sciences, research, and other technology sectors. The IEEE career resources page presents articles that guide prospective engineers, as well as job-related services such as resume posting and job searches. Members may also access the USA Employment and Career Strategies Forum. The Engineers Guide to Lifelong Employability is another helpful resource to prospective engineers, providing strategies vital to being a successful engineer. Additional career-related webinars and videos are also provided, as are volunteer opportunities.

The International Society for Optics and Photonics
www.spie.org
SPIE or the International Society for Optics and Photonics' career center covers an assortment of topics related to careers in optics and photonics. Apart from the basic job search tools, information regarding SPIE job fairs is presented. Also available is SPIE's salary survey, the result of a 2011 survey of optics and photonics professionals. The results of this report are displayed by location, employer type, discipline, gender, and other factors. The Advice and Tools page provides information about a typical workplace and offers career and recruiting/hiring advice.

The Oceanography Society

www.tos.org

The Oceanography Society's site provides perspectives on a variety of career options in an effort to guide ocean sciences graduates on the right career path. Scientifically Speaking: Tips for Preparing and Delivering Scientific Talks and Using Visual Aids is a booklet which helps students develop successful visual aids, oral presentations, and longer lectures in an effort to facilitate effective scientific communication. Educational resources are also available for current students, as well as a traditional job board.

Physics Today

www.physicstoday.org

Physics Today prides itself on being the flagship publication of The American Institute of Physics, one of the most prominent and closely followed physics magazines in the world. The Three Rules for Transitioning, written by Lawrence Berkeley National Laboratory scientist and AAS member Louis-Benoit Desroches, provides helpful advice about changing career paths while working on a degree. The Career Profiles page outlines detailed information about some of the most popular and exciting career paths in the field of physics; over thirty different jobs are described in detail. The Current Scientific Employment and Education Data page presents the latest employment and education data regarding physicists and related scientists compiled by the Statistical Research Center of the American Institute of Physics. The Careers Using Physics page displays many possible career paths. Also available is career advice from Peter Weddle, a recruiter, HR consultant, and business CEO, who provides guidance and advice on career decisions.

The Society of Nuclear Medicine and Molecular Imaging

www.snm.org

The Society of Nuclear Medicine and Molecular Imaging supplies basic job and resume banks, as well as numerous other resources to assist users with career needs. The Career Tips page has a wealth of information related to different career stages, ranging from choosing the right coach, negotiating an offer, and closing the deal. The organization supplies professional resume writing services and analysis for all job levels. The career center also provides coaching pages, where informed coaches (all of whom are members of the International Coach Federation) from a variety of professional backgrounds work with users to help them advance their careers. The site also presents tips for profile development for social networking sites such as LinkedIn and Twitter.

Occupational Resources

Below is an alphabetized list of list of websites that students and readers alike can turn to for further research and information about the particular occupations profiled. In selecting the following websites, efforts have been made to identify sites of occupational interest.

Academy of Geo-Professionals
1801 Alexander Bell Drive
Reston, VA 20191
www.geoprofessionals.org

Aerospace Industries Association
1000 Wilson Boulevard, Suite 1700
Arlington, VA 22209
www.aia-aerospace.org

American Academy of Environmental Engineers
130 Holiday Court, Suite 100
Annapolis, MD 21401
www.aaee.net

American Astronomical Society
2000 Florida Avenue NW, Suite 400
Washington, DC 20009-1231
aas.org

American Fisheries Society
5410 Grosvenor Lane
Bethesda, MD 20814
www.fisheries.org

American Institute of Aeronautics and Astronautics
1801 Alexander Bell Drive, Suite 500
Reston, VA 20191-4344
www.aiaa.org

American Institute of Hydrology (AIH)
Southern Illinois University Carbondale,
1230 Lincoln Drive Carbondale, IL 62901
www.aihydrology.org

American Institute of Physics
1 Physics Ellipse
College Park, Maryland 20740-3843
www.aip.org

American Meteorological Society
45 Beacon Street
Boston, MA 02108-3693
www.ametsoc.org

American Nuclear Society
555 North Kensington Avenue
La Grange Park, IL 60526
www.new.ans.org

American Physics Society
1 Physics Ellipse
College Park, MD 20740-3844
www.aps.org

American Registry of Radiologic Technologists
1255 Northland Drive
St. Paul, MN 55120
www.arrt.org

American Society for Cell Biology
8120 Woodmont Avenue, Suite 750
Bethesda, MD 20814-2762
www.ascb.org

American Society for Engineering
  Education
1818 N Street NW, Suite 600
Washington, DC 20036
www.asee.org

American Society of Civil Engineers
1801 Alexander Bell Drive
Reston, VA 20191
www.asce.org

American Society of Mechanical
  Engineers
3 Park Avenue
New York, NY 10016
www.asme.org

Argonne Accelerator Institute
9700 S. Class Avenue
Argonne, IL 60439
www.aai.anl.gov

Association for the Sciences of
  Limnology and Oceanography
5400 Bosque Boulevard, Suite 680
Waco, TX 76710-4446
www.aslo.org

Audio Engineering Society
International Headquarters
60 East 42nd Street, Room 2520
New York, NY 10165
www.aes.org

Biophysical Society
11400 Rockville Pike, Suite 800
Rockville, MD 20852
www.biophysics.org

Brookhaven National Laboratory
P.O. Box 5000
Upton, NY 11973
www.bnl.gov

Cryogenic Society of America
218 Lake Street
Oak Park, IL 60302
www.cryogenicsociety.org

Cryogenics Technologies Group
National Institute of Standards and
  Technology
Mail Stop 638.00
325 Broadway
Boulder, CO 80305
www.cryogenics.nist.gov

FIRST
200 Bedford Street
Manchester, NH 03101
www.usfirst.org

Institute of Electrical and
  Electronics Engineers
2001 L Street NW
Suite 700
Washington, DC 20036
www.ieee.org

International Association of
  Machinists and Aerospace
  Workers
9000 Machinists Place
Upper Marlboro, MD 20772-2867
www.iamaw.org

MarineBio
PO Box 235273
Encinitas, CA 92023
www.marinebio.org

Marine Technology Society
1100 H Street NW, Suite LL-100
Washington, DC 20005
www.mtsociety.org

National Aeronautics and Space
Administration (NASA)
Public Communications Office
NASA Headquarters
Suite 5K39
Washington, DC 20546-000
www.nasa.gov

National Council of Structural
Engineers Associations
645 North Michigan Avenue, Suite
540
Chicago, IL 60611
www.ncsea.com

National Ground Water Association
601 Dempsey Road
Westerville, OH 43081
www.ngwa.org/Pages/default.aspx

National Institute of Standards and
Technology
100 Bureau Drive, Stop 1070
Gaithersburg, MD 20899
www.nist.gov

National Nanotechnology Initiative
4201 Wilson Boulevard
Stafford II Room 405
Arlington, VA 22230
www.nano.gov

National Oceanic and Atmospheric
Administration
1401 Constitution Avenue NW,
Room 5128
Washington, DC 20230
www.noaa.gov

National Robotics Engineering
Center
Carnegie Mellon University
Robotics Institute
10 Fortieth Street
Pittsburgh, PA 15201
www.rec.ri.cmu.edu

National Society of Professional
Engineers
1420 King Street
Alexandria, VA 22314-2794
www.nspe.org

National Weather Association
228 West Millbrook Road
Raleigh, NC 27609-4304
www.nwas.org

National Weather Service
1325 East West Highway
Silver Spring, MD 20910
www.weather.gov

Nuclear Medicine Technology
Certification Board
3558 Habersham at Northlake
Building I
Tucker, GA 30084
www.nmtcb.org

Oceanography Society
PO Box 1931
Rockville, MD 20849-1931
www.tos.org

Optical Society of America
2010 Massachusetts Avenue NW
Washington, DC 20036
www.osa.org

Radiological Society of North
America
820 Jorie Boulevard
Oak Brook, IL 60523
www.rsna.org

Recording Academy
Producers and Engineers Wing
3030 Olympic Boulevard
Santa Monica, CA 90404
www.grammy.org/recording-
academy

Recording Connection Audio Institute
1201 West 5th Street, Suite M130
Los Angeles, CA 90017
www.recordingconnection.com

SLAC National Accelerator
Laboratory
2575 Sand Hill Road
Menlo Park, CA 94025
www.slac.stanford.edu

Society of Broadcast Engineers
9102 North Meridian Street, Suite
150
Indianapolis, IN 46260
www.sbe.org

Society of Naval Architects and
Marine Engineers
601 Pavonia Avenue
Jersey City, NJ 07306
www.sname.org

Society of Nuclear Medicine and
Molecular Imaging
1850 Samuel Morse Drive
Reston, VA 20190
www.snm.org

Society of Physics Students
1 Physics Ellipse
College Park, MD 20740
www.spsnational.org

SPIE
PO Box 10
Bellingham, WA 98227
www.spie.org

Sustainable Nanotechnology
Organization
www.susnano.org
American Board of Science in
Nuclear Medicine
3000 Spout Run Parkway
D-401
Arlington, VA 22201
www.snm.org/absnm

United States Environmental
Protection Agency
Ariel Rios Building
1200 Pennsylvania Avenue NW
Washington, DC 20460
www.epa.gov

United States Geological Survey
(USGS)
12201 Sunrise Valley Drive
Reston, VA 20192
www.usgs.gov

Nobel Prizes in Physics

1901	Röntgen, Wilhelm Conrad		1925	Hertz, Gustav Ludwig
1902	Lorentz, Hendrik Antoon		1926	Perrin, Jean Baptiste
1902	Zeeman, Pieter		1927	Compton, Arthur Holly
1903	Becquerel, Antoine Henri		1927	Rees Wilson, Charles Thomson
1903	Curie, Pierre		1928	Richardson, Owen Willans
1903	Curie née Sklodowska, Marie		1929	de Broglie, Prince Louis-Victor Pierre Raymond
1904	Rayleigh, Lord (Strutt, John William)		1930	Venkata Raman, Sir Chandrasekhara
1905	Anton von lenard, Philipp Eduard		1932	Heisenberg, Werner Karl
1906	Thomson, Joseph John		1933	Schrödinger, Erwin
1907	Michelson, Albert Abraham		1933	Dirac, Paul Adrien Maurice
1908	Lippman, Gabriel		1935	Chadwick, James
1909	Marconi, Guglielmo		1936	Hess, Victor Franz
1909	Braun, Karl Ferdinand		1936	Anderson, Carl David
1910	van der Waals, Johannes Diderik		1937	Davisson, Clinton Joseph
1911	Wien, Wilhelm		1937	Thomson, George Paget
1912	Dalén, Nils Gustaf		1938	Fermi, Enrico
1913	Onnes, Heike Kamerlingh		1939	Lawrence, Ernest Orlando
1914	von Laue, Max		1943	Stern, Otto
1915	Bragg, Sir William Henry		1944	Rabi, Isidor Isaac
1915	Bragg, William Lawrence		1945	Pauli, Wolfgang
1917	Barkla, Charles Glover		1946	Bridgman, Percy Williams
1918	Ludwig Planck, Max Karl Ernst		1947	Appleton, Sir Edward Victor
1919	Stark, Johannes		1948	Stuart Blackett, Patrick Maynard
1920	Guillaume, Charles Edouard		1949	Yukawa, Hideki
1921	Einstein, Albert		1950	Powell, Cecil Frank
1922	Bohr, Niels Henrik David		1951	Cockcroft, Sir John Douglas
1923	Millikan, Robert Andrews		1951	Sinton Walton, Ernest Thomas
1924	Siegbahn, Karl Manne Georg		1952	Bloch, Felix
1925	Franck, James		1952	Purcell, Edward Mills
			1953	Zernike, Frits (Frederik)

1954	Born, Max	1971	Gabor, Dennis
1954	Bothe, Walther	1972	Bardeen, John
1955	Lamb, Willis Eugene	1972	Cooper, Leon Neil
1955	Kusch, Polykarp	1972	Schrieffer, John Robert
1956	Shockley, William Bradford	1973	Esaki, Leo
1956	Bardeen, John	1973	Giaever, Ivar
1956	Brattain, Walter Houser	1973	Josephson, Brian David
1957	Yang, Chen Ning	1974	Ryle, Sir Martin
1957	Lee, Tsung-Dao (T.D.)	1974	Hewish, Antony
1958	Cherenkov, Pavel Alekseyevich	1975	Bohr, Aage Niels
1958	Frank, Il'ja Mikhailovich	1975	Mottelson, Ben Roy
1958	Tamm, Igor Yevgenyevich	1975	Rainwater, Leo James
1959	Segrè, Emilio Gino	1976	Richter, Burton
1959	Chamberlain, Owen	1976	Ting, Samuel Chao Chung
1960	Glaser, Donald Arthur	1977	Anderson, Philip Warren
1961	Hofstadter, Robert	1977	Mott, Sir Nevill Francis
1961	Mössbauer, Rudolph Ludwig	1977	van Vleck, John Hasbrouck
1962	Landau, Lev Davidovich	1978	Kapitsa, Pyotr Leonidovich
1963	Wigner, Eugene Paul	1978	Penzias, Arno Allan
1963	Mayer, Maria Goeppert	1978	Wilson, Robert Woodrow
1963	Jensen, J. Hans D.	1979	Glashow, Sheldon Lee
1964	Townes, Charles Hard	1979	Salam, Abdus
1964	Basov, Nicolay Gennadiyevich	1979	Weinberg, Steven
1964	Prokhorov, Aleksandr Mikhailovich	1980	Cronin, James Watson
1965	Tomonaga, Sin-Itiro	1980	Fitch, Val Logsdon
1965	Schwinger, Julian	1981	Bloembergen, Nicolaas
1965	Feynman, Richard P.	1981	Schawlow, Arthur Leonard
1966	Kastler, Alfred	1981	Siegbahn, Kai M.
1967	Bethe, Hans Albrecht	1982	Wilson, Kenneth G.
1968	Alvarez, Luis Walter	1983	Chandrasekhar, Subramanyan
1969	Gell-Mann, Murray	1984	Rubbia, Carlo
1970	Alfvén, Hannes Olof Gösta	1984	van der Meer, Simon
1970	Néel, Louis Eugène Félix	1985	von Klitzing, Klaus
		1986	Ruska, Ernst
		1986	Binnig, Gerd

1986	Rohrer, Heinrich	2000	Kilby, Jack S.
1987	Bednorz, J. Georg	2001	Cornell, Eric A.
1987	Müller, K. Alexander	2001	Ketterle, Wolfgang
1988	Lederman, Leon M.	2001	Wieman, Carl E.
1988	Schwartz, Melvin	2002	Davis, Raymond Jr.
1988	Steinberger, Jack	2002	Koshiba, Masatoshi
1989	Ramsey, Norman F.	2002	Giacconi, Riccardo
1989	Dehmelt, Hans G.	2003	Abrikosov, Alexei A.
1989	Paul, Wolfgang	2003	Ginzburg, Vitaly L.
1990	Friedman, Jerome I.	2003	Leggett, Anthony J.
1990	Kendall, Henry W.	2004	Gross, David J
1990	Taylor, Richard E.	2004	Politzer, H. David
1991	de Gennes, Pierre-Gilles	2004	Wilczek, Frank
1992	Charpak, Georges	2005	Glauber, Roy J.
1993	Hulse, Russell A.	2005	Hall, John L.
1993	Taylor, Joseph H. Jr.	2005	Hänsch, Theodore W.
1994	Brockhouse, Bertram N.	2006	Mather, John C.
1994	Shull, Clifford G.	2006	Smoot, George F.
1995	Perl, Martin L.	2007	Fert, Albert
1995	Reines, Frederick	2007	Grünberg, Peter
1996	Lee, David M.	2008	Nambu, Yoichiro
1996	Osheroff, Douglas D.	2008	Kobayashi, Makoto
1996	Richardson, Robert C.	2008	Maskawa, Toshihide
1997	Chu, Steven	2009	Kao, Charles Kuen
1997	Cohen-Tannoudji, Claude	2009	Boyle, Willard S.
1997	Philliphs, William D.	2009	Smith, George E.
1998	Laughlin, Robert B.	2010	Geim, Andre
1998	Störmer, Horst L.	2010	Novoselov, Konstantin
1998	Tsui, Daniel C.	2011	Saul Perlmutter
1999	Hooft, Gerardus 't	2011	Brian P. Schmidt
1999	Veltman, Martinus J.G	2011	Adam G. Riess
2000	Alferov, Zhores I.	2012	Serge Haroche
2000	Kroemer, Herbert	2012	David J. Wineland

Indexes

Occupational Index

Accelerator Physicist, 181–189
Aeronautical Engineer, 167
Aerospace Engineer, 33, 38–46, 203, 224, 359, 412, 430
Aerospace Stress Engineer, 430
Agricultural Engineer, 245
Agricultural Scientist, 126
Astronautical Engineer, 167
Astronomer, 65, 88, 107, 186, 341
Astrophysicist, 60, 68, 107
Atomic and Molecular Physicist, 102–108
Atmospheric Physicist, 69, 78

Biochemist, 65, 125
Biological Engineer, 107, 301
Biological Technician, 126
Biomedical Engineer, 203, 224, 412
Biophysicist, 65, 107, 119–127, 302, 376
Broadcast Technician, 22

Cardiovascular Technologist, 321
Chemical Engineer, 301, 395
Chemist, 107, 186, 395
Civil Engineer, 130–131, 140–147, 165, 186, 245, 395, 430
Computer and Information Research Scientists, 65
Computer Engineer, 223
Computer Hardware Engineer, 412
Computer Scientist, 376
Cryogenic Engineer, 199–204

Diagnostic Medical Sonographer, 321

Electrical Engineer, 43, 186, 208, 217–225, 359, 422, 431
Electrician, 412
Electronics Engineer, 376

Environmental Engineer, 146, 240
Environmental Engineering Technician, 245
Environmental Physicist, 226
Environmental Scientist, 88, 245
Epidemiologist, 126

Film and Video Editors, 22
Food Scientist, 126, 203

Geologists, 264
Geophysicist, 264, 285, 422
Geoscientist, 88, 264

Health and Safety Engineer, 341
Hydraulic Engineer, 43, 146, 155
Hydrologist, 88, 245, 260–266, 285

Industrial Engineer, 431
Information Research Scientist, 376

Laser Technician, 359

Manufacturing Engineer, 45, 167, 223
Marine Archaeologist, 285
Marine Engineer, 431
Marine Policy Specialist, 285
Materials Physicist, 389–396
Materials Scientist, 107, 186, 301, 359, 395
Mathematician, 376
Mechanical Engineer, 43, 161–168, 203, 224, 395, 412, 422, 430
Medical Assistant, 321
Medical Doctor, 125
Meteorologist, 75, 82, 90, 264
Motion Picture Projectionist, 22
Musical Instrument Repair Technician, 22

Nanosystems Engineer, 203, 296, 304–393

Natural Sciences Managers, 65

Nuclear Engineer, 341, 359, 376

Nuclear Medicine Technologist, 317–323, 341

Nuclear Monitoring Technician, 336–343

Ocean Engineer, 285

Oceanographer, 279–287

Photonics Engineer, 355–360

Physicist, 65, 186, 266, 341

Power Distributor, 341

Power Plant Operator, 341

Power Plant Operator and Distributor, 186, 395

Quantum Physicist, 371–378

Radiation Therapist, 321

Radiologic Technologist, 321

Robotics Engineer, 407–413

Sanitary Engineer, 146

Solid Mechanics, 379–389

Sound Engineering Technician, 17–23

Structural Engineer, 146, 165

Thermodynamics Engineer, 426–432

Thermodynamics Physicist, 425

Thermodynamics Specialist, 425

Transportation Engineer, 146

Weather Forecaster. *See* Meteorologist

Index

acoustics, 3–16, 76; musical, 6, 12; physiological, 5, 10; psychological, 5, 10; speech, 6, 11; underwater, 6, 12

adiabatic demagnetization, 192

aerodynamics, 76

aeroelasticity, 30

aeronautics, 25–28, 429

aerospace industry, 195

AIAA. See American Institute of Aeronautics and Astronautics (AIAA)

air pollution, 81, 95

Alpha Magnetic Spectrometer, 68

alternative energy, 96, 126, 203, 232–234, 237, 300, 303, 422

American Astronomical Society (AAS), 63

American Institute of Aeronautics and Astronautics (AIAA), 40–41

American Institute of Physics (AIP), 63, 104

American Physical Society (APS), 63, 105

American Society of Mechanical Engineers (ASME), 163

Apollo space program, 401

archaeology, 331, 334

astrophysics, 47–60

atmosphere; composition of, 71; zones of, 73

atmospheric dynamics, 69

atmospheric physics, 69–82

atomic and molecular physics, 91–102

atomic clock. See timekeeping

atomic structure, 93

atomic theory RT, 91–92

aurora borealis, 72

automotive industry, 194

aviation, 25–38

avionics, 32

big bang theory, 55

binary code, 367

biomedicine, 176

biomolecular structure, 112

biophysics, 109–119

black holes, 54

calorimetry, 417

CAM. See computer-aided manufacturing

celestial mapping and exploration, 153

Census of Marine Life, 2000–2010, 286

CERN (European Organization for Nuclear Research), 183, 186

Chandra X-Ray Observatory, 63

chaotic systems, 160

Chernobyl disaster, 342

civil engineering, 128–139

climate change, 76, 80, 89, 107, 231, 247, 286, 421

climate modeling, 231

climatology, 275

clouds, noctilucent, 72

computational chemistry, 368

computer-aided manufacturing (CAM), 410

computer programming, 404

computers, 367

condensed matter physics, 169–180

conduction. See thermal conduction

construction, 272

cosmic microwave background radiation, 55

cosmic rays, 50

Cryogenic Society of America (CSA), 201
cryogenics, 190–199
cryonics, 191
crystallography, 169
Curiosity (Mars rover), 412
cybersecurity, 369

deformation, 381
differential equations, 150
digital signal processing, 207
double-slit experiment, 361

eddy covariance, 229
Edison, Thomas, 210, 211
elasticity, 381
electrical engineering, 205–217
electricity, 172
electromagnetism, 271, 362
electronics, 292, 367
electron microscopes, 111, 289–290
energy; conservation of, 415
energy bands, 172
energy-efficient technology, 96, 291
entanglement. *See* quantum entanglement
entropy, 415
environmental physics, 226–239
Environmental Protection Agency (EPA), 277
environmental technology, 224
Euler, Leonhard, 249
European Organization for Nuclear Research. *See* CERN
evaporative cooling, 191
expanding-universe theory, 55

fiber optics, 351
fluid dynamics, 249–259
fluid mechanics, 130, 270
food and beverage preservation, 194
forcings and feedbacks, 80–81

frequency analyzers, 326
Fukushima Daiichi disaster, 342

Galilei, Galileo, 52, 419
gamma-ray astronomy, 50
Gemini-Scout mine rescue robot, 412
genes, 110
genetically modified (GM) food, 126
geographic information system (GIS), 85
geomechanics, 384
geophysics, 268–278
geothermal energy, 233
geothermal power, 274
Giacconi, Riccardo, 49
Global Positioning System (GPS), 52
global warming. *See* climate change
GPS. *See* Global Positioning System (GPS)
graphene, 175, 179
gravitational theory. *See* gravity
gravity, 151
Great Lisbon Earthquake. *See* Lisbon earthquake, 1755
green energy. *See* alternative energy
green technology. *See* alternative energy

heat conduction. *See* thermal conduction
heat transfer, 270
Hubble Space Telescope, 54, 63
hydraulic engineering, 155
hydroelectric dams, 155

infrared astronomy, 50
Institute of Electrical and Electronics Engineers (IEEE), 219
instrument design, 51
instrument manufacture, 195
Intergovernmental Panel on Climate Change, 231

internal combustion engine, 420
International Association of Nano-
    technology (IANT), 299
International Space Station, 68
International Union for Pure and
    Applied Biophysics (IUPAB),
    116
ionosphere, 81

jet engine, 421
Joule-Thomson effect, 192

Keck telescopes, 63
Kepler, Johannes, 47

Lagrange, Joseph-Louis, 70
Large Hadron Collider (LHC), 375
lasers, 96, 366, 368
    free-electron, 186
LCD. *See* liquid crystal display
lightning, 72
light scattering, 171
liquid crystal display, 175
Lisbon earthquake, 1755, 272–274

Manhattan Project, 403
mass spectrometry, 228
materials science, 156, 382
mathematics, advanced, 363
matter, states of, 95
Max Planck Institute of Biophysics,
    115
measuring instruments, 150
mechanical engineering, 382
mechanics; applied, 148–160;
    classical, 148–160; continuum,
    153
medical school, 121
medical technology, 97, 107, 194,
    291, 303
membrane structure, 113
mesosphere, 74

meteorology, 69, 75, 276
mineral physics, 269
mining, 274
molecular imaging, 312
molecular structure, 93
moon landing. *See* Apollo space
    program
multiphysics, 159

nanobiology, 115
nanotechnology, 168, 169–180,
    288–296, 382
National Aeronautics and Space
    Administration (NASA), 158,
    195
National Math and Science Initiative
    (NMSI), 80
National Nanotechnology Initiative
    (NNI), 294
Navier-Stokes equation, 250
navigation, 52
neutrinos, 51
neutrons; probing technology, 171
Newton, Isaac, 148, 152
Newton's law of universal gravita-
    tion, 151
Newton's laws of motion, 149–150
newton (unit), 152
noise, 8, 12
nuclear energy, 328, 334
nuclear magnetic resonance, 111, 331
nuclear medicine, 305–316, 330,
    333–334
nuclear physics, 324–336
nuclear weapons, 329, 332–333

oceanography, 275
optical astronomy, 48
optics, 344–354; geometric, 346;
    physical, 345; quantum, 347
orbital motion, 153–154
ozone, 71

particle accelerators, 181, 184, 326, 370
particle-wave duality. *See* wave-particle duality
pharmaceutical development, 114
phonon, 173
photosynthesis, 109
physical cosmology, 51
piezoelectricity, 152
planetary motion. *See* orbital motion
planetary science, 54
plasticity, 382
polymer, 385
positron emission tomography, 307
Projectionist, 22
professional engineer (PE) license, 41, 141, 163, 220, 242, 299, 410

quantum biology, 368
quantum computing, 98
quantum entanglement, 98, 364, 377
quantum field theory, 362
quantum mechanics, 92
quantum physics, 361–371
quantum tunneling, 364, 377
quasars, 53
qubits, 367

radar, ground penetrating, 230
radioactivity, 272
radio astronomy, 49
radiometric dating, 230
radiometry, 227
radionuclides, 306–307
radiopharmaceuticals, 305
rapid-expansion cooling. *See* Joule-Thomson effect
reaction control, 98

reaction engine, 420
refrigeration, 421
renewable energy. *See* alternative energy
rheology, 254

satellites; remote sensing and, 74
Schrödinger's cat, 364
seismology, 271
semiconductors, 326, 365
sensors, 291
smart materials, 156, 291
software design, 404
soil mechanics, 130
solid rocket boosters (SRBs), 152
solid state physics, 172
sound waves. *See* acoustics
sources and sinks, 418
spacecraft, 154
Space Physics and Atmospheric Research Center (SPARC), 79
space plasma physics, 54
spectrometers, 326
spectroscopy, 93, 228, 417; circular dichroism, 111; nuclear magnetic resonance, 111
SPIE (professional organization), 356
sports engineering, 154
Sputnik I, 74
statics, 129
steam engine, 418
stellar dynamics, 51
strain. *See* deformation
stratosphere, 74
subatomic particles, 325
superconductivity, 194
superposition, 364
synthetic biology, 114
systems engineering, 397–407

telescopes, 58. *See* also instrument design; infrared, 50; optical, 48; radio, 49
thermal conduction, 191
thermal equilibrium, 77
thermodynamics, 73, 151, 414–426, 427
thermosphere, 73
time-domain reflectometry, 229
timekeeping, 97
transistors, 369
troposphere, 74
tunneling. *See* quantum tunneling

ultrasonics, 4, 9
ultraviolet astronomy, 49
uncertainty principle, 363

Unified Modeling Language (UML), 400
United States Geological Survey (USGS), 276

Video Editors, 22

water; movement of, 71
wave-particle duality, 361
wave-power generators, 155
weather, 75; military and, 78

x-ray astronomy, 49, 54
x-ray crystallography, 112
x-ray machines, 330
x-rays; probing technology, 171